Photo courtesy Himalayan Packs

HAVE YOU been repressing an urge to learn to climb mountains? Let up long enough to read page 1721, where you'll get some very valuable tips on equipment and techniques. What you learn there may be enough to get you started

LAWNS LIKE THIS don't just happen. Find out about keeping your lawn velvety in the story on page 1601

Photo courtesy Scott Seeds

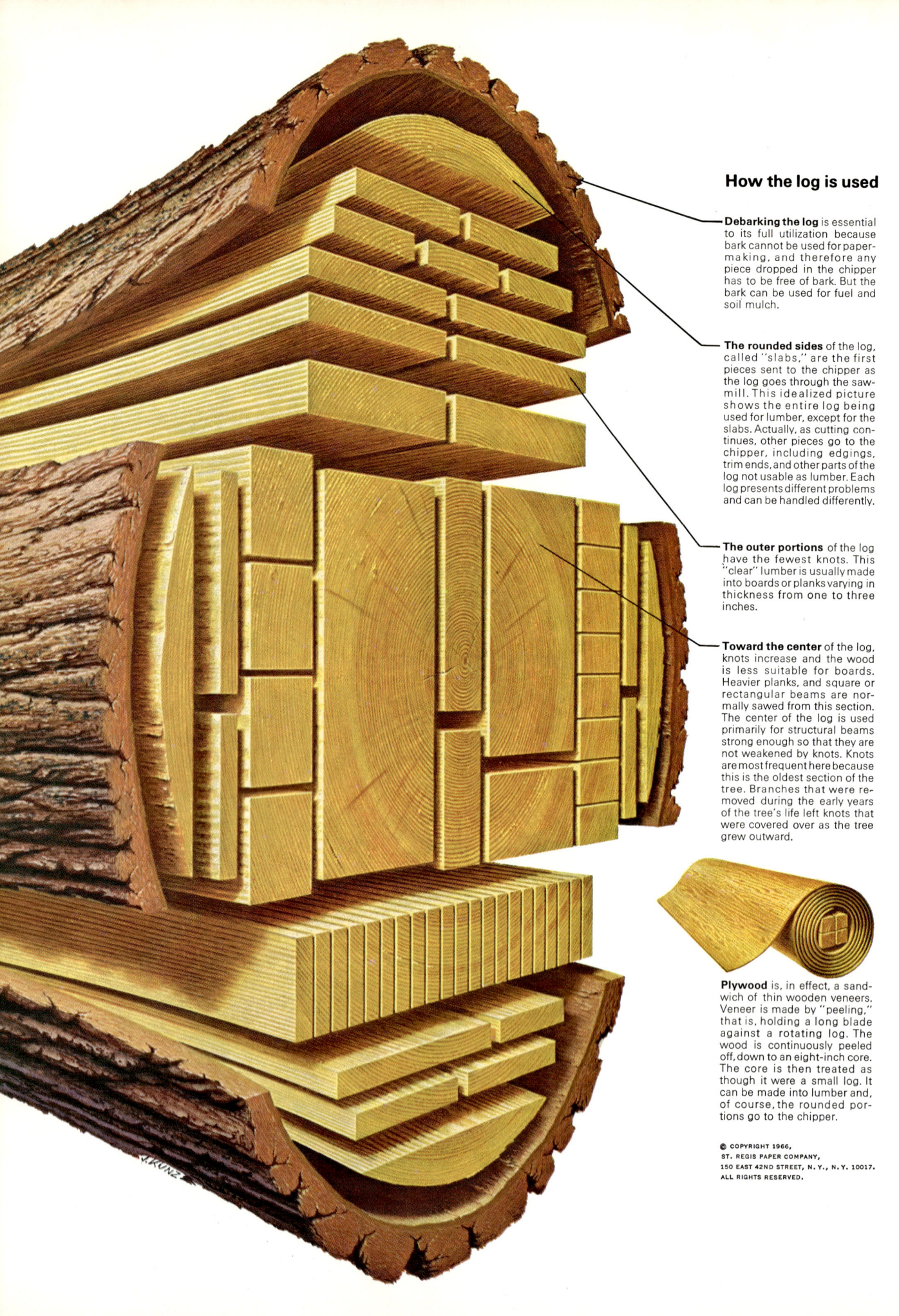

How the log is used

Debarking the log is essential to its full utilization because bark cannot be used for papermaking, and therefore any piece dropped in the chipper has to be free of bark. But the bark can be used for fuel and soil mulch.

The rounded sides of the log, called "slabs," are the first pieces sent to the chipper as the log goes through the sawmill. This idealized picture shows the entire log being used for lumber, except for the slabs. Actually, as cutting continues, other pieces go to the chipper, including edgings, trim ends, and other parts of the log not usable as lumber. Each log presents different problems and can be handled differently.

The outer portions of the log have the fewest knots. This "clear" lumber is usually made into boards or planks varying in thickness from one to three inches.

Toward the center of the log, knots increase and the wood is less suitable for boards. Heavier planks, and square or rectangular beams are normally sawed from this section. The center of the log is used primarily for structural beams strong enough so that they are not weakened by knots. Knots are most frequent here because this is the oldest section of the tree. Branches that were removed during the early years of the tree's life left knots that were covered over as the tree grew outward.

Plywood is, in effect, a sandwich of thin wooden veneers. Veneer is made by "peeling," that is, holding a long blade against a rotating log. The wood is continuously peeled off, down to an eight-inch core. The core is then treated as though it were a small log. It can be made into lumber and, of course, the rounded portions go to the chipper.

© COPYRIGHT 1966,
ST. REGIS PAPER COMPANY,
150 EAST 42ND STREET, N.Y., N.Y. 10017.
ALL RIGHTS RESERVED.

■ **EASTERN WHITE PINE** — An important tree in Colonial America, for homes and for the masts and spars of ships. It is still an important timber tree, and one source of knotty pine decorative paneling.

■■ **DOUGLAS FIR** — Averaging 150 to 200 feet in height, the Douglas fir is considered the most important timber tree in the world. It is used principally for construction lumber and plywood, and for telephone poles.

■ **WESTERN HEMLOCK** — A tall, graceful tree, the western hemlock is important for timber and is also a prime source of pulpwood; and tannin, used in tanning leather, can be extracted from its bright red inner bark.

■■ **YELLOW POPLAR** — The yellow poplar, the tallest hardwood in the east, is a favorite ornamental tree, and an important source of wood for musical instruments, television cabinets, and other furniture.

■■ **PONDEROSA PINE** — A tall, straight tree found in many parts of western U.S.; second only to Douglas fir as a timber tree. Its wood is used for lumber, railroad ties, telephone poles, posts, and mine timbers.

■■■ **WHITE OAK** — The oaks have always been our most important hardwood timber trees. Early American mansions, public buildings, and ships' hulls, were of oak. White oak was the traditional wood for whiskey barrels.

■■■ **SHAGBARK HICKORY** — Tough hickory lumber supplied spokes for the wheels that crossed the continent and the ax handles that cleared the wilderness. Hickory smoke is used for curing ham.

THESE EIGHT TREES helped build America. They became American homes, supplied the ties under the rails across the continent and the poles for the wires for power and communications. On the opposite page, you see how a typical log is handled so that we get the highest utilization to supply the nation's lumber needs. See page 1656 for information on the kinds and sizes of lumber

■■ **SUGAR MAPLE** — This is the tree that maple syrup and maple sugar come from. But it is also an important source of fine hardwood, prized for furniture. It grows in the eastern half of the U.S., and Canada.

FISHERMEN HAVE SELECTED 12 all-time favorite fish-killing lures. Read about them on page 1661

THERE'S MORE to a long ladder than a lot of rungs, as you can see in the story on page 1553

Popular Mechanics
Do-It-Yourself Encyclopedia

in 16 volumes

A complete guide to

- home maintenance
- home improvement
- hand-tool skills
- craft projects
- power-tool know-how
- hobbies
- automotive upkeep
- automotive repair
- shop shortcuts
- boating
- fishing
- hunting
- model making
- outdoor living
- radio, TV and electronics

Volume 9

Book Division, Hearst Magazines, New York, N.Y. 10019

© 1968, The Hearst Corporation
All Rights Reserved

No part of the text or illustrations in this work may be used without written permission by the Hearst Corporation.

Printed in the United States of America

VOLUME 9

kites
    Go fly a kite   1541
    These kites fly high   1546

kite winders
    Kite winders give better flight control   1548

knurling
    "Nutcracker" knurler for your lathe   1549

ladders
    A long look at long ladders   1553
    How to stay alive on a ladder   1558

ladders, boat
    Swing-up ladder mounts on transom   1562

lamps
    Lamps are reminders of earlier days   1564
    Lamp base is ideograph meaning "thought"   1565
    Spotlight on modern lamps   1566
    Cask lamp goes with rustic decor   1567

landscaping
    You can have a lazy-man's lawn   1568

land yacht models
    Racing land yachts is exciting fun   1576

lathe accessories
    Convert discards to metal-lathe accessories   1578
    Lathe pinch-hits as disk sander   1580
    Add these to your metal lathe   1581

lathe techniques
    Short course in metal turning   1582

laundry
    Give your wife a break   1596

lawns
    Velvety green lawns don't just happen   1601

lawn sweeper
    Lawn sweeper from an old hand mower   1610

leaf blower
    Windrow those leaves—it beats raking   1616

leaf burner
    Leaf burner rolls to the job   1620

lectern
    Take this folding lectern along   1625

legs, furniture
    A dozen ways to attach legs   1626

lifesaving
    Just four minutes to save a life   1628

lighting
    You can't buy these lighting fixtures   1634
    Switch on your dimmers at home   1636
    Beams by day, lights by night   1640

light stand
    A stand for your photo spot   1642

linoleum-block press
    Linoleum-block press from at-hand materials   1644

locks
    Tricks that foil lock pickers   1653

lumber
    Lumber basics for the craftsman   1656

lures
    Experts pick fishing's deadly dozen lures   1661

machine gun, toy
    Machine gun "fires" water bursts   1665

magic
    "Squozen" sponges come to life   1666
    There's magic in these tricks   1668

magnetos, outboard
    Magneto how-to for outboards   1673

maintenance center
    Home maintenance center built into a wall   1678

marble
    How to mend, trim and polish marble   1684

marksmanship
    Duffer to expert wingshot in minutes   1688

measurements
    Guide to the right measurement   1690

merry-go-rounds
    This go-round puts kids in orbit   1692

microphones
    Choose your mike for the job   1698

microphotography
    Nearsighted camera shoots fine detail   1703

mirrors
    Makeup mirror for powder rooms   1704

mixers, food
    How to fix a food mixer   1706

moldings
    Moldings—the finishing touch   1708
    How to cope-cut moldings   1711

motorcycles
    Winter tune-up for trouble-free cycling   1712

mountain climbing
    The up and down of mountain climbing   1721

movies, sound
    Soundtrack your home movies   1726

How to use your Encyclopedia

Browse. Glance through this volume, or any other volume of the Encyclopedia. Likely you will find the solution to a particular home-maintenance problem that has been bothering you, or a shop project so appealing that you will immediately head for your bench. Browsing not only is enjoyable, but is a source of ideas.

Seek specific information. Perhaps you want to find out how to cure that leak in your basement, how to keep the exterior paint from peeling, or how to tune and set the carburetor on your car.

Four reader aids, all cross-referenced, will enable you to find specific information:

1. *Alphabetical headings.* Located at the top of the page, these headings cover broad classifications of information. If you are looking for information on how to keep paint from peeling, for example, look up "Paints" alphabetically, then find the particular section dealing with peeling paint.

2. *Alphabetical cross-references.* These are shown in a box at the bottom of the page. Some material can logically be classified under more than one alphabetical heading, so if you don't find what you are seeking alphabetically (as described above), be sure to check the *alphabetical cross-references* at the bottom of the page; there you may find precisely the classification you are seeking. For example, you and your son decide to build a model airplane, and are looking for plans. You look up "Model airplanes" and find nothing under that alphabetical heading. However, if you glance at the bottom *of that same page* you will find an alphabetical cross-reference that reads: **model airplanes,** see airplane models.

3. *See also references.* These are shown at the end of many articles. They refer you to related articles which may also be of interest.

4. *Instant index.* Located at the end of Volume 16, it is thoroughly cross-referenced to help you find information under any heading.

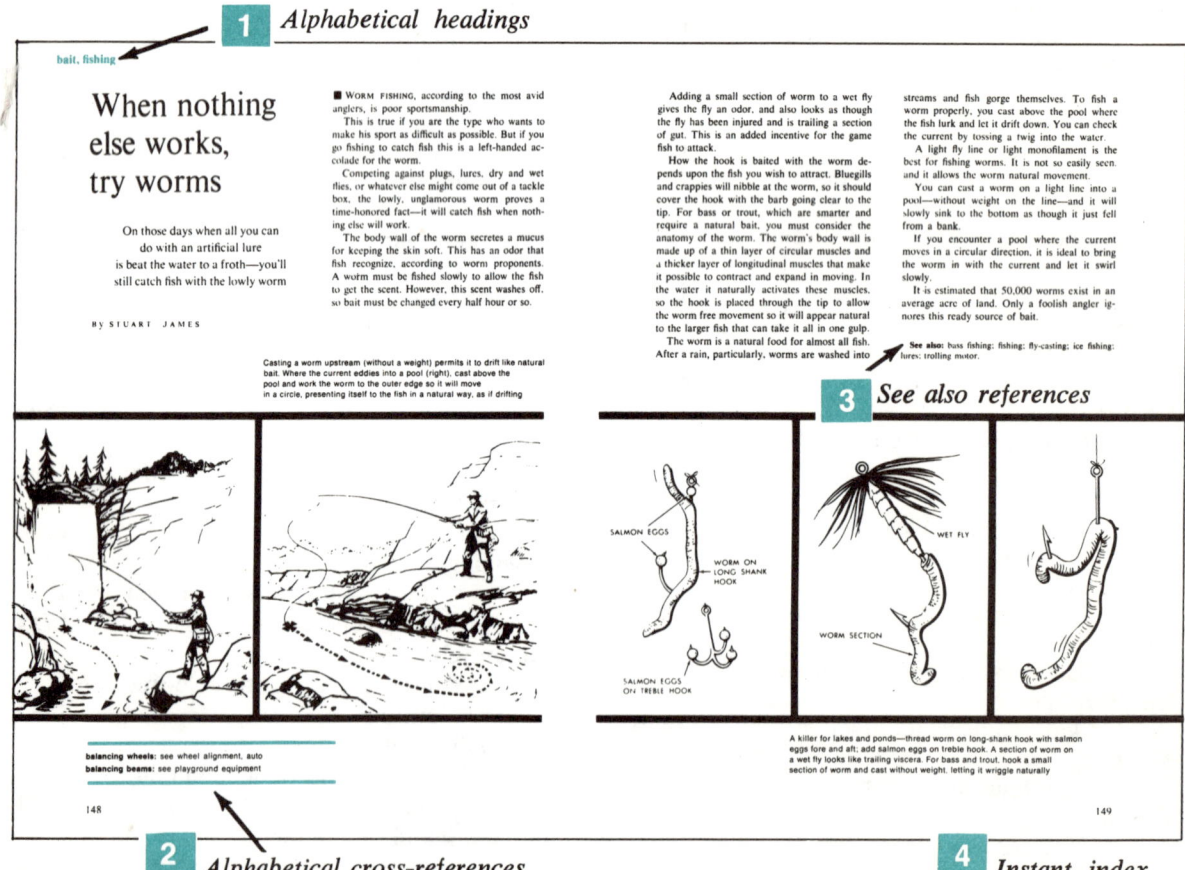

The bat-winged triangular box kite is so dependable a flyer it's been used to tow strings across chasms at the start of bridge-construction. That floating hoop kite you see at the right has a printed-plastic covering

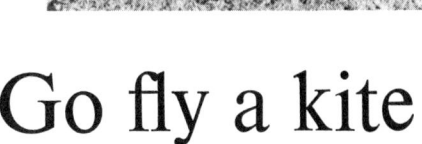

WHO STARTED the whole thing? Legend has it that the first kite-flyer was Archytas, a Greek philosopher and friend of Plato, 400 years before the birth of Christ. Others credit the ancient Chinese general Hao Sin with the idea.

However, kites were in existence long before either of these men lived. The earliest travelers to Malaya reported that natives flew large leaves and worshipped them as gods. There's evidence, too, that the Egyptians flew kites centuries before Cleopatra.

Kites have not been merely playthings, but

Go fly a kite

BY WILLARD and
ELMA WALTNER

These four novel designs make the most of March winds. There's also a variation on the box kite that you can fly from a "control" line

kites

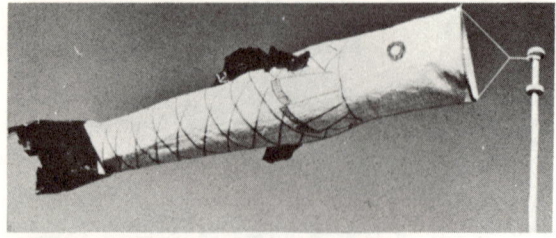

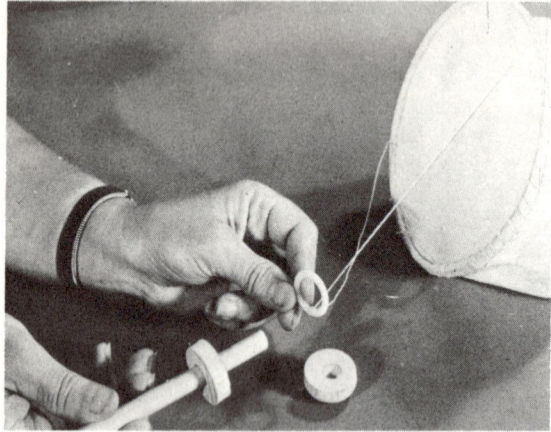

The fish wind vane (top) is a pole kite — popular in the Orient. The mouth is formed by whip-stitching cloth to a reed hoop. The ring, tied into the bridle string, lets the fish show which way the wind is blowing

four kite designs, continued

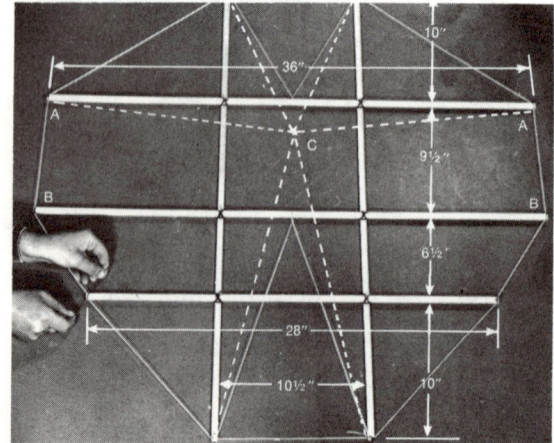

have served man in practical ways. Polynesians still use them for fishing. Ancient Chinese flew them as signaling devices during wartime. A kite laid the first line of the bridge that now spans Niagara's gorge, and until recently the U.S. Weather Bureau sent kites high into the upper air to record temperature, wind velocity and humidity. America's most famous kite-flier, Ben Franklin, put one up in the midst of a thunderstorm in 1792 to prove that lightning was electricity.

Most of us, though, simply accept the principles of what makes a kite fly and just enjoy the thrill of a high flyer's tug on the line. And the thrill's double when you've made the kite yourself. Materials are easy to come by. For the sticks, a strong, light wood with straight grain is best; it can be soft pine, spruce, basswood or redwood. Sticks 3/8 x 3/16 in. are suitable for most kites except very large ones that require heavier frames.

The covering material is usually paper. Ordinary brown wrapping paper is fine. Lightweight cloth, such as silk or nylon, is less likely to tear, if you don't mind the extra cost. Some plastics work well—an old shower curtain makes a strong, colorful covering. Plastic should be fastened to the framework with masking or freezer tape. Paper is attached by spreading glue on the top surface of the sticks and laying the framework onto the paper. Smooth out face-down on a flat surface. Cut the paper at least ½ in. larger than the kite's outline on all sides. Apply glue to this projection and lap it back around the frame or outline string.

string is needed

String is needed both for flying and building the kite. For flight lines, the larger the kite, the stronger the string must be. Mason's chalk line is fine.

Rigid lashing of the frame is essential. After crossing the sticks at the desired angle lash diagonally both ways, forming an X. Many turns of thread do a better job than a few turns of heavier cord.

The butterfly kite has a flat stick frame with outlining string tied around notched ends. Its bow strings run between points A-A and B-B and are tied at the center. The dotted lines show how bridle strings are attached. The flight string is tied at point C, which should be 15 to 19 in. from the kite's face

A common misconception about kiteflying is that you need a strong wind. Actually, kites fly best in a light, steady breeze of from 8 to 15 mph. Launching a kite is easier if you have help, as in the photo at the top of page 1541. The helper, downwind about 50 to 100 ft. from the stringholder, raises the kite until he feels it being lifted by the wind. A light upward toss should launch it without your having to dash away with the string. A well-balanced kite will climb steadily as string is gradually paid out. If a kite won't rise in a good breeze, it's probably too heavy for its surface area.

A kite usually flies best if the bridle is adjusted so the kite's at an angle of 30 to 40 deg. from horizontal. Most kites need a tail for balance. The only one of the designs shown here that will fly its best without one is the box kite. An effective tail can be made of light material; it's not the weight but the bulk and surface that give the balance. Accordion-pleated sheets of typing paper, cinched at their center to make them fan out, work very well. So do scraps of plastic or cloth. A good tail may be made of pieces about 1½ in. wide, tied to cord about every 5 or 6 in. The stronger the wind, the more tail is needed to balance the kite. Tails are attached at the kite's lowest point. In the case of the butterfly kite, a second string is required to center a tail between the two points.

The floating hoop kite differs from the others

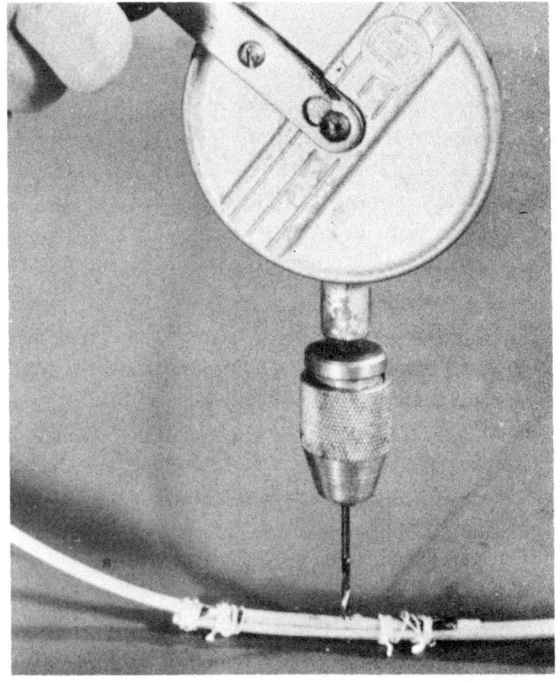

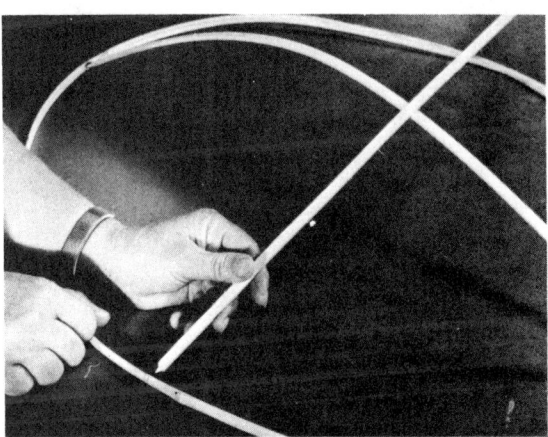

Form the hoop by lapping the ends of a ¼-in.-wide bamboo strip 77 in. long. At the center (top) drill one of four socket holes for pointed cross sticks. These will bow when they are inserted

Lash the sticks at the center and cut a circle from plastic curtain material, big enough so the edge can be folded around the hoop (right). Apply tape at four cross-stick points and at midpoints to stretch the cover

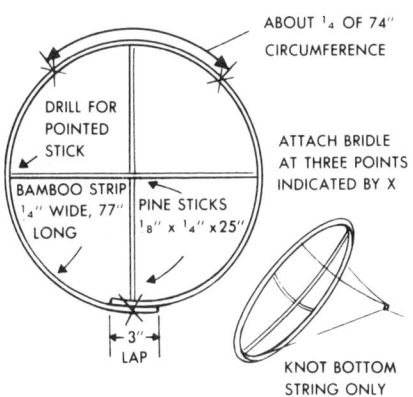

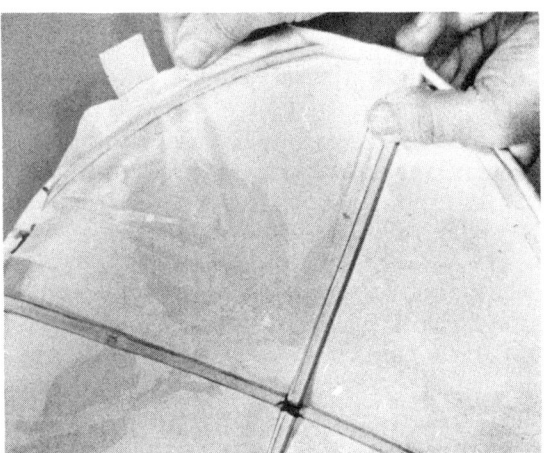

1543

kites

four kite designs, continued

presented in that its outline is formed by bamboo. Since you'll need a strip 77 in. long, you'll probably have to join two shorter pieces by tapering, lapping and gluing the ends; let the glue set under clamping pressure. Also glue (and lash) the 3-in. lap that brings the strip into a hoop. After stretching the plastic covering by taping at eight equidistant points, tape all around the frame.

The Chinese Fish kite is a wind sock, so it needs no body frame. In the Orient, such kites are carried in holiday processions at the top of long poles. Cut the two pieces of the body from cloth; draw the simple markings with crayons and set the color by placing the cloth between two layers of paper and pressing with a warm iron. Lay the two pieces together, right side in. Cut fins of plastic cloth and lay them between the two body pieces. Stitch along the top and bottom, leaving the ends open. Turn right-side-out and stitch the basket-reed hoop inside the large end. Attach the bridle at top and bottom seams and tie it to a bone ring large enough to turn freely on the pole you've selected.

Since the framework for the box kite can't be lashed, use a good grade of wood glue in the assembly. Fasten paper around the two end triangles, leaving the center section open. Then, glue the cross stick at right angles and lash the joints where it crosses the body sticks.

Plans for the maneuverable version of the box kite call for the glued joints to be reinforced with staples and pins because this frame will be subjected to unusual movement in flight. Once you learn how to twist a double reel to pivot the rudder right or left, you can send the kite plummeting all over the sky or swooping in lazy figure-eights against the clouds. The fact that it can be guided (plus its load-carrying abilities) means you can even put it to practical use. It'll carry a small camera aloft for aerial photography—or a sheaf of circulars for your next church bazaar, to be released when a separate trigger line is tugged from the ground.

use rubber cement

For the covering, use the heaviest grade of model-airplane tissue, or light cloth such as handkerchief silk or cambric. Rubber cement is best for attaching since it won't shrink or pull anything out of shape. The rudder is covered on one side only. Its control horn is fastened to the bottom stick with glue and small airplane

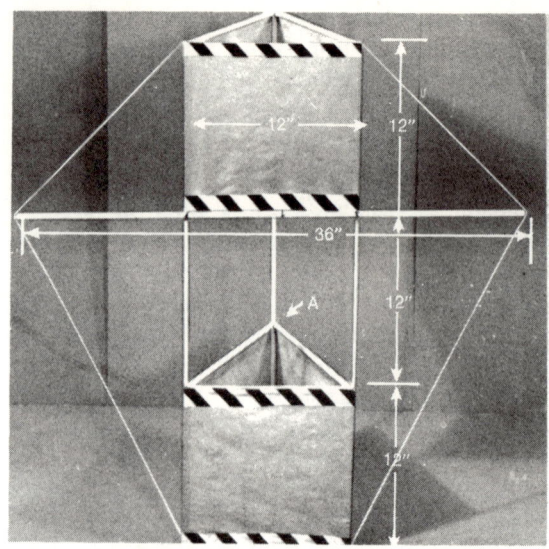

After covering the kite's top and bottom (leaving center open), form bat-wings' outline with string and cover it separately. Attach the bridle at point A. The diagram below shows how the rudder version is controlled by lines from the ground

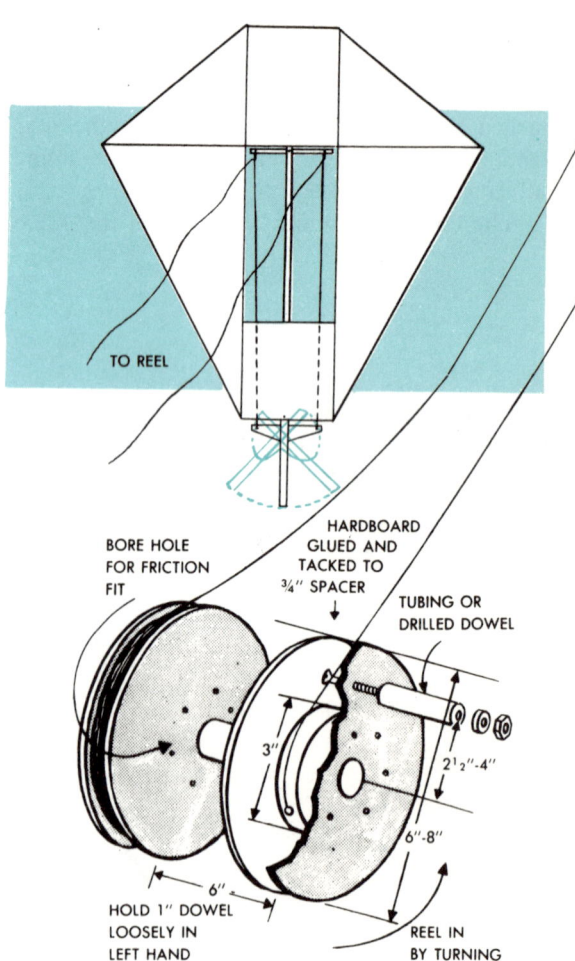

1544

bolts, and is set back from the leading edge to permit free pivot action.

When launching the kite, let it gain some altitude before you attempt to control its flight. The two flight strings are tied to opposite ends of the control horn and run through screw eyes turned into the bottom edge of the lower crossbar which is nailed and glued to the second V-frame. The opposite ends of these lines are tacked to the core disks of the reel spools. When the lines are taut, merely twisting this double reel swings the rudder right or left.

The kite can also be flown from a single string. You don't even have to tie down the rudder—just remove its control lines and let it swing free.

Designer Roy Clough test-flew this model in New Hampshire, to let us know how high the kite would climb on a single string. He'd paid out 1000 ft. of line when the string broke. "Far as I know," he says, "it's still going."

See also: archery; boomerang; boys' projects; doghouse; kite winders; magic play bouncers; playground equipment; sleds; stilts; toboggan; tree houses.

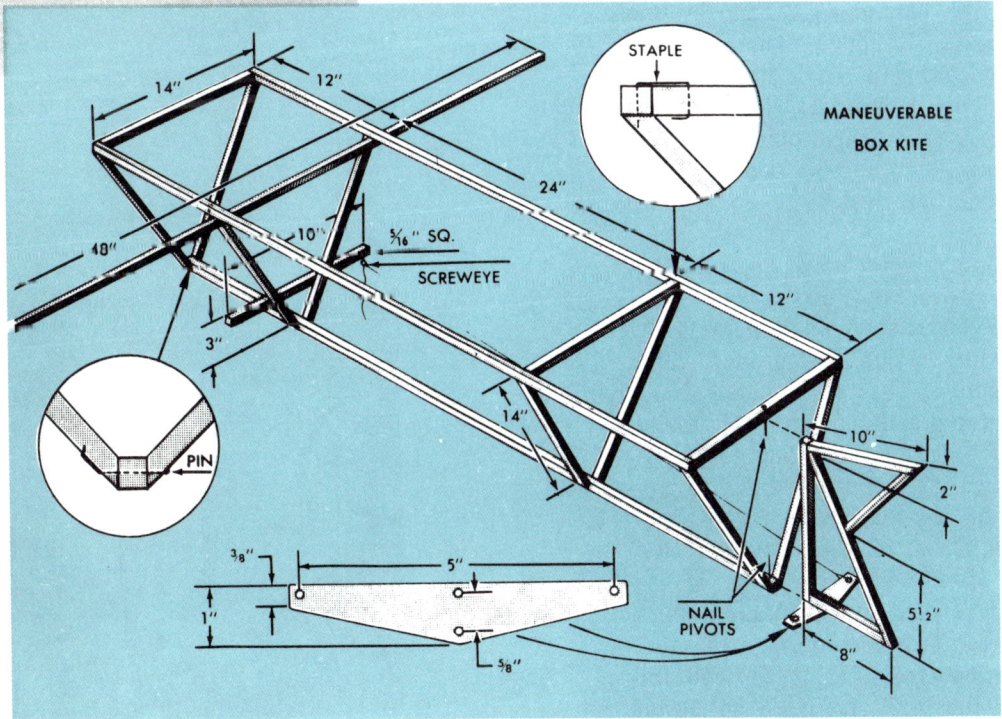

The maneuverable version of the triangular box kite is by Roy L. Clough, Jr. The frame dimensions differ from those given for the conventional type, but the main feature of the maneuverable version's design is the fish-tail rudder at the rear

kites

These kites fly high

1. Flexible Kite. As simple a kite as you could hope to make, this one consists of a single piece of acetate or aluminum foil which is lofted at the end of a fly rod. In a stiff breeze it billows like a parachute, and a 5-ft. balancing tail with three 15-in. foil streamers tied to the end keeps it heading into the wind. Cut the foil to the size and shape indicated, punch the shroudline holes at the points given and fold the foil down the center to provide a sharp crease when the foil is placed flat. The converging six-leg bridle of braided fishline, knotted on the back of the kite, extends out from the face of the kite about 12 in.

2. Fighter Kite. Shaped like an arrowhead and measuring nearly 2 ft. across, the India fighter kite flies with a rapid oscillating (jerky) motion. The drawing details the kite from the rear. As shown, the framework consists of two reed ribs lashed together in the form of a cross. One is bound to the other with thread at a point 4 in. down from the top. Tabs of paper affix the vertical reed to a covering of rice or tissue paper which is first cut to the shape shown, and hemmed all around by folding over the edge 1/8 in. and gluing. The horizontal reed is curved to suit the width of the kite and is held to the paper covering with tape and glue. Finally, the tissue-paper tail, A, is added. This is made double thick by gluing a single thickness to each side of the kite. A toothpick rib is inserted between the two layers of paper along the outer edges at the sides. An adjustable two-leg bridle is attached to the vertical reed.

3. Bird Kite. Resembling a falcon in flight this kite flies like a bird because dowel wing spars are pivoted on a central shaft which permits the wings to flap with varying air currents. First make a paper pattern from the squared drawing, trace it on muslin and cut out. Form a hem along the leading edge of each wing and overcast all other edges of the fabric by hand to prevent fraying. Then sew on pockets for spars at the points shown. Detail A shows how the wing spars are pivoted. Holes in the ends of the dowels are made oversize to fit freely over a headless nail forced crosswise through the vertical dowel. Cotton string is run through the wing hems, and the bridle is rigged as shown.

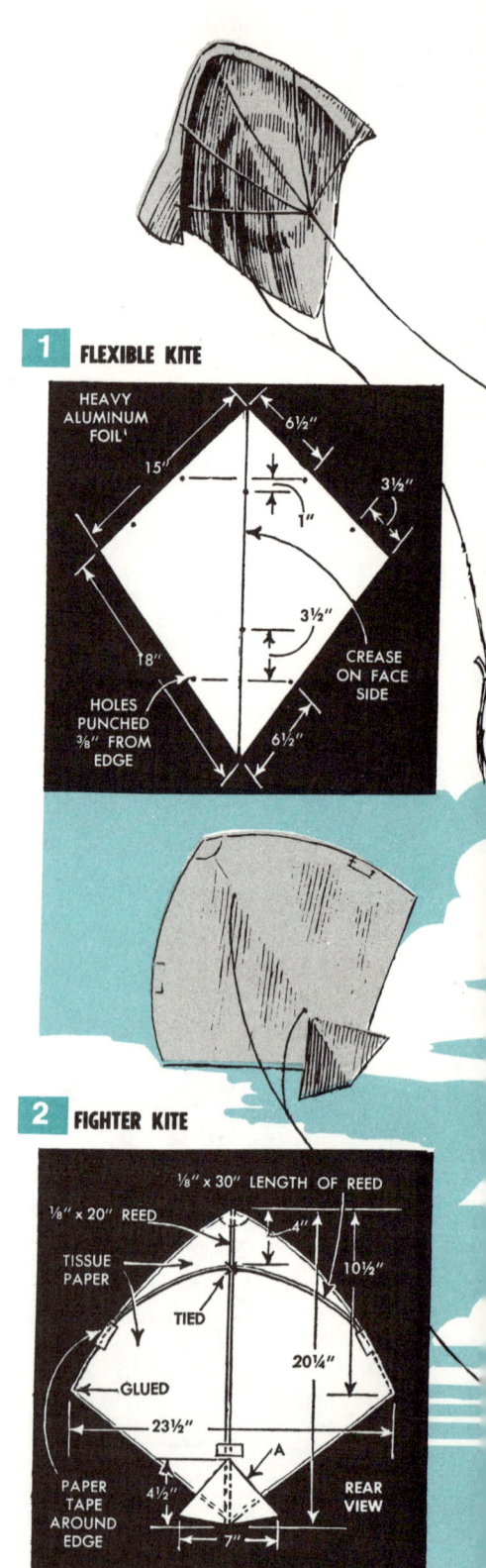

kite winders

Kite winders give better flight control

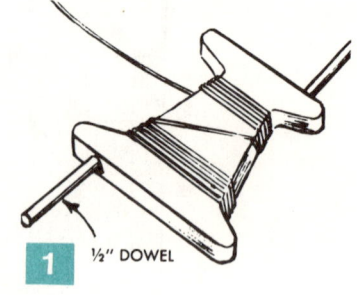

1. Better control of a kite in wind gusts is possible with this tapered reel. Automatic decrease or increase of take-up and let-out speeds are obtained simply by angling the reel so as to direct the windings to the narrow or wide end of the spool respectively.

2. Here is a standard-type kite-string reel that can be made in a few minutes, using a 4 x 8-in. board cut from one end of a wooden fruit crate for the reel and two empty thread spools for handles. The concave ends of the reel curve to a maximum depth of ½ in. The end of the string is tied in a loop around the reel, so that it can't be lost accidentally when the last turn is let out.

3. Mounted on a saw-horse-type seat and made to swivel from side to side in a pipe post, this clever chain-driven winder will appeal to the serious kite flyer. As you see, it is made from parts of an old bicycle. The front half of the frame is cut away at the seat post and at the sprocket hub, and the coaster brake from the rear wheel is made into a reel, or drum, by bolting two 8-in. hardboard disks to the flanges of the hub. The rubber treads are removed from the pedals and the spindles used for handles. With the bike braking action retained through the use of the coaster brake, you can pay out the kite string as fast or a slow as you wish.

See also: archery; boomerang; boys' projects; doghouse; kites; magic; play bouncers; sleds; stilts; toboggan; tree houses.

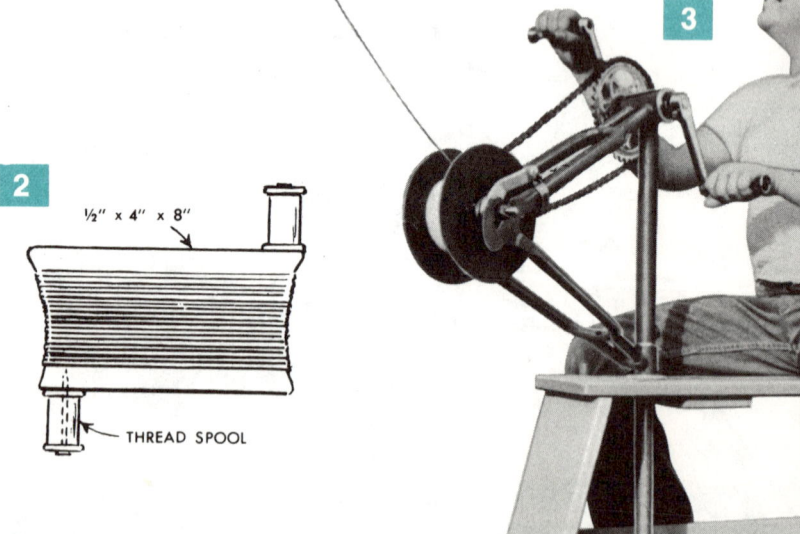

---

knapsacks: see packs, camping
knives: see honing
knobs, drawer: see hardware
knots: see rope

knurling

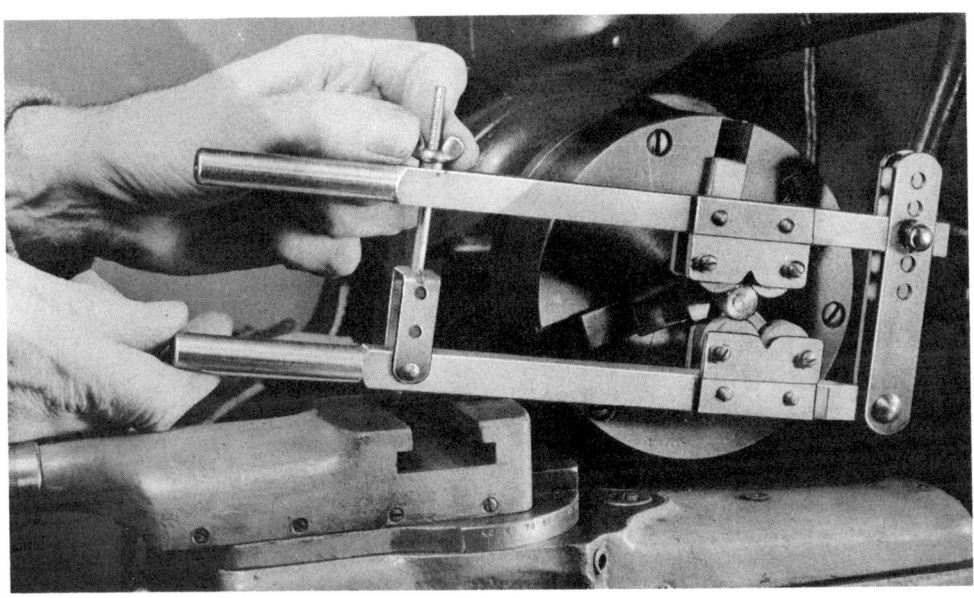

"Nutcracker" knurler for your lathe

BY WALTER E. BURTON

■ WITH THIS HAND-HELD KNURLER you can do straight or diagonal knurling, using one, two or three knurls at a time, on rods, tubes, knobs, etc., mounted in a lathe, drill press, portable electric drill, bench vise or even in final position on a machine.

Its normal capacity is about 3/16 to 2-in. diameter. However, by using smaller knurls and rollers closer together, somewhat smaller diameters could be accommodated, and by increasing lengths of the connector strips, larger diameters could be knurled.

The tool uses 3/4-in. knurls 3/8 in. wide, together with soft back-up rollers. Knurls are obtainable through most hardware dealers and generally come in pairs, either straight or diagonal, in fine, medium and coarse cuts. Straight knurls emboss longitudinal grooves parallel to the axis of the work. Diagonal ones produce diagonal grooves when used singly, diamond patterns when used in

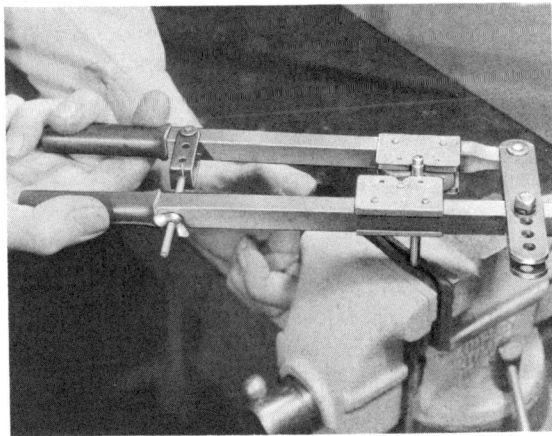

This hand-held model also can be used to knurl material held in a vise by placing the knurler around the work, tightening the clamp screw, and rotating

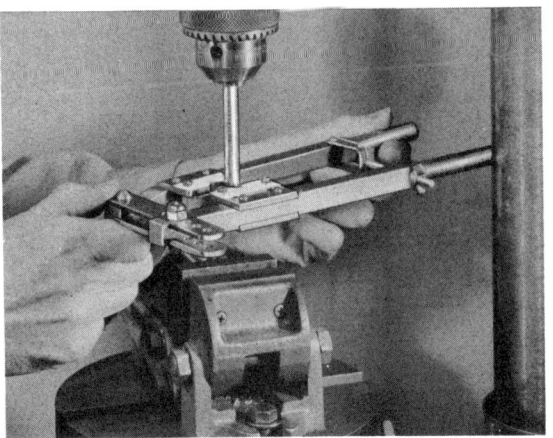

When knurling material on a drill press, the knurler is held so that one handle is steadied against the column. Operate the drill press at slow speed

1549

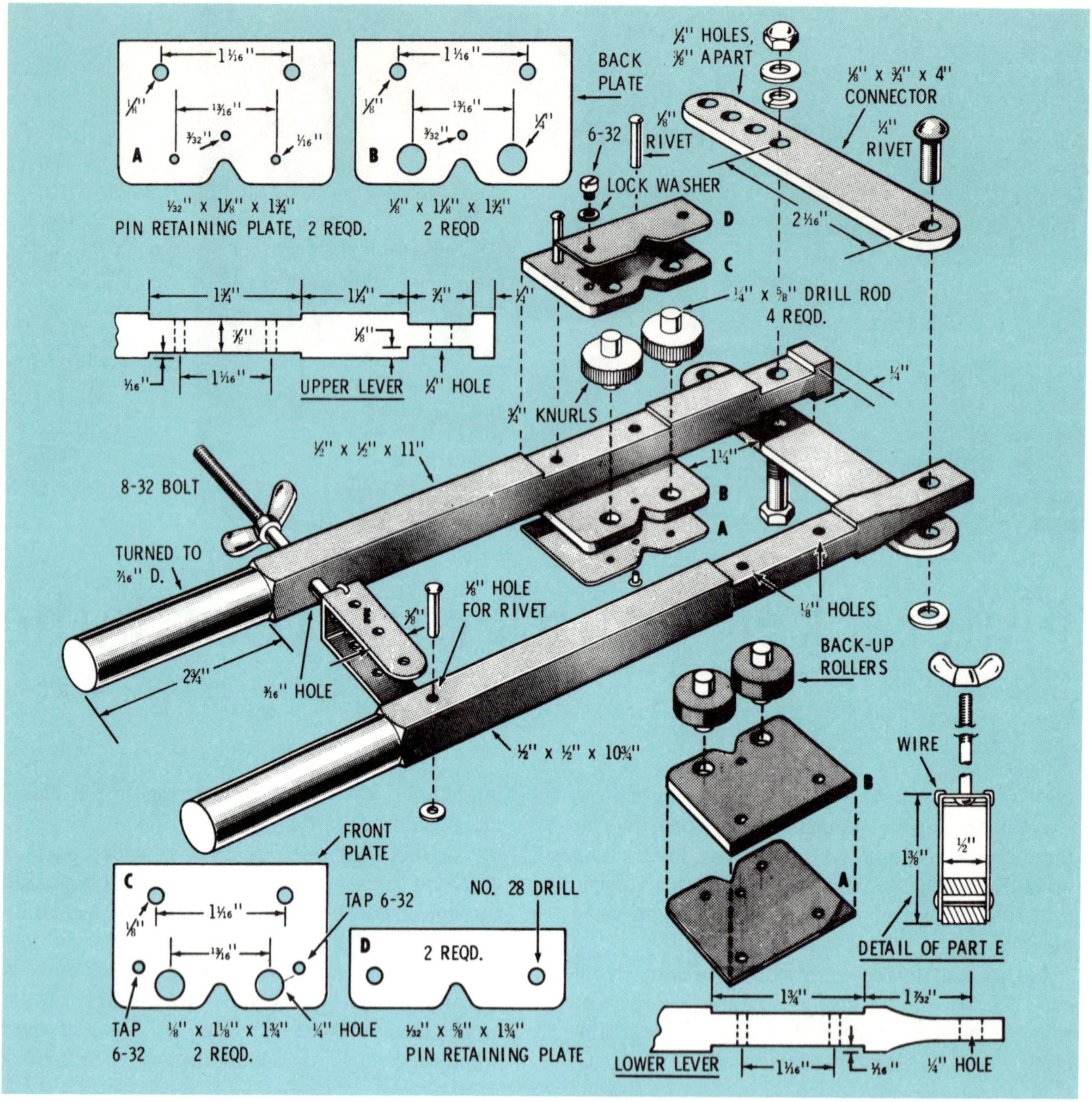

knurling

"nutcracker" knurler for your lathe, continued

The first step in machining the levers is to turn down one end of each to a 7/16 in. diameter

multiple. The knurls used in the original were Armstrong's No. 8275 (straight) and No. 8225 —right and left (diagonal).

Chief material required for this hand knurler is mild steel—about 24 in. of ½ x ½-in. bar, 9 in. of ⅛ x ¾-in. strip and about 8 in. of ⅛ x 1⅛-in. strip or plate. Ground flat stock can be substituted for the ⅛-in. strip, if desired.

The two levers, or arms, differ slightly in length. The upper lever is notched to produce a rigid right-angle joint between it and the two strips that connect the lever ends. You can cut both these notches and the shallower ones for the knurl-holder plates by milling, shaping, or filing. Depths of the plate recesses should be such that knurls have clearance to turn freely.

For ⅜-in. knurls, you'll find ⅛-in. recesses provide sufficient clearance.

Outer ends of the levers are machined round to ½-in. diameter, to serve as handles. Rubber or plastic grips may be added, or pieces of plastic garden hose can be used as grips. Just heat the hose and handles before assembly with an infrared lamp or other means, so the plastic will soften and conform to the handle shape.

Two steel connector strips are pivot-joined to the lower lever with a ¼-in. rivet. Toward the opposite end of each strip is a series of ¼-in. holes permitting adjustment of the separation between the levers in order to accommodate various diameters of work. If you wish, slots can be used instead of holes. A ¼-in. bolt, with a cap (acorn) nut for a more finished appearance, fastens the connectors to the upper lever.

The knurl holders are pairs of ⅛-in. steel plates between which knurls or back-up rollers are installed. One pair of plates is offset along its lever (with respect to the other pair) a distance equivalent to one half the spacing between knurl centers in a pair. Thus, one knurl or roller in each holder is positioned midway between the two knurls or rollers in the other holder. Center-to-center knurl spacing in the tool shown is 13/16 in., so the offset is 13/32 in.

plates marked "front" and "back"

For convenience, plates are marked "front" and "back" on the drawing. Each plate is provided with a thin (about 1/32 in.) piece, whose purpose is to hold the ¼-in. pins that serve as knurl axles, in position. The cover for each back plate is the same size as the plate, and is riveted permanently to it. The front cover is only half as wide and is held by two 6–32 machine screws and lock washers, so it can be removed when knurls are to be changed.

To assure alignment of knurl-pin holes, rivet the two knurl-holding plates temporarily to each lever before drilling the ¼-in. holes for the pins. Later, rivet them permanently, with the back covers in position. Each back cover has a small hole opposite each pin end, so a punch can be used to force out stubborn pins.

The clamp screw is an arrangement for applying constant pressure other than by squeezing with the hands. The screw-and-yoke arrangement shown consists of a U-shaped steel strip pivoted to the lower lever with an 8–32 or slightly larger bolt extending from it, and passing through a hole in the upper lever. A wire through the yoke and screw-head slot prevents

After milling the recesses for the connectors near the lever end, mill recesses for the knurl-holder plates, positioning by measuring from the bolt hole in each. End recesses are 1/8 in. deep. Others are 1/16 in.

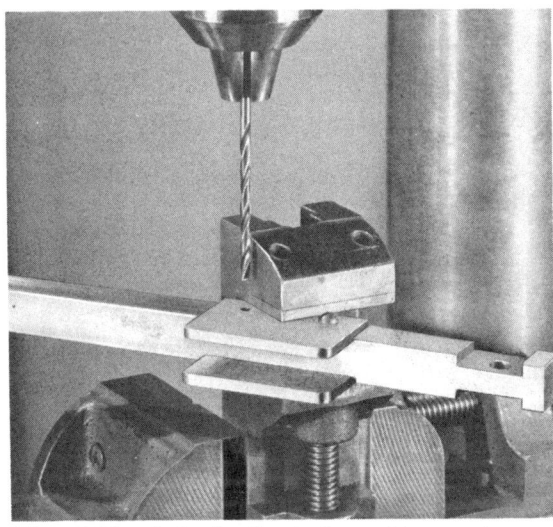

When drilling holes for the rivets used to mount the knurl-holder plates, align the plates on the lever and drill one hole, then slip a rivet into it to hold them in place while drilling the second

Holes for knurl pins can be drilled with the milling attachment in your lathe or on your drill press. Positioning is slightly easier on the lathe

knurling

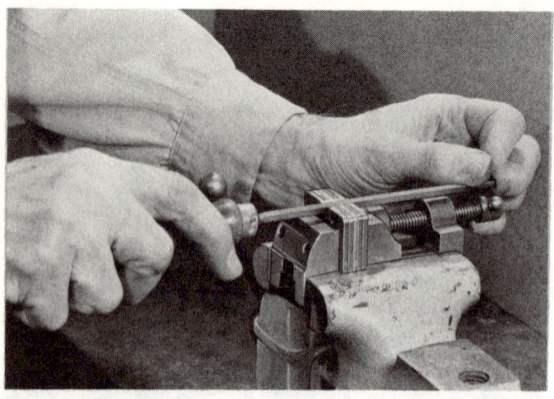

After cutting the rounded notches in the knurl-holder and pin-retaining plates, stack them and clamp them in a vise for finish-filing. Once this is done, the plates can be riveted to the levers

Drill both connectors simultaneously in the milling attachment of your lathe. Though you see five adjustment holes in this photo, it was later determined that only four holes would be required

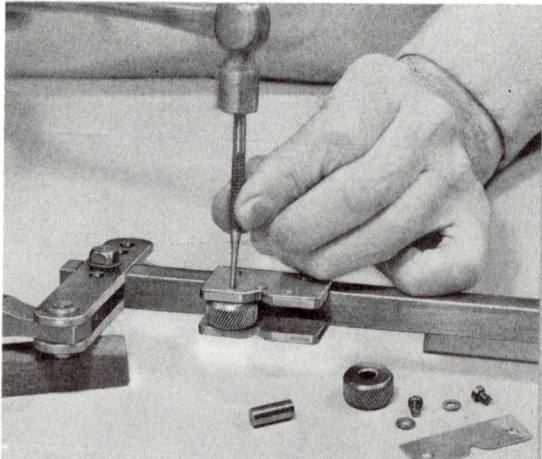

To change the knurls, remove the front pin-retaining plate and drive out the pins by inserting a punch through the holes in the rear pin-retaining plate. The same procedure is used to replace worn rollers

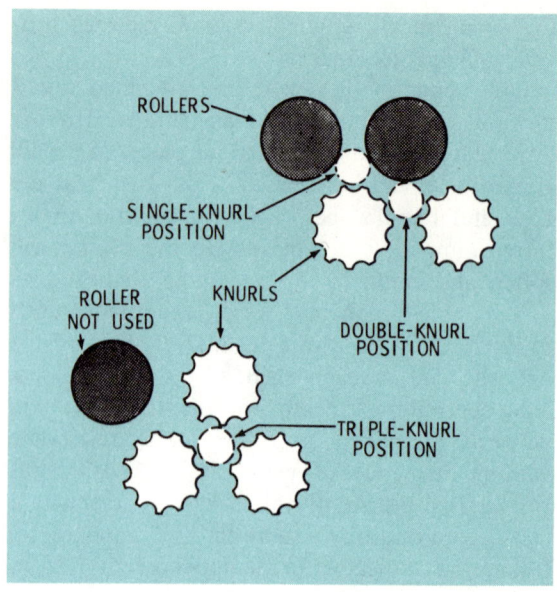

the screw from turning when the wingnut is turned. The 2½-in. bolt shown is adequate for the small and medium-diameter work for which this particular knurler was intended. For larger work a length of 4 in. or so is desirable.

The tool holds two pairs of knurls or rollers. If you are using three knurls of a kind simultaneously, install two in one holder and one opposite them in the other. If you intend to use one or two knurls at a time, install two knurls in one holder and two back-up rollers in the other. Then merely switch from one position to the other, as required, for single or double-knurl patterns, as sketched above.

The back-up rollers are made of relatively soft material that will not flatten the knurled pattern as fast as it is formed. Each roller is machined to the same size as a knurl. The rollers shown were turned from a phenol-formaldehyde resin that happened to be in the shop scrap box. They have worked well with aluminum, brass and steel, and do not appear to wear away at an excessive rate. Of course, some wearing away can be expected, so it's a good idea to make up spare rollers for quick replacements. Other materials that might be used for rollers (depending somewhat on the materials to be knurled) include aluminum, various plastics and steel faced with a softer material.

Always lubricate the knurls, rollers and work, as in conventional machine knurling. Use slow speeds when knurling work on a lathe or other power tool, and steady the knurler against some fixed part of the machine or the bench.

See also: circular cutters; dial indicator; inlaying; keyways; lathe techniques.

A long look at long ladders

BY JACKSON HAND

■ LADDER SHOPPERS too hungry for a bargain risk getting tripped by cheap manufacturing and merchandising methods. In their scramble to undersell each other, many dealers search out ladders they can sell cheaply. At first glance, these rigs seem as good as those costing 25 percent or so more. But let's take a closer look.

The matter of length, for example, is trickier than you might think. A 24-foot extension ladder has two 12-foot sections—the "base" and the "fly" (see drawing, p. 1554). According to the American Standards Assn. (A.S.A.), these

Is that ladder a bargain? Or a shortcut to the hospital?
Does it have enough rungs?
Enough muscle? Will it give you the usable length you're paying for?

A common way of fastening aluminum rungs into place in the side rails makes what amounts to a giant rivet of each rung. The collared rung goes into the rail (left) and is then peened over as shown in the cutaway section

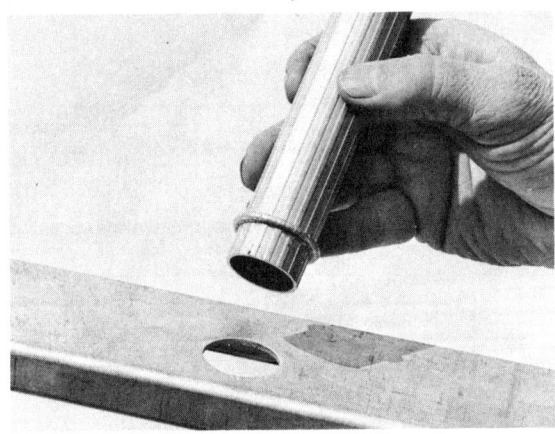

The rungs of magnesium ladders are often welded in place (left). Before buying a ladder, try to twist each rung. They shouldn't budge. Photo at right shows a swivel mount for ladder feet; note the non-skid rubber "soles"

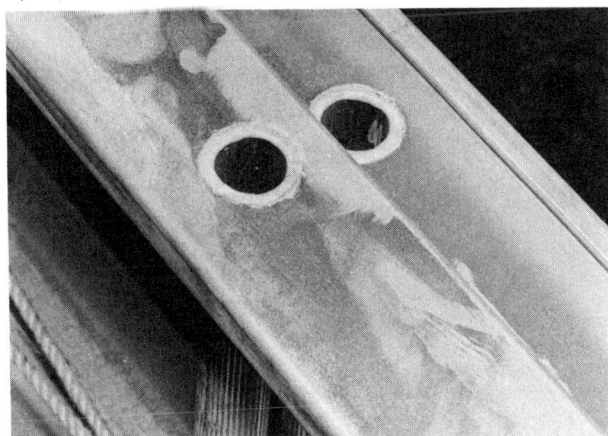

ladders

long ladders, continued

sections should overlap 3 feet, giving you 21 feet of usable length. Sometimes, especially in cheaper ladders, this overlap is greater to increase rigidity. A tip-off here would be the location of the pulley. Normally, it would be on the top or second rung of the base. On a cheap ladder, the manufacturer may put it two or three rungs away to prevent you from extending the ladder farther than is safe.

The best ladders have one rung per foot of nominal length. For instance, a 12-foot section of a 24-footer has 12 rungs, the lowest one 7 in. from the bottom, the top one 5 in. from the top. Cheaper ladders may have 11 rungs, starting up 1 ft. from the bottom and ending a ft. from the top. This is no great inconvenience, but it leaves 1 ft. of side rail at each end which is not supported by a rung. To reinforce the unsupported rails, some such ladders may have a brace beneath the bottom rung. While the braces may give added strength, check to be sure they don't prevent maximum extension by interfering with the operation of the pulley.

Experts say that the longer a ladder is, the more you should pay for it, by the foot. One ladder-component manufacturer puts it this way: "The longer the side rails, the stronger they must be. The extra strength can come from only one thing—extra metal or wood."

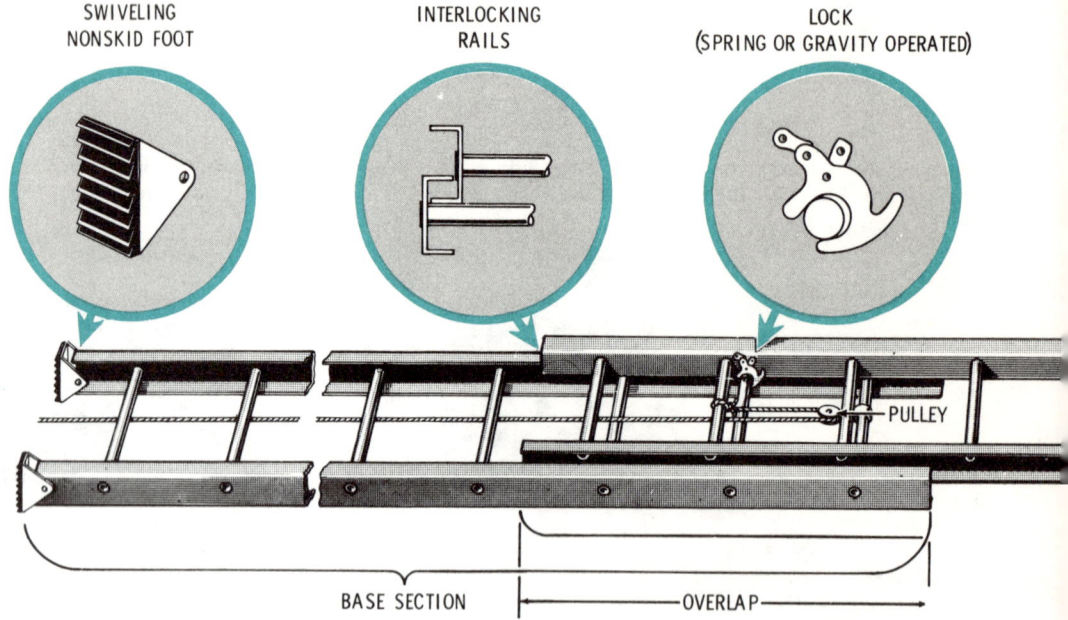

The drawing above shows the basics of metal ladder assembly. Many will have rungs and feet shaped somewhat differently from the illustration. Some shorter models may have neither pulleys nor ropes

The chart below lists the approximate specifications of well-made extension ladders. Height-in-place is less than nominal height because ladders are used at an angle and the sections overlap to a degree

TYPICAL DIMENSIONS OF METAL EXTENSION LADDERS

NOMINAL HEIGHT	ACTUAL HEIGHT IN PLACE	Utility-household grade				Industrial-commercial grade			
		WIDTH	CROSS SECTION OF RAIL	SIZE OF RUNG	WEIGHT	WIDTH	CROSS SECTION OF RAIL	SIZE OF RUNG	WEIGHT
16'	12'	15"	2½"x ¾"	1³⁄₁₆"	20 lbs	18-20"	3"x 1½"	1⁵⁄₁₆"	36 lbs
20'	16'	15"	2½"x ¾"	1³⁄₁₆"	25 lbs	18-20"	3"x 1½"	1⁵⁄₁₆"	44 lbs
24'	20'	15"	2½"x ¾"	1³⁄₁₆"	30 lbs	18-20"	3"x 1½"	1⁵⁄₁₆"	52 lbs
28'	24'	15"	2½"x ¾"	1³⁄₁₆"	35 lbs	18-20"	3"x 1½"	1⁵⁄₁₆"	59 lbs
32'	28'	15"	2½"x ¾"	1³⁄₁₆"	40 lbs	18-20"	3½"x 1½"	1⁵⁄₁₆"	73 lbs
36'	32'	Not recommended				18-20"	3½"x 1½"	1⁵⁄₁₆"	82 lbs
40'	34'	Not recommended				18-20"	3½"x 1½"	1⁵⁄₁₆"	90 lbs

Straight grain is important. This typical break followed the grain from edge to edge of the rail

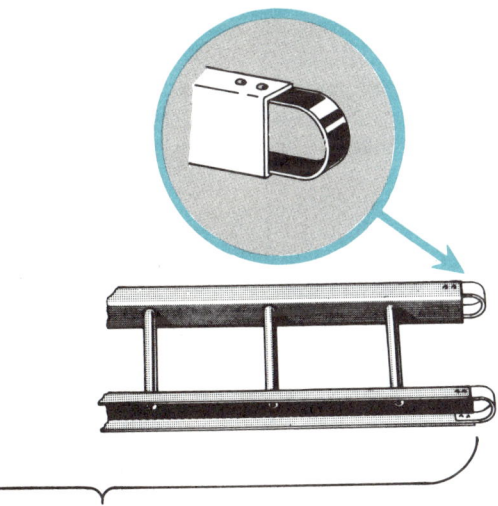

FLY SECTION

The height-to-weight ratio is a guide to quality in stepladders and extensions. Ladders much lighter than indicated in the charts below and at left may have skimped on strength, stability and safety

Stepladders: typical sizes and weights		
Light duty	3 feet 4 5 6	6 lbs 9 10½ 12
Utility	3 feet 4 5 6 7 8	7 lbs 10 11½ 14½ 18 21
Industrial	4 feet 5 6 8 10 12 14	14 lbs 16½ 20 26½ 35 42 50

Of course, there is nothing to keep someone from making a cheap 32-ft. ladder using rail stock meant for a 24-footer. As long as such a ladder is never twisted, never set up on uneven ground, never overloaded and never set up at too flat an angle everything may be fine and dandy. But the limitations easily cancel out the low price.

weight per running foot

Metal ladder stock is graded by weight per running foot of rail. A good 24-footer may have rails that go .391 lbs. per foot. A higher ladder or a better 24-footer may go .440 lbs. per foot. Tops for homeowner equipment is around .550. It's hard to measure this weight on the dealer's floor, of course. All you can do is appraise the gauge of the metal by studying the ends of the rails. There are, in addition, two ways you can judge strength intelligently.

First, don't be so all-fired interested in lightness. Any good aluminum or magnesium rig is light enough. If it is too light, it may also be too weak for safety.

Second, here is an A.S.A. test for ladder rigidity: Extend the ladder to its permissible overlap. Place it flat on two supports spaced 6 in. from each end. Put a 2 x 4 or something similar across the ladder at midpoint and apply a 200-lb. load. The ladder must withstand the load without permanent bending or other visible weakening. Obviously, few dealers will let you perform this test on their merchandise. But it's worth a try.

Ladder experts agree that you should buy a ladder long enough to reach the highest point around your home. But, think twice about skinning up a 32- or 40-footer to reach the gable ends of a two-story house, especially if you're overweight, under-agile or inexperienced.

How wide should a ladder be? They generally run as narrow as 12 in., which is a bit skimpy. Good ones run 15 in. or more. A worthwhile industrial grade goes 20 in. Extra width, of course, provides greater stability and comfort for the user.

Incidentally, the once common practice of flaring the base section does little, if anything, for stability. It's impossible to flare the interlocking sections of a metal ladder, anyway, and the practice has even grown rare among wood-ladder makers.

Good rungs are important to quality. Wooden rungs should be pretty close to 1¼ in. in diameter. Grain should be straight and clear. Edge grain should face the top of the ladder.

Metal rungs should be closed tubes which may

ladders

To stiffen the side rails, the bottom two or three rungs of a metal stepladder, depending on its height, should have diagonal braces like these

Both of these wood ladders have straight grain, braced back section, and reinforcing rods under the rungs, but only one has non-skid rubber feet

long ladders, continued

be round or D-shaped, with the flat surface upward. Cheap ladders may have tubular rungs with open seams. A metal rung under 1 3/16 in. in diameter is too light. Good ladders usually have 1 5/16-in. rungs.

Some ladders have flat treads, riveted to the sides, or tubular rungs with flat treads welded on top. Both are more comfortable than plain rungs. The rivet construction, however, does not give the strength found in properly made round-rung ladders, and should, therefore, be reinforced with braces under several steps.

A ladder derives its basic strength from its side rails. In metal rigs, it's immaterial whether these are channel, I-beam, etc., as long as the metal is properly distributed between flanges and web. In simplest terms, the web provides the strength to keep the ladder from "bellying" when you stand on it. The flanges keep the ladder from bending sidewise. More critically, they hold the web in perfect plane, because the slightest bend or wave might let the web buckle.

Be suspicious of a side rail that measures less than 3/4 x 2 1/2 in. overall. Also, compare the dimensions with the weights in the chart mentioned previously, because a rail can be made with good dimensions, but with thin webs and flanges.

Hardware varies greatly from ladder to ladder. Feet should swivel freely, to seat firmly on the ground. In some good ladders, they fasten to toothed projections. In icy conditions, you remove the rubber-soled feet and let the teeth take over. Locks may be gravity-operated or spring-loaded. In either case, try them out. If they are tricky or temperamental, the fly section might crash down unexpectedly as you raise or lower it.

Some metal ladders have little wheels at the top to facilitate raising and lowering of the fly. Make sure such wheels are solidly made. An alternative to wheels is skids, usually in the form of an arch over the top of each rail or a curved nosing at the end of each rail. Sometimes these are covered with plastic to keep aluminum from marking the side of the house. Magnesium doesn't mark, needs no such cover.

So far, we've talked mostly about metal extension ladders. What's the story on metal vs. wood? Essentially, wood ladders cost less and weigh more, as shown by this comparison of typical "homeowner" grade rigs:

	Wood	Aluminum	Magnesium
Height	24 ft.	24 ft.	24 ft.
Weight	48 lbs.	29 lbs.	27 lbs.
Price	$26	$31	$47

check side rail quality

In judging the quality of a wooden ladder, look for side rails of straight-grained fir, hemlock, pine or spruce. Spruce is best, but getting scarce. The edge of the grain must fall on the edge of the rail. Ash or oak (especially red or scrub oak) make the best rungs. There are probably fewer bad wooden ladders on the market than bad metal ones, since there is less price competition.

Is wood safer than metal around high-voltage wires? Well, it is true that you can electrocute yourself by touching a metal ladder to a high-voltage wire, but the antidote is to avoid the wires, not the metal ladders.

Which brings us to stepladders. Because women frequently buy and use them, there has been considerable effort by manufacturers to reduce weights in this group. That should, after all, make their product more appealing to their gentle customers.

But the result is that many stepladders on the market today are virtually worthless—or even dangerous to use. Light weight can hardly be that important.

And anyway, a little lady used to muscling around —say— an 18-lb. turkey or controlling an obstreperous 40-lb. youngster needn't quail at the thought of a 12-lb. stepladder. Yet that's all a good aluminum or magnesium version usually weighs.

Actually, the vast majority of feminine around-the-house jobs can best be handled from a 24- or 27-in. step stool.

The back rails of a good metal stepladder are usually made of channel. Angle can be adequate, however, if the rails are heavy enough. In many cases, you'll find X-bracing between the rear rails, for rigidity, but some products have rungs you could stand on in a pinch. The X-brace breaks up the geometry into triangles—the strongest and most rigid form possible, so the best models have X-bracing as well as rungs.

When you're sizing up a stepladder, open it up and flip down the pail shelf. Then pull down on it. The A.S.A. says it should be able to handle a 50-lb. load without failing. And don't be hesitant about checking it out thoroughly; if the retailer isn't confident enough of his merchandise to let you test it, you're better off to get your ladder someplace else. After all, the few bucks you might save with a "bargain" can hardly compensate you for the pain and financial cost of injuries from a ladder that can't handle the job.

The ladder's overall dimensions indicate a lot about its stability. Further, they can help you recognize the product of a manufacturer that has tried to cut corners a bit here and there.

start with the profile

Start out with a look at the ladder's profile. Unless it was especially designed for working unusually close to a wall (a technique that demands special care and is usually better left to professionals), it should follow a minimum spread proportion: The front and back should spread about 5½ in. farther apart for each foot of height. Thus the rear feet should be nearly 36 in. from the front ones for a 6-ft. ladder. The proportion should be even greater for short ladders, to insure enough stability.

Now take a head-on look. The ladder should be at least 1 ft. wide at the top, and each side should spread away from vertical at the rate of an inch per foot. Thus, a 6-footer will spread to around 24 in. at the base. Again, the degree of splay is greater for short ladders.

Finally, a word about a few special-purpose stepladders. At least one—the platform type—is often more comfortable than the standard variety. It has a platform near the top for you to stand on. Such ladders are classified by height. A "No 8," for example, will be around 8 ft. high, with the platform about 6 ft. from the ground when in use.

The double-front, or trestle, ladder has two fronts instead of a front and back, permitting two people to stand on it simultaneously. Such models are usually strong and stable, and prove handy for such jobs as applying gypsum board to a ceiling.

As you can imagine, there aren't many instances when you'll need this extra versatility. Since there is little call for a double-front ladder in the home handyman market, these are usually available only in commercial or industrial grades. The extra convenience is rather costly.

See also: building; crawl space; fire ladders; gutters; ladders, boat; painting; roofs.

ladders

Rubber-faced feet keep metal ladders from slipping. On soft ground, a plank provides footing

No home accessory looks so harmless—yet has greater accident potential. But if you're savvy, you're safe

1558

To perch safely on the roof, lay the ladder flat and hook brackets over the ridge as in inset

A pair of rented ladder jacks lets you rig a scaffold and save lots of ladder moving

How to stay alive on a ladder

BY BERNARD GLADSTONE

It's an essential tool for many jobs, but the ordinary ladder can lay you low if you ignore these basic rules

■ WHAT GOES UP must come down—but not always at the same speed. To make sure *you* will always come down a ladder the way you went up—a step at a time:

• Don't climb anything but a top-quality ladder which you know is in good repair.

• When using any type of ladder, be sure to follow established common-sense rules on setting it up and working from it.

Before using a ladder—especially a borrowed, rented, or rarely used one—inspect it carefully. Check rungs or steps for cracks or splitting. Test rungs on a long ladder by laying it flat and bounc-

A multi-purpose ladder leads three lives: At left, it's a double-fronted stepladder. Or the back swings up (center) to convert to a small extension ladder. The back can also be removed to serve as a separate straight ladder. An adjustable provision lets you offset the back (right)

1559

ladders

HOW TO CARRY A LADDER

Horizontal carry is safest if you're moving a long ladder any distance. Lift the ladder at the balance point and rest a rail on your shoulder. For short moves, lift it vertically (right) and steady the top with a good, high grip

stay alive on a ladder, continued

ing your full weight lightly on each rung. Then stand it in working position to see if it's solid. And inspect pivots, locks, and other hardware.

If you're buying a new ladder, don't let price alone determine your selection. Even with a small stepladder this can be foolhardy. Remember that more injuries are caused by falls from a 3 or 4-ft. height than by falls from a tall extension ladder. Since a good ladder will last many years, the few dollars saved is hardly worth the increased risk inherent in a "bargain" of inferior quality. Check the ladder before you buy it. The side rails should be free of knots or other defects.

To preserve a new wood ladder, coat it with a clear penetrating wood sealer or spar varnish before you expose it to the weather. Never use paint—an opaque finish may hide cracks so they'll be difficult to spot later on. It's a good precaution to lubricate all hardware at least once a year, and spray exposed metal with a clear plastic or lacquer to prevent rusting. Ladders of magnesium or aluminum need no special maintenance (except for lubrication of pivots), but they should be permanently equipped with rubber-faced safety feet to prevent slipping on hard surfaces. Such metal ladders are lighter and easier to handle than comparable wood ladders, but be careful when using them near power lines.

Before climbing to any height on a ladder, mount a step or two and bounce lightly up and down to see if there's any sign of shifting or sliding. When positioning a tall extension ladder against the side of a house, one obvious caution is to avoid resting the top end against a window pane or screen. If you must place the ladder in a spot where a window is located, nail a wide board across the opening first, and rest the ladder against this. If it's not practical to nail the board in place from inside the window, nail or clamp it across the upper end of your ladder, instead, before you raise it. To keep the top of an extension ladder from marring a freshly-painted surface, wrap the ends in heavy rags, or slip a pair of old wool socks or work gloves over them. Be sure to scrape all mud or grease off your shoes before you start up.

When climbing, descending or working from any ladder, always face *toward* it, never away from it. While climbing, hold on with both hands. Try to tuck tools in your pockets or clip them to your belt to leave your hands free. If there are too many items to handle, climb the ladder first, then haul the load up with light rope. You can keep most small tools in a pail hooked onto a rung. While working, hold on with at least one hand; if that's impractical, hook one leg through a rung.

For certain jobs, a long working platform is more convenient than working from a single ladder. The quickest way to rig up a simple scaffold is to rent a couple of ladder jacks. At relatively low heights such as the setup shown on a preceding page, you have the option of mounting such jacks on the *inside* of the ladders, as well, for an underslung platform closer to the wall. Though ladder jacks are made in various styles, the safest type is the kind that hooks onto the ladder rails rather than the rungs. You can also rent an adjustable extension plank of the kind shown, or just use a 2 x 10 or 2 x 12.

If a ladder must be placed in front of a door, either lock the door shut or tie it open so that no one can come charging through and slam into the ladder while you're on it. If you're working indoors—particularly on polished-tile or hardwood floors—you can keep a ladder from slipping (or marring the floor) by fastening a piece of rubber heel or a split section of hose to each leg.

HOW TO RAISE A TALL LADDER . . .

Raise it alone by butting the foot against the wall and lifting the other end.
Bring the "high" end to head level, grasp the top rung as shown, and "walk" your hands toward the building.
Moving toward the building, go hand over hand along the rungs until the ladder is vertical.
The ladder can now be moved to either side as needed or, if you're located right, just bring the foot out.
For a safe climbing angle, the distance from the wall to the foot should be a fourth of the ladder's height.

. . . AND HOW TO ADJUST IT AFTER IT'S UP

Never reach beyond a comfortable arm's length to the side; stand straight on the rungs and don't strain overhead. Raise the extension to working height by pulling down on the rope; bracket hooks over rungs (inset)

To lower the ladder, tug the line until the hook is free; the pivoting bar will close the hook so it slides past rungs on the way down. To shift the ladder sideways (right), move the top a bit, then the foot

1561

ladders, boat

Swing-up ladder mounts on transom

BY HANK CLARK

■ IF YOU'VE EVER TRIED to climb into a boat from the water without using a boarding ladder, you know just how necessary this accessory can be. It's almost a must for skiing or swimming. The swing-up model shown here has one advantage over portable ladders—it's permanently mounted on the transom, thus self-storing.

The choice of materials is up to you. The model shown is ¾-in. mahogany, although white oak would make a somewhat stronger ladder. You can determine the proper angle for the upper sides by dropping a plumb bob from the transom and measuring the triangle thus formed. The entire ladder must be tailored to match the transom height of your boat, so plan on running it from the deck down to a point slightly above the waterline when the boat is on plane.

Cut the sides of the lower section the same length as those of the upper part to form an even joint when the ladder is folded. For appearance, the rungs should also be spaced to butt against each other when the ladder is swung up.

After determining the rung locations, cut notches in the sides and mount the rungs with glue and screws. If you use brass or bronze screws, the heads may be set flush with the surface and left exposed. For a deluxe job, however, countersink them and cover with wood plugs.

Finally, assemble the ladder according to the plan and paint or varnish it to match your boat.

See also: anchors, boat; boat repair; cover, boat; deck, boat; fire ladders; ladders; propellers, boat; sterns, boat; tools, boat.

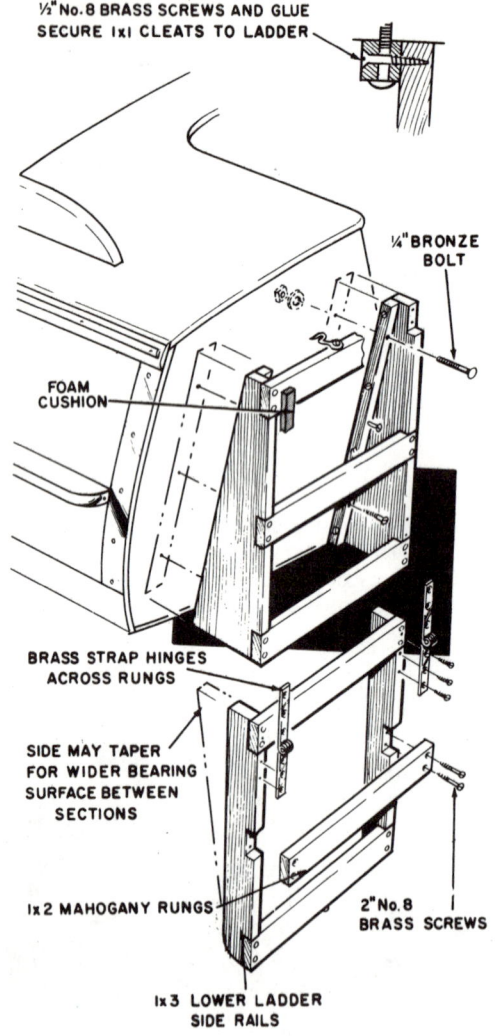

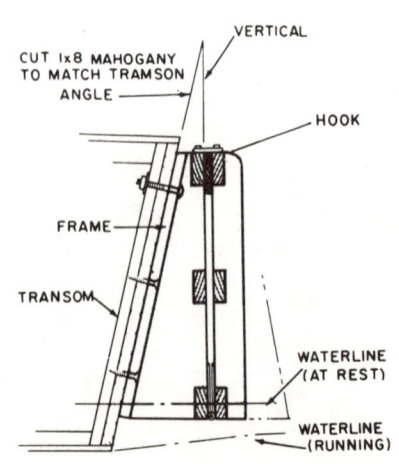

ladders, fire: see fire ladders
lamp, pole: see pole-lamp table

clever ideas

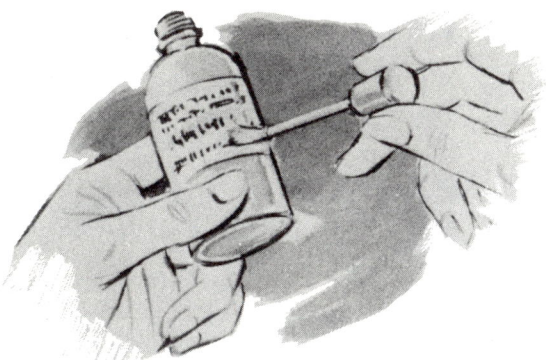

Labels on medicine bottles will often become so smudged and blurred as to be unreadable. You can protect the label by applying a coat of colorless nail polish right after purchasing the medicine.

This handy doorside rack for milk and bread deliveries can be made by attaching a discarded bicycle basket next to the back door. The rack will also be handy for holding bundles while you unlock the door.

Following a recipe can be especially difficult if you're interrupted by phone calls or delivery men. To avoid overlooking an important step, mark your stopping point with a bobby pin.

A pin-up board for gardeners provides a place to post planting schedules, special seed packets, and seasonal memos. Make it from a narrow carton with the sides and ends cut away to form a bin.

When location requires that there be a space between a washer and dryer, installation can be made more pleasing by building a matching filler unit of 1 x 2s and plywood cut and fitted to the contour of the space.

lamps

Lamps are reminders of earlier days

BY ART TRAUFFER

■ HERE ARE two novel lamp bases which are built around nostalgic items of the past—a sadiron and a horseshoe.

The sadiron is converted into a lamp by drilling a ⅜-in. hole through the wooden handle for a length of ⅛-in. electrical fixture pipe, threaded at each end. The upper end is fitted with a standard pushbutton socket and the lower end is attached to the wooden handle with a round and a hex nut. A bit of rubber tape is wrapped around the lampcord where it enters the pipe. The lamp is completed by brightening the pipe standard with steel wool, cementing felt pads to the iron bottom and adding a clip-on shade.

The second lamp is a cute one for a young cowpoke's room. Here both the horseshoe and the toy pistol are drilled for a ¼-20 stove bolt, the hole in the shoe being tapped. It is important that the hole in the pistol handle be drilled parallel with the barrel so that the revolver will stand vertically when bolted to the shoe. A short ⅛-in. pipe nipple is cemented in the end of the barrel with epoxy for attaching a socket. Finally, a hole is made in the cap of the socket for the lampcord.

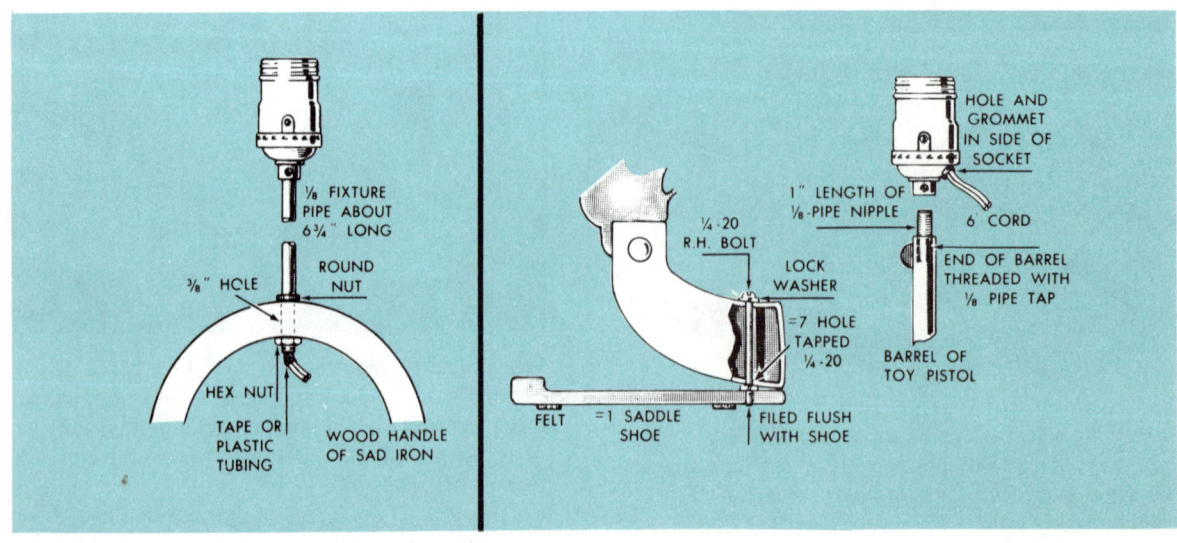

1564

lamps

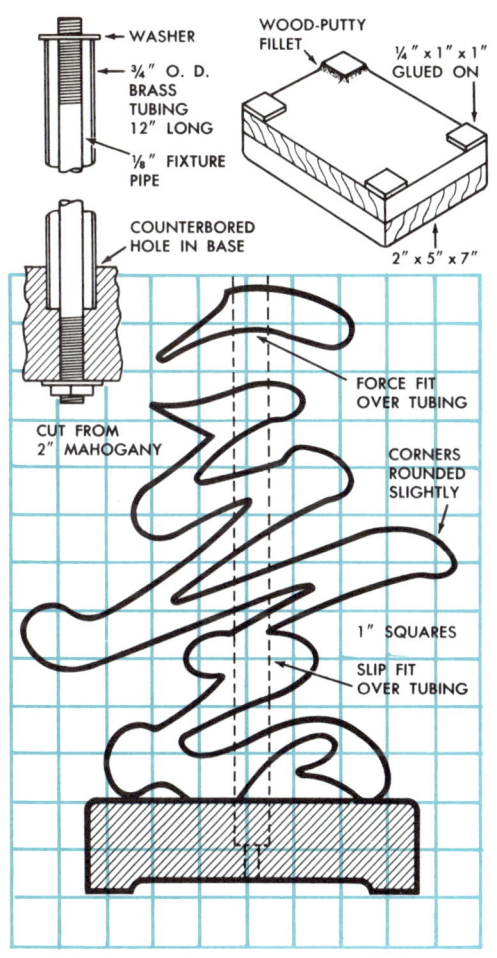

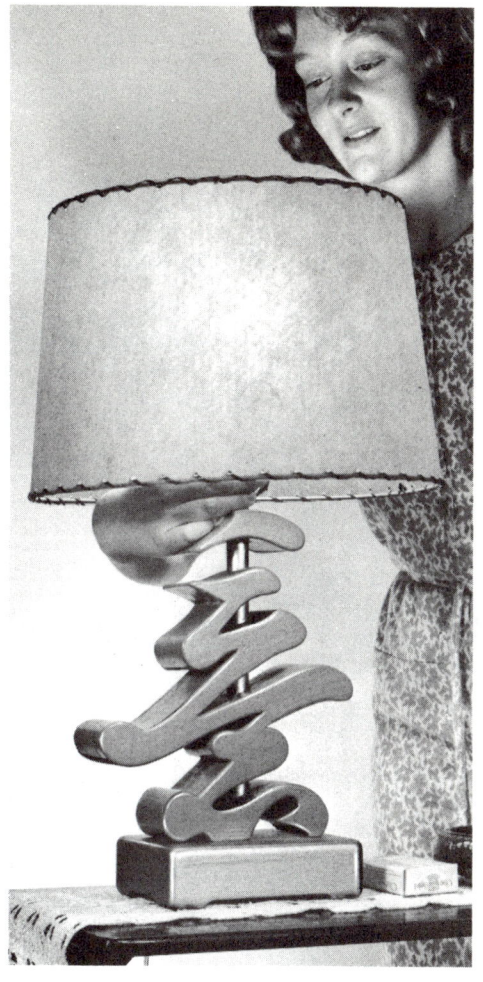

Lamp base is ideograph meaning "thought"

BY JOHN BURROUGHS

■ YOU MIGHT THINK that this lamp is simply a sort of free-form design, but actually it's the Chinese ideograph "I," which means "thought." To make the lamp you'll need a piece of mahogany or other hardwood about 11-in. long. If you find it difficult to obtain a block a full 2 in. thick, you can glue together two or more pieces. Before bandsawing, drill the block endwise for the ¾-in. tubing through which the lamp cord and threaded pipe pass. The lower end of the tubing seats in a counter-bored hole made in the built-up wooden base. All corners should be rounded with a rasp and sandpaper.

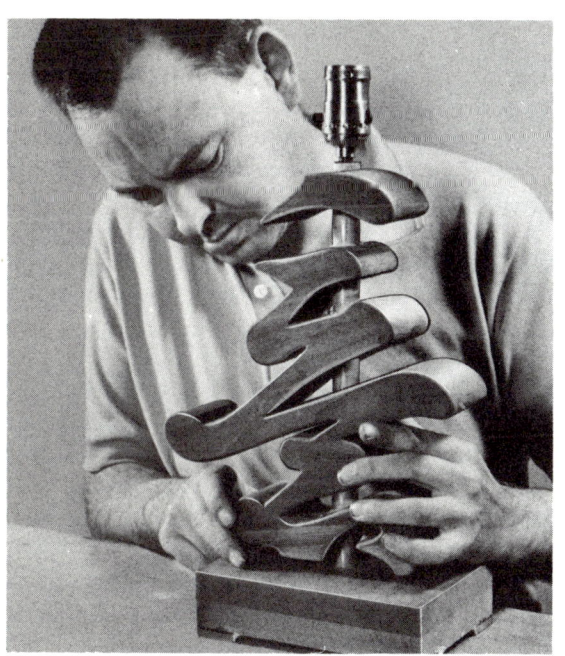

1565

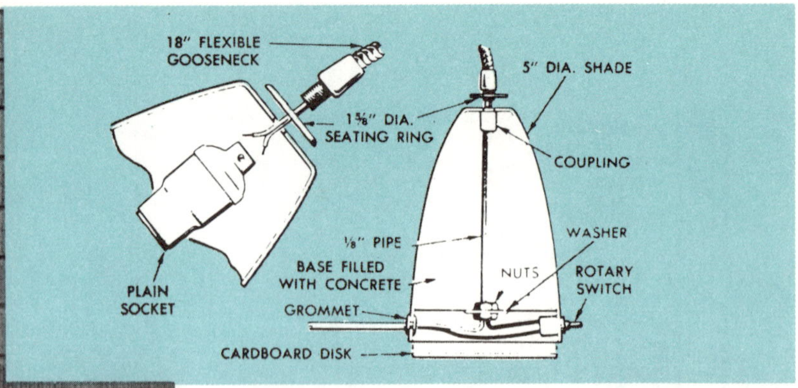

lamps

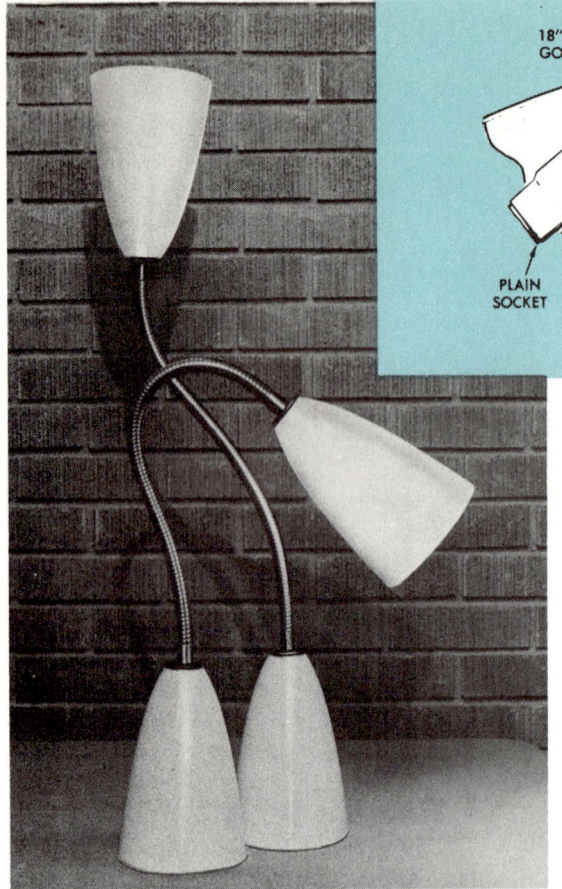

Use cardboard and tape for recess forms around switch and bushing. Curved strip set in concrete carries cord

Spotlight on modern lamps

BY RON ANDERSON

Decorative and flexible, these modern lamps won't tip over in the wind

■ TWO SHADES ARE BETTER than one, particularly in the case of these modern gooseneck table lamps, for one of the shades forms the base. Each lamp is assembled from standard lamp fittings, fiberglass bullet shades, a regular flexible brass arm and, of all things, concrete.

As you see in the detail, the concrete is used to weight the base and keep it from tipping. It will take about 11 lb. of concrete, the kind you buy dry-mixed in a paper bag. The details show quite clearly how you assemble the parts to make a single lamp. Be especially careful when drilling the holes through the shade that serves as the base not to crack or otherwise damage the material. Install switch, bushing, grommet, pipe and coupling in the shade as detailed. Now notice in the right-hand photo that the switch and bushing are protected by pieces of light cardboard when pouring the concrete and that after pouring, a groove, or channel, is formed for the cord with a strip of cardboard or sheet metal. This done, allow the concrete to harden (keep it damp for several hours after it sets) and then assemble the wiring and the shade, using a plain, or keyless, socket as detailed. Finally, fit a disk of cardboard into the bottom of the base shade, glue it in place and cover with felt so the base will not scratch table tops.

Cask lamp goes with rustic decor

This decorative lamp is half made before you start

■ CALL IT A LAZY MAN'S LAMP if you will, but it's a quickie which is half made for you since the base is an empty fig cask. All you really need to make it is a turned wood hub and a new cask head; the rest of the parts are standard lamp fittings. Where do you get the cask? Go to a health-food store. Of course it will be up to you to empty the cask. The sketch shows how the turned hub, or riser, is attached to the cask head with screws, after which a hole is bored through the center for a length of ⅛-in. electrical fixture pipe, threaded at the ends. A socket and harp are added at the top and a washer and locknut at the bottom. A hole is bored in the side of the cask and the lamp is wired with a 6-ft. lampcord before the cask head is forced back into place. Fitted with an appropriate shade, your finished lamp will fit in perfectly with the rustic decor of a den or vacation cabin.

land, federal: see home sites

landscaping

A professional landscape architect shows you how to design your yard for easy care and eye-pleasing beauty. Follow his advice for an all-play and no-work showplace

You can have a lazy-man's lawn

BY CLAYTON W. STEEN

■ HUMAN NATURE being what it is, most home owners today would like their private real estate to resemble a nursery exhibit at the National Flower Show. But the care of this neatly manicured arboretum mustn't interfere with golf, sailing, social engagements or family vacations. Briefly, it should take care of itself. Is this wishful thinking? Not entirely. The answer, like many in our complex modern civilization, is neither black nor white.

Whatever is said about landscaping, one thing

Pebbles, concrete and ground cover turned a woodland lot into a graceful low-maintenance garden built from the plan below

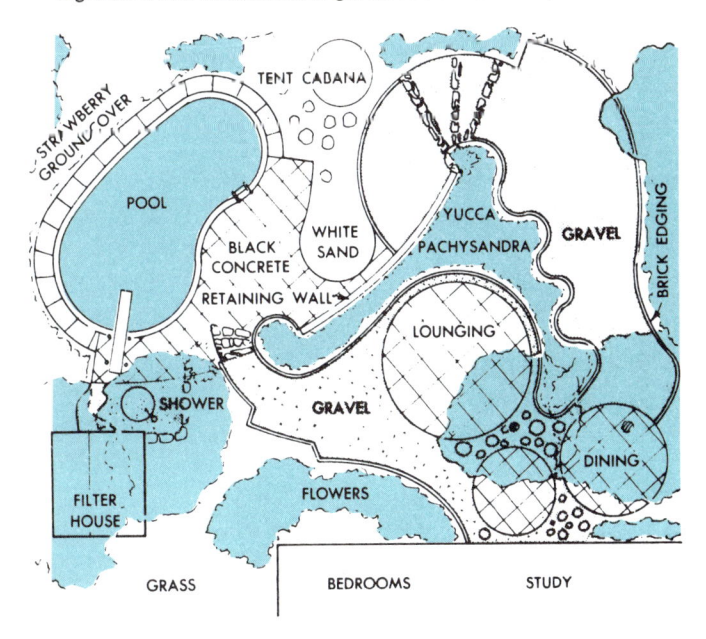

landscaping

Terracing with low walls divides yard areas, creates a pleasing effect and permits the use of decorative steps. The lawn area is edged with brick to aid in trimming the grass

lazy-man's lawn, continued

is certain: Maintenance is never *completely* eliminated. Plants, whether grass, trees or shrubs, are living, growing things. As such, they require feeding, weeding, spraying and pruning. Fortunately, however, many plants are sympathetic to the demands made upon harassed modern man and are able to put on a good show without much help. Whether you think in terms of lawn or plantings, the job is to separate for use the best performers demanding the least attention. These are "easy maintenance" qualifications:
1. Neat growth habit.
2. Relatively free of disease and insect attack.
3. Seasonal interest.
4. Hardy resistance to temperature change or drouth.
5. Slow-growing, or easily restricted.

By choosing such plants carefully, employing a few tricks in the planning of beds, and restricting lawn areas with sweeping, maintenance-free patio spaces, no one need be a slave to a weedy jungle.

The job of creating easy maintenance landscape on any site, however, begins with planning. This is a must. No two sites are alike, nor are the needs of any two families. Whatever else it may be—from showplace to eyesore—the area around any house is for people to use and enjoy. It should be designed with this in mind.

One of my recent problems involved a retired gentleman and his wife with a small house on two acres. They wanted freedom to play golf, fish and travel. They weren't interested in decorative settings, but the place had to look perpetually tidy. So we preserved the site's natural, irregular contours with interesting rocks and gnarled old trees. A farmer cuts the meadow-type lawn three times a year. With maintenance slashed to the bone, these people can take a slow boat around the world and come home to find the landscape unchanged.

Another family with three energetic young-

Stepping stones of concrete, planted at random through a gravel "lawn," serve a practical and decorative purpose by providing firm footing and an eye-appealing pattern

sters in a new tract house presented a different problem. They wanted decor, easy maintenance, a place for the kids to play, "practically no lawn to mow, please—and do something about the swamp." Today you enter this home via a spacious court of screened bluestone and rectangular flag stepping-stones, contained by long, low railroad tie walls that terrace an embankment rock garden. A steep bank on the far end is cloaked in a blanket of evergreen periwinkle that never needs trimming. A king-size area beside the house is paved in asphalt and marked out for games. A drainage ditch beyond it takes the ex-swamp water off into a winding brooklet behind the house. Here, long, curving gravel areas with circular concrete stepping-stones embedded at random surround a circular concrete patio and terraced gravel picnic area. A graceful weeping willow shades the patio, and evergreen shrubs soften hard lines. With little to maintain, these people can devote their time to family activities, and a rock garden they enjoy.

So, once the needs of the family are known, the first thing to do is to make a scale plan sketch of house and site, positioning all existing trees, rock outcrops and slopes. Before you start pushing the ground around, remember that many existing shrubs, trees, ground cover, rocks and terrain may be worked into your plan as is. The danger to root systems of major trees, possible erosion resulting from grade changes—and cost —are sound reasons to think twice before "shaping" a site to fit a theoretical plan. You can exploit rocks in the garden areas, and plan patio areas in the shade of existing trees, for instance.

Don't overlook the pleasing effect of low terracing to divide areas. Nearly every plot has a grade change of at least eight inches somewhere. That's enough to terrace. The slope can be banked with railroad ties, old brick, or dry stone walls. With the areas established—for lounging, outdoor eating, garden, play—you can "dress up" for easy maintenance.

The majority of landscape maintenance prob-

landscaping

In lawns where the slope does not exceed one foot in four, mowing is easy. Crowns and swales should curve away gently so that you avoid "scalping" the turf with the mower blades as you cut

Steep slopes are hard to mow but are easily maintained under ground cover, or when broken into stepped terraces with retaining walls of stone, brick or block

Existing trees often can be worked into your landscape plan when used as the shady centers of lounging areas. They also can create spots for ground-cover beds

Mowing strips of brick or tile separating all grass areas from gravel and planting beds help to eliminate trimming. Set the bricks on the flat side

Natural rock outcrops left intact create no mowing problem if they are dressed with rock plants or gravel and edged with a decorative curbing

PEBBLES

landscaping

There are a variety of ground covers, such as Ajuga, that require little or no care under proper conditions and can be used as an excellent lawn substitute. Learn about the best types for your climate

lazy-man's lawn, continued

Shady areas like the one below lend themselves to beds of ground cover such as this evergreen pachysandra that stays low to the ground, needs little trimming, thrives without sun

lems hinge on three things—drainage, lawn and plantings. Solutions for each must be thought of in relation to the others, plus things like driveways and walks.

Drainage: An area improperly drained can provide a perpetual maintenance headache by causing constant erosion or by creating a soggy bog too wet for lawn or plantings. Erosion of gentle slopes is easily controlled with lawn. If the grade is too steep, try a heavy planting of ground covers such as Hall's honeysuckle, English ivy, creeping junipers or the Memorial Rose. Often the best and most pleasing effect is to interrupt a steep slope with terracing, using a series of those low retaining walls. Another solution is to rip-rap the embankment with stone, and to plant the areas between rocks with rock garden plants or ground covers.

One hint for planting embankments: Cover the tilled slope with jute matting or burlap, pegged to the earth before the plants are set. Make a small cut for each plant.

This will retard soil washout until roots are established.

correct boggy areas

Boggy areas aren't so easy, but are even more important to correct. High water tables flood septic systems. The hydrostatic pressure they induce can crack and tumble retaining walls, heave terraces and driveways. The best solution is a curtain drain along one side of the property, with lateral drains leading into it. You may find it less expensive to raise low areas with porous fill. The important thing to remember is that most plants won't tolerate wet feet.

Lawns: The biggest beef I hear regarding care and upkeep of landscape is: ". . . if only I could eliminate the mowing, trimming and edging of that (unmentionable) lawn, I wouldn't mind the rest . . ." etc. Oddly, when questioned closely, the grumblers don't mind the mowing as much as the trimming and edging!

The fact is that well-established lawn—provided there isn't too much of it—is one of the best low maintenance covers going. It is also the least expensive solution to ground stabilization and beautification. When worked into a landscape plan judiciously in conjunction with other substitutes we'll come to, it can relieve severity of line and add a softening touch of cool color.

Most of us are not ready to accept green asphalt as a suitable substitute for grass, even if it must be crabgrass. There are ways to reduce the size of lawn areas, however, and they will be considered after a few hints on where grass *should* be used, and how to prepare for it.

1. Limit grass to level areas and slopes—not exceeding a rise of one foot in four—for easy mowing.

2. Use ground cover, such as pachysandra or myrtle, under shade trees where grass is difficult to maintain. If you'd like to lounge in the shade of favorite trees, spread out a two-inch layer of builder's sand as a cushion for a brick or flagstone terrace. Do not mortar the joints. Water and air must get to the roots!

3. Much work can be saved in mowing lawn and preserving the design of a garden if all grass areas are restricted with a border mowing strip of brick, concrete or tile. Be sure to avoid sharp corners, not easily maneuvered with a mower. The strip should be wide enough so the mower blade laps it without having the wheels slip off the edge (see sketch).

4. Prepare the seed bed with generous amounts of humus for good moisture retention. Seed in late August and early September. Water established lawns every 7 to 10 days, unless supplied by rainfall. This encourages deep roots. Two complete feedings a year are sufficient—in mid-March and early September.

5. Select grass varieties suited to the demands made upon it. *Poa Trivialis* is good for wet, shady areas while *Chewing Fescues* are good where it is drier and partly shaded. *Kentucky Bluegrass,* especially the *Merion* variety, is excellent in full sun—or where a playproof turf is required. Farther south *Meyer Zoysia* is a good all-purpose lawn grass.

6. Checking weeds and grubs with chemicals the first year will eliminate trouble.

Lawn substitute areas. Many materials can be used to reduce lawn area. When thoughtfully handled they can produce attractive, unusual effects—and they involve little upkeep. Proven materials include beach pebbles, pit gravel, crushed stone, sand, tanbark, wood chips, and buckwheat hulls. For one client, whose yard is pictured here, we used ½-inch screened multi-colored gravel in sweeping patterns to integrate his deeply shaded two-level garden. Set into the gravel are cross-hatched circles of concrete for eating and lounging terraces. Random size circular concrete stepping-stones are scattered through the gravel to make walking easy for high heels.

On irregular land with rocky outcrops, pea-size gravel can be used to eliminate difficult-to-cut grass areas. And in heavy shade where grass won't grow, it can be highly dramatic when used in combination with beds of pachysandra or myrtle.

Warning! Unless your plan is strictly geometric, large areas of gravel without compensating areas of grass, ground cover or shrubbery may look austere. And unless you run to straight lines and rectangles, bold, sweeping curves are more pleasing than tight corners and circles where one area joins another.

control weed growth

Don't get the idea that gravel and crushed stone are entirely maintenance free. Seeds sift between stones, grow into weeds, and must be plucked. But it's not as bad as it sounds, either. Weed growth can be controlled in one of two ways. If the roots of desirable shrubs and trees are not in the area, an arsenic solution may be sprayed over the pebbles each spring to kill any weeds that are sprouting, otherwise heavy tarpaper or polyethylene film can be spread over the ground before the gravel is laid.

Shrubs and plant materials. Next up on the maintenance gripe list are plant materials selected to beautify the grounds. Too often, those cute little plants from the supermarket grow to tree-like proportions—right in front of the picture window.

There are a variety of good ground cover, vines, shrubs and trees that are well adapted to form the backbone of any garden scheme. Farther south the list may vary so consult your local nurseryman.

There is one all-important piece of advice in regard to foundation plantings: *UNDER-PLANT.* It is always easier to add another plant than to remove an overgrown, misplaced one. Those selected should, for the most part, be evergreen and slow growing. If you're in a hurry for that "finished" look, buy larger plants.

The maintenance ogre need not rob you of the pleasures of homeownership if planning is done before spending. The money saved in avoiding mistakes can buy an automatic lawn sprinkling system, so you can golf with no concern about the lawn burning up. Then, you will always be assured of having lawn to mow in a few small areas, and you'll never need feel unneighborly when you see everyone else on the block sweating over his less cleverly planned patch of paradise.

See also: edger, lawn; fences; lawns; lawn sweeper; mulchmaker; propagating, shrubs; retaining walls; tree felling; tree stumps; weed killers.

land yacht models

Racing land yachts is exciting fun

BY HI SIBLEY

Whether you build a fleet or just one, these boats make for summer enjoyment

---

lanterns, camping: see camping
lap board: see drafting equipment
latex paint: see house paints

1576

■ LAND YACHTS are fun to make and exciting to race. Teamed up with a breezy day and some smooth pavement, they will provide your youngsters with hours of amusement.

Their construction is strong but surprisingly light. Thus, a strip of lead ballast must be tacked to the bottom of the cross beam if capsizing is to be avoided. With the exception of the capstan, which is made to be a snug, friction fit, all wooden parts are nailed and glued. The sail is secured with celluloid loops cemented in place.

The housing for the rudder wheel is made from a scrap of tin. Piano wire soldered to the housing forms the steering post which is bent downward so that it bears strongly against a balsa crossbar. This assures that the rudder wheel will remain in the desired position.

Much of the yacht's performance depends on the wheels. For best results use 1-in. model airplane wheels. They are designed for lightweight objects and are easily obtained. Wire nails make good axles, but you'll have to solder the nail to the housing of the rudder wheel.

Colorful shades of enamel will result in an attractive finish; you might try painting the deck yellow and the cross beam and rudder housing red. Top off the sail with a red star.

Once finished, your youngsters will be able to compete in sidewalk races or driveway regattas with land yachts that can be constructed from materials available in any hobby store.

See also: air-car model; railroad model; road racing, model; stick-model planes.

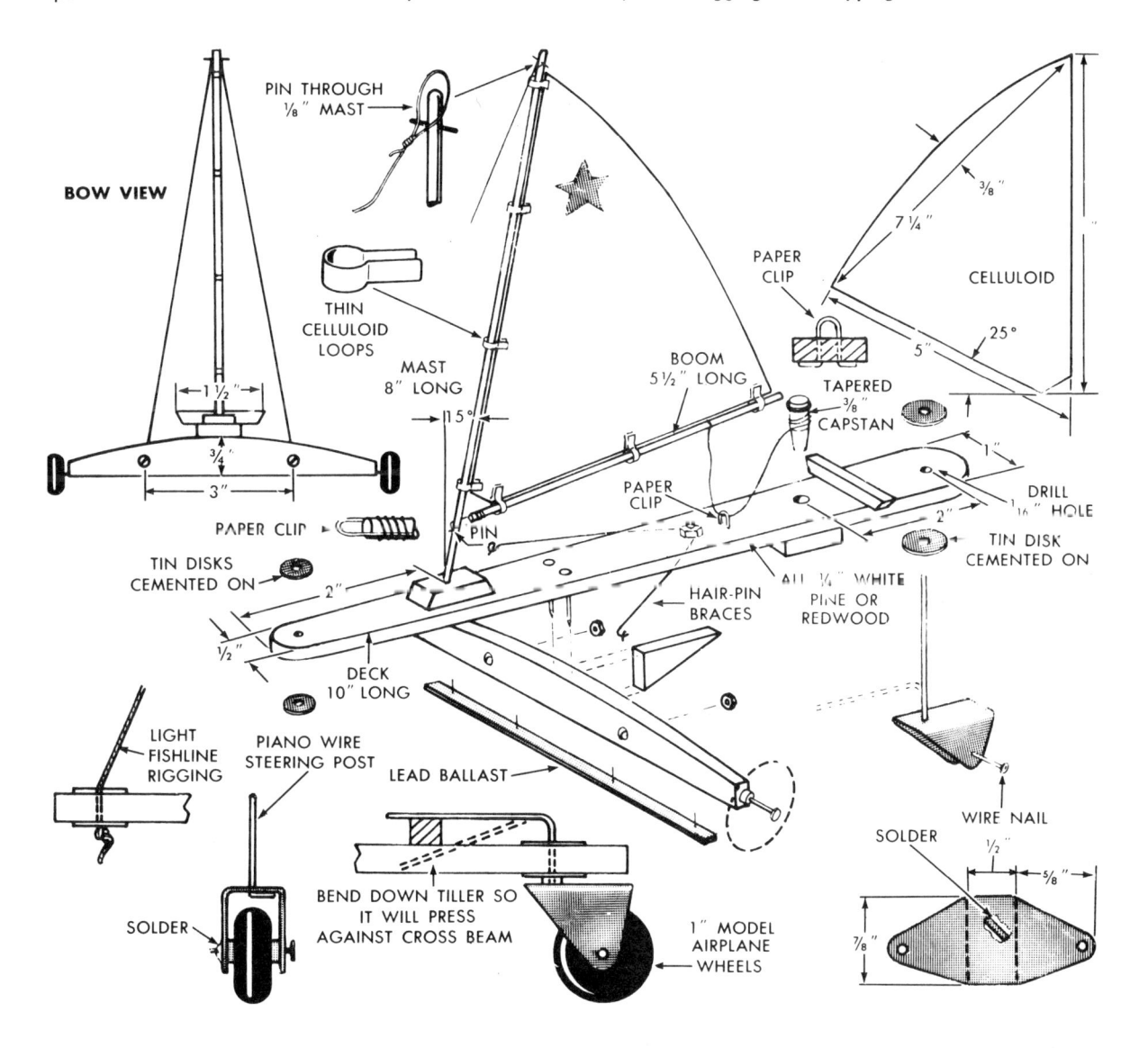

Cut parts to the dimensions shown. The cross beam should be 6-in. long and attached at a point 3-in. from the deck end. Drive pins into the mast to prevent rigging from slipping

lathe accessories

1 LATHE CENTER — INSERT
2 HALF CENTER
3 FEMALE CENTER

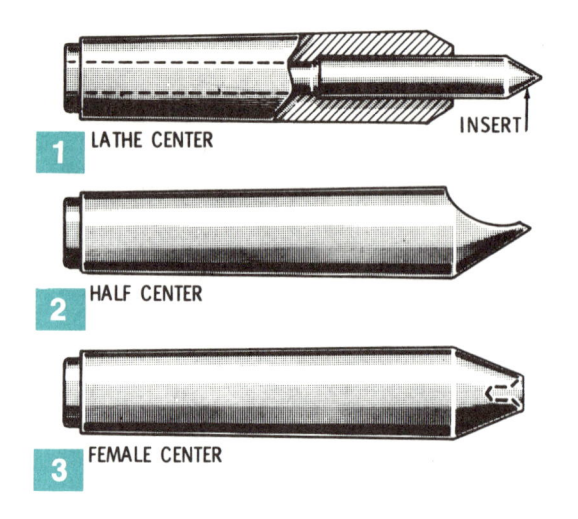

Convert discards into metal-lathe accessories

BY C. W. WOODSON

4 SMALL EXPANDING MANDREL — TAPER PIN
5 LARGE EXPANDING MANDREL
6 SCREW-TYPE EXPANDING MANDREL — PIPE PLUG
7 LARGE FEMALE CENTER
8 CUP CENTER FOR WOOD

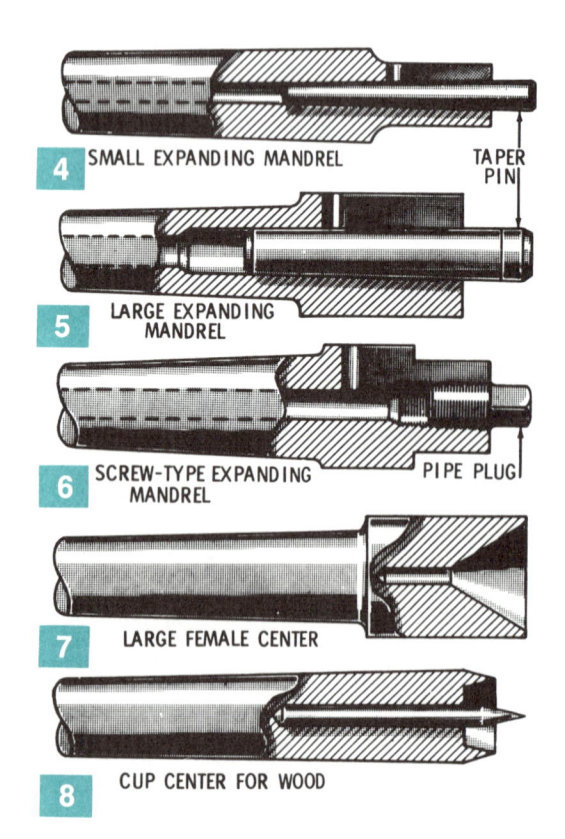

DON'T TOSS OUT the Morse taper shanks of worn-out twist drills. You can convert these discards into useful accessories for your metal lathe—such as the three centers and the small expanding mandrel sketched at the left.

The larger mandrels, the crotch center and the live center require bigger heads, so are best made from blank centers or semi-machined chuck arbors. You can buy these with No. 2 or No. 3 Morse tapers, and heads of various sizes that are soft enough to machine to any shape.

Taper-shank twist drills and reamers aren't usually hardened as far back as the shank, so the old tool can be cut off with a hacksaw or parting tool by inserting the shank directly into your lathe's headstock spindle. The projecting end can then be turned to shape and end-drilled as required. The mill holder (11) and drill chucks (12) are cross-drilled by using the tailstock's crotch center for support.

The outer diameter of the mandrels should be turned to an easy press fit in the center hole of the work to be mounted. After drilling for the taper pin or plug, cut the expansion slots last. Driving in the pin or turning plug expands the mandrel to center the work.

See also: belt sander; circular cutters; dial indicator; headstock brake, lathe; lathe techniques; slide rest, lathe; tool-post grinder; tool tray, lathe.

1. LATHE CENTER for light precision work. High-speed steel insert is driven in place. Harden the center point and grind to 60-deg. included angle

2. HALF CENTER, milled to provide tool clearance for facing end of work or extended grinding of small diameters. Point is hardened and ground

3. FEMALE CENTER is head-hardened for small diameter or pointed work, after turning it to 60-deg. incl. angle and center-drilling to the same angle

4. EXPANDING MANDREL, for small-diameter work. Drill and ream for a standard taper pin. Three saw cuts allow expansion. See sketch of item 9

5. EXPANDING MANDREL, turned from a blank center. Drill and ream for a Morse taper. Again, saw cuts into the radially-drilled holes allow expansion

6. EXPANDING MANDREL, turned from a blank center. It is end-drilled and tapped for a tapered plug. The end is sectioned with a slitting saw

7. LARGE FEMALE CENTER, drilled and bored to 60-deg. included angle. It is hardened to support armature shafts and other centerless work in tailstock

8. CUP CENTER, for wood turning. Turn the cup to shape and end-drill to take replaceable steel point. Both the cup and point are hardened after assembly

9. PERSPECTIVE VIEW of item 6 with cutting details for expandability. If a slitting saw is not available, use a hacksaw to cut the slots

10. LIVE CENTER, with head bored for a press fit of a ball bearing. Turn the center point to 60-deg. incl. angle, harden and grind. Drop ball in shank hole

11. WOODRUFF CHUCK, for mounting cutters with ½-in. shanks. The head is cross-drilled and tapped for a setscrew to lock a cutter or end mill in place

12. CENTER-DRILL CHUCKS. Make three sizes to permanently convert most-used center drills for quick mounting in a lathe headstock or tailstock

13. SPUR CENTER, milled to shape in a milling attachment and end-drilled for a replaceable hardened center. Driver tips are beveled, hardened and ground

14. CROTCH CENTER, for accurately centering round work to be cross-drilled in tailstock. Mill groove to 60-deg. incl. angle, and end-drill a ¼-in. relief

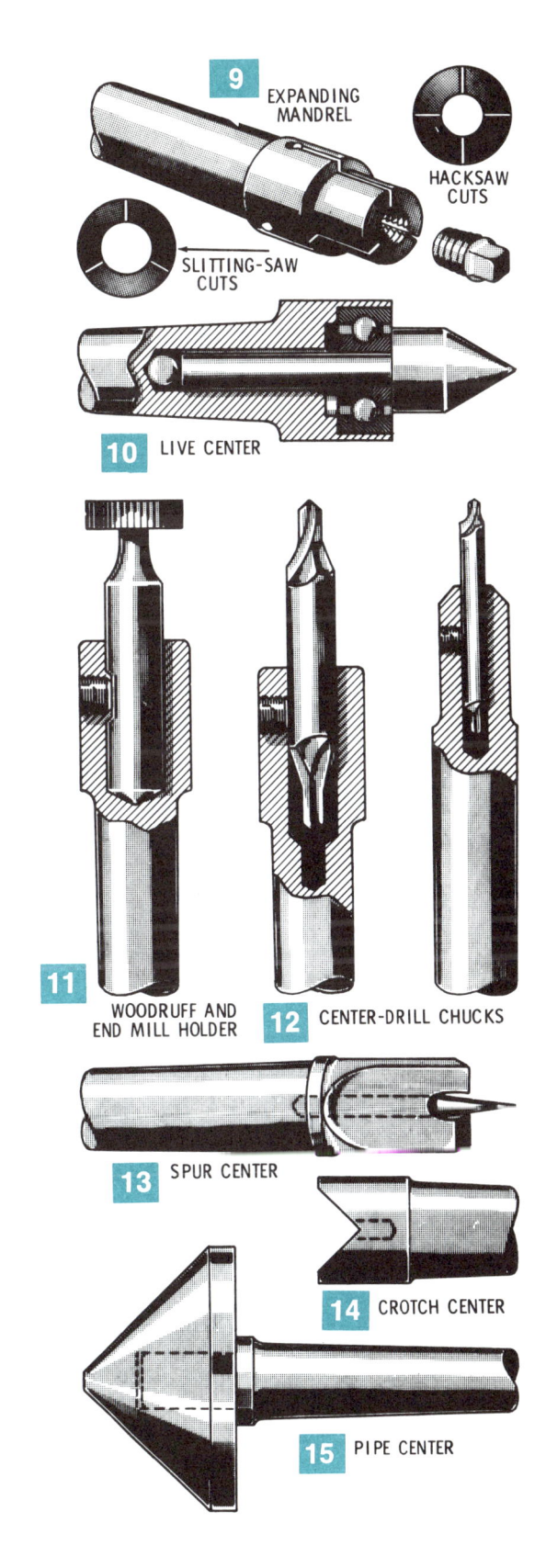

15. PIPE CENTER, for mounting tubular work between centers. Turn 90-deg. cone from steel and bore it to spin without shake on a tailstock-mounted straight shank. The cone takes ⅜ to 3-in. diameter

lathe accessories

Lathe pinch-hits as disk sander

BY C. W. WOODSON

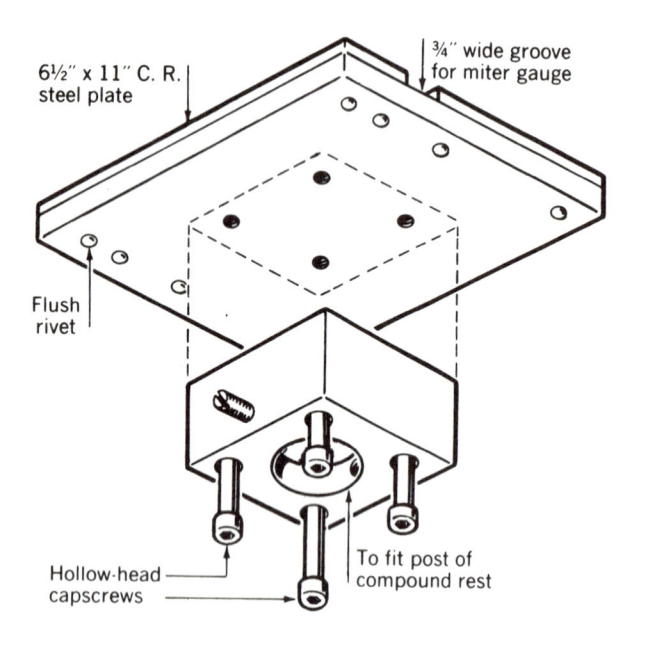

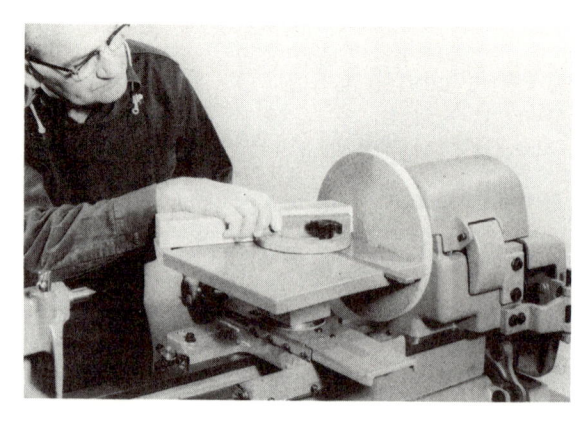

■ YOUR METAL-TURNING LATHE can pinch-hit as a fine disk sander when fitted with this handy shop-made accessory. The entire unit is fabricated from cold-rolled steel flats or heavy plate. Have the ½-in. disk flame-cut to the maximum lathe-swing diameter. Four capscrews fasten it to a faceplate for mounting on the lathe spindle. In this position, true the edge and face off.

Then bore a block of mild-steel bar stock for the table standard and mill to fit the dovetail post of the lathe's compound rest. Drill and tap for the anchoring screws, and drill and countersink for hollow-head capscrews to bolt it to the sander table.

The table top is three pieces of steel plate riveted together. The one-piece bottom is ½-in. stock and the two top pieces are ⅜-in. These two must be cut to fit flush with the bottom and parallel to the disk, while allowing a ¾-in. groove for your miter gauge. Be sure that all fasteners are snugged up firm. On the faceplate, make sure the capscrews are filed flush; smooth the filing grooves with a piece of emery paper.

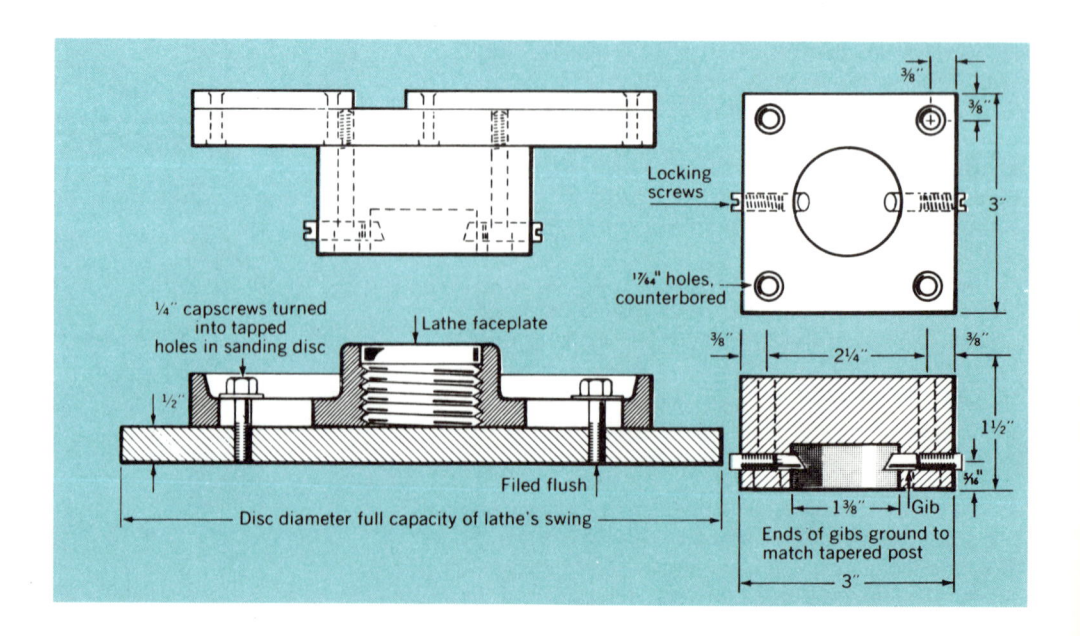

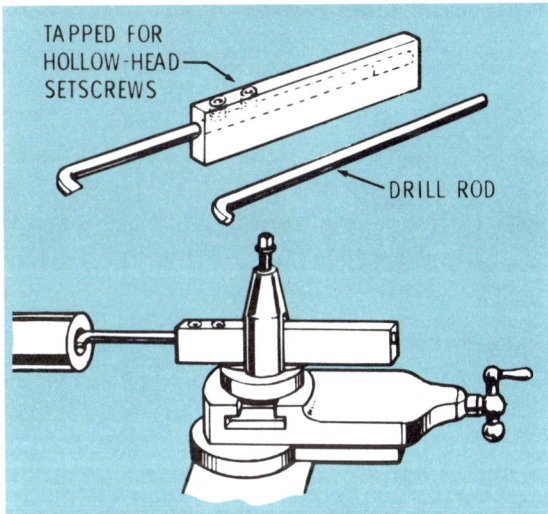

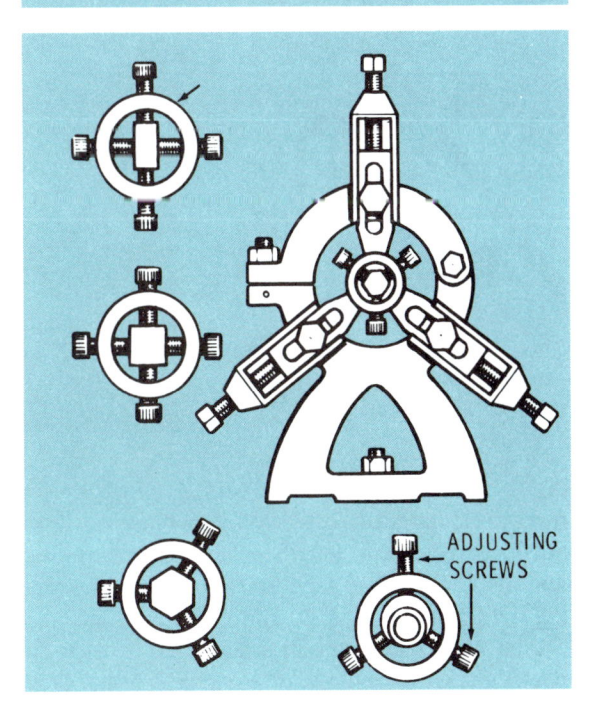

Add these to your metal lathe

■ Long lengths of small-diameter stock tend to chatter while being machined. This difficulty can be overcome by using a follower rest made from a cold-rolled-steel blank drilled to fit the tapped holes in the tailstock side of the carriage. The blank is temporarily mounted and the carriage moved until the tailstock center makes contact. The back of the blank is then lightly center-punched to mark the exact lathe-center axis. From this mark the layout can be made and the bushing hole drilled. The bushing, of bronze, should be an easy running fit on the work. A setscrew holds the bushing in place. In use, the rest travels with the carriage.

■ Boring tool holders for small diameter, close-tolerance work can be made from cold-rolled steel flats. The holder is drilled lengthwise to accommodate the boring bar. It is then cross-drilled and tapped at one end for two hollow-head setscrews as indicated in the drawing. The boring bars, and internal threading tools as well, can be easily made from drill rod. One end is heated and bent at right angles, filed roughly to shape, hardened and the temper drawn. The tool is brought to final shape on a grinding wheel and honed to a keen cutting edge with a hard oilstone. In clamping such bars in the tool-post holder, watch to see that they engage the work at lathe-center height.

■ Long, out-of-round or odd shaped rods and shafts are easy to support and machine between centers if you use a cathead in conjunction with a lathe steady rest. The cathead is nothing more than a short length of thick-wall seamless tubing fitted with lock screws, which when slipped over the work provide a smooth true surface for the jaws of the steady rest to ride on, regardless of its sectional shape. Three adjusting screws are needed on each end of the tube for gripping out-of-round, hexagonal or offset work. For square or flat stock, four screws on each end are required. The two rows of screws must be set far enough apart to clear the steady-rest jaws.

lathe bits: see circular cutters
lathe brake: see headstock, lathe

1581

lathe techniques

Short course in metal turning

BY W. CLYDE LAMMEY

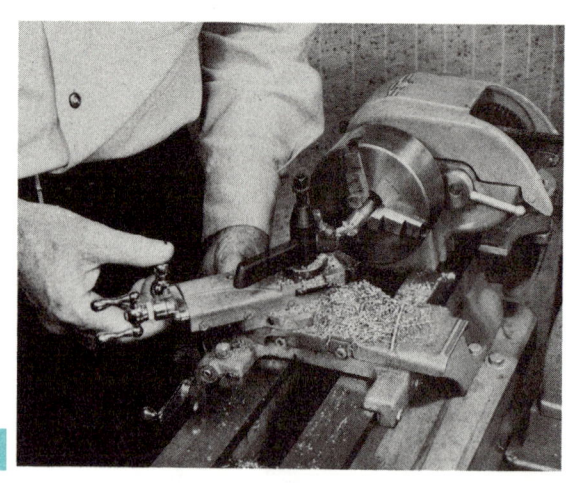

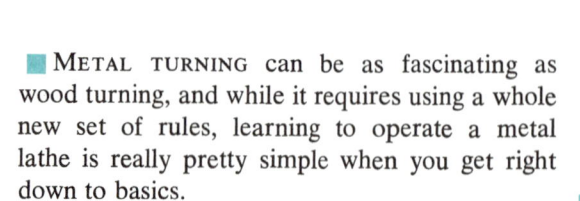

METAL TURNING can be as fascinating as wood turning, and while it requires using a whole new set of rules, learning to operate a metal lathe is really pretty simple when you get right down to basics.

Learning how to set up work for turning between centers and on a faceplate is lesson number one.

The first step is to rough-cut the workpiece to length with an allowance for facing both ends, when facing is required. For practical purposes this can be done with a hacksaw, using care to cut the ends square. Or, if the nature of the work and the material available permit, cut the workpiece over-length so that you can machine it to finish diameter and length up to the driving dog and then cut off and face the end. When measuring the length, be sure to allow for the dog.

The next step is centering. If the work will pass through the hollow, headstock spindle, then

1582

chuck it in the lathe's three-jaw chuck, letting it project a minimum amount. Now face off and center-drill the ends with a combination center drill and countersink as pictured and detailed in Figs. 2, 3 and 10.

If the workpiece is too large to pass through

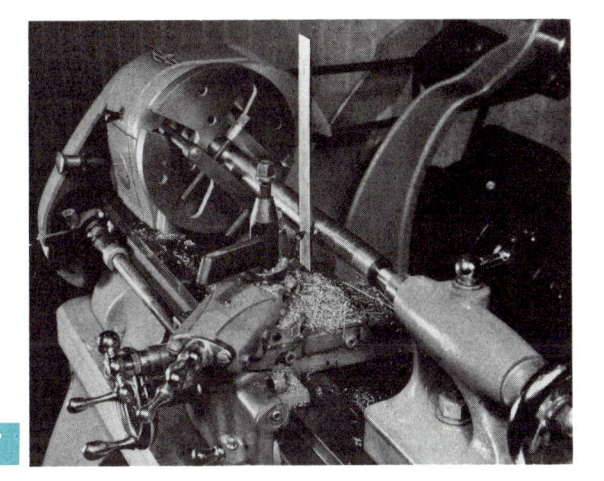

1. The first step in mounting between centers is facing the ends of the workpiece square. Indent the center so the center drill will start accurately

2. When the workpiece will pass through the lathe spindle, center-drilling is done in the lathe. Chuck the work and feed the center drill slowly

3. If the work is too large for the lathe spindle, chuck it and center-drill in a drill press. Center-punch the work first and feed slowly

4. After center-drilling, attach a driving dog and mount on centers. Make sure tail of the dog clears and the work turns freely without play

5. When turning between centers, use screw or automatic carriage feed to get smoother work, and to prevent gouging and overloading of the bit

6. Use a rule to locate the cutting tool on the axis of the lathe. Here, rule tilts away, indicating the point set too high. Recheck and reset the tool

7. The vertical rule indicates that the tool is set dead on center. Some machinists prefer the cutting tool set slightly above center on some work

8. When turning ferrous metals, an occasional drop of light oil at the cutting point will give a smoother cut and help to prevent undue heating

lathe techniques

HOW TO GET STARTED IN METAL TURNING

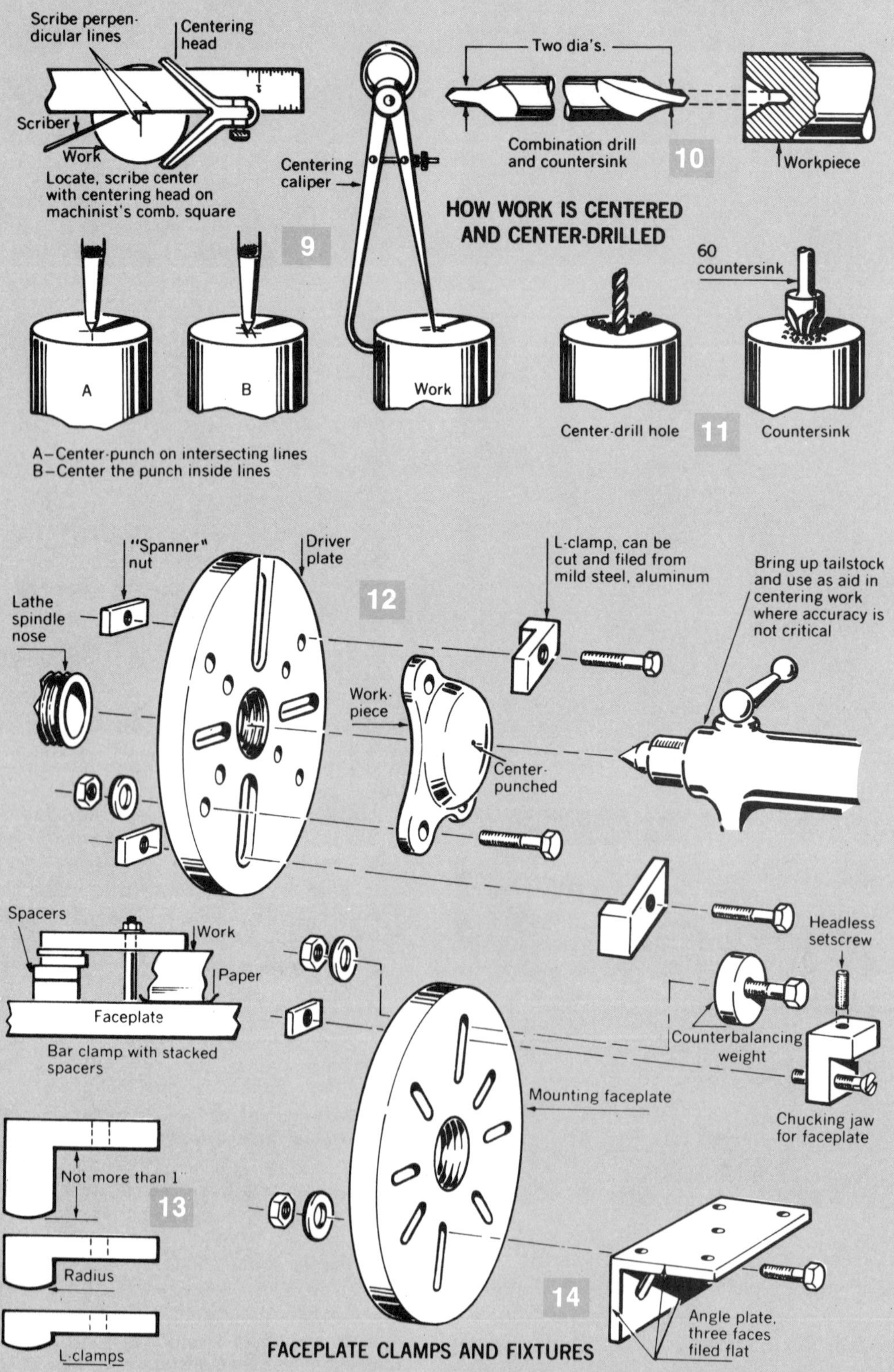

HOW WORK IS CENTERED AND CENTER-DRILLED

Scribe perpendicular lines — Centering head — Scriber — Work
Locate, scribe center with centering head on machinist's comb. square

Centering caliper — Work

Two dia's. — Combination drill and countersink — Workpiece [10]

[9]

A — Center-punch on intersecting lines
B — Center the punch inside lines

Center-drill hole — 60° countersink — Countersink [11]

FACEPLATE CLAMPS AND FIXTURES

"Spanner" nut — Driver plate — Lathe spindle nose — Workpiece — Center-punched

L-clamp, can be cut and filed from mild steel, aluminum

Bring up tailstock and use as aid in centering work where accuracy is not critical

[12]

Spacers — Work — Paper — Faceplate
Bar clamp with stacked spacers

Not more than 1" — Radius — L-clamps [13]

Mounting faceplate

Headless setscrew — Counterbalancing weight — Chucking jaw for faceplate

Angle plate, three faces filed flat [14]

CORRECT BIT PROFILES

Side — 20°. Tool must be ground with zero top rake for brass, bronze.

Top — Flat gives zero top rake.

15

Top (back) rake angle. Nose. Relief angle. 8° Side rake. 5-6° End view. Tool ground for rough cut in mild steel, mach. aluminum. 5° Side. 30° Top. Radius. 15°.

16

Groove curls chip. End. 8°. 20° Side. 30°. 3° Top. Tool ground with curling groove for facing, finishing.

TOOL SETUPS

Tool on centerline of work. 20°. Workpiece. Setup with Armstrong tool holder for turning between centers.

Not more than 1/16" on work under 1" dia. Workpiece. Feed. Minimum overhang. Normally tool is set perpendicular to axis of work.

Drip light oil on work (when cutting steel). Chamfer (break) corner. Groove curls chip. Set tool to cut square shoulder.

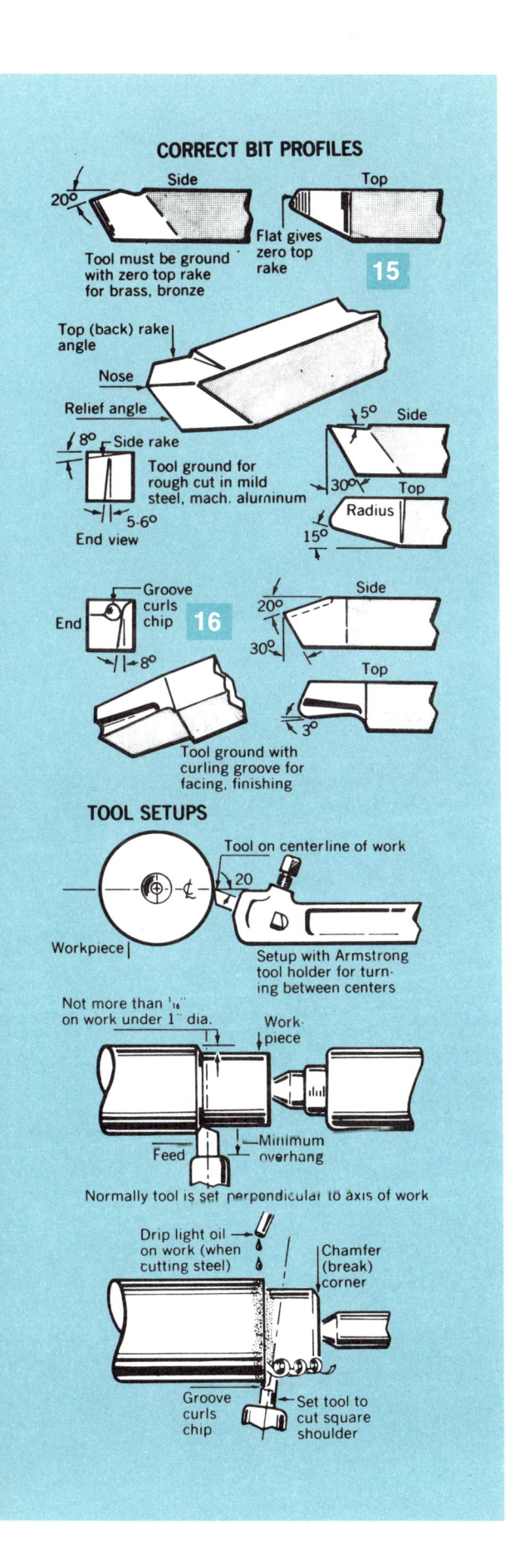

the spindle but will drop through the hole in your drill-press table, locate and scribe the centers, using either a centering head on a machinist's combination square or a centering (hermaphrodite) caliper as detailed (Fig. 9.) Then, using the lathe chuck, hold the workpiece and drill the center with the combination drill and countersink in the drill press as pictured in Fig. 3.

If too large in diameter for either operation, lay off and scribe the centers as described, then drill and countersink in two operations as in Fig. 11. The facing cuts can be taken after the work is mounted between centers. When mounting the workpiece between centers, be sure that the tail of the dog engages the slot in the faceplate properly and that the end clears the headstock before you start the lathe. Turn the work by hand to make sure everything is in the clear.

Small metal lathes, under 9-in. swing, usually are supplied with one large faceplate which can serve both as a work mounting plate and as a driving plate. Such a plate has one open-end slot for driving the dog and several closed-end slots to which work of irregular shape may be bolted or clamped for machining operations such as facing, drilling and boring. See Fig. 12.

types of plates

Lathes of 9-in. swing and up are usually furnished with a small plate having a single open-end slot for driving the dog. Larger plates with closed-end slots and spaced holes are supplied as accessories. Such plates are useful for mounting a wide range of workpieces of such shape that they cannot be chucked. Both types are shown in the details, Fig. 12. A typical, irregularly shaped small casting is shown, being of a shape that cannot be chucked in either a three-jaw universal chuck or a four-jaw chuck having individually adjustable jaws. Such a piece can be mounted and worked on a driving plate such as that supplied with small lathes by using two, three, or more L-clamps and bolts (Fig. 13), if the work permits, as fastenings. Although similar clamps are available ready-made, you can make them yourself, using mild steel which is easily cut with a hacksaw, filed and ground as needed. Make them in several sizes to accommodate work of varying proportions and thicknesses. If desirable, you can improvise a chuck for noncritical machining by making L-shaped chucking jaws for the faceplate.

On large faceplates, machinists sometimes find it convenient to mount the work on an angle plate (Fig. 14), bolted to the faceplate. Like the

lathe techniques

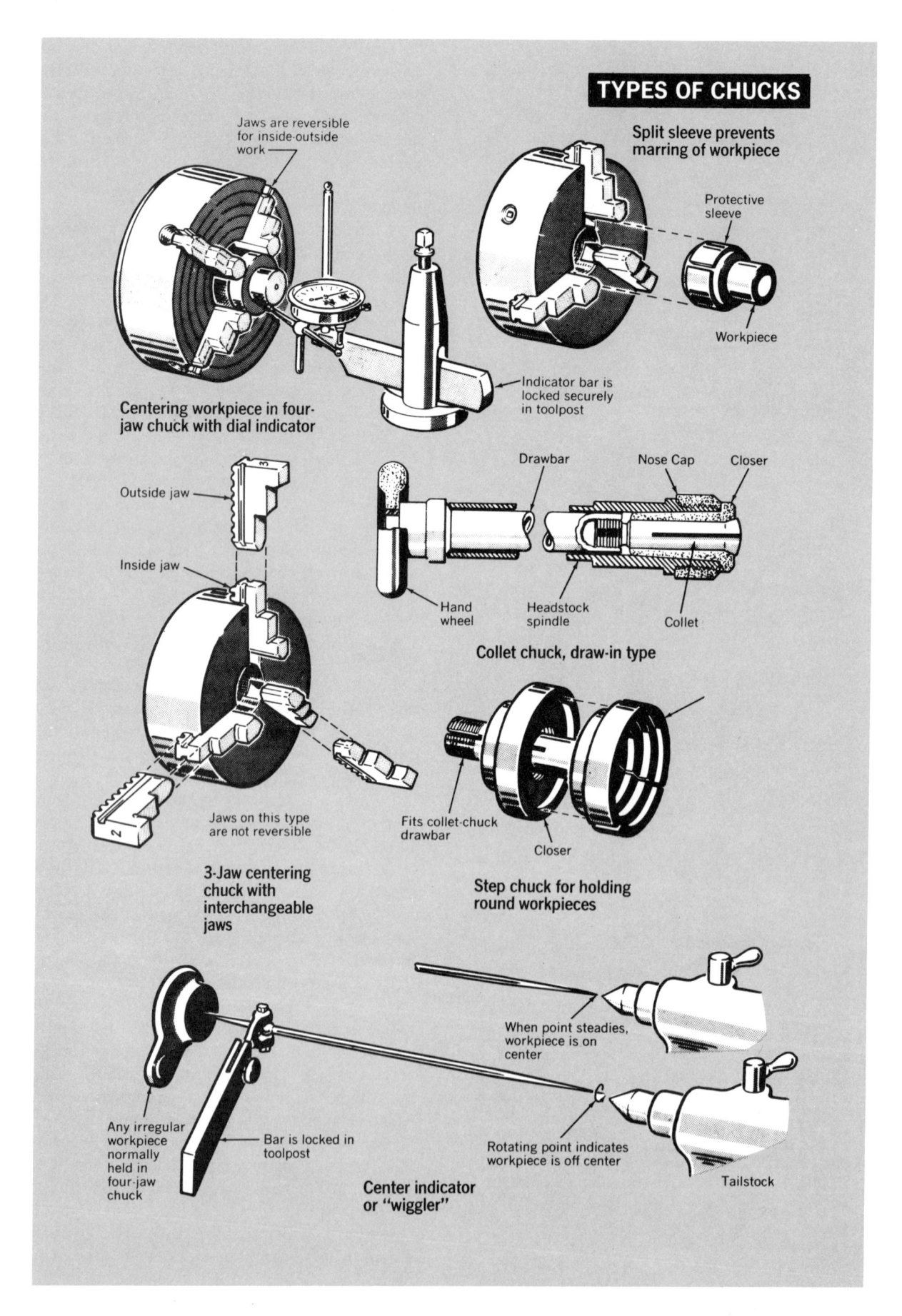

L-clamps, angle plates are available ready-made, but you can make one suitable for noncritical work from a short length of ordinary steel angle. This should be filed or ground, or both, on three faces as indicated, with special care taken to maintain the outside angle at 90 deg. and all surfaces flat.

When you're mounting work on an angle plate —or, in some instances, clamping work to the faceplate—it is necessary to provide a counterbalancing weight. These are easily made from round steel stock by cutting and machining disks of varying diameters and thicknesses and center-drilling to take a small bolt for attachment. After mounting the counterbalance, make short test runs to make sure the setup is in close balance.

Correct grinding, honing and mounting the tool in the toolholder and on the toolpost come next. To cut properly in ferrous metals, such as ordinary steels and certain machining aluminums, the tool should be ground with a top (back) rake, side rake and relief angle as detailed (Fig. 15). The angles given are used in general practice, but some machinists vary these slightly for certain purposes.

For common nonferrous metals, such as brass and bronze, the cutting tool should generally be ground with a negative, or zero, top rake and little, if any, side rake. In all cases, except for threading, the nose should be ground with a very slight radius. Use a medium-fine grinding wheel (preferably a vitreous wheel) and be careful not to overheat the cutting edge. Carbide-tipped tools must be ground on a specially made wheel.

For finishing cuts, tools may be ground with a round-bottom chip groove as detailed (Fig. 16). Properly ground (this is, of course, rather difficult on tools less than ¼-in. square), such a tool leaves a smooth finish, as it curls away a continuous chip, generates somewhat less heat when cutting and requires less power. Although shown with negative top rake, some machinists prefer it ground with a slight top rake.

Lathe tools generally will cut more smoothly if honed on a fine oilstone, such as a hard Arkansas stone. Be careful not to alter the rake angles when honing. Tool settings are those common for ordinary work. Tools ground with a chip groove should generally be set to cut a square shoulder. Don't permit any tool to undercut; it may tend to dig in without warning and damage the work.

Use of geared chucks is the next step in learning to operate a metal lathe.

Work that cannot be mounted between centers and driven with a dog usually is chucked for

To avoid dropping the chuck during mounting, clamp it on round stock that will pass through the spindle and provide a "handle"

1587

lathe techniques

Headstock spindle nose

Geared chuck for small workpieces

Standard mandrel
- Body tapered .004 to .006 per ft.
- Flat

Mandrel improvised from mild steel round or drill rod
- Large end
- Taper .004 to .006
- Workpiece such as flanged bushing

1

2

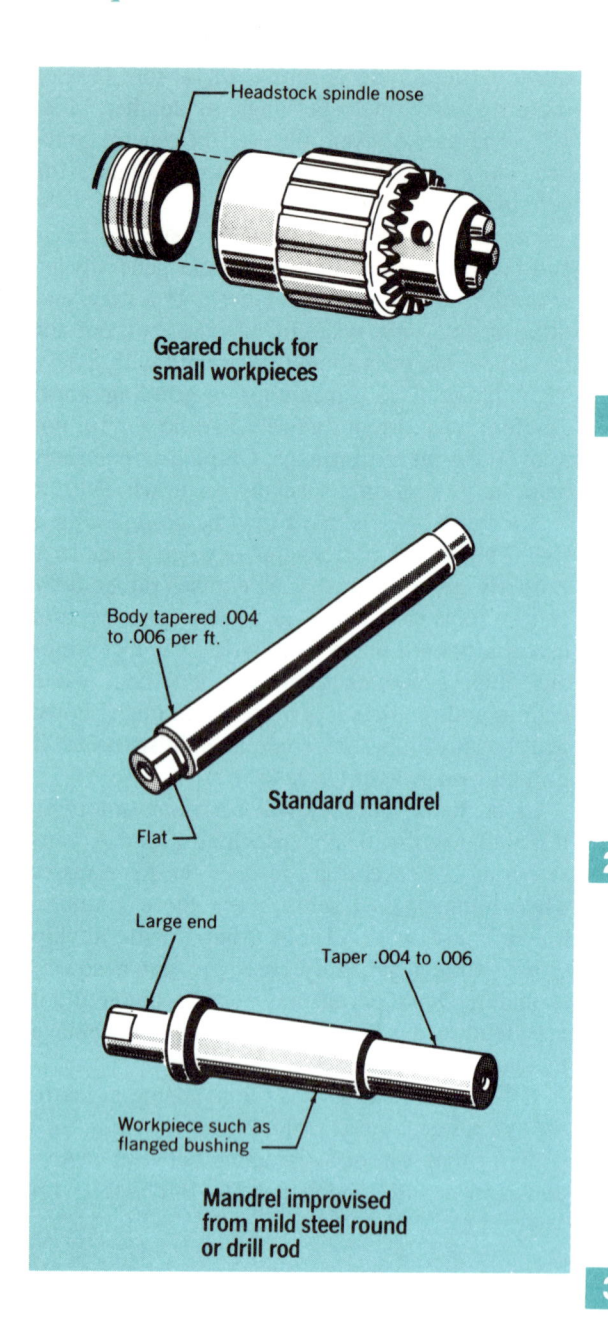

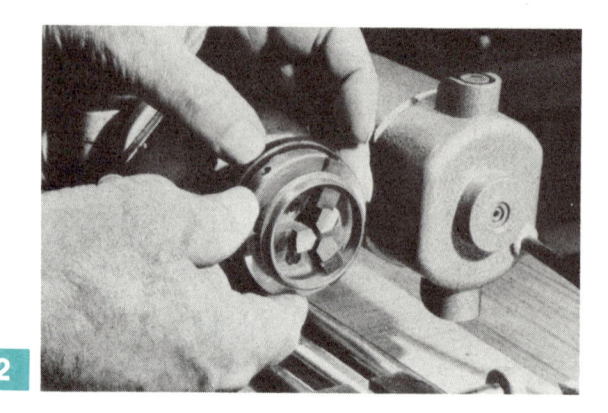

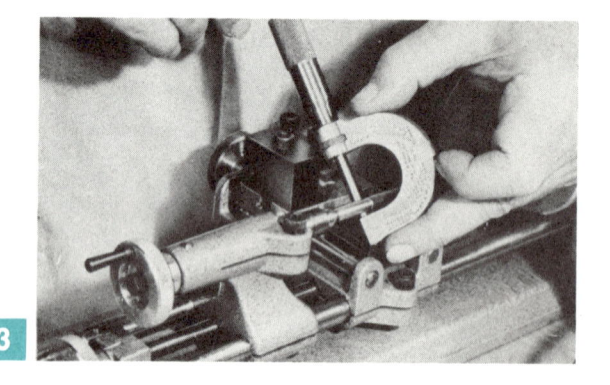

3

short course in metal turning, continued

machining. Chucks for everyday work are of several types, all operated manually with a special wrench.

Perhaps the most common is the four-jaw chuck on which each jaw is operated individually. These usually come with a set of jaws that can be reversed to hold inside or outside work ("inside" and "outside" refer to the way in which the jaws engage the workpiece). Concentric rings, equally spaced, are machined on the face of the chuck to help center the work.

Next in common usage is the universal, or scroll, chuck on which the three jaws are self-centering. Turning the T-wrench in the single actuating socket on the chuck body moves all three jaws simultaneously. When they close on the workpiece it is automatically centered. Such chucks are accurate within .003 or less and come with two sets of jaws—for inside and outside work. Some miniature scroll chucks have one reversible set.

In addition to these two common types there are spring collet and step chucks; both are actuated by a spindle drawbar and also a geared chuck (similar to a drill chuck) that turns onto the spindle nose and is ordinarily used for "live"

1588

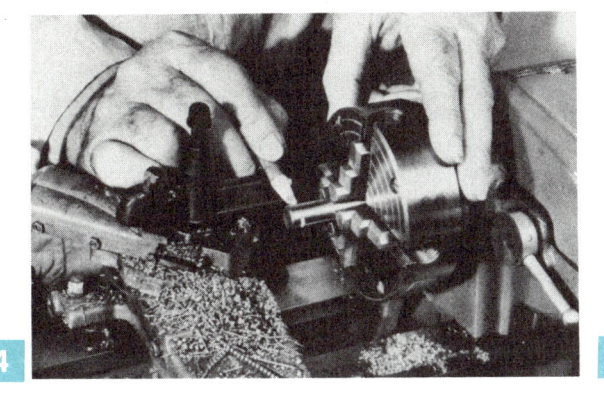

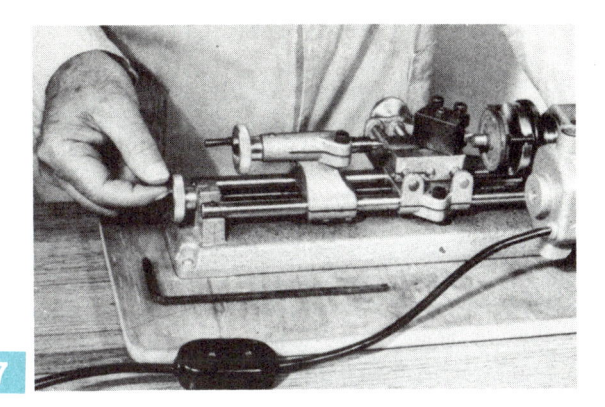

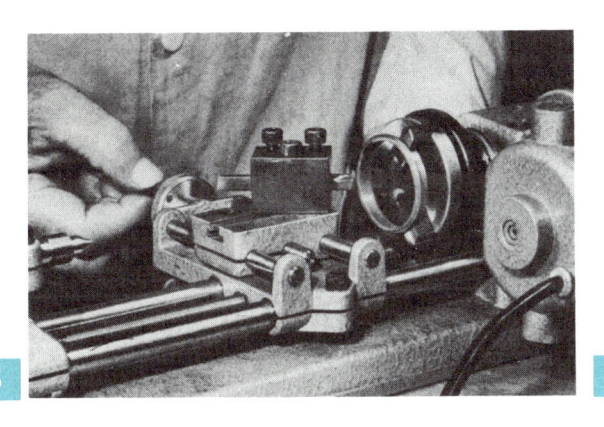

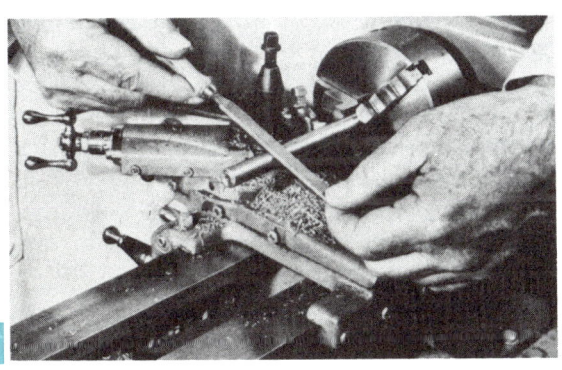

1. The tailstock center is used as an indicator for centering in a four-jaw chuck. The workpiece is center-punched or center-drilled. Not for close work

2. Grip the inside of the workpiece with jaws of a universal chuck by backing them out rather than running in, to permit both edging and facing of work

3. When you must come close, use a mike, especially on small-diameter work where it is more difficult to "feel" a caliper. Be sure of the reading

4. This shows the chalk or pencil-mark method of centering in a four-jaw chuck. Here the line is not continuous, showing that the work is off center

5. Grip the outside of the workpiece for a final backfacing operation by reversing the jaws. On most universal chucks, the jaws should be interchanged

6. Make a mandrel for average work when you don't have a ready-made one handy by filing a taper on the round of a drill rod that has been center-drilled

7. Here is the machining of a chucking lug on model-locomotive drive wheel. The work is held in the outside of three-jaw chuck with reversible jaws

8. On ordinary work not requiring close tolerances, diameters can be checked quite accurately with calipers. Finger sensitivity largely determines accuracy

9. Finish the taper by smoothing with a loop of fine abrasive cloth, checking the diameter frequently until you have the correct taper of .004 to .006

lathe techniques

short course in metal turning, continued

drilling operations, with the work supported by a pad held in the tailstock.

The collet chuck also is widely used in the machining of small parts requiring close tolerances. Spring collets range from about ⅛ in. up, the sizes usually increasing by 16ths.

The step chuck is really a collet-chuck accessory. It is threaded to fit the collet-chuck drawbar and each unit is designed to hold two or more sizes of rounds, such as disks or small gear blanks, for machining. Both collet and step chucks are especially useful for repetitive work; the workpiece can be locked quickly in place in the collet, where it is automatically centered, then machined and released by a short turn of the handwheel. Modelmakers, experimenters and metal-working hobbyists find these chucks useful for machining small parts.

rough-center the workpiece

When working with the independent four-jaw chuck, you rough-center the workpiece, with the concentric rings on the face of the chuck aiding in placement. For ordinary work not requiring close tolerances you can use the tailstock center as an indicator when the workpiece has been center-drilled or center-punched. The usual procedure is to set two adjacent jaws and then work the third and finally the fourth to bring the workpiece to dead center. With care, this can be done quite accurately.

Another fairly accurate method is to rough-center the work and then hold a piece of colored chalk or a china-marking pencil on the toolholder. The pencil point should just touch the high point of the workpiece when the lathe spindle is rotated by hand. Move jaws slightly until the pencil scribes a continuous line.

When a machining job requires working within close limits, you must use more accurate centering methods. A center indicator, or "wiggler," gives good results when set up as shown on page 1586. Center-punch the workpiece, rough-center it, and move the chuck jaws slightly until the indicator arm steadies as the work is rotated and you have it very close.

The dial indicator is more sensitive and faster, and it can be used on a greater range of work shapes. The workpiece need not be center-punched, since the actuating arm of the instrument can be located to ride on any smooth surface, inside or outside or on the face when it is necessary to test for out-of-true axially or radially. When the needle steadies you are quite sure the work is dead-centered.

A note of caution: Use a protective sleeve when chucking or rechucking workpieces that are fragile or partially machined. To protect the machined surface from the chuck jaws, cut a short sleeve from tubing with an inside diameter that will slip-fit the workpiece (or machine a sleeve to fit). Slot it as shown at the top of page 1586 and slip on the part of the workpiece to be gripped in the chuck. The sleeve protects from marring and gives support to fragile work that might be crushed out of round in the chuck. Avoid overtightening the jaws, or both chuck and work may be damaged.

All-over machining sometimes presents a problem in holding the workpiece, such as a bushing. The first step is to bore, ream and face to specifications, with the bushing held in the chuck. Then remove the bushing and mount it on a mandrel that will take the bore of the bushing in a close press fit.

how to make a mandrel

Ready-made mandrels come in many sizes, usually tapered from .004 to .006 per ft. For work not requiring extreme precision, you can make a mandrel as shown in the two bottom photos on page 1589, tapering it to take the bushing. The latter should be a fairly tight press fit after the mandrel has cooled to normal temperature. Of course, the mandrel must be center-drilled and a flat filed or ground at the big end to assure that the driving dog does not slip when the work is mounted between centers for final all-over machining.

The many extra jobs your metal lathe can do, in addition to all the standard metal-turning operations are taken up in this part of our story. Even the small machines can be set up to do such work as drilling, reaming, milling, thread-cutting, knurling and turning tapers. And, you can turn the harder woods by replacing the 60-deg. centers with the spur and cup centers and substituting a short metal bar for the toolholder. You just swing the toolpost so that the bar is parallel with the workpiece.

Drilling is perhaps the most common "side" operation done on a metal lathe. On a small lathe you can use drill bits from needle size to ½ in. or more as the tailstock, fitted with a precision drill chuck, gives an extremely sensitive feed.

When drilling the larger diameters, it's advisable to run in a pilot hole first, using a small-diameter bit that you are sure is perfectly straight and correctly ground. The hole will serve as a guide for the larger bit. Ordinarily the pilot hole should not be more than one fourth the diameter of the larger hole—sometimes, less is preferable. Before drilling either hole, make sure the tailstock quill (or sleeve) taper is clean, with no chips or grime. Also wipe the tapered drill shank and place a drop of very light oil on it before inserting it.

You won't need a lubricant to drill most nonferrous metals and cast iron, but when drilling steel an occasional drop of light oil will result in a smoother job and prevent undue heating. When the finish hole is to be of large diameter, it's often best to drill undersize and then finish to the required diameter with a boring tool.

reaming to final size

Work specs frequently call for reaming to final size. In any case, if you are working to close limits it's well to follow through with this step. Drill the hole slightly undersize—about 1/64 in. in the larger sizes—then go through with a straight reamer of the final diameter desired. This will give you a smooth, true hole of exact diameter as long as you don't remove the work from the chuck between the two operations.

Accurate screw threads can be cut on a lathe equipped with a lead screw. The cutting tool must be ground with a 60-deg. point and the compound turned 29 deg. to the right for cutting the common external threads. The tool must be set at right angles to the axis of the workpiece. If you have a center gauge, use it to obtain an accurate setting as detailed in the third sketch on page 1594. Also, the cutting tool must be set exactly on the center line, or axis, of the workpiece to produce the best work. Somewhere on your lathe—usually on the inside of the gear cover or on the quick-change gearbox—you'll see an index chart listing the correct change gears to use in the train to cut a given number of threads per inch.

Diagrams on the change-gear lathe will show position of the change gears for cutting any thread within the lathe's capacity. With the gear train arranged to cut the thread desired, center-drill the workpiece and mount it between centers. Drive with a dog as in the left center threading photo on page 1593. Usually it is desirable, when the lathe carriage has no threading stop, to run in a shallow groove with a cut-off tool at the finish end of the thread to get clearance to back off the threading tool at the end of the cut.

On the simple threading dial you'll see four (some have eight) equally spaced marks. All pass a single witness mark as the dial slowly rotates. To start any even-numbered thread, such as 12 or 24 per inch, with the lathe running, engage the half nuts just as the rotating zero mark coincides with the witness mark.

After the first scoring cut, back off the tool, disengage the half nuts, return the carriage to the starting point by hand and re-engage the half nuts at the *same* mark used previously on the rotating dial.

Normally the common threads—even finer ones—should be cut in several passes, feeding the tool in from 1/64 to 1/32 in. at each pass, the depth depending on the thread size.

Cutting an internal thread requires much the same procedure as does the external thread, except that the feed is toward you, and you use a different type of threading tool. Also, there must be clearance in the bore for backing off the tool, and the compound is set 29 deg. to the *left* instead of the right.

Milling, tapping, knurling, taper turning and cutting off are less frequently encountered, yet all can be done on a metal-turning lathe with available accessories. The main problem in hand tapping is getting the tap started accurately. The lower left photo on page 1593 shows how; you use the lathe as a support for the work and tap wrench.

knurling and taper turning

A considerable range of accurate milling operations can be done with accessories shown in the photos and sketches. Knurling, which provides that neat gripping surface on small screws and other hand-turned parts, is done with the special tool sketched, page 1594. To knurl any small part, you first turn it to diameter, chuck it (or mount it between centers), set the knurling tool on center in the toolpost and run up to the work. Apply enough pressure to score the work surface and make the first pass, using the lead-screw feed. Then, just before the knurling "wheels" clear the work surface, reverse the lead screw, turn up the cross-feed screw slightly to apply more pressure and allow knurls to feed back in a reverse pass. Continue until the knurl is cut in to the desired depth.

On small lathes without a taper-turning attachment, tapers may be formed by setting over the tailstock. A machinist's handbook (check your library) will give formulas for taper per foot to any degree.

Long workpieces to be turned to small dia-

lathe techniques

short course in metal turning, continued

meters between centers tend to spring away from the cutting tool. To prevent this you'll need a follower rest, one type of which is sketched on page 1594. The cutting-off tool is useful mainly when a number of pieces are to be duplicated. It must be set exactly at right angles to the workpiece and precisely on center. Don't try this on work supported at both ends.

You'll get a great deal of satisfaction from

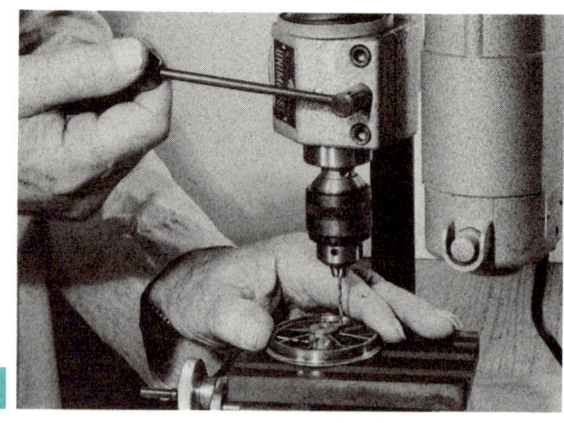

1. Sensitive drilling can be done on a small lathe with the headstock clamped to the vertical column that is an accessory with some makes

2. The first step in thread cutting is to engage the dial with the lead screw. The dial saves returning the carriage with the lead screw on each pass

To drill with a ⅝-in. twist drill in a small lathe, grip work in a three-jawed universal chuck. A small-diameter pilot hole serves as guide for the larger bit. Use light, uniform feed

1592

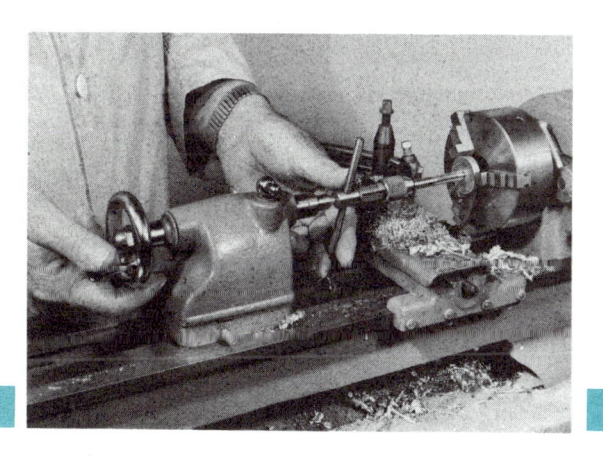

3. Finish boring of an off-center job shows that it is often best to drill large-sized holes undersized, then finish to the required diameter with a boring tool

4. At the end of the pass disengage half nuts from lead screw and return carriage by hand to start, with point of cutting tool clearing threaded section

5. In hand tapping, the main problem is to get tap started straight and true. This setup utilizes lathe as an accurate support for tap wrench and workpiece

6. To drill and ream you first drill an undersize hole, then go through with a reamer— backing off a bit at intervals to clear the chips

7. For the next pass, in-feed the tool a given amount on the cross-feed dial and re-engage half nuts on lead screw as index marks on thread dial coincide

8. Convert the lathe to a vertical mill with accessory vise, column and table. Here both the cross and the longitudinal feeds are utilized

lathe techniques

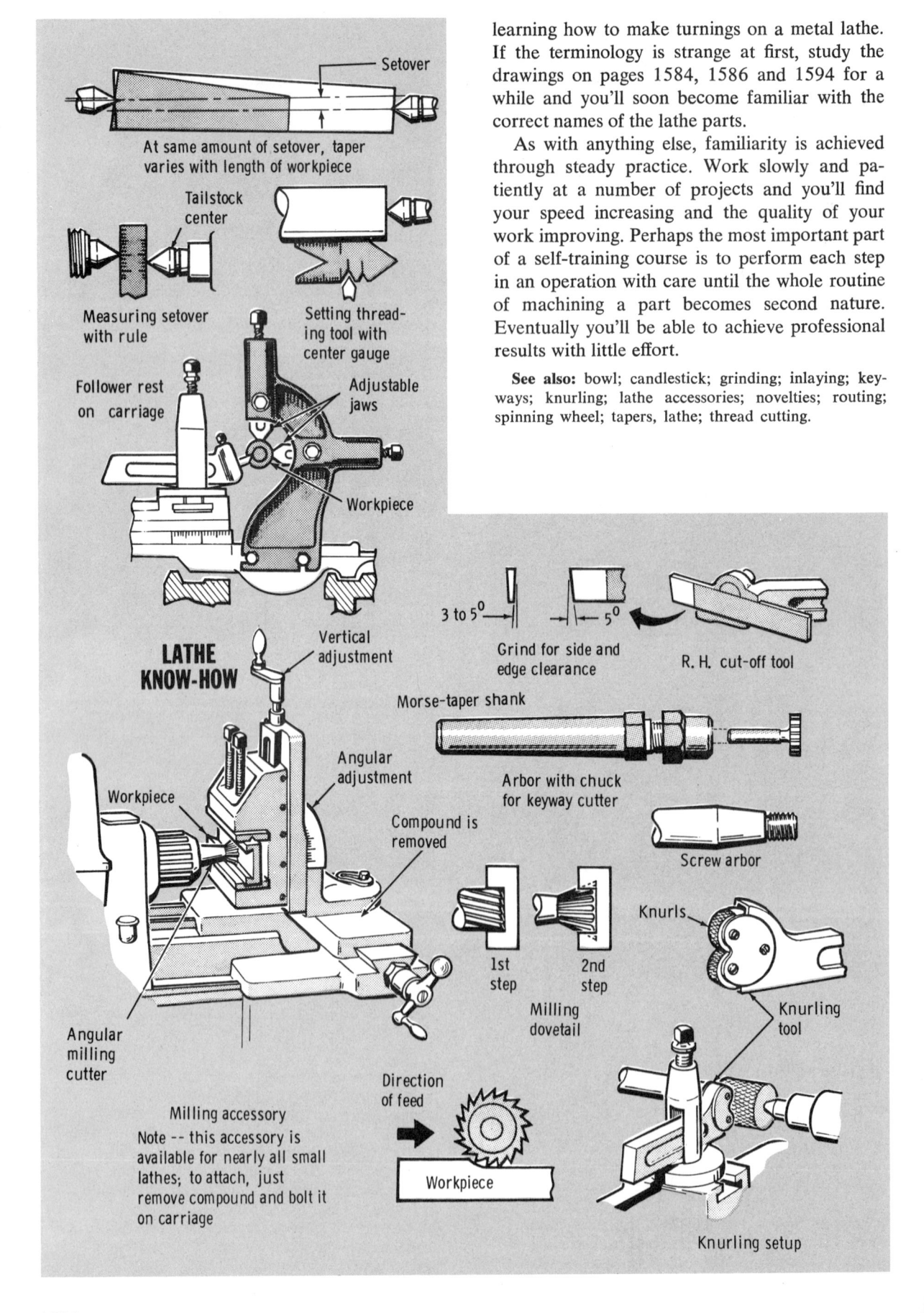

learning how to make turnings on a metal lathe. If the terminology is strange at first, study the drawings on pages 1584, 1586 and 1594 for a while and you'll soon become familiar with the correct names of the lathe parts.

As with anything else, familiarity is achieved through steady practice. Work slowly and patiently at a number of projects and you'll find your speed increasing and the quality of your work improving. Perhaps the most important part of a self-training course is to perform each step in an operation with care until the whole routine of machining a part becomes second nature. Eventually you'll be able to achieve professional results with little effort.

See also: bowl; candlestick; grinding; inlaying; keyways; knurling; lathe accessories; novelties; routing; spinning wheel; tapers, lathe; thread cutting.

clever ideas

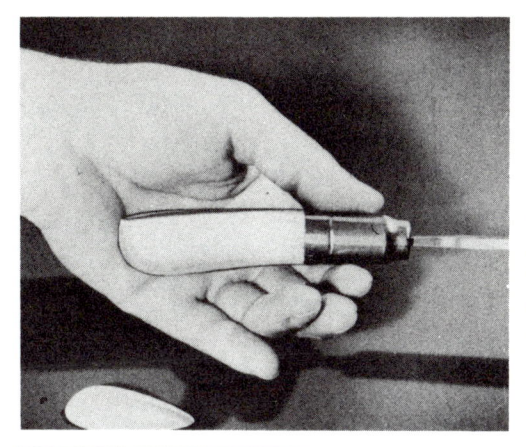

You get better control of a file on a delicate job by cutting away a portion of the handle, leaving it flat as pictured. This not only gives a better and surer sense of lateral tilt of the file, but offers a somewhat easier and more comfortable grip when doing heavier work, such as filing a flat surface. Cut away only the wood portion of the handle back of the metal ferrule and sand the flat surface smooth, rounding the edges of the handle only slightly.

You've known for a long time about using a short length of dowel as a pilot for an auger bit when enlarging a hole concentrically, but did you ever think of using a faucet washer? It accomplishes the same thing as the dowel—pilots the bit accurately—and it does not split or wedge tightly in the smaller hole, making it necessary to drive it out and start all over again. All you have to do is select a faucet washer of the right size, turn it onto the screw point of the bit and proceed to bore the hole to a larger diameter.

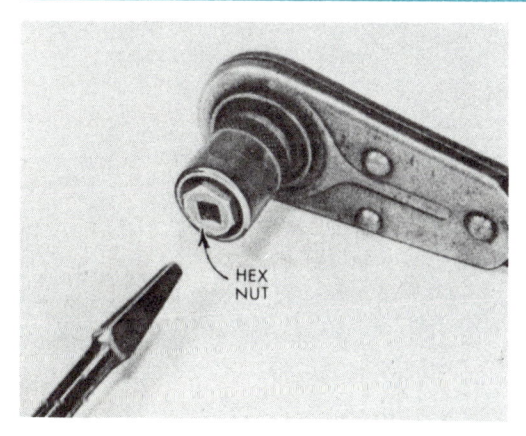

Of course, a regular ratchet brace takes care of most problems in boring holes where there isn't room for a full swing of the sweep. But there are times when even the ratchet brace won't do the trick, and then you have to improvise. Square the threaded hole in a hex nut, drop it into a wrench socket, snap the socket onto a ratchet driver and you've got the short ratchet pictured. Fit the squared hole in the nut over the shank of an auger bit and you can bore a hole in places it's impossible to reach with any other tool.

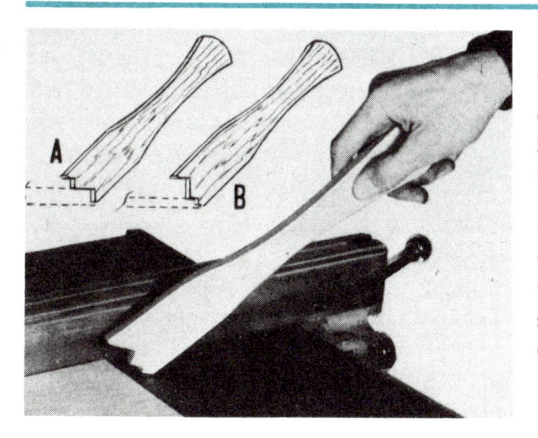

When you make a push stick—and there should always be one handy at the circular saw—cut two notches instead of one in the end as is the usual practice. The extra notch is not only an added utility feature, it's a safety bonus as you can safely handle stock in a wide range of thicknesses. Note the two sizes of notches in details A and B. The smaller notch takes stock ¼ in. thick with just enough clearance to prevent the corner from riding on the saw table, permitting the stock to chatter as it is pushed past the blade. Flip the stick over and you have a ½-in. notch for stock up to 2 in.

laundry

Give your wife a break

BY HANK CLARK

Here are two work centers to make her housework easier

laundry chute: see home improvement
lavatory remodeling: see bathrooms

■ IT MAKES SO MUCH SENSE to locate the home laundry in the kitchen that I'm surprised more people haven't done so. Modern washers and dryers are as smartly styled as any stove or refrigerator, and most of them are whisper-quiet. But the best argument is convenience.

I installed our washer and dryer in the space originally planned to hold a dinette set. The one problem was finding a place to store all those laundry necessities—soap, bleach, a sorting hamper for dirty clothes, and other odds and ends—but I had a solution.

Special-purpose cabinets above and on either

Broom closet at the end of the laundry wall holds vacuum cleaner, floor polisher, a broom

Double hamper features a partitioned bottom section for sorting clothes

Kitchen desk above hamper has pigeon-holes for household accounts, correspondence

End cabinet is a handy place to store detergents and bleaches handy to the washer

side of the washer and dryer provided plenty of storage space for all of these things. There was even some extra shelf space to take the overflow from other kitchen cabinets. Since all the cabinets were styled to match the kitchen decor and dimensioned to fill the available space, the whole thing ended up looking like an efficient built-in laundry center which might well have been a part of the original kitchen plan.

Now that it's finished, I can see that this laundry wall could just as well be built as an island divider wall or a partition with one end against a regular wall to form an alcove. It depends on your floor plan.

The only real requirement is access to the

Cookbook shelves have sliding doors of opaque plastic to diffuse light from fluorescent fixtures

1597

laundry

laundry lifelines—hot and cold water for the washer, a drain line to a trap, a 20-amp outlet to plug in the washer, a 50-amp circuit to the dryer (or a gas line, if you have a gas dryer) and an outside exhaust duct for the dryer.

The water lines should have shut-off valves at the outlets, since washer manufacturers recommend that the water be shut off between loads to take pressure off the hoses. I installed an access panel in the opposite side of the wall from the laundry center for this purpose.

All building codes require a trap in the drainage line to prevent sewer odors from backing up. Instead of installing a separate drain with a trap, I led a hose down through the floor to our unfinished basement so that the washer would drain into a stationary laundry tub which is equipped with a trap.

The plans for the cabinetry are self-explanatory, with exact dimensions determined by the space available. Most washers are top-loading so the bottom of the wall cabinet above should be high enough to allow the lid to swing up. Shallow cookbook cupboards with inclined sliding doors of translucent plastic fill this space nicely without obstructing the lid. Fluorescent fixtures mounted in the top of these cupboards and wired to a wall switch provide plenty of light.

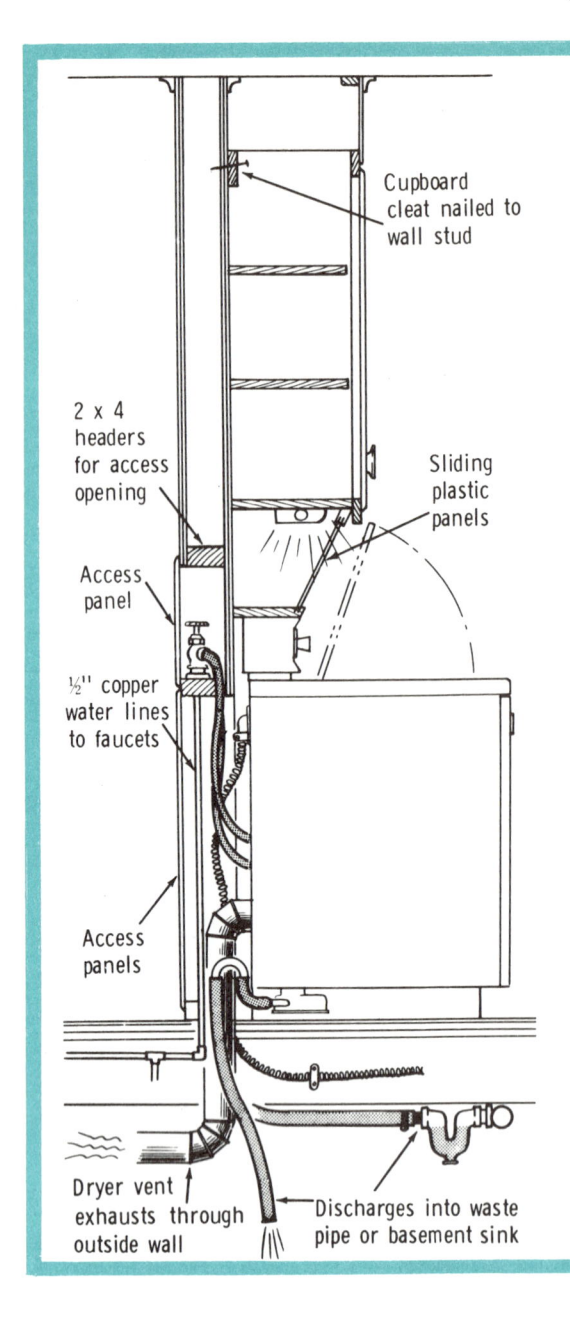

dormer sewing center

Has your wife's sewing graduated from the sewing basket stage? If her sewing paraphernalia is now scattered all over the house, here's a solution:

Basically, it's just a compact free-standing cabinet equipped with a number of special-purpose storage compartments and a spacious worktable. And while it could be used anywhere, it was originally designed to suit a rather unusual situation in which the only possible location for a sewing area proved to be in a large double-windowed dormer at one end of the master bedroom. While the lighting situation was ideal, potential storage space seemed quite limited.

To take full advantage of the light, a spacious worktable was installed in the dormer directly

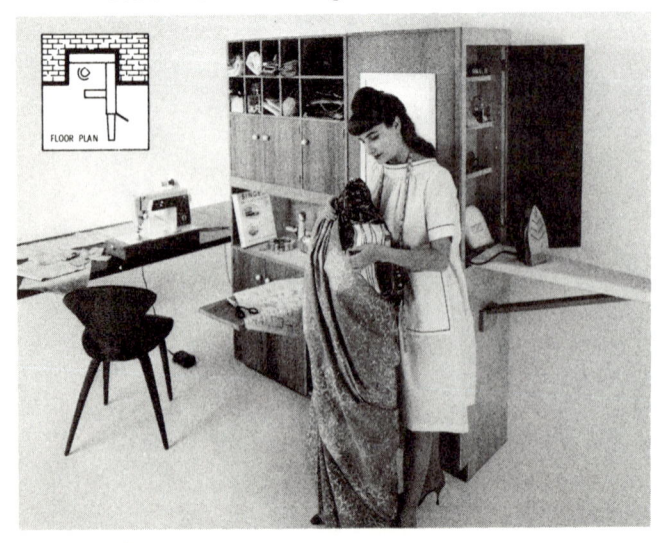

Designed to fit the alcove of a dormer (inset), sewing center makes use of light from the window

under the windows. It rested on cleats secured to the wall.

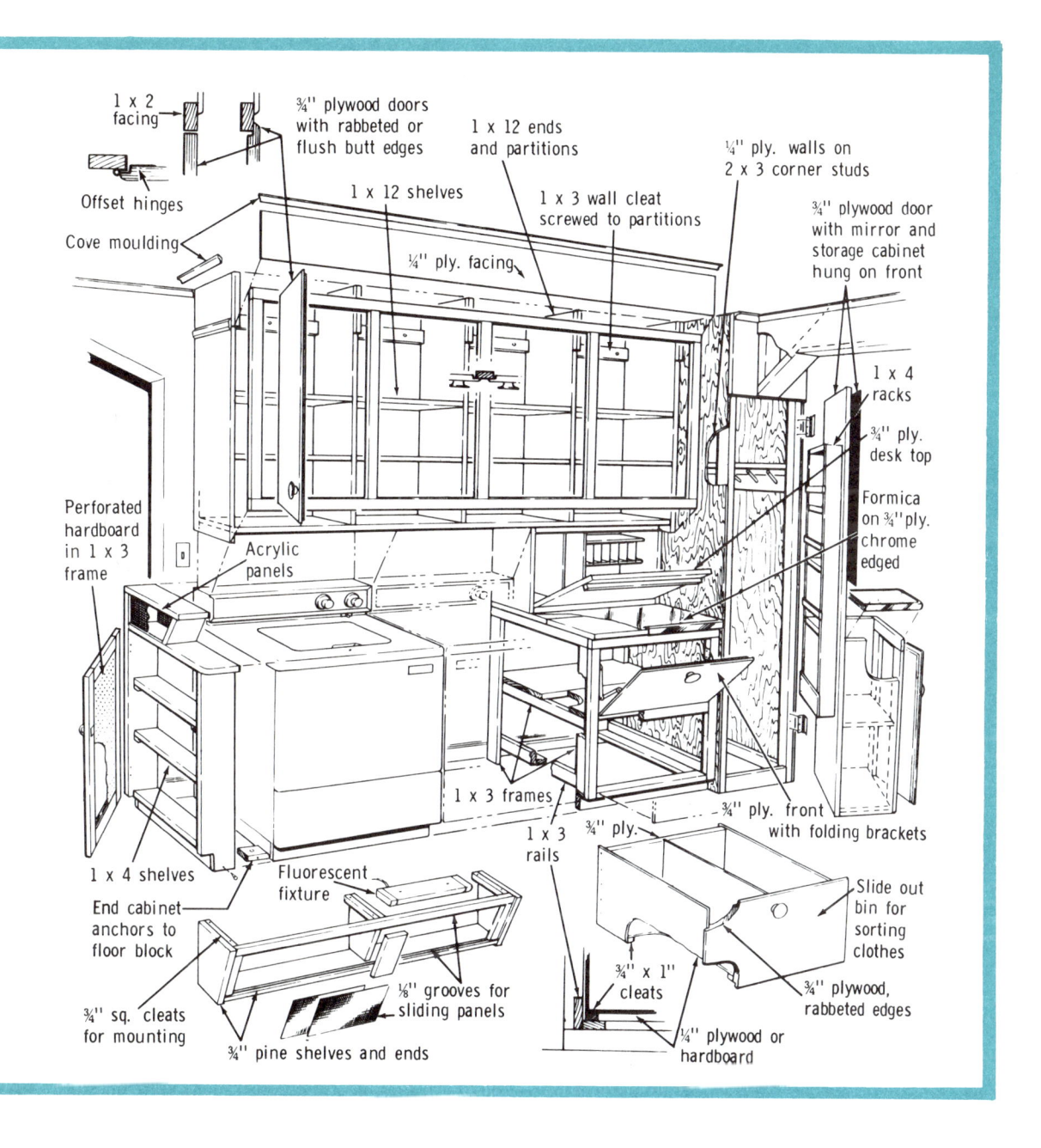

Providing adequate storage space seemed to be an almost impossible problem at first glance. The dormer was too narrow to accommodate storage cabinets on both walls, and the slanting roof line made it impractical to locate cabinets along both sides.

The solution was actually quite simple—a single large cabinet along one wall of the dormer extending out into the room to partition off that corner and turn it into a sewing alcove. Designed specifically for this storage job, the cabinet's an ingenious combination of different-sized bins and shelves to hold all the needfuls. It includes a miniature swing-down ironing board, a swing-up work table and a closet for partially finished garments, and a dress form.

Of course, the worktable and storage cabinet could be located anywhere in the house, either as an L-shaped unit in a corner or with the end of the cabinet against a wall to partition off a sewing corner. By adding legs to the worktable, the two units can be made independent of each other and arranged to suit your floor plan.

See also: clothes dryer; clothes dryer, electric; home improvement; kitchens; irons; remodeling ideas; weekend projects.

1599

clever ideas

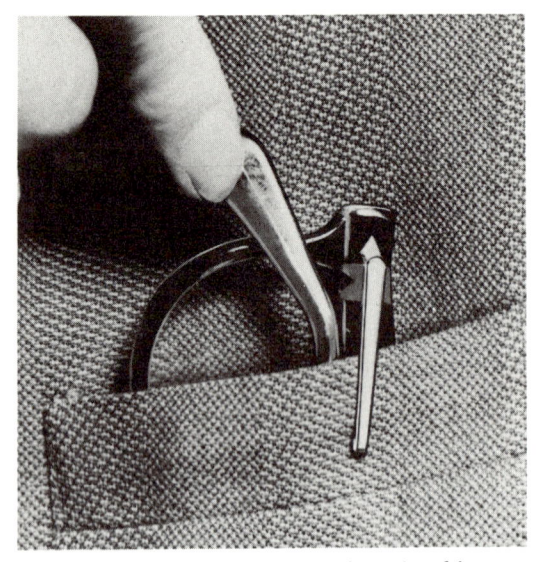

Eyeglasses carried in the breast pocket of a shirt or jacket may slip out when you stoop over. To prevent costly breakage, bend the barrel of a pencil clip to fit the bow.

Got an old venetian blind you don't know what to do with? Use it as a smart summertime screen for your fireplace. Discard the tape and insert the slats in slanting slots cut in 1 x 2 frame.

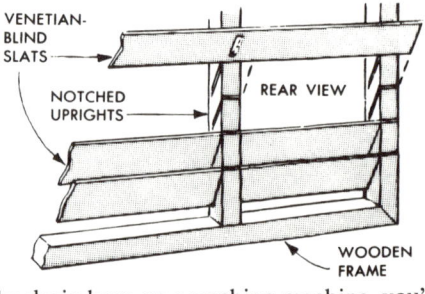

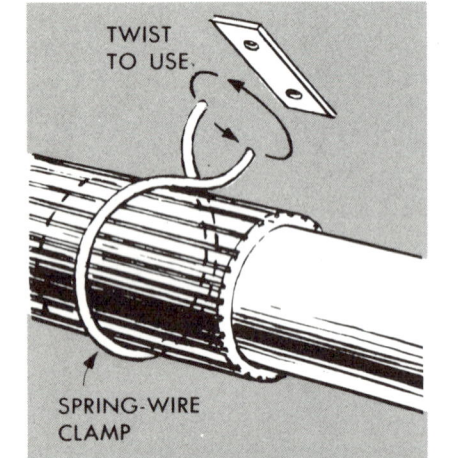

When replacing the drain hose on a washing machine, you'll find that it's much easier to remove the spring-type clamp if you drill a metal plate to fit over the ends. A twist of the wrist will open the clamp.

Clotheslines will stay taut if you secure them to spring-mounted eyebolts. Drill a hole in the crosspiece for a 6-in. eyebolt and slip a 2-in. spring over the bolt before adding the nut and washer. The result? No slack.

This improvised door stop is just a large rubber electrical plug with the prongs bent outward. Mount it by driving small screws through the holes in the prongs and into the baseboard. It's fine for basement or laundry doors.

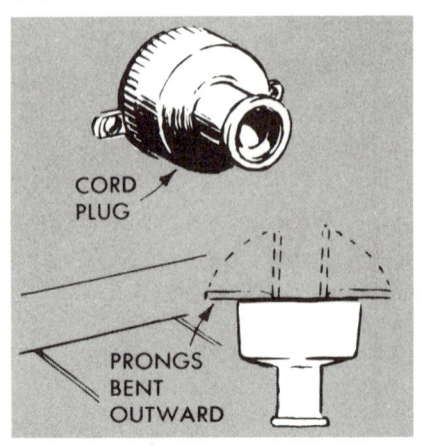

1600

lawns

Velvety green lawns don't just happen

BY CLIFFORD B. HICKS

THE NO. 1 PROBLEM of most lawns is not scraggly weeds, grasping crabgrass or hungry insects. The No. 1 problem is human nature.

Come spring, most homeowners can hardly wait to get in the warm sun and begin rolling the still-soggy turf, reseeding bare spots, spreading fertilizer, and swinging the first punch at crabgrass. Their enthusiasm carries into summer.

But come fall, most homeowners have had it. Mowing has become a tiresome chore, and crabgrass is fighting back. Besides, there are storm windows to hang and the kids are beginning to holler for help with their homework. Suddenly it's much easier to forget everything that needs to be done, including lawn work.

Yet fall is the prime time for renovating a lawn. A little work invested then will pay off in a vastly improved lawn the next year. Lawn care is a round-the-calendar operation, but fall offers real opportunity.

Autumn is the key time because it is nature's own season for renovation. Get in step with her rhythm. In the fall:

• Nature is shedding seeds herself, and offers a big boost to your own efforts.

continued

lawn blower: see leaf blower
lawn curbing: see concrete
lawn edger: see edger, lawn
lawnmowers: see mowers
lawnmower shelter: see shelters

1601

lawns

ARE YOU MISTREATING YOUR LAWN?

Problem lawns become problems in most cases because they are mistreated. Over many years, Dr. Juska has found that most problems are caused by the same errors. If you have a tired, disloyal lawn, you are probably committing one or more of these seven sins

1. Improper use of fertilizer. Too little nitrogen starves your lawn, too much weakens the root structure. See the section, "What's So Mysterious About Fertilizer," on page 1605. Also check the chart, "Best Grass for Your Lawn," on page 1604 for the recommended amount of fertilizer for your turf

2. Improper watering. Wait to water your lawn until the grass actually shows signs of wilting; then water to a depth of 6 in. Sandy soils require frequent watering in small amounts; clay soils require infrequent watering in larger amounts. Never apply less than an inch of water to an established lawn. To know how much water you are applying, simply place a coffee can in the sprinkled area and wait for an inch of water to appear in it. This is the minimum amount. And if you live in map area 1A, an occasional watering won't keep your lawn green during hot weather. Virtually all cool-season grasses in this area go dormant in midsummer. They'll turn green again in the fall

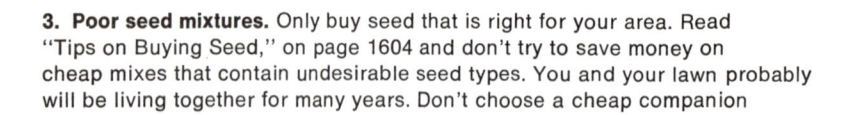

3. Poor seed mixtures. Only buy seed that is right for your area. Read "Tips on Buying Seed," on page 1604 and don't try to save money on cheap mixes that contain undesirable seed types. You and your lawn probably will be living together for many years. Don't choose a cheap companion

FIND YOUR AREA ON THIS LAWN-CARE MAP

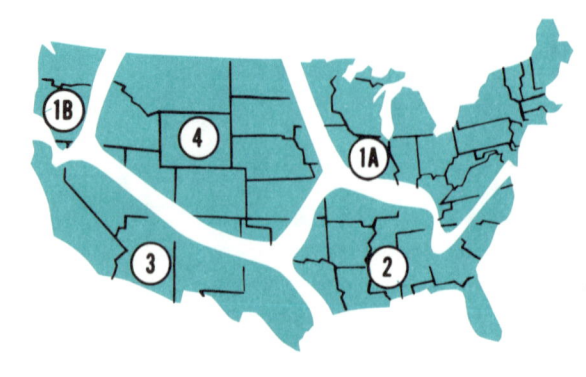

The environment determines every step of good lawn care. Spot your location on this map. In the charts on the following pages, geographical areas are referred to by number.

Obviously the lines on the map are arbitrary, and lawn-care information suited to a spot on one side of a line may be equally applicable to a spot 20 miles away on the other side of the line. However, the lines are the result of long-term research; the map serves as the key to information for your particular spot of ground.

4. Poor mowing practice. Many homeowners mow too closely. As a result, there is not enough leaf area left to provide food for good root development. Never remove more than half the blade of grass at one time. See the recommended mowing height on the chart of lawn grasses on page 1604

5. Too much traffic. Most homeowners believe that lawns are to be played on and enjoyed. Normal activity won't harm a good lawn. However, heavy traffic across certain areas, particularly during winter and early spring, will so compact the soil that it can no longer support grass.
Don't fight the system. Pave or lay stone in areas that always get heavy traffic

6. Too much shade. Most grasses are not adapted to shady areas, and those that are recommended for shade must still compete for sun, water and nutrients. To help your grass in this fight for life, fertilize shady areas frequently but not too heavily; prune low branches from trees to allow more light (even indirect light) to fall on the grass; fertilize the trees 4 to 5 ft. deep, so they won't steal the grass food; apply lime if needed (shady areas are more likely to become acid); remove fallen leaves and clippings frequently. In watering your lawn, remember that in shady areas, trees are often competing for moisture

7. Poorly drained soils. Water will gather in natural depressions in your lawn; then the grass plants drown, or the continually moist soil becomes compacted. On the other hand, many slopes are so steep that water runs right off; the grass gets little water and the soil erodes. In either case, it is best to regrade the lawn

lawn, continued

• Grass has come out of its summer dormancy and is growing vigorously in an unconscious urge to prepare itself for the winter.

• Weeds are again growing vigorously, and thus are prime targets for weed killers. If you kill weeds in spring and summer, the resulting bare spots are likely to be infested with an even worse enemy—crabgrass. If you kill weeds in the fall, crabgrass has begun to go dormant, and fine grasses will spread to fill bare spots.

Furthermore, seedlings established in the fall are much more likely to survive. Heat, not cold, is the biggest environmental threat to a seedling. If you reseed in the spring, some of your tender new plants will inevitably be killed by summer heat and drought; on the other hand, if you sow seed in early fall, seedlings will be well established by the time they are covered with an insulating blanket of snow, and will emerge healthy and vigorous in the spring, when they will have three or four months to mature before they are exposed to the summer sun.

So if you want the finest lawn in your neighborhood, overcome your late-summer lethargy and start your lawn renovation now. On these pages you'll find all the information you'll need.

Every neighborhood has a quiet, competent man to whom others look for authoritative advice. Such a man is Dr. Felix V. Juska—except that his neighborhood is the entire country. Dr. Juska is responsible for lawn-grass research in the Crops Research Division of the U.S. Department of Agriculture. As such, he is the nation's No. 1 authority on home lawns.

Much of the grass-roots information on these pages has been provided by Dr. Juska and his research department at Beltsville, Md.

Start on a program of lawn renovation in late summer and early fall. That's the time to keep your lawn loyal.

lawns

TIPS ON BUYING SEED

BEST TIP OF ALL is to *study labels*. Look on the label for:

1. *The kinds of seed in the mixture.* Any type of seed present in excess of 5 percent must be listed. Beware of seed mixtures containing very high percentages of annual ryegrass, tall fescue and bentgrass. On the other hand, some mixtures are good. Most of the bluegrasses mix well together, and a bluegrass-red fescue mix is good for shady areas and sandy soils. Often a mixture is superior in disease resistance to a single variety.

2. *The percentage of weed seeds present.* This must be shown on the label. Compare labels, and avoid seed with large amounts of weed seed.

3. *The percentage of germination of each type of seed present.* This is, in effect, your guarantee of performance, for it insures the viability of the seed at the time it was tested.

4. *The date of the germination test.* This must also be shown on the label, and is of equal importance to the percentage of germination. The viability of seed declines fairly rapidly with the passage of time. For this reason the law requires that seed be shipped within 5 months of the date of the germination test. The more recent the date of this test, the more seeds will germinate. *Buy fresh seed.* Be particularly careful of grass seed on sale. It may legitimately be on sale; on the other hand, it may be so old that it is rapidly becoming worthless. Reputable seed companies regularly replace aging stocks in stores but, of course, there are disreputable suppliers.

NAME	GEOGRAPHICAL AREA
1. KENTUCKY BLUEGRASS	
Common	1A, 1B, 4 under irrigation
Merion	1A, 1B, northern 2
Park	1A, 1B
2. RED FESCUES	
Common	1A
Pennlawn	1A
3. ASTORIA	1B
4. ZOYSIAS	
Meyer	southern 1A, northern 2
Emerald	2
Manilagrass	2
5. BERMUDAGRASSES	
Everglades 1	southern 2
Ormond	southern 2
Texturf 10	2 and 3 in Texas
Tifgreen	2, 3
Tiflawn	2
6. ST. AUGUSTINES	
Floratine	2
Bitter blue	2
7. BAHIAGRASS	2
8. CENTIPEDE	2
9. BUFFALOGRASS	southern 4
10. BLUE GRAMA	4
11. WHEATGRASS	northern 4

YOUR LAWN-CARE CALENDAR
(For regions 1A, 1B and most of region 4. Warm-season grasses grown in regions 2 and 3 require care only during the hot summer months.)

Early fall—If your lawn needs a complete renovation, do it now (see separate section). Apply herbicide to eliminate broadleaf weeds. Apply lime if needed. In September, apply half of your fall fertilizer allotment. Rake bare areas and reseed; water lightly but often.

Late fall—In mid-October, apply the other half of the fall fertilizer allotment. Continue mowing as long as the grass grows; do not leave the grass tall for the winter months. Mulch the leaves as they fall, or if they tend to clot on the lawn, rake and remove them.

Early spring—Rake trash from lawn. Apply lime if needed, and if you were too lazy to do it last fall. Apply a pre-emergent crabgrass killer. In late February or early March, spread a light application of fertilizer, or a heavier application of slow-release fertilizer. Reseed any bare spots you missed last fall. If the soil has heaved from frost, use a light roller but not a heavy one. Apply a herbicide for chickweed if that weed is a problem in your lawn.

Late spring—Give your lawn another light shot of fertilizer. Kill the broadleaf weeds. Mow according to the recommended practice for your type of grass. You should have used a pre-emergent crabgrass killer months ago. If you didn't, do it now.

Summer—If you have a zoysia or Bermuda-grass lawn, feed it in July and again in August. Mow frequently enough that you remove no more than one-half the total leaf length. If you have a bluegrass lawn, don't worry if it turns brown—it's dormant as nature intended it to be. In long periods of drought, water deeply once a week. Take a vacation. When you return, if the grass is so long that the clippings may smother the lawn, remove them as you mow.

HERE YOU'LL FIND THE BEST GRASS FOR YOUR LAWN

CHARACTERISTICS	MOWING HEIGHT	BEST SEEDING OR PLANTING TIME	NITROGEN, LBS./ 1000 SQ. FT. ANNUALLY
Excellent cool-area grass; withstands abuse; not good for heavy shade.	1½-2"	Fall	3-4
Low-growing, short leaves, good color; thick turf; leaf-spot-resistant.	1½-2"	Fall	6-8
Vigorous and resistant to rust, particularly in far north.	1½-2"	Fall	3-4
More tolerant of shade than bluegrass, narrow leaf, good color.	1-2"	Fall	2-3
Better turf than common red fescues, more tolerant of leaf spot.	1-2"	Fall	2-3
Beautiful bentgrass lawn, but requires continuous and expensive care.	¾" or less	Fall	4-6
Dense turf able to withstand hot, humid summer.	¾-1"	Spring	5-10
Dense, relatively weed-free turf. Very slow to establish.	¾-1"	Spring	5-10
Very dense, stands considerable shade.	¾-1"	Spring	5-10
Dark green, fine textured, vigorous; excellent for Florida.	¾-1"	Spring	5-10
Blue-green, slow growing; resists leaf spot, but not dollar spot; excellent for Florida.	¾-1"	Spring	5-10
Medium texture, dark green; makes early spring recovery; slow spreading.	¾-1"	Spring	5-10
Dark green, fine texture, disease resistant.	¾-1"	Spring	5-10
Dense, weed-free turf; tolerates heavy wear, used on many football fields.	¾-1"	Spring	5-10
Thick growth; adapted to sandy soils; year-round color.	2-2½"	Spring	4-5
Blue-green; excellent ornamental turf, but does not withstand heavy wear.	2-2½"	Spring	4-5
Coarse, relatively unattractive turf, but easy to maintain.	2"	Spring	4
Easily maintained, good for heavy soils; has unattractive brown winter color.	1-1½"	Spring	2
Best grass where water is unavailable; thrives when mowed low.	1-2"	Spring	Seldom required.
Bunch-type grass, not as desirable as buffalograss, but drought-resistant.	1-2"	Spring	Seldom required.
Withstands long, dry periods and heavy traffic if not mowed closely.	2"	Fall	Seldom required.

WHAT'S SO MYSTERIOUS ABOUT FERTILIZER?

THERE HAVE BEEN so many claims and counterclaims about fertilizers that most homeowners have blindly settled on one brand that seems to do the job, and continue to use it year after year. There is a better, cheaper way to select fertilizer.

A complete fertilizer contains three elements: nitrogen, for stimulating leaf growth; phosphorus, for the formation of strong roots; and potash, which gives plants stamina and disease resistance. Every bag of fertilizer is labeled with the percentages of each of these elements. For example, a 10-6-4 fertilizer consists of 10 percent available nitrogen, 6 percent phosphorus, 4 percent potash —and 80 percent inert carrying material.

Since nitrogen is the most vital of these elements, and also the most expensive, the *first* figure on the label is the one on which you should focus your attention. Simply divide this figure into 100. The answer is the number of *pounds* of fertilizer you must buy to apply 1 lb. of nitrogen to 1000 square feet of lawn. And a good rule of thumb is to apply no more than 1 lb. of nitrogen per 1000 sq. ft. of established turf at any one time.

One specific example: Suppose you have 5000 sq. ft. of lawn. You look at one bag of fertilizer priced at $3.98. It weighs 50 lb., and has a 10-6-4 formula. Divide the first figure (10) into 100 and you find that you'll need 10 lb. of fertilizer per 1000 sq. ft. Because you have 5000 sq. ft. of lawn, you'll need 50 lb. of this fertilizer (one bag), priced at $3.98.

Down the counter is another brand, this one on sale. It is an 8-6-4 mixture, with a 35-lb. bag priced at $2.25. Divide the 8 into 100 and you get 13, the number of pounds you'll need per 1000 sq. ft. Multiply by 5 (because you have 5000 sq. ft.) and you find you need 65 lb. to treat your lawn, or two bags of this fertilizer. The on-sale brand thus will cost you $4.58. Obviously this on-sale fertilizer isn't as good a buy as the first. Prices are average, of course.

There are two basic *types* of fertilizer: organic and inorganic. Organic fertilizers are processed from such plant or animal materials as sewage sludge and bonemeal. After application, they are broken down by the action of soil bacteria, a process which takes place over a period of time. In this respect organic fertilizers may be slightly preferable to inorganic.

Urea-form and *resin form* fertilizers are synthetic nitrogen fertilizers that release their nitrogen slowly throughout the season, which is a big advantage. However, it is still possible to overstimulate the grass with slow-release fertilizer. Suppose you apply a healthy dose of one of the fertilizers in the spring. During the summer you decide that the lawn needs another light shot, so you apply either a smaller dose of the same, or a shot of quick-release fertilizer. Along comes a period of hot weather combined with good rains. *Both* fertilizers then are accelerated to release their nitrogen. This may well overstimulate and weaken the lawn.

The chart shows various combinations of inorganic fertilizers, and some of the more common organic fertilizers. It indicates how much *total* fertilizer you'll have to buy to apply 1 lb. of nitrogen per 1000 sq. ft. of your lawn.

FERTILIZER

FERTILIZER	FERTILIZER NEEDED TO SPREAD 1 POUND OF NITROGEN OVER 1000 SQ. FT. AREA
5-10-5	20 Pounds
4-12-4	25 Pounds
5-10-10	20 Pounds
10-10-10	10 Pounds
8-8-8	13 Pounds
10-6-4	10 Pounds
8-6-4	13 Pounds
4-8-4	25 Pounds
6-12-4	17 Pounds
Processed sewage sludge	17 Pounds
Ammonium nitrate	4 Pounds
Ammonium sulfate	5 Pounds
Nitrate of soda	7 Pounds
Steamed bonemeal	50 Pounds
Cottonseed meal	17 Pounds
Peanut hull meal	50 Pounds
Cocoa shell meal	50 Pounds
Dried cattle manure	50 Pounds
Dried sheep manure	70 Pounds
Sewage sludge	50 Pounds
Tobacco stems	50 Pounds
Urea	3 Pounds
Processed tankage	13 Pounds
Soybean meal	17 Pounds
Urea-form	3 Pounds

WEED CONTROL

THE BEST WEED CONTROL is a thick stand of vigorous grass. Close mowing allows weeds to come into the turf, and frequent light watering helps the weeds more than the grass.

Chemical science has come up with a broad range of selective herbicides that make weed control much easier than it was a generation ago. These herbicides are available in liquid, powder and granular forms. All are effective.

Individual manufacturers package herbicides under their own brand names, and in differing concentrations. The chemical names which appear on the weed-control chart will be on the label, despite trade names. *Always use the manufacturer's recommended dosage,* as it is the result of long research with that particular concentration. Never apply more of a herbicide than is recommended; you won't kill any more weeds, and you may well kill desirable turf.

Spraying and spreading are the easiest ways to cover large areas with a herbicide. For spot treatment at low cost, simply tie a small sponge to a stick. Dip the sponge in a solution of the herbicide and press it at the base of individual weeds.

Pre-emergent herbicides must be applied before weed seeds have a chance to germinate. A good rule of thumb is to apply such herbicides before the lilacs bloom or magnolia petals fall.

Broadleaf weeds can be treated spring or fall; again, fall is the most satisfactory time. As weeds curl their ugly arms and die, bare spots appear. After fall treatment, lawn grasses will fill such bare spots; after spring treatment, they are more likely to be plugged with crabgrass.

Any sprayer used to spread a herbicide should be thoroughly washed with a strong solution of household ammonia before other use.

YOU CAN WIN THE BATTLE AGAINST CRABGRASS

NO QUESTION ABOUT IT, with modern chemical controls you can eliminate all signs of crabgrass from your lawn.

The first weapons developed for the homeowner's crabgrass arsenal were post-emergent herbicides. These have the unique ability to recognize growing crabgrass plants and kill them. Two such chemicals are DMA (disodium, monomethylarsonate) and PMA phenylmercuric acetate). They are best applied in late spring and early summer, when crabgrass is actively reaching out its ugly tentacles. Usually two or three

HOW TO CONTROL COMMON LAWN WEEDS

WEED	BEST TIME TO TREAT	CONTROL	EFFECT
Bermudagrass	Spring or summer	Methyl bromide (kills all plants)	Good
Bindweed, field	Spring, fall	2,4-D; silvex; MCPA	Good
Chickweed, common	Spring, fall	Silvex; 2,4,5-T	Good
Chickweed, mouse-eared	Spring, fall	Silvex; 2,4,5-T	Good
Crabgrass	Winter, spring, summer	See separate crabgrass section	Fair to good
Dandelion	Spring and fall	2,4-D; MCPA; 2,4,5-T; silvex	Good
Garlic, wild	Late fall, early spring	2,4-D	Good
Goosegrass	Spring, early summer	2,4-D	Poor
Ground-ivy	Spring, fall	Silvex	Good
Henbit	Spring, summer	Silvex	Good
Knotweed	Late winter, early spring	2,4-D; silvex; 2,4,5-T	Good
Nimblewill	Spring	Zytron (repeated treatments)	Fair
Plantain, Buckhorn	Spring	2,4-D	Good
Plantain, rugel	Spring	2,4-D	Good
Quackgrass	Spring, summer, fall	Dalapon (kills all plants)	Fair
Sorrel, red	Spring	Silvex	Fair
Woodsorrel, yellow	Spring	Silvex	Good

HOW TO CONTROL COMMON LAWN DISEASES

DISEASE	SYMPTOMS	CONTROL
Helminthosporium leaf spot	Kentucky bluegrass susceptible. Reddish-brown spots appear on leaves, which shrivel, and plant discolors and rots.	Acti-dione-thiram, Captan, Dyrene, Ortho Lawn and Turf Fungicide, PMA
Dollar spot	Affects many species, but particularly destructive to bentgrasses. Appears during cool, wet weather. Silver-dollar-size spots appear on lawn, black at first, then brown, then white. Grass dies.	Cadmium-containing fungicides, Dyrene, Ortho Lawn and Turf Fungicide, Tersan OM
Brown patch	Attacks virtually all species. Prevalent in warm, humid areas. Irregular circular spots from few inches to several feet in diameter appear and turn brown. If weather stays hot and humid, grass dies but leaves remain erect.	Mercury-containing fungicides, Dyrene, Ortho Lawn and Turf Fungicide, Tersan OM
Rust	Attacks many grasses, but particularly destructive to Kentucky bluegrass. Usually occurs late in summer. Yellow-orange powdery spots appear on leaves. If cloth is rubbed across leaf, spores will leave a yellowish or orange stain.	Acti-dione-thiram, zineb
Snow mold	Affects many grasses, but particularly bentgrasses. Appears on grass which is growing while still covered with snow. White cottony growth appears on leaves.	Dyrene, mercury-containing fungicides, Ortho Lawn and Turf Fungicide
Curvularia fading-out	Attacks many southern grasses when humidity is high. Damage severe on grass that has been covered by water. Older leaves die, but tips of new growth remain green.	Acti-dione-thiram, Captan, Dyrene, Ortho Lawn and Turf Fungicide, PMA
Gray leaf spot	Attacks St. Augustine grass. Small gray circular or elliptical spots appear on leaves. May spread to kill large areas of turf.	Acti-dione-thiram, Captan, Dyrene, Ortho Lawn and Turf Fungicide, PMA

lawns

lawn, continued

applications are required at 7 to 10-day intervals. They may cause a slight discoloration.

The big weapons developed more recently are pre-emergent crabgrass killers. These are applied in late winter or early spring. They offer excellent control because they kill each crabgrass seedling as it pokes its head through the ground. Crabgrass thus has no opportunity to go to seed and provide a crop next year.

If you genuinely want to get rid of crabgrass, apply a pre-emergent control for two or three successive years. Crabgrass seeds can lie dormant in the ground for 50 years, and then germinate. However, in two or three years most of them will be killed by pre-emergent control. You then can skip a year or two.

Some pre-emergents are available under trade names only; some by generic terms. They include calcium arsenate, Dacthal, Zytron, Betasan, Bandane and Azak.

One important point to note in connection with application of these killer chemicals: Usually you will be warned on the labels not to sow new grass seed until 30-60 days after application.

One new herbicide which solves this problem has been marketed under the trade name Tupersan. This product clearly distinguishes friend from foe in your lawn. It kills up to 99 percent of all crabgrass seedlings before they get more than ½ in. long, yet you can sow seed at the same time.

Tupersan, under that name, is not generally available to homeowners. However, other herbicides that can be bought at your garden supply dealer contain Tupersan.

HOW TO REJUVENATE A TIRED LAWN

ACCORDING TO DR. JUSKA, you can materially improve a shabby lawn *if approximately half of the area is still covered with good perennial grasses.* Crabgrass may be reaching its greedy fingers across the other half, or weeds may be clotted here and there, but if you have half a lawn, it's worth saving. Start in mid-August.

Here are the steps in the process:

1. Apply 2,4-D (according to the manufacturer's directions) to wipe out broadleaf weeds. If crabgrass is a major problem, make two or three applications of DMA. Don't apply grass seed for at least a month.

2. If no lime has been applied for four to six years, apply agricultural limestone, preferably dolomitic (calcium and magnesium) at the rate of 50 to 75 lb. per 1000 sq. ft. of ground. Your garden-supply dealer will have it.

3. Apply a strong dose of fertilizer—10 to 15 lb. per 1000 sq. ft., if the first number on the bag is a 10. If it's less than 10, you'll need correspondingly more fertilizer.

4. Mow closely, and rake the bare areas to loosen the soil.

5. Seed perennial grasses—bluegrasses and red fescue—in bare areas at the rate of 1 or 2 lb. per 1000 sq. ft., and rake lightly. If you live in map areas 2 or 3 you may plant stolons instead of sowing seed; it depends upon the type of grass you have, and the type you want to establish.

6. Water seeded areas lightly, and keep soil moist until seedlings are established.

7. Continue to mow whenever the older grass requires it.

8. Early in the spring, apply a pre-emergent crabgrass killer, and another shot of fertilizer.

THINGS YOU MAY HAVE WONDERED ABOUT

Is it right—or wrong—to leave the clippings on the lawn?

If they are not too thick, grass clippings make a desirable mulch that retains moisture. They also decompose over a period of time to provide nutrients to the lawn. On the other hand, clippings that are too thick tend to smother the lawn and foster fungus diseases. A good rule of thumb, according to Dr. Juska, is to let the clippings lie 24 hours. If, from a short distance away, they have become invisible, you're better off to leave them. If they are still readily visible, they should be removed.

How about fallen leaves? Should I mulch or remove them?

If leaves sift down from trees gradually, remain dry, and leave few traces after they are mulched, it is better to mulch them. They provide excellent humus for the grass. However, if they are so thick and wet that they remain in globs on the lawn, even after mulching, it is best to remove them. Often it is a good practice to rake and remove the leaves immediately under thick shade trees, and mulch the remainder of your lawn. If you mulch the leaves instead of removing them, you should add lime ⅓ to ½ again as frequently as normal, because decaying leaves tend to make the soil much more acid.

How can I tell whether my lawn needs lime?

The only certain method is to test lawn soil yourself or send a sample of it to your county agent, state agricultural college, or state department of agriculture for testing. In some states, such tests are made free; in others, there is a nominal charge, but you can be sure it *will* be nominal. (See next question for further information.) However, for about a buck you can get a soil-test kit that will tell you whether your lawn needs lime. It's a simple test that you can make in three minutes. If you need lime and your soil is sandy, you should apply ground agricultural limestone every two or three years. In clay soils, apply it every five or six years. The rate of application should be 50 to 75 lb. per 1000 sq. ft.

Where can I get answers to specific questions about my lawn?

Most homeowners fail to realize the information and help that is available to them at state and local levels. Every state publishes bulletins and other information to answer specific questions for particular areas. In most states this information comes from the state agricultural college. Furthermore, most states have extension services which go right down to the county level. Very likely there is a man in your county called a county agent or farm advisor (depending upon the state) whose function is to help answer questions concerning agricultural crops. And grass definitely is considered an agricultural crop; as a matter of fact, in terms of investment, more money is spent on turf than on corn, wheat, cotton or any other crop. In most cases, a call to the man at the county level will yield an answer to your specific question, or bring the man right to your home to analyze your problem. The titles of such public servants and the departments they represent vary from state to state. Try a local telephone listing for your state college of agriculture, or the department of agriculture for your state. If you still can't pin down your man, drop a postcard to your local state department of agriculture, and ask for the name, address and phone number of your local county agent.

Is there any way to speed up the germination of grass seed?

Some types of grass, such as Merion blue, have very long germinating periods, up to a month or more. Keeping them well-watered during this period can be a chore. You can appreciably shorten this time by a pre-germination treatment. Put the seed in a cloth bag and soak it in cold water overnight. Then wash the bag, with the seed still in it, under a faucet until the water runs clear. Finally, spread the seed in the sunlight and let it dry thoroughly, turning it occasionally during the drying. When dry, it is ready for sowing.

Why is it necessary to keep lawnmower blades sharp? What difference does it make?

A mower with dull blades will cut your lawn. But professional lawn men insist on keeping mower blades sharp, no matter which type—reel or rotary. The reason is that a dull blade crushes or frays the leaves as it cuts, and the damage this causes will move down the leaf. It encourages disease and may cause the grass plant to die. The "crushed" cut of a dull mower gives a lawn a brown cast within a few hours after mowing.

Does aeration really do a lawn any good? Doesn't it damage the grass?

When the soil in a lawn becomes compacted, aeration can be of considerable value. Aeration, of course, simply means spiking holes into the soil. These holes permit water and fertilizer to penetrate deeply to promote heavy root growth. Penetration in compacted soil is difficult, if not impossible, and as a result, roots frequently are starved. Aeration can be done with hand tools, or you can rent a machine from an equipment dealer or landscape gardener.

What is the best time of day for watering the lawn?

Improper watering can be one of the causes of disease in a lawn. Water the lawn early enough in the day so that the grass leaves have time to dry out before nightfall. Avoid frequent light waterings, especially during warm weather. The best rule is: don't water the grass until it begins to wilt, and then soak the soil to a depth of 6 in. or more. Light waterings only encourage shallow root development, which in turn makes the grass especially vulnerable during very hot weather.

See also: concrete; edger, lawn; landscaping; lawn sweeper; leaf blower; leaf burner; mowers; mulchmaker; retaining walls; weed killers; wheelbarrow.

lawn sweeper

Lawn sweeper from an old hand mower

BY MANLY BANISTER

You've gone to power for your weekly grass-cutting chore? Don't throw away your push-type machine until you've considered this practical use for some of its parts

■ MAYBE YOU hadn't thought of it, but the parts from the old hand mower you've been ready to toss out since you bought a new power mower can be used to make an excellent lawn sweeper. You dismantle the mower and throw away everything but the wheels, wheel plates (in older hand mowers these are castings), the pinions and clutch pins and the bolts and retainers that hold the wheels on the spindles, and in some cases the reel bearings. Clean these parts thoroughly in a solvent to remove accumulations of grime and lubricant.

The brush which picks up leaves and trash must run in a direction opposite to that of the grass-cutting reel. This is accomplished by reversing the normal position of the wheel plates and driving the brush through spur gears and a roller chain as in Figs. 1 and 3. The former detail of the assembly and the photos show how the mower is altered and reassembled with a new drive shaft, a jackshaft, to give the brush shaft a reverse rotation to the direction of travel. The

---

lawn weeds: see lawns
laying brick: see brickwork
lazy-susan hardware rack: see rack, hardware
lazy-susan necktie rack: see tie rack

1 GENERAL ASSEMBLY

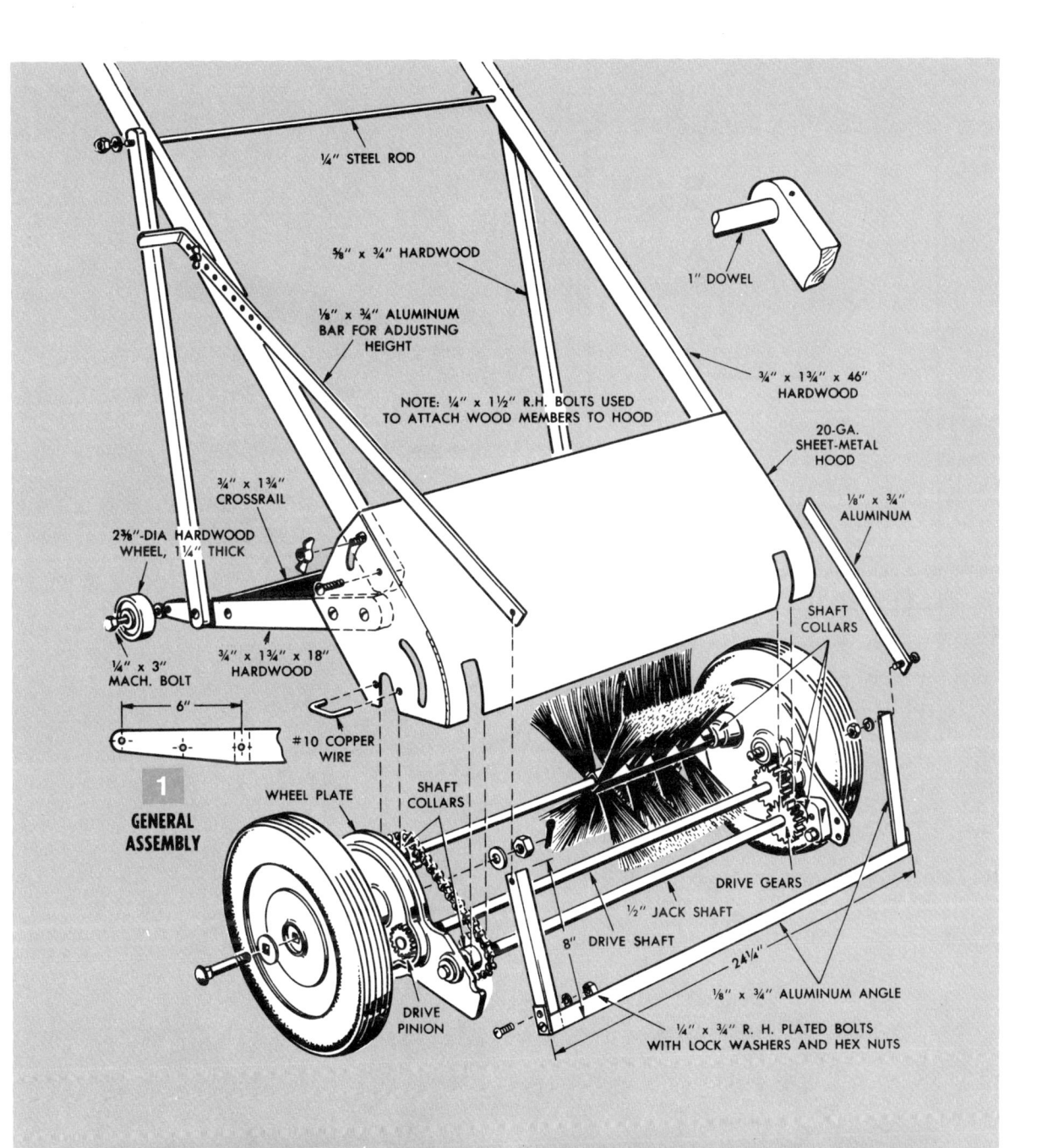

Labels on diagram:
- ¼" STEEL ROD
- ⅜" × ¾" HARDWOOD
- ⅛" × ¾" ALUMINUM BAR FOR ADJUSTING HEIGHT
- 1" DOWEL
- NOTE: ¼" × 1½" R.H. BOLTS USED TO ATTACH WOOD MEMBERS TO HOOD
- ¾" × 1¾" × 46" HARDWOOD
- ¾" × 1¾" CROSSRAIL
- 20-GA. SHEET-METAL HOOD
- 2⅜"-DIA HARDWOOD WHEEL, 1¼" THICK
- ⅛" × ¾" ALUMINUM
- ¼" × 3" MACH. BOLT
- ¾" × 1¾" × 18" HARDWOOD
- SHAFT COLLARS
- 6"
- #10 COPPER WIRE
- WHEEL PLATE
- SHAFT COLLARS
- DRIVE GEARS
- ½" JACK SHAFT
- 8" DRIVE SHAFT
- 24¼"
- ⅛" × ¾" ALUMINUM ANGLE
- DRIVE PINION
- ¼" × ¾" R.H. PLATED BOLTS WITH LOCK WASHERS AND HEX NUTS

The original wheel, with wheel plate and spur gears, brush shaft, jackshaft and drive shaft

On the opposite wheel, the roller-chain drive to the brush shaft reverses brush rotation

lawn sweeper

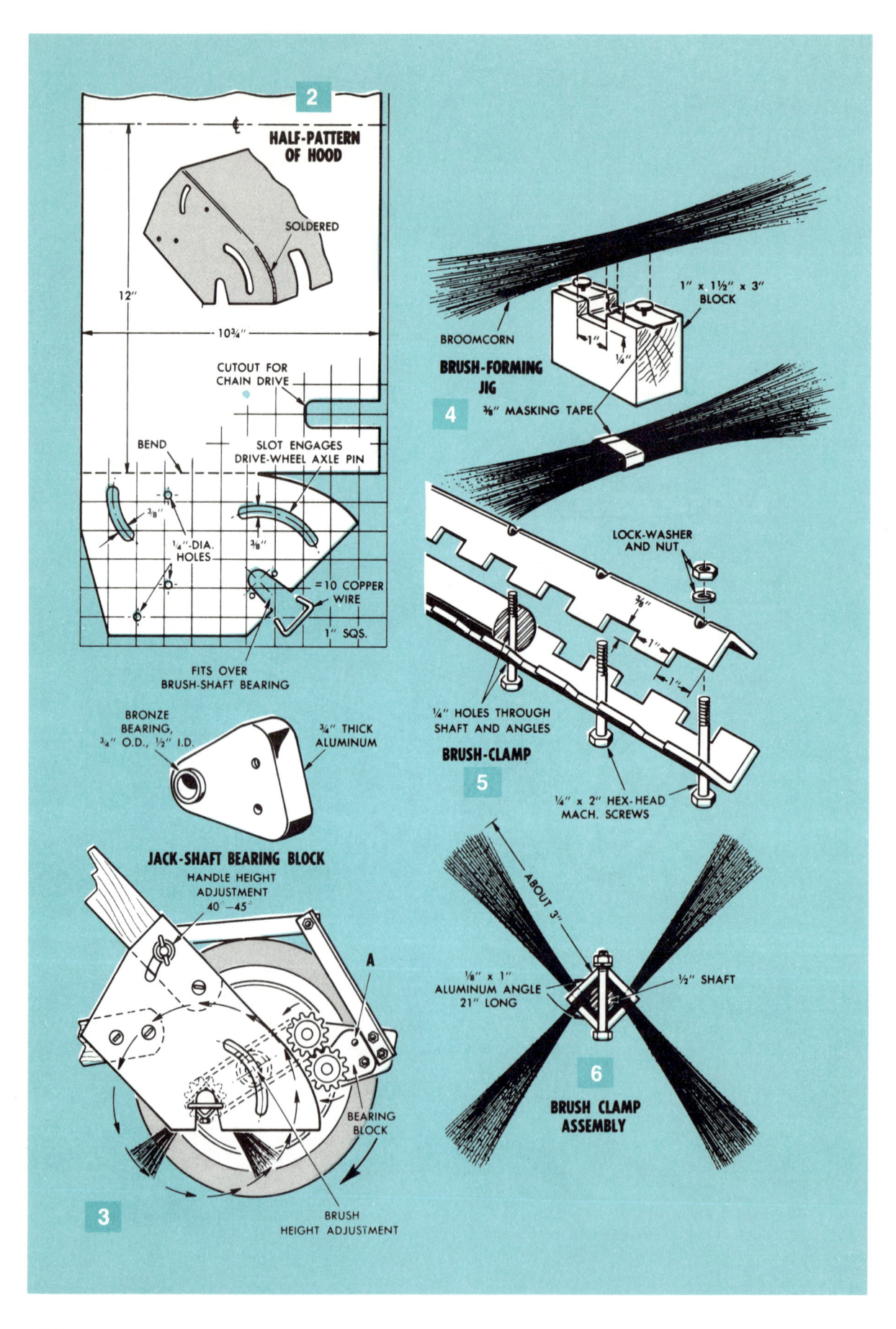

1612

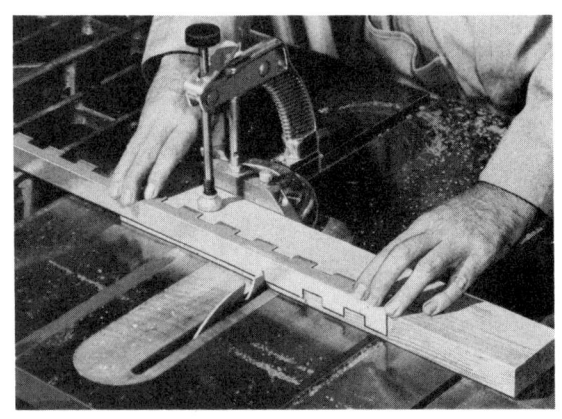

Aluminum angles that hold the brush sections in place are notched on a table saw. Note the backing strip

Broomstraws are bundled in a jig, then taped and sewed. Keep the bundles as uniform as possible

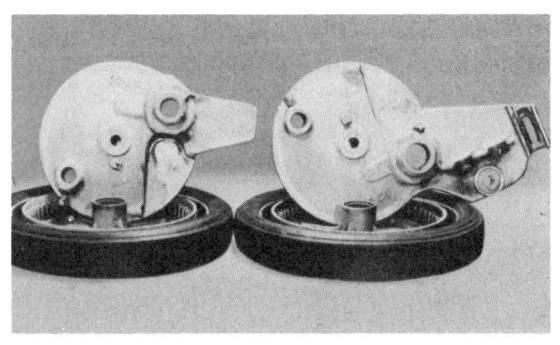

From the mower, only the wheels, wheel plates, pinions, clutch pins, bolts and retainers are used

A partially assembled brush with all bundles in place ready for the second angle forming the complete hub

bosses on the wheel plates which normally take the ends of the shrub bar are utilized as seats for bronze sleeve bearings in which the brush shaft rotates.

Now, from the mower you use you will have to determine the diameter of the drive shaft and the brush shaft. Of course, these are longer than the originals, that is, if the original mower was, say, a 16-in. cut, you can open it out to 24 in. or slightly more in sweeper width, and the 18-in. mower in proportion. The jackshaft can be ½ in. diameter as in Fig. 1. But the diameters of the other two shafts will be governed by the size of the sleeve bushings you can seat (by reaming) in the shrub-bar bosses and also by what size bushings can be seated in the drive-shaft bores. On some old mowers the reel is carried on self-aligning ball bearings and it may be that these can be utilized in the conversion. The clutch mechanism of the mower is retained; only the shaft is replaced by a longer one.

Note closely in Fig. 1, the photos below Fig. 1, and also the detail A, Fig. 3, that the jackshaft is carried in pivoting bearing blocks. In the first stage of the assembly these blocks are attached with only one bolt through the mower plates. This permits you to adjust the spur gears for proper running clearance. Once this has been determined—with all parts in position in a trial assembly—the blocks and plates are drilled and tapped for small capscrews, labeled A in Fig. 3. The spur gears were taken from an old mower, the clutch collars, or hubs, machined flush and the body of each drilled between adjacent teeth and tapped for a hollow setscrew. Normally, these gears are 1½ to 1¾ in. in diameter, an average being 1⅝ in. Of course, any pair of spur gears near these sizes can be used. Chain sprockets are ⅜-in pitch, 1⅝ in. total diameter and have 11 teeth.

Next you make the hood, or brush housing. Fig. 2 shows the development of half of the hood from a center line and indicates where and how to bend the metal to obtain the necessary shape;

lawn sweeper

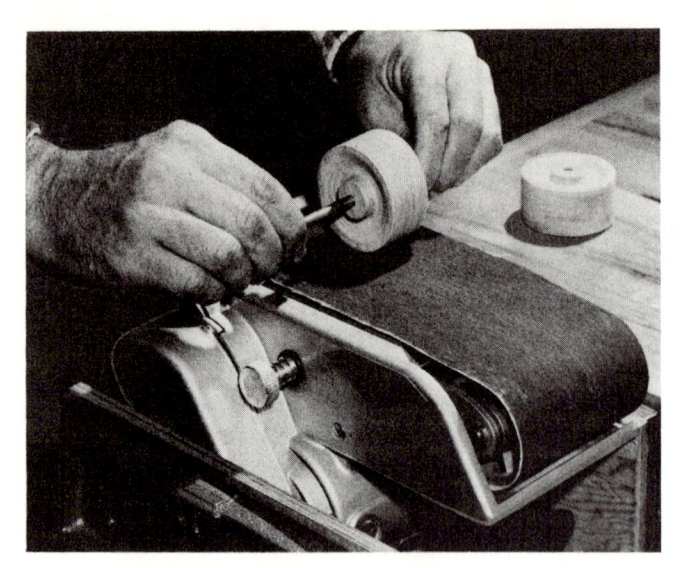

True up the dolly, or trailer, wheel treads on belt sander. Use hex-head machine bolts as wheel spindles

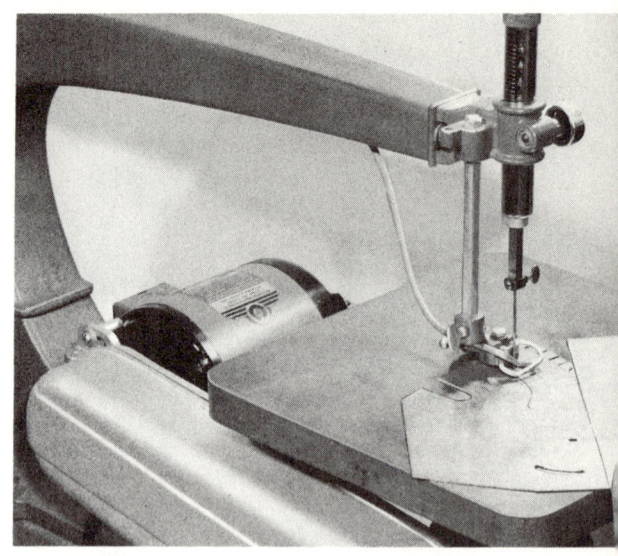

Much of the work of cutting out the hood can be done on a jigsaw with a metal-cutting blade

Hold wood parts against sheet-metal parts and drill through both. This locates holes accurately

An under view of the finished sweeper shows the dolly that supports the hopper and push bar

mower to sweeper, continued

mowers differ in construction, so before you make the cuts and slots indicated, run a check on all parts of the assembly, just to make sure you get them properly located. Don't solder, slot, cut or drill holes until you're sure of location. Note the relationship of parts in Fig. 3, also the positions they assume when the unit is in operation. Compare also with the pulled-apart detail, Fig. 1. You might also correlate these views with the photo of the finished sweeper. The adjusting bar, Fig. 1, raises and lowers the brush, the assembly pivoting on the wheel retaining pin. In some mowers this is a bolt and in this case the hex nut can be replaced with a wingnut which is more easily loosened when adjustment is made. Note also in Fig. 3 that when assembled, the tips of the four-section brush are trimmed so that they just clear the hood. The clearance can be $1/16$ to $1/8$ in. but no more for leaf sweeping. For some mowers you may have to make a full-size drawing of one wheel and wheel plate in order to determine the locations of the bearing and axle center. By projecting the shape of the hood on the drawing you can then determine the clearance needed for gears, bearing bosses and locations of the brush shaft and wheel-spindle slots.

The length of the brush is determined by the

distance between the wheel plates (unit assembled) less the space on the brush shaft required for the two shaft collars and the sprocket. For leaf sweeping and ordinary lawn grooming, regular broom straws will do for the brush sections. If there's a broom factory near you, then your supply problem is solved. If not, the straws from a couple of old brooms will do. To make the individual brushes you first make a jig, Fig. 4. Then clamp the jig in a vise, lay a 3-in. length of ⅜-in. tape across the groove and thumbtack the ends. Then make uniform bundles of broomstraws by pressing them tightly into the groove as in the photo and taping them tightly together as indicated. Sew each bundle of broomstraws along the center line of the tape, using a heavy linen thread and a backstitch. The purpose of taping is to hold the bundle in shape for sewing; the sewing holds it in shape until it can be clamped in the hub.

how to make brush hub

The brush hub, or holder, is made as in Figs. 5 and 6. Notches are cut in both webs of each of the two aluminum angles, each notch ⅜ in. deep and offset 1 in. Notching can be done on a table saw as in the photo on page 1613. Place the angles over the brush shaft (it should be removed from the assembly, of course) and drill ¼-in. holes through both angles and the shaft for hex-head bolts, the holes equally spaced.

Bundles of broomstraw won't take the bend required without breaking, so you coat them lightly with No. 10 motor oil and place them in the kitchen-range oven at about 250 degrees for an hour or so. The heat drives the oil into the straws, making the bundles sufficiently flexible to take the bend. Hex head machine bolts, ¼ x 2 in., are about the right length to draw the brush assembly tight, but in the first step in assembly you'll need two longer ¼-in. bolts at the ends of the steel angles so you can draw the angles down sufficiently to permit use of one shorter bolt at the center of the assembly. Once the shorter 2-in. bolt is in place and drawn down, the two longer bolts at the ends can be removed and the 2-in. bolts substituted.

The brush is a little tricky to assemble but perhaps the best way to go about it is to attach the end of one angle loosely to the shaft with one of the longer bolts. Then support the ends of the shaft on blocks (or wooden V-blocks) and place one row of brush bundles, pulling each one under the shaft and pressing into the notches in the angle. Lay the alternate bundles on top of the shaft and the assembly will appear as in the lower right-hand photo on page 1613. Now, place the second angle, insert the bolts at the ends and draw down the nuts just enough to permit inserting a shorter bolt at the center. Draw this bolt down but not so tightly that the angles are bent. Now, insert the shorter bolts each way from the center (you'll have to drill through the broomstraws blocking the holes) and draw the bolts tight by stages until the brush bundles assume the form shown in Fig. 6. Replace the unit in the assembly.

height adjustment

Now back to Fig. 1. The aluminum angle bar you see across the front of the pulled-apart unit is fitted with uprights of the same material. The lower ends of these are bolted to the ends of the wheel plates and the upper ends are joined to a locking bar on the left side (looked at from the rear) and to an adjusting bar on the right. The end of the locking bar is simply clamped under the washer on the handle-adjustment bolt, or it can be slotted 5/16 x 2½ in. The upper end of the adjusting bar is bent at right angles to form a handle and is drilled just below the handle with spaced ¼-in. holes for a bolt and wingnut.

This arrangement provides for height adjustment of the brush.

The handle bars, handle-bar supports and the trailing members which carry the dolly wheels are cut from hardwood such as oak. The handlebars are cut 46 to 48 in. long, ends are rounded and the corners are softened by sanding. The push bar is a 1-in. dowel, and a ¼-in. steel tie rod, threaded at both ends, joins the supports to the handle bars. A crossrail, or spreader, joins the trailing members. The dolly wheels are turned from hardwood. Machine bolts, with washers to protect the wooden hubs, serve as spindles. As detailed the push bar is about average height. It will not raise or lower. If you wish it to raise or lower then slot the upper ends of the handlebar supports so that the push bar can be adjusted to any desired height.

And that's it, except that the grass catcher pictured in use with the unit on page 1610 is inadequate for leaf sweeping. You'll need to make a much larger fabric hopper for leaf gathering. Attach the leading edge to the forward ends of the trailing bars with wire hooks and screw eyes.

See also: edger, lawn; lawns; leaf blower; leaf burner; mowers; mulchmaker.

leaf blower

Windrow those leaves —it beats raking

BY MANLY BANISTER

Your yard and patio will stay clean as a whistle this fall when you make yourself a leaf blower that whips up an 80-mph wind. You buy the parts that are hard to build

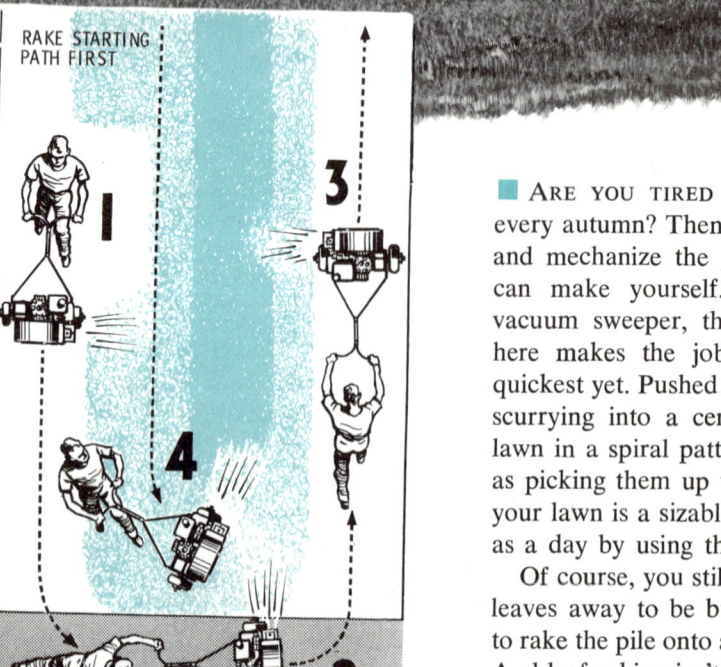

RAKE STARTING PATH FIRST

■ ARE YOU TIRED of being a slave to a rake every autumn? Then leave the rake in the garage and mechanize the job with a leaf blower you can make yourself. Next to having a giant vacuum sweeper, the tornado-on-wheels shown here makes the job of raking your lawn the quickest yet. Pushed like a mower, it sends leaves scurrying into a central pile as you circle the lawn in a spiral pattern. It is three times as fast as picking them up with a lawn sweeper, and if your lawn is a sizable one you can save as much as a day by using the blower instead of a rake.

Of course, you still have the job of lugging the leaves away to be burned, but the time it takes to rake the pile onto a tarp is a matter of minutes. And leaf-raking isn't the only job the blower will do. The 80-mph airstream kicked up by the engine will scoot sticks and twigs right along with

1616

Radial-arm saw simplifies accurate cutting of steel angle. Stop block (left) assures an equal-length pair. Miter is cut in one pass by feeding aluminum-oxide blade slowly to prevent undue heating

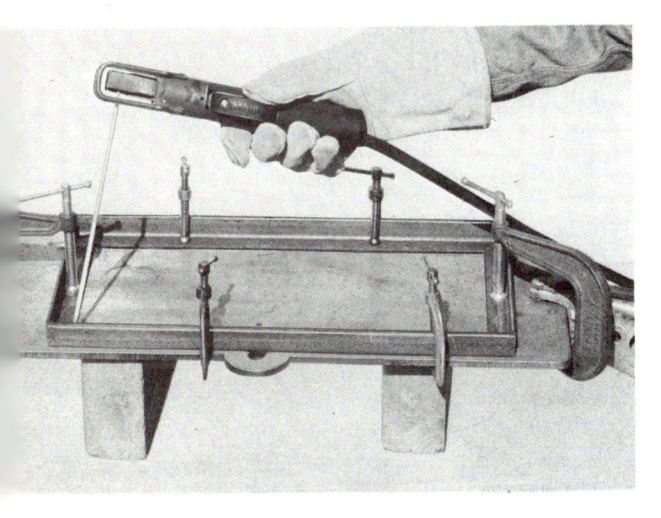

the leaves, and the blower is great, too, for gathering grass clippings after mowing—in case you want to use them for compost. Also, a broom is no match for it in sweeping a drive or patio.

The machine consists of three main parts—the blower and housing assembly, a gasoline engine, and a carriage with a push handle. I bought my fan from a factory specializing in ventilating equipment; you can order an identical unit, complete with housing, through the W. J. Darm Co., 1313 S.E. 12th Ave., Portland, Ore., 97214. This fan is designed to spin clockwise when viewed from the hub-side, so it'll rotate counter-clockwise when seen from the power-takeoff side of the engine, and that's the direction the engine-shaft turns. I find my 3-hp Briggs & Stratton just right for the job. Less horsepower might not rev the fan up enough, and too much could damage the blower blades. I bought the engine from a standard mail-order catalog for $44.

Because of its short shaft, the engine must be set flush with the leading edge of the carriage, and smack against the blower housing. You must make an adapter to mate the ¾-in. shaft to the 1-in. bore of the fan hub, as shown in the detail. In assembling, be sure that one of the hub set-screws bears directly on the key in the engine

Setup for welding outside frame has pieces squared and clamped to steel plate (if no plate is available, use plywood and ground to angle). Weld inside only, leave clamped till welds cool to prevent buckle

Custom-made grille for air intake is simple matter of silver-soldering wire ring to existing baking rack, trimmed to rough circle. Use blower wheel as form for bending ring. Brick keeps heated wires from lifting. When cool, cut wires flush with ring, grind ends smooth, attach to housing with three clips

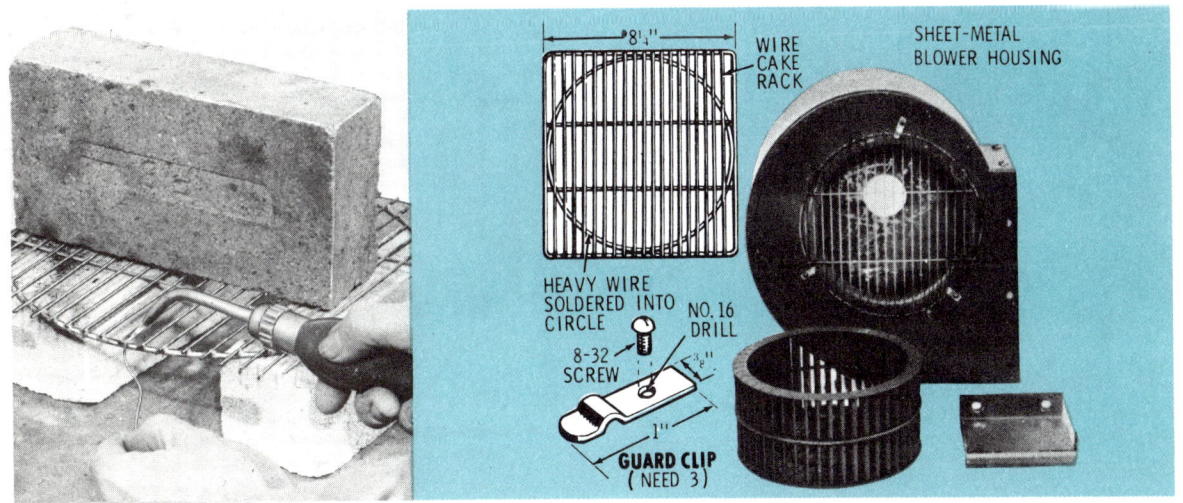

leaf blower

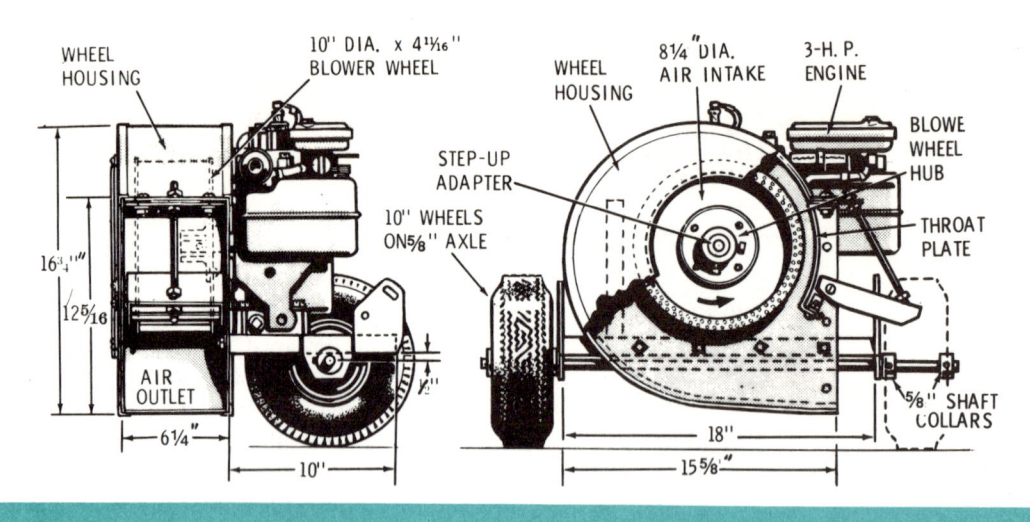

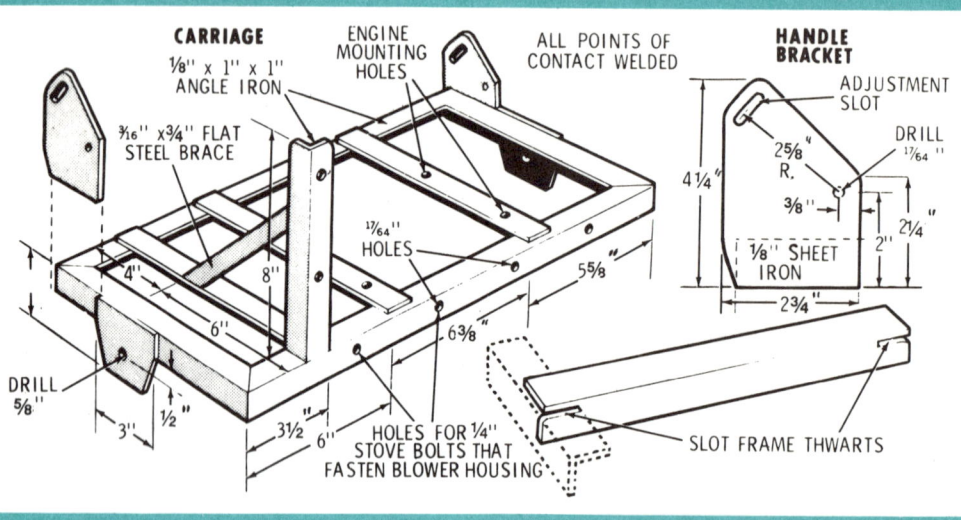

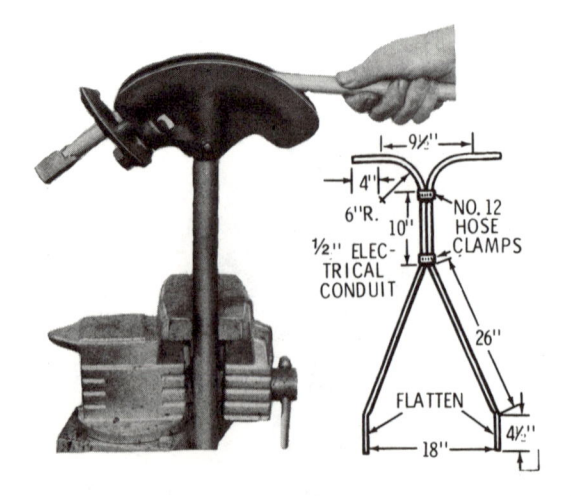

WHEEL HOUSING — 10" DIA. x 4 11/16" BLOWER WHEEL — WHEEL HOUSING — 8¼" DIA. AIR INTAKE — 3-H.P. ENGINE — BLOWER WHEEL HUB — STEP-UP ADAPTER — THROAT PLATE — 10" WHEELS ON 5/8" AXLE — 16¾" — 12 5/16" — AIR OUTLET — 6¼" — 10" — 18" — 15 5/8" — ½" — 5/8" SHAFT COLLARS

CARRIAGE — ENGINE MOUNTING HOLES — ALL POINTS OF CONTACT WELDED — **HANDLE BRACKET** — 1/8" x 1" x 1" ANGLE IRON — ADJUSTMENT SLOT — 3/16" x ¾" FLAT STEEL BRACE — 2 5/8" R. — DRILL 17/64" — 17/64" HOLES — 3/8" — 4¼" — 2¼" — 4" — 8" — 55 5/8" — 1/8" SHEET IRON — 2" — 6" — 6 3/8" — 2¾" — DRILL 5/8" — 3" — ½" — 3½" — 6" — HOLES FOR ¼" STOVE BOLTS THAT FASTEN BLOWER HOUSING — SLOT FRAME THWARTS

9½" — 4" — 6" R. — 10" — NO. 12 HOSE CLAMPS — ½" ELECTRICAL CONDUIT — 26" — FLATTEN — 18" — 4½"

Slot adapter with two passes on metal-cutting bandsaw; hold the blank vertical in drill-press vise. Adapter mates ¾-in. engine shaft and 1-in. fan hub

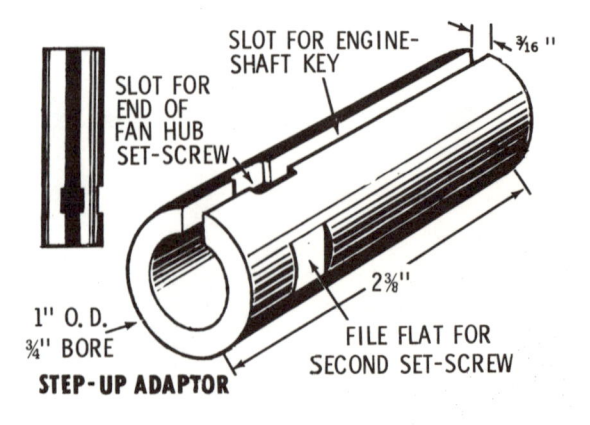

SLOT FOR ENGINE-SHAFT KEY — 3/16" — SLOT FOR END OF FAN HUB SET-SCREW — 1" O.D. ¾" BORE — 2 3/8" — FILE FLAT FOR SECOND SET-SCREW — **STEP-UP ADAPTOR**

Deflector is hung from retainer plate cut from sheet metal and driven between housing and throat plate. Rod has two nuts clamped against slot at each end

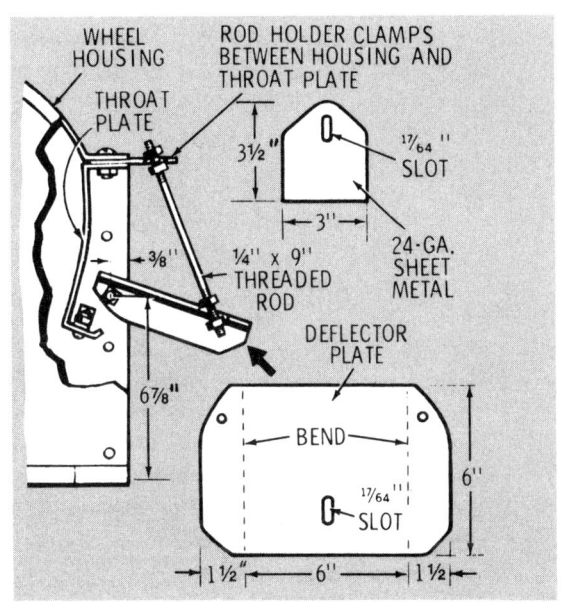

Arrangement of nuts on threaded adjusting rod permits a wide range of airstream control. When adjustment is best for job at hand, nuts are turned up tight

shaft, and not on the adapter. You'll have to drill the slot wider to pass this setscrew; you can locate this accurately by trying the fan on the shaft with the setscrew removed so you can mark through its hole. The fan is correctly adjusted on the shaft when the adapter is slipped on as far as it will go and the outboard end of the fan hub is flush with the end of the adapter.

I made the push handle from a 10-ft. length of ½-in. conduit. After cutting it into two 5-ft. pieces, I hammered a wooden plug into one end of each length, filled both with dry sand, then plugged the open ends. At a point 4 in. from one end I bent each length at right angles with the aid of a conduit bender. Next, using a carpenter's square and chalk, I drew on the shop floor the shape of the lower part of the handle. Then, carefully lining up the second bend with the first, I bent it as far as I thought necessary and compared the bend with the pattern drawn on the floor. Any overbending is easy to correct by simply reversing the work in the bender. Bend the second length to match.

I sawed off both tubes at a point 31 in. from the second bend, then flattened the final 4½ in., first by a series of squeezes in the vise, followed by hammering on a steel plate. The flattened ends were finally bent around into position by clamping them in the vise and applying leverage to the remainder of the now-empty conduit.

I joined the two tubes with stainless-steel hose clamps (the kind that work with a wormgear and screwdriver) by placing them flat on the floor. They were then marked and drilled for ¼-in. stud bolts for attaching to the carriage bosses.

A safety grille for the fan blade is a must. The fan sucks air with terrific force and the grille keeps out foreign objects which might damage the fan, as well as hands, small dogs, etc.

The airstream deflector directs the gale parallel to the ground with little force being felt at ground level within several feet of the outlet. Everything beyond that point, however, can be felt in the next county. The main purpose of the deflector is to keep the force of the air within bounds. When directed downward, the airstream strikes the ground full force, close to the outlet and becomes fan shape like a bamboo rake. The main force of the airstream is thus kept within a distance of about 6 ft. so that it will blow the leaves into a pile but without blowing the pile itself into the neighbor's yard.

I used 10-in. pneumatic wheels for easy wheeling over rough ground and curbs. If you use smaller wheels, remember to change the height of the axle hanger so that the lower edge of the blower housing rides about 2 in. above the ground when the carriage is level.

See also: edger, lawn; lawns; lawn sweeper; leaf burner; mowers; mulch-maker.

leaf burner

Leaf burner rolls to the job

BY MANLY BANISTER

Where to burn the leaves?
Let this incinerator-on-wheels
help solve the problem next autumn.
And when it's not being used
for yard work it'll come in handy
—the year 'round—as a trash burner.
Its 30-gal. steel drum gives you
a capacity of almost 3 bushels

■ HANDY AS IT IS in autumn, this mobile leaf burner won't stand idle the rest of the year. It makes a fine roll-away trash burner that dumps ashes from the bottom with a flip of a lever.

leaks, auto radiator: see cooling system, auto
leaks, basement wall: see basements
leaks, eaves: see gutters
lean-to shelter: see shelters
lean-to storage: see storage buildings

The 30-gal. steel drum is 31 in. high and has an inside diameter of 18 in., giving the burner a capacity of almost three bushels above the 7-in.-deep ash pit. Wheels for the pilot model were salvaged from an old hand lawnmower and have the advantage of being an exact fit for the $15/16$-in. dia. of ¾-in. thin-wall conduit used for the axle. If you decide to use regular 10-in. utility wheels with ½-in. bearings, substitute ½-in. steel rod.

All joints in the carriage and ash-dumping

1620

Ash-dumping doors fit into a 10-in.-wide opening sawed out of the bottom of the 30-gal. drum. Orient the cutout so drum seam will be at rear of burner

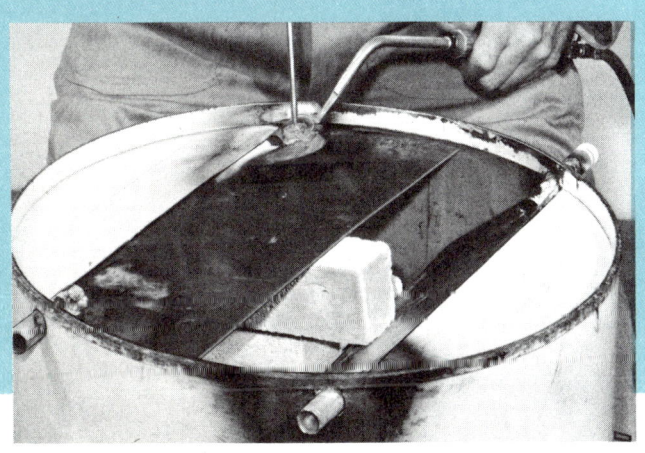

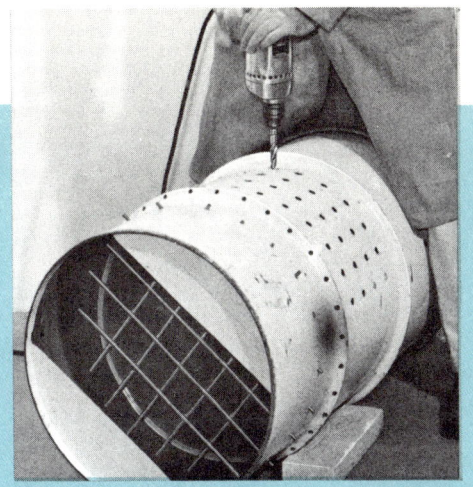

Holes in side of drum should be drilled with ½-in. bit in ⅜-in. slow-speed drill. To locate them, tape paper pattern over the drum

Levers controlling ash-dumping mechanism are brazed to door pivots and connected by linking bar. Note cotter pins in linking-bar pivots

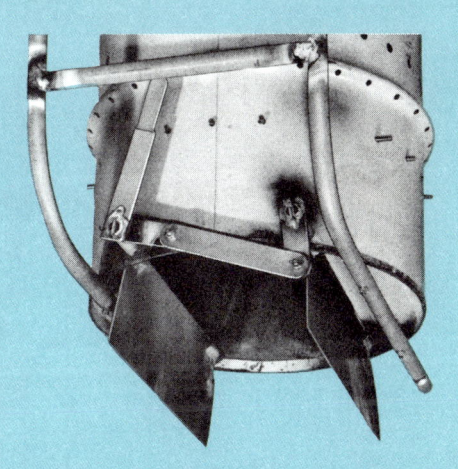

When brazing the ash doors to their ½-in. conduit pivots, support them horizontally on insulation bricks piled on the grate. These bricks won't conduct the heat

mechanism should be brazed with a bronze brazing rod (Oxweld 25M, or similar). In building the pilot model, a Prest-O-Lite air-acetylene torch with a #4 burning tip was used. If welding equipment is available, the joints may be welded.

The first step is to cut a 10-in-wide opening in the bottom of the drum for the ash-dumping doors. (Save the cut-out piece to use as a pattern for the doors.) Next, install the grate. This is composed of 10 lengths of ¼-in. steel welding rod—five installed crosswise to the opening and five parallel to it. While you should braze or weld the rods at each crossing to make a solid unit, it isn't necessary to braze the grate to the drum. Now, with the drum upside down, drill ⁵⁄₁₆-in. holes every 2 in. around the under surface of the rolling flange. Then lay out and drill the pattern of ½-in. holes on each side of the drum.

Make the ash doors from 14-ga. ungalvanized sheet metal, using the cutout from the drum

1621

leaf burner

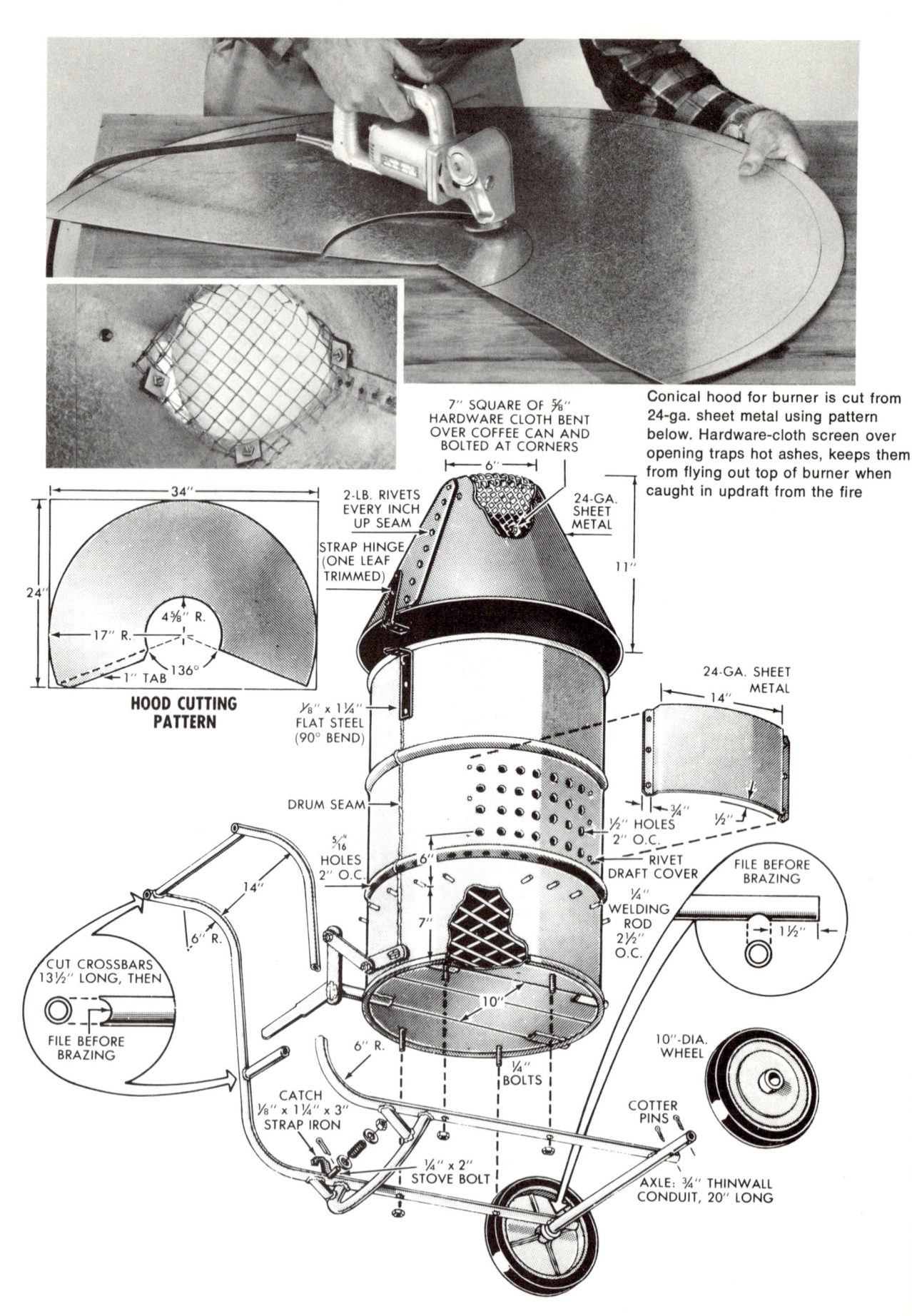

Conical hood for burner is cut from 24-ga. sheet metal using pattern below. Hardware-cloth screen over opening traps hot ashes, keeps them from flying out top of burner when caught in updraft from the fire

HOOD CUTTING PATTERN
- 34"
- 24"
- 17" R.
- 4 5/8" R.
- 136°
- 1" TAB

7" SQUARE OF 5/8" HARDWARE CLOTH BENT OVER COFFEE CAN AND BOLTED AT CORNERS — 6"

2-LB. RIVETS EVERY INCH UP SEAM

24-GA. SHEET METAL

STRAP HINGE (ONE LEAF TRIMMED)

11"

1/8" x 1 1/4" FLAT STEEL (90° BEND)

DRUM SEAM

5/16" HOLES 2" O.C.

24-GA. SHEET METAL — 14"

1/2" HOLES 2" O.C. — 3/4" — 1/2"

RIVET DRAFT COVER

FILE BEFORE BRAZING — 1 1/2"

1/4" WELDING ROD 2 1/2" O.C.

6"

7"

10"

CUT CROSSBARS 13 1/2" LONG, THEN FILE BEFORE BRAZING

14"

6" R.

6" R.

CATCH 1/8" x 1 1/4" x 3" STRAP IRON

1/4" x 2" STOVE BOLT

1/4" BOLTS

10"-DIA. WHEEL

COTTER PINS

AXLE: 3/4" THINWALL CONDUIT, 20" LONG

The burner may be used anywhere on your lawn without damaging the grass. When the 7-in. ash dump in the bottom is full, you merely wheel the cart to the trash heap and dump it with the flip of a lever

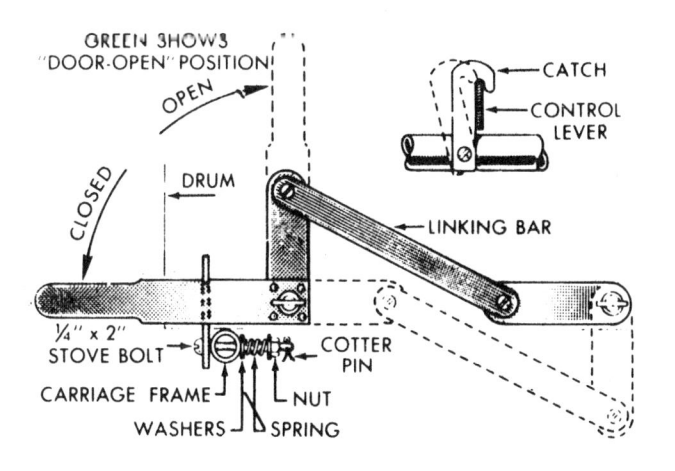

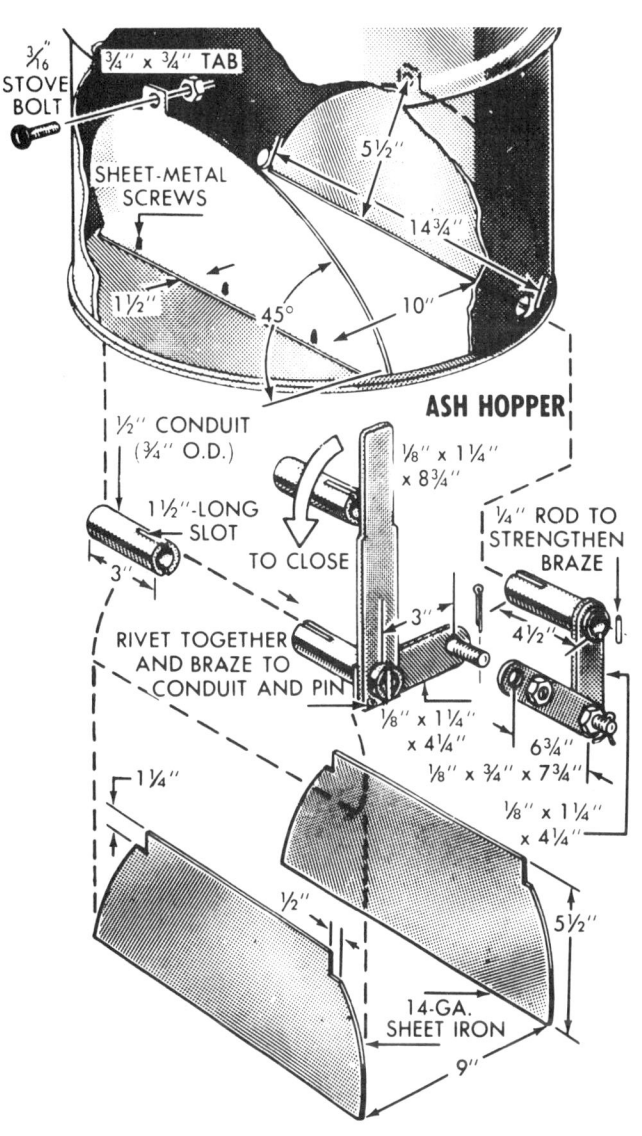

bottom as a pattern. The doors should swing 90 deg. in the opening provided. First, determine the amount to be ground from the shoulders for clearance by trial. Locate the pivot holes in the base of the drum. Drill these out to ½-in. dia., then file them with a round file to ¾-in. dia. to fit the pivots of ½-in. thin-wall conduit. The door pivots are of two different lengths. Slit the two shorter ones with a hacksaw, braze them to their respective doors and install the doors in the drum to check for ease of opening and closing. If necessary, correct the fit by grinding or filing, then prop the doors in a horizontal position, slit the longer pivots and install in the drum, brazing them to the doors.

All strap-iron requirements of the construction can be met with one 36-in. length of ⅛-in. x 1½-in. strap. Make the ash-dumping mechanism as shown on this page. Braze or weld the levers to the door pivots with the drum

1623

leaf burner

on its side and the doors open. You'll find it easier to position and hold the levers in place if you mount the linking bar and run the nuts up tight. Braze a short length of ¼-in. steel welding rod into each joint to strengthen it. Also, braze the fulcrum pins in the levers before the unit is mounted, and drill these for cotter pins to prevent losing nuts.

To make the carriage, you'll use most of two 10-ft. lengths of ¾-in. thin-wall conduit. Bend the side members of the frame before cutting to length so as to have plenty of leverage. A standard ¾-in. conduit bender, which has a 6-in. radius, is the best tool for making these bends. (If you don't own a bender, you can rent one from your local hardware store.) Cut the first side frame 20½ in. from the second bend, then bend the other frame and cut it to length. Check these frames for congruency.

mount bent frames

Mount the bent frames on the drum bottom 14 in. apart, center-to-center, using ¼-in. machine bolts with lock washers under both head and nut. Install these bolts as close to the side of the drum as practical. Cut the crossbars 13½ in. long to allow ¼ in. on each end for fitting. To install the handle, turn the drum upside down and squeeze the side members of the frame to the handle with a bar clamp. Then braze the handle in place. Install, clamp and braze the crossbar in the same manner.

Next, mark and file the side members of the carriage, and braze the axle in place. The wheels can be positioned and retained on the axle with shaft collars. If you are using ¾-in. conduit for an axle, make shaft collars by cutting slices from standard ¾-in. pipe coupling. Face them with a file and fit with setscrews. With wheels mounted, turn the unit right side up and block up the back of the drum until it is level. Bend the rear support from ¾-in. thin wall, starting the second bend where the first leaves off. Fitting the support and Y-braces is a matter of trial-and-error. When the parts fit correctly, braze them together.

Now turn the unit upside down again and install the ash-hopper inserts. These are 24-ga., sheet-metal plates mounted at a 45-deg. angle to facilitate dumping ashes. Their outline is an elongated arc like that of the end of an oval. Make a cardboard pattern first and try it for size. When you arrive at an outline that fits, transfer it to sheet metal and cut it out, remembering to leave a ¾-in. x ¾-in. tab at the top for bolting to the sidewall of the drum. Leave a 1½-in. wide tab across the bottom and bend it over at a 45-deg. angle. Fasten these hopper inserts with 3/16-in. stove bolts through the side of the drum and three sheet-metal screws through the drum bottom.

Next, lay out a pattern for the conical hood on a piece of 24-ga. sheet metal and cut it out. If a sheet-metal-forming machine is not available, you can form the cone easily by hand. Just clamp the edge opposite the riveting tab to the edge of a table, roll the tab side over until the tab overlaps the opposite edge, and clamp the two ends together with a pair of clamping pliers. Adjust the small end of the cone to the correct overlap and clamp it. Rivet the overlap every inch, drilling each hole and riveting it before going to the next. You can either use 2-lb. tinned rivets and a rivet set, or small roundhead machine screws, tightening the nuts, then peening over the ends.

attach hood

Attach the hood to the drum with a strap hinge, one leaf of which has been cut off and mounted on a piece of bent strap iron which is bolted to the drum. Mount a barn-door pull on the hood opposite the hinge. To keep hot ashes from flying out of the top, install a screen of 5/8-in. mesh hardware cloth in the hood. Form this screen over a coffee can so that it fits inside the top of the hood, cutting the wires where they buckle. Install the screen with 3/16-in. stove bolts, using 1-in. squares of sheet metal for washers inside. In installing the draft cover, lay out the sheet metal and bend the end tabs first. Clamp the tab between a board and the edge of a table and bend it by hand. Hammer the bend with a mallet to sharpen it, then move the tab out to the second mark and bend it in the opposite direction to a 45-deg. angle.

To make the draft cover fit, give it a radius bend before installing. Then attach it to the drum with 3/16-in. stove bolts. The notched catch which holds the ash-dump lever in place is mounted on the outside of the side frame. Drill a 5/16-in. hole through the conduit and strap-iron catch for a ¼-in. x 2-in. stove bolt, then mount the catch, using a compression spring between two washers to hold the catch tight to the frame while allowing it to be turned back when necessary. Install a cotter pin in the end of the bolt to keep the nut tight.

See also: edger, lawn; lawns; lawn sweeper; leaf blower; mowers; mulchmaker.

Take this folding lectern along

BY P. L. STOTLER

■ FOR PERSONS THAT SPEAK, it never seems to fail: there's no lectern in the restaurant or hall in which the engagement is scheduled. If this is your problem, the easy solution is your own lectern, and you can make it quickly yourself.

The drawings on this page show how to cut and assemble the component parts. The sides are ½-in., the legs ¾-in. pine; the bearing blocks are ¾-in. maple. The top panel sets in ½-in. rabbets; it is a 16½ x 19½-in. piece of ¼-in. hardboard. The front leg unit folds over the rear one, and one friction clamp holds both.

The slight incline of the top will allow you to glance repeatedly at your notes without losing eye contact with the audience. The lectern can be painted or stained. Apply two finish coats.

See also: drafting equipment

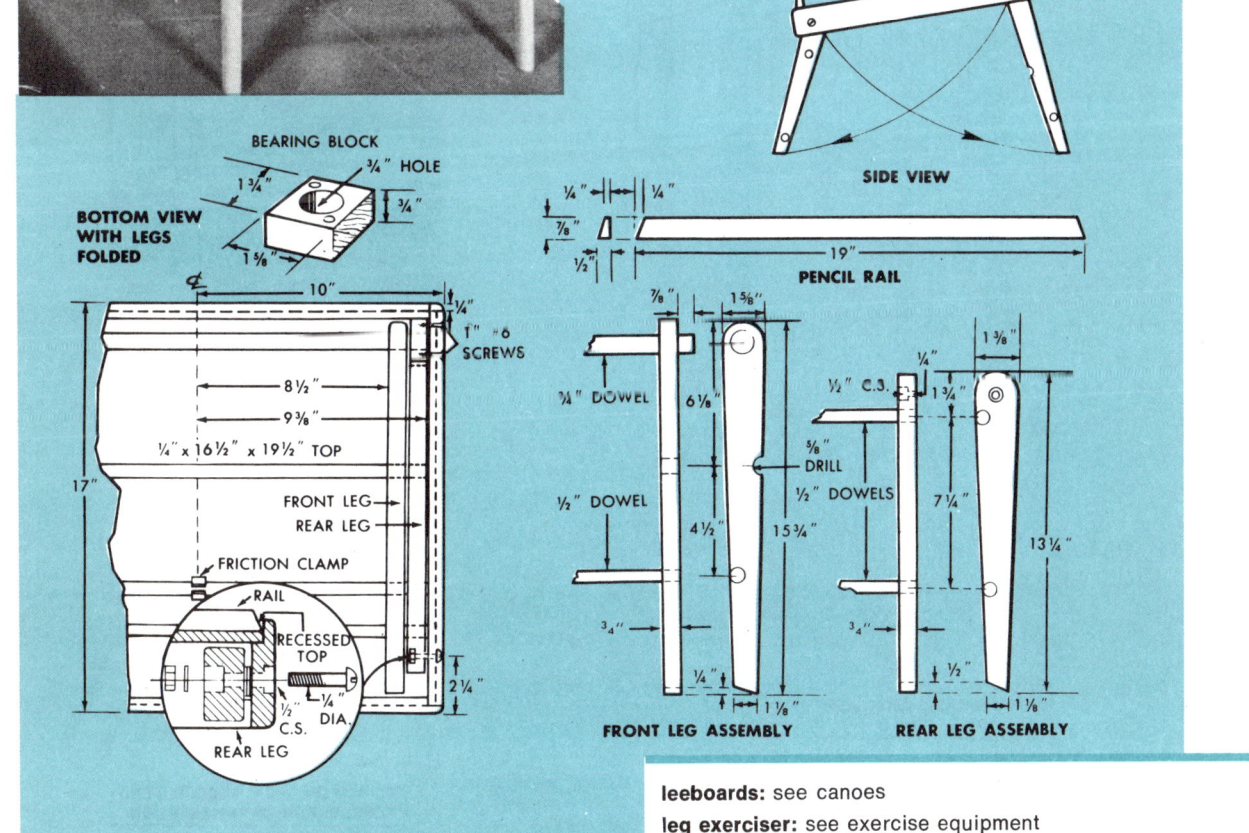

---

leeboards: see canoes

leg exerciser: see exercise equipment

legs, furniture

A dozen ways to attach legs

BY W. CLYDE LAMMEY

Whether you're building new furniture or restoring the old, sturdy legs are essential

YOUR CHOICE of methods for attaching legs depends on the piece of furniture and its style. If you're building a simple modern chest or slab table, you can get by with purchased legs that screw into their own mounting plates. But if you're reproducing or refurbishing a period piece, you'll most likely have to go to hand joinery.

The dozen methods sketched on these pages cover most means of attaching legs to rails and aprons or flat undersides. Say you want to build a workbench that won't jiggle or "walk" when you plane stock or do some hammering. For this, use the butt joint with a drawbolt to join the legs to the rails of the frame. You'll get a job that will take the roughest usage—even without bracing or gluing.

In making a cabinet or table with turned legs, use rails-to-legs joints with mitered, wedged or draw-pinned tenons.

See also: bedroom furniture; bolts; children's furniture; dovetailing; hardware; screws; tables.

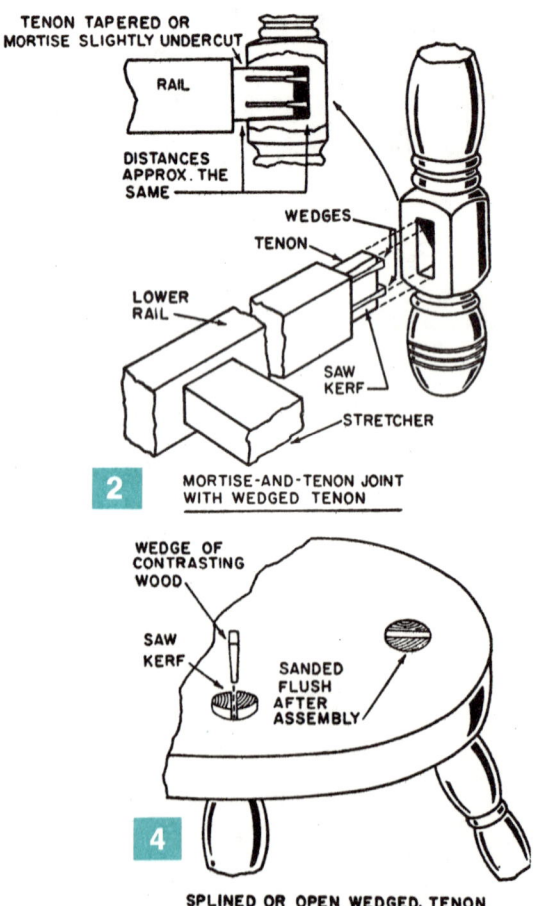

1 MORTISE-AND-TENON JOINT WITH MITERED TENONS

2 MORTISE-AND-TENON JOINT WITH WEDGED TENON

3 MORTISE-AND-TENON JOINT DRAW-PINNED

4 SPLINED OR OPEN WEDGED, TENON EXPOSED FOR ORNAMENTATION

letters: see alphabets; signs

1626

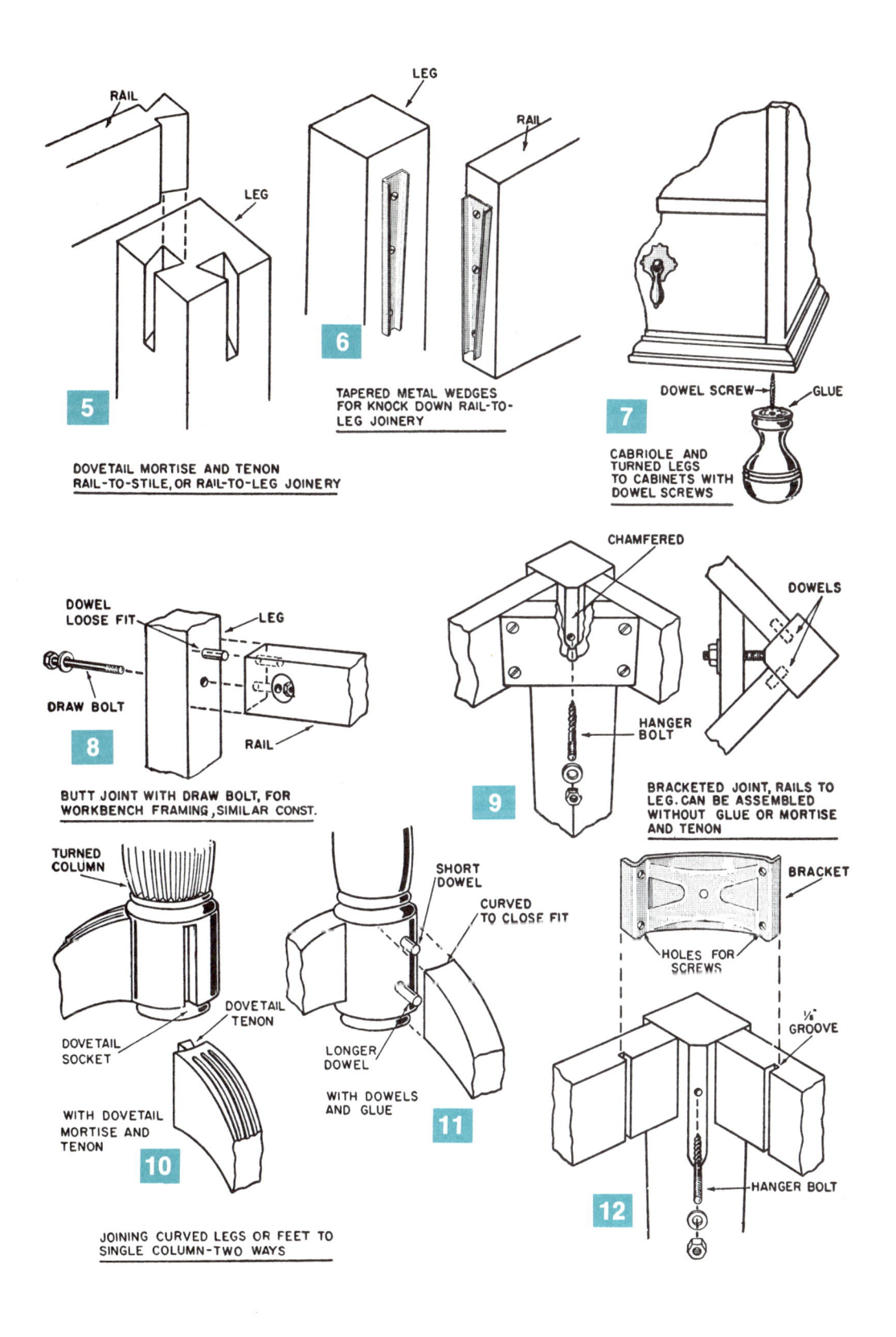

5 DOVETAIL MORTISE AND TENON RAIL-TO-STILE, OR RAIL-TO-LEG JOINERY

6 TAPERED METAL WEDGES FOR KNOCK DOWN RAIL-TO-LEG JOINERY

7 CABRIOLE AND TURNED LEGS TO CABINETS WITH DOWEL SCREWS

8 BUTT JOINT WITH DRAW BOLT, FOR WORKBENCH FRAMING, SIMILAR CONST.

9 BRACKETED JOINT, RAILS TO LEG. CAN BE ASSEMBLED WITHOUT GLUE OR MORTISE AND TENON

10 WITH DOVETAIL MORTISE AND TENON

11 WITH DOWELS AND GLUE

JOINING CURVED LEGS OR FEET TO SINGLE COLUMN—TWO WAYS

12

1627

lifesaving

What can you do when someone collapses with a heart stoppage or asthma attack? You only have about four minutes after his heart stops before he'll be dead or injured beyond repair. Here is an approved way to help him

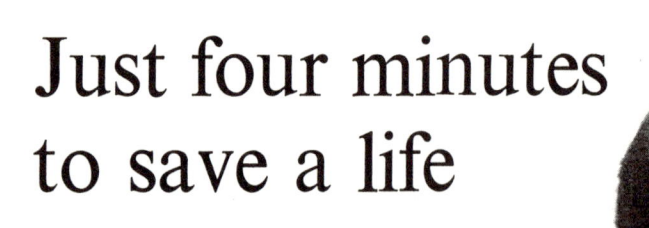

Just four minutes to save a life

BY PAUL W. KEARNEY

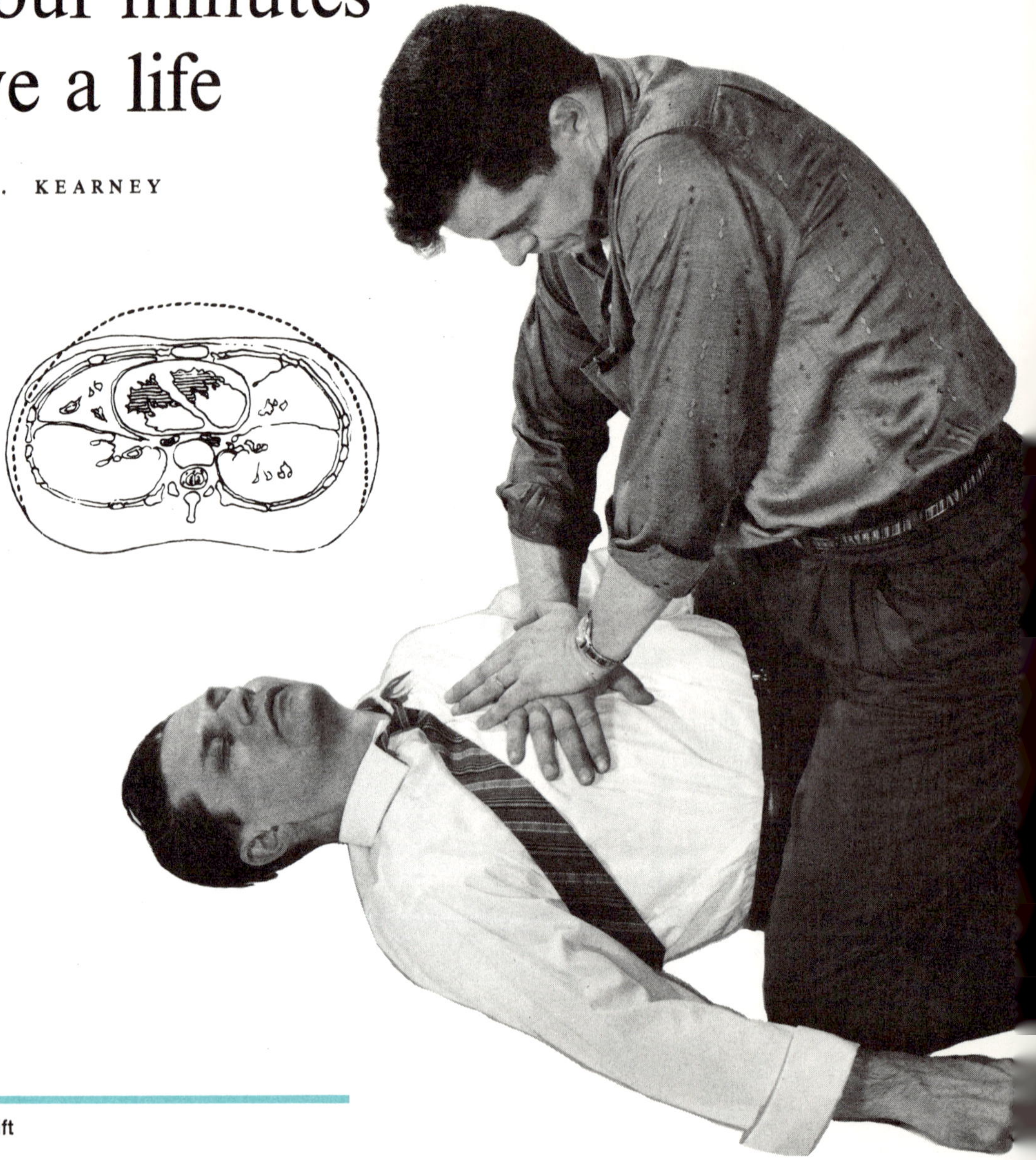

The technique for closed-chest heart massage. The drawing shows how outside pressure forces the heart to pump

lift, stairway: see elevator lift
lift, stern: see sterns, boat
lifters, valve: see valve lifters, auto
light control: see darkroom light control
light detector: see electronics
light dimmer: see electric power control

■ ON THE EVENING of November 20, 1961, Capt. William E. Moberley, a USAF officer, read an article in a service publication on "external cardiac massage." At 3:15 the next morning, he used his brand-new knowledge to save the life of his next-door neighbor.

Awakened by the screams of his neighbor's wife, the Captain rushed over to be told hysterically that the husband was dead. Prostrate on the bathroom floor, with no heartbeat, no respiration, and the gray-blue pallor of cyanosis already tinging his cheeks, he certainly looked gone.

The Captain, a Supply Officer at Hickam Air Force Base, Honolulu, recalled what he had read the night before. He instructed the distraught wife to phone for an ambulance; then he rolled the victim on his back on the floor and went to work. He placed his hands on the victim's breastbone. Then, using a firm, quick thrust, he pushed the unconscious man's chest down about an inch, and quickly released it. In a rapid cadence, the movement was repeated.

Moments dragged by and nothing happened. But through Moberley's mind raced the article's admonition: "Don't quit until rigor mortis sets in." So he kept going. Then, almost imperceptibly, the still heart seemed to stir. The faint beat persisted. So the rescuer kept on—*for 45 minutes* before an ambulance finally arrived to transport the patient to Leeward Hospital. With pulse and respiration re-established by the first-aid work, medical treatment kept him going even though he didn't regain consciousness for another 12 hours. The lucky man was discharged a week later and returned to his job. According to Dr. Howard Lilijestrand, hospital director, he owes his life to the intelligent action and physical stamina of a neighbor.

That is "closed chest heart massage" in action, newest thing in resuscitation and the first effective weapon that any *layman* can use in cases of heart standstill.

simple to apply

The method was developed at Johns Hopkins Hospital through years of research and experiment, and was reported in the *Journal of the American Medical Association* in July, 1960, on the strength of 44 successes in 56 cases of heart arrest. This report observes: "The method of closed chest cardiac massage . . . is simple to apply; it is one that needs no complex equipment. Only the human hand is required. . . . Its real value lies in the fact that it can be used wherever the emergency arises . . . in or out of a hospital."

Here are the simple basic steps:

1. Lay the patient on his back on a firm support, such as a floor or a table. A bed is too soft and should not be used.

2. *It is imperative to tilt the victim's head well back so his chin is pointed toward the ceiling.* This keeps the windpipe free from obstruction by the tongue, which may result if the head sags forward. Lolling tongues can cause asphyxiation.

3. Straddle the victim and place your right hand on his breastbone, right at the junction point of the two lowest ribs. Then place your left hand directly on top of the right.

4. Press downward firmly to compress the victim's chest about an inch.

5. Release pressure sharply after each thrust, and spread the fingers up off the chest to avoid rib injury.

6. Thrust and release should be repeated continuously at a cadence of about 60 to 80 thrusts per minute. This simulates the normal heartbeat closely enough to "crank the stalled engine" in many cases that may appear hopeless. Don't stop until: (a) help arrives, (b) the victim resumes breathing regularly, or (c) you are sure the subject is past saving.

The method described applies to adults. For children, one hand is enough, and half to three quarters of an inch compression is sufficient.

What makes this system practical is the fact that the human heart is not entirely on the left side as popularly supposed. The greater part of it lies directly beneath the sternum, or breastbone. Hence, your simple hand pressure compresses the heart between sternum and backbone, forcing blood out of it and into the arteries. Releasing pressure allows the heart to expand and pull in more blood from the large veins.

7. Check occasionally to see if the victim's heart is actually working again under its own steam. You do this by taking his pulse. The best place for a layman to check a pulse is *not* in the wrist, but in the throat where the big carotid artery passes on either side of the windpipe near the collarbone.

8. Get the victim to a hospital as soon as possible, even if pulse and breathing have been restored. The patient is sorely in need of professional aid. In cardiac arrest cases, attempts to re-start the heart may result in fibrillation (a sort of helter-skelter heart flutter) which no layman can detect. Unless checked, it is fatal,

lifesaving

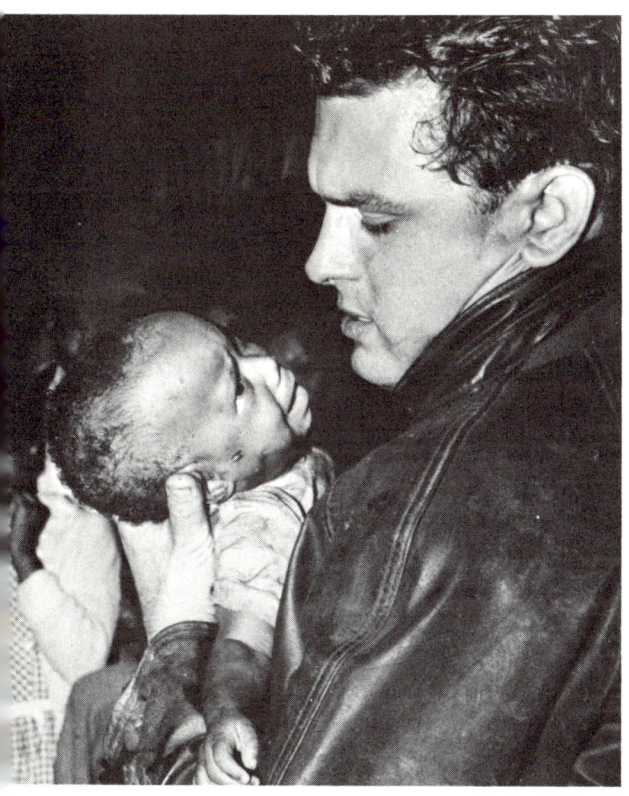

Mouth-to-mouth insufflation can be applied almost anywhere; here a fireman saves a life on the spot

anyone can learn rescue breathing; remember these three steps

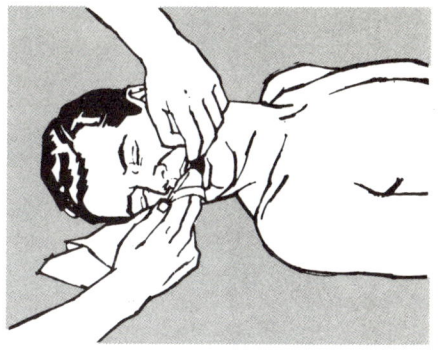

1 Clear the victim's throat with two fingers, using a cloth if handy. If he's choking, pick him up by the waist, head down in a jackknife position, and strike a sharp blow between his shoulder blades to dislodge the object choking him

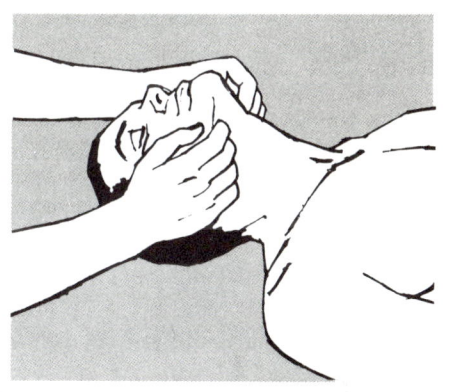

2 With the victim on his back, lift his chin until his jaw points straight up to keep him from choking or gagging on his tongue. This may get breathing started, but if the tongue is blue or gray, begin mouth-to-mouth rescue breathing

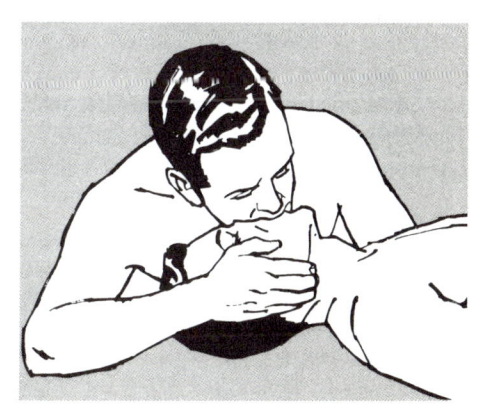

3 Cover the victim's lips with your own to make an airtight seal; close his nose with one hand. Don't just breathe, but blow hard enough to make his chest expand (more gently for children) 12 to 20 times per minute, letting him exhale normally

and the only place to check it is in a well-equipped hospital emergency room. But external massage may well keep the victim alive until he gets there.

So much for procedure. Despite the simplicity of the method and its impressive record of success, medical men offer a number of stern warnings about using it.

First, if the external heart massage is not begun within about four minutes after the pulse has stopped, the chances are high that irreparable brain damage will be done by lack of oxygen.

Second, do not look for the impossible. Not infrequently, even hospital patients revived by it may die a day or so later from the same thing that caused the original heart stoppage.

The new technique is of proven value not only for cardiac cases or asthma attacks, but in drowning, electrical shock or lightning stroke, smoke or gas asphyxiation, overdose of drugs, or any other mishap which causes the heart to stop. A real bonus provided by the technique is that the chest pressure will force some ventilation of the lungs. This is a vital factor since, in cardiac arrest, breathing also stops and some

lifesaving

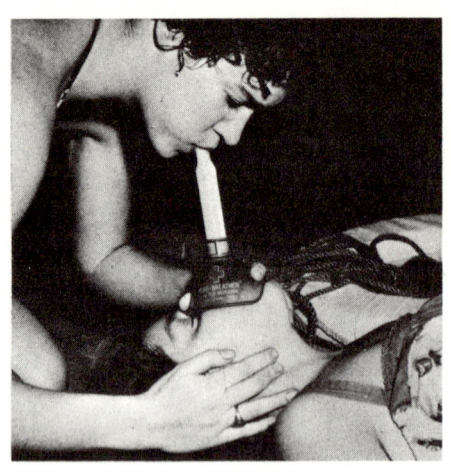

More efficient and requiring less personal contact, resuscitation tubes simplify rescue

save a life, continued

form of artificial respiration must be applied.

All of which brings up another first-aid technique for the accident victim with a pulse but no respiration. Such a victim also is in dire need of air within the aforementioned four minutes. And the easiest, quickest, most efficient method of providing that air is by "rescue breathing"—blowing it out of your lungs into his.

After lying dormant for generations, the technique, actually the oldest effective resuscitation method known to man, was revived and perfected in 1958 by Dr. Peter Safar, chief anesthesiologist for the Baltimore City Hospitals. The National Academy of Sciences has declared it to be the most practical method of artificial respiration for first aid in the field, and it has been adopted by the American Red Cross and countless other rescue agencies.

In the surge of publicity following these acknowledgments, practically everybody has read something about "mouth-to-mouth insufflation." Hundreds of rescues have been achieved with it by laymen who had no more practice than the captain at Hickman Field with heart massage.

Although expired air from the lungs contains only about 16 percent oxygen—as against some 21 percent for inhaled air—even a briefly trained novice using "rescue breathing" can move 10 to 12 times as much air into a victim's lungs as can a trained first aider using the old pressure methods. And this air is at exactly the proper temperature and moisture content for instant use.

The major objective is to get the *maximum* volume of air *directly* into the lungs without any waste, and this involves several important points.

1. The victim's mouth and throat must be cleared of any foreign obstruction such as water, blood, or regurgitated matter, using the first two fingers of your hand. In the common family emergency of a child (or an adult) choking on some solid object, don't waste time *patting* him on the back! Pick up a child with your arm around his abdomen; jack-knife him head down; and hit him a lusty wallop between the shoulder blades to dislodge the object. The adult victim should be folded double, head down. Then hit him a sharp blow on the back.

2. Once the victim's airway is cleared, it is again vital that the chin be kept straight up to keep him from "swallowing his tongue." This cannot be overemphasized.

3. If the victim starts breathing naturally after the obstruction is removed, this "chin up" position may be all that need be done. But, if his tongue is blue or gray, rather than pink, start rescue breathing immediately, *even if he is breathing on his own.*

4. Do not merely *breathe* into an adult victim's mouth. *Blow*—hard enough to make his chest expand.

5. Do not hold the victim's mouth wide open: you must take his lips *inside* of yours with an airtight seal. You should also close the victim's nose with one hand. With a baby, you take both its nose and mouth inside your lips.

6. Blow gently for children; for babies, use only *puffs* of air from your cheeks, not from your lungs.

one final warning

Take extra care with a bloody, drooling or regurgitating accident victim. Mouth-to-mouth breathing would blow foreign material into his airways and kill him either immediately by asphyxiation or later by "aspiration pneumonia." For drowning victims you should start out with the old prone-pressure method until you are sure there is not going to be any regurgitation of liquid that could get down into the patient's airways. In the prone position such liquid can run out of the mouth. Once this danger is past, the victim can be turned into the supine position for mouth-to-mouth insufflation.

If close personal contact is repellent, use a Resuscitube, a tube one end of which fits over the victim's mouth while you breath into the other end.

See also: fire ladders; ladders; mufflers, auto; skin diving; swimming pools; water skiing.

clever ideas

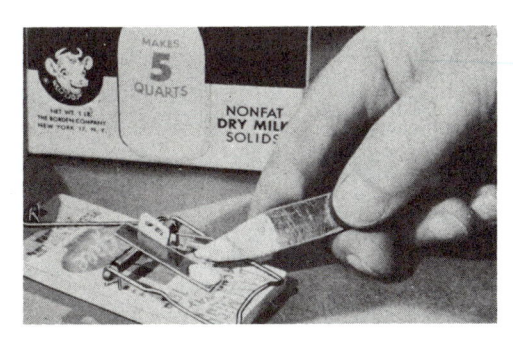

This sure-fire bait for mouse traps is made by mixing a little powdered skim milk with water to form a thick paste. Apply this to the bait holder with a knife.

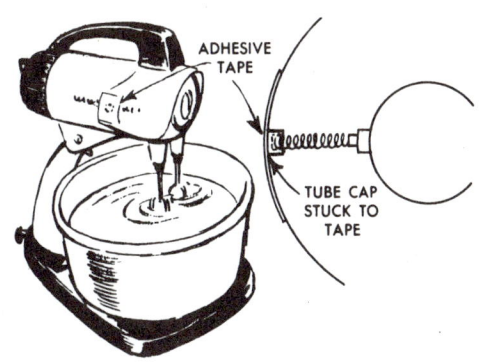

A temporary replacement for the hard-rubber, brush-spring retainer on a mixer can be made by taping the plastic cap from a small cosmetic tube over the spring.

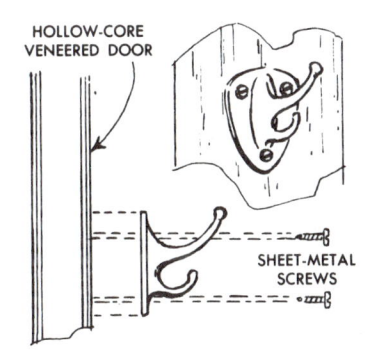

If you have to attach a robe hook to the thin facing on a hollow-core door, you'll find that sheet-metal screws will hold where ordinary screws won't.

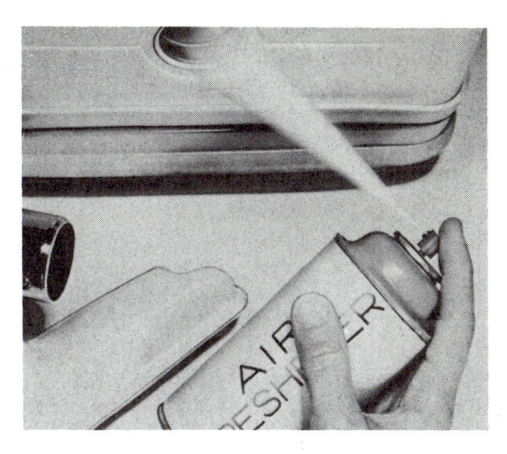

Kill odors from a vacuum-cleaner dust bag at the source. With the cleaner running, disconnect the hose and spray room deodorizer into the intake hole.

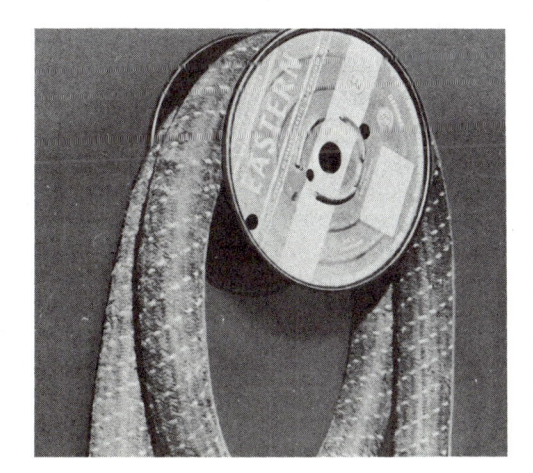

Make a wall holder for your vacuum-cleaner hose from a discarded electrical wire spool. Mount the spool on the wall or inside the broom-closet door.

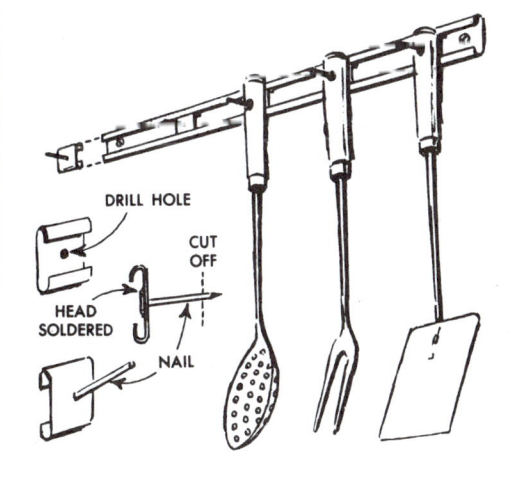

This adjustable rack for utensils was originally a curtain rod. Make the sliding hooks by sawing the inner section into 1-in. lengths and soldering a nail to each.

1633

lighting

You can't buy these lighting fixtures

They're made from auto coil springs, plastic cake covers and electrical fittings

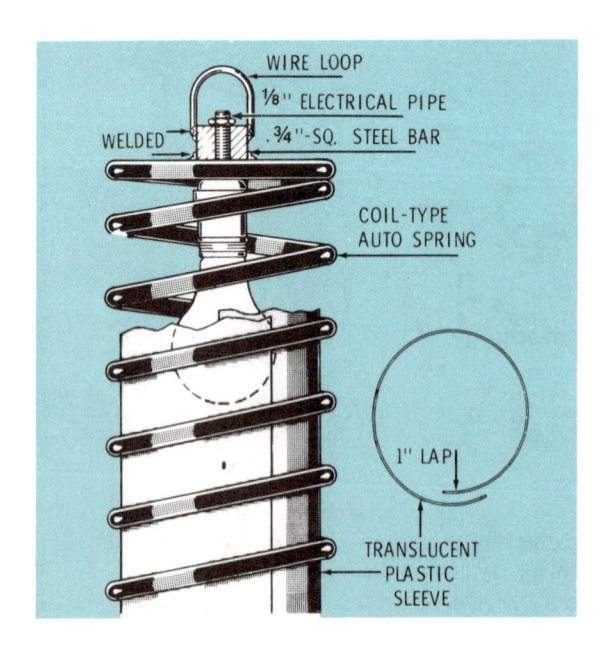

YOU'D PAY a pretty penny in a store for any one of these smart light fixtures, yet they cost only "pennies" when made from such common items as auto coil springs, plastic cake covers and electrical fittings.

Robert Shaffer of Canyonville, Ore., made the attractive spring fixture shown above from coil springs from junked cars. When three springs are joined together by welding them to a horizontal bar, then sprayed copper and fitted with white plastic liners, you wind up with the most stunning fixture you ever saw. The detail at the left shows how the sockets are attached and the wires are brought through holes drilled through the bar.

Equally stunning are the two ceiling fixtures made from plastic cake covers. Designed by Joseph Braunstein, Forest Hills, N.Y., one fixture uses the cover, while the other uses the tray. The detail shows how you add the sockets using standard fittings.

See also: electrical power control; electrical wiring; lamps; night light; switches, light; yard lights.

Both cover and tray are used to make this elegant fixture. The locknut on the end of the center post permits the cover to "hang" ¼-in. below the trap to provide ventilation. The hole is drilled through the knob of the cake cover for pipe post

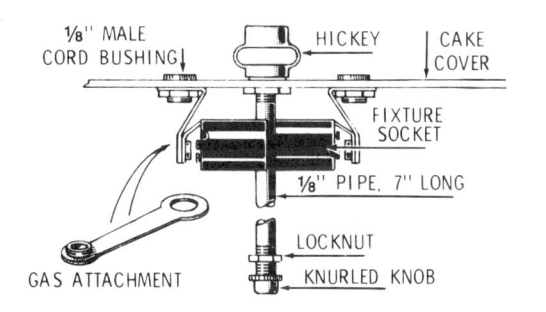

Photo above and drawing at left show how sockets are attached to the tray. Center post holds cover in place, while tray is attached to outlet (flat against ceiling) with standard pipe nipple and hickey

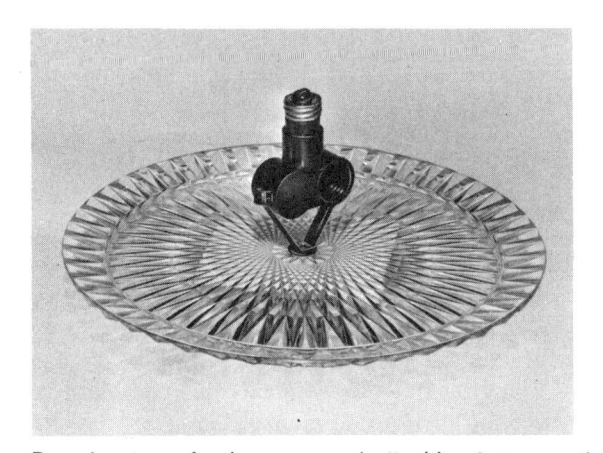

By using tray of cake cover and attaching two-way, standard socket to center with nipple and knurled knob, you can make an attractive fixture that can be screwed into an overhead socket. Since the material is plastic, you can easily drill holes for the nipple

lighting

Here's a quick review
of the many ways you can vary
the intensity of home lighting
to suit the occasion
and set the mood

Switch on your dimmers at home

BY HANK STOCKERT

■ COURTESY OF THE ROAD has long dictated that you dim your headlights so you won't dazzle approaching motorists. Have you ever thought of applying a similar courtesy to guests in your home? Why subject them to the blaze of light required to prepare for their arrival? Especially when it's easy and economical to control lighting to create a friendlier atmosphere.

This concept applies not only to the living room serenade, demonstrated above. If you've admired the effect of gently dimming light in restaurants and theaters, you can put the same principle to work in various parts of your home. For example, if you are giving an informal dinner party, you may need bright light to set the table, but once guests are seated, you could change the glare to a candle-glow.

Likewise, when you assemble friends in the rumpus room for slides or movies, you want full illumination while you set up projector and screen, but it often seems rude to halt conversation by plunging the room into darkness for the show. With a dimmer setup, you could prepare your audience by gradually diminishing the light. A selection of light levels is also a boon in the nursery and for television viewing.

Dimming equipment is no longer a luxury that involves fussy installation. The latest units will slip into your present light boxes, in place of the standard on-off switch. And most types *save* you money through lower power consumption and longer bulb life. You can even dim fluorescent lights with presently available equipment.

Some commercial systems are unsuited to home installations, of course. The latest types of remote-controlled, solid-state units designed for TV studios are too costly and complex. The resistance units used in theaters generate too

by providing (through a special switch and socket) electricity to either or both filaments. The bulb in the diagram offers a choice of 50, 100 or 150 watts.

2. A variation on this first system may be of more value to you. A multiple-poled rotary switch lets a special wiper progressively supply electricity to more and more small separate bulbs. The problem is to devise a practical housing for the number of bulbs you want, since each requires a separately wired socket.

3. Amateur photographers will find that a circuit like this will extend the life of photoflood bulbs. Throwing the center off-switch one way gives you a series hookup in which each bulb burns at about one-third its normal output—providing plenty of light for setups and focusing. When you're ready to shoot, flip the switch to the opposite side for a parallel hookup that gives you normal output from all bulbs. This system works only when each branch has equal total wattage. If you tried to use a 7-watt night light in one branch and a 100-watt bulb in the other, you'd find that the big bulb simply went out in the "low" (series) hookup, while the other burned normally.

4. One of the newer methods of home light control is a three-position wall switch that directly replaces your current toggle switches. Containing a miniature silicon-controlled rectifier, this switch, in low position, only passes every other half-cycle of your 60-cycle current. Since the bulb is literally "turned off" half the time, it gives only about 30 to 40 percent of its normal light. A second position of the switch disconnects the rectifier and supplies current in the normal manner. While this system offers you a choice of only two light levels, it can be used with any number or combination of incandescent bulbs up to its rated capacity. Typical units handle 300 to 500 watts.

vary light smoothly

The dimming methods discussed so far have one disadvantage in common: they only give a specific number of light levels in distinct steps. Now, let's vary light smoothly from full-bright to off.

Resistance dimmers have been around a long time. Earliest types had a lot in common with a pickle barrel. They were, in fact, brine-filled wooden barrels into which two metal plates were lowered. One plate was connected to the current source, the other to the load of lights. As the plates descended, their surface areas

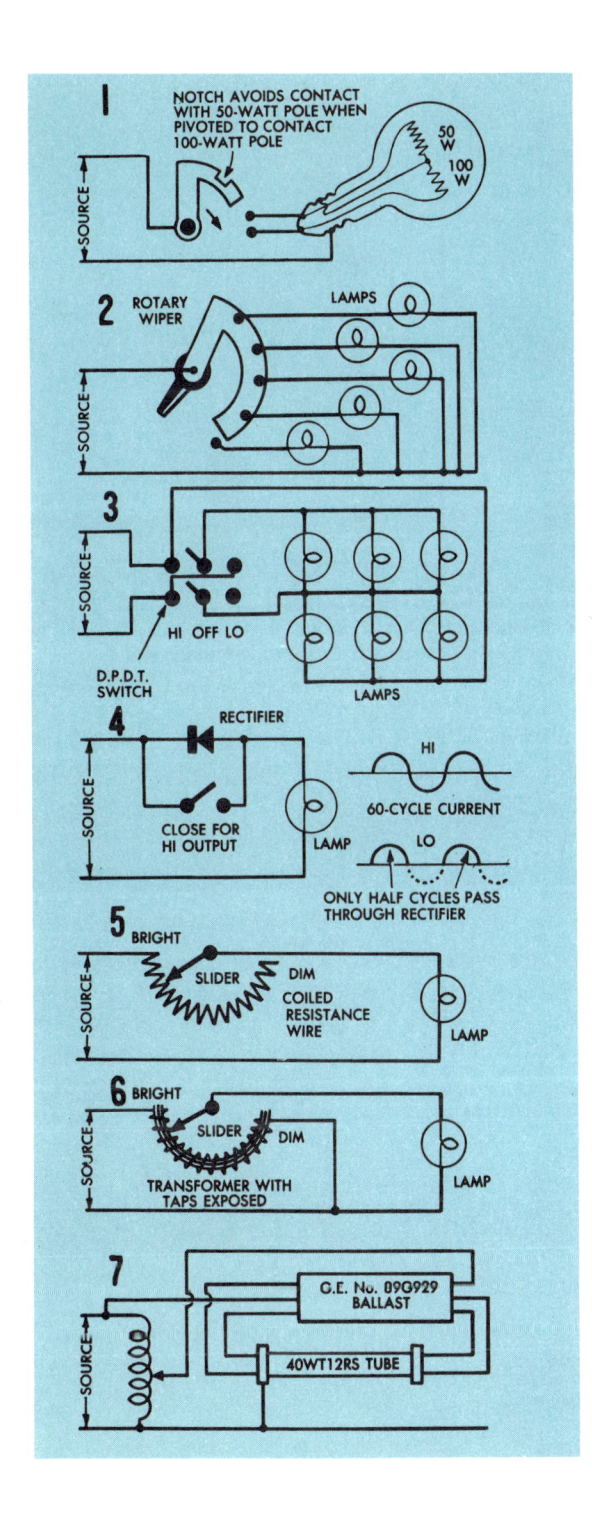

much heat to be practical or safe for the home. But let's survey the various dimming methods you *can* adapt to domestic use. Numbers refer to sketches above.

1. Your home probably already has the first type of controllable light shown—the dual-filament bulb that's found in many floor and table lamps. Three distinct levels of light are possible

1637

lighting

Modern miniaturization shrinks dimmer controls to a compact size. The auto-transformer at the left and the solid-state dimmer at the right have nearly the same capacity. While the former uses less juice it can be a problem to enclose it in a conventional wall

dimming lights, continued

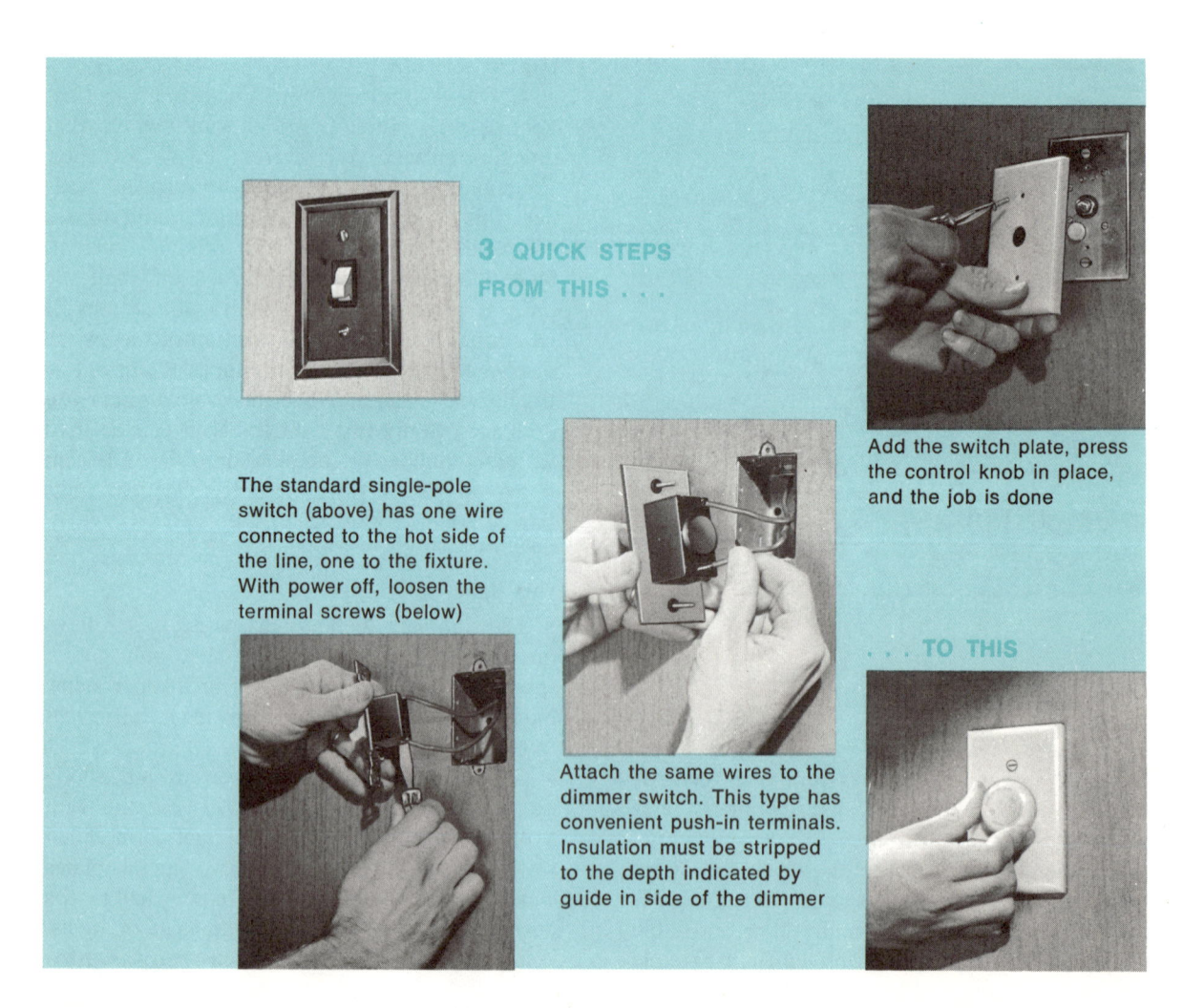

3 QUICK STEPS FROM THIS . . .

The standard single-pole switch (above) has one wire connected to the hot side of the line, one to the fixture. With power off, loosen the terminal screws (below)

Attach the same wires to the dimmer switch. This type has convenient push-in terminals. Insulation must be stripped to the depth indicated by guide in side of the dimmer

Add the switch plate, press the control knob in place, and the job is done

. . . TO THIS

1638

within the brine increased, and a proportionately increasing amount of electricity could pass between them. This crude system did the job, but the shock hazard of the brine—and the fuss of maintaining the brine level—led to the adoption of "dry" resistance units. These took the form of a king-size radio volume control, with a sliding contact moving along a length of coiled resistance wire.

5. In the simplest of these units, bulbs wired to the slider can be dimmed from full output (with the slider resting on the end of the coil that's connected to the current source) to off (when the resistance in the circuit is so high it doesn't pass enough electricity to heat the

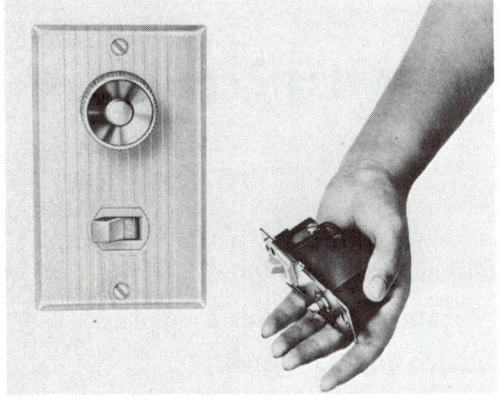

An on-off switch, built into this 500-watt dimmer by Thomas Industries, lets you shut off the light without disturbing the dial setting. This saves readjusting the light level next time you use it

bulb's filament). The following chart lists typical values of resistance and current ratings for home-sized dimmers:

LAMP WATTAGE	DIMMER RESISTANCE	DIMMER CAPACITY
7	5500 ohms	.06 amps.
25	1450 "	.23 "
60	600 "	.55 "
75	500 "	.68 "
100	360 "	.91 "
150	250 "	1.36 "
300	175 "	2.73 "
500	75 "	4.5 "

Aside from the waste of electricity suggested by these figures, such resistor units aren't very practical for the home since this waste must be carried away in the form of heat. Well-ventilated, fireproof enclosures are a must.

6. This system evolved from the resistance dimmer. But instead of moving along a resistance bank, the slide moves along the coils of wire in a transformer. This results in a voltage that can be tapped from the transformer at any value from zero to (in most variable transformers) about 30 percent above normal line voltage. Since these transformers are designed for maximum efficiency, they draw only slightly more current than the lamps actually use. Typical units waste as little as 5 to 12 watts of current in their lowest position, allowing them to be hooked up all the time.

These variable auto-transformers are available in sizes to handle from 100 watts (or less) to over 7500 watts. (A 600-watt size is shown in the photo at top of page 1638.) The size you need depends on the total wattage drain on the circuit the dimmer will control. A chandelier with eight 60-watt bulbs is too big a load for a 450-watt dimmer. You can buy the units uncased, or in a portable enclosure, or mounted in a permanent enclosure accepting conduits, or in a special box—with an attached switch plate —to recess in the wall of your home. Uncased units can be mounted in large lamp bases.

Most of these units can be used with either incandescent or fluorescent bulbs—but never *both,* intermixed, on the same circuit.

7. While existing wiring from a standard on-off switch is fine for incandescent bulbs, an extra —as shown in the diagram—must be run from the dimmer to a fluorescent fixture. The fixture can be the conventional type, but you must add the special dimming ballast indicated. The bulbs must be the 40-watt rapid-start (not instant) type, and in this case an on-off switch is required in the input line, since the dimmer won't de-energize fluorescent filaments. You can't get extremely low levels of fluorescent light because a point is reached where the tube "cuts out."

how new dimmers work

The very latest form of full-range household dimmers use silicon controlled rectifiers in a package that will slip into a standard switch box. A dial control sets the level at which the rectifier "fires" and starts conducting current. Set it to fire only at the *peaks* of each cycle of AC current, and the rectifier lets only a small amount of electricity pass. As the voltage level at which the rectifier fires is lowered, more and more current can pass, up to the point of normal consumption of the lamp. An incandescent type SCR dimmer is shown on this page. Another, made by Superior Electric Co., Bristol, Conn., has a continuous off-to-bright dial.

lighting

Beams by day, lights by night

BY DOROTHY SWANSON

■ COMBINING THE DECORATIVE effect of an exposed beam ceiling with room-width strip lighting, this ingenious remodeling idea was developed by a building contractor for use in his own kitchen.

H. D. Roach, Reidsville, N.C., worked out the simple plan in an evening. After nailing a mounting board to the ceiling for each "dummy" beam, he mounted three fluorescent fixtures, end to end, onto each board. Sides of the open-bottom beams were stock 1 x 8s from which thin strips had been cut to serve as support molding for the frosted glass. This molding was secured with brads and glue to the bottom edges of the side pieces, offset slightly to form a lip for the glass.

Sides were attached by nailing into the edge grain of the mounting board, after which the nail heads were concealed with cove molding. Finally, three strips of frosted glass were cut to fit loosely inside the bottom of each beam.

To simplify finishing, Roach applied stain and clear varnish to all exposed surfaces before assembling the beams. The same procedure can be followed for painted beams.

Here's a clever way in which false ceiling beams can be put to work as kitchen light fixtures to give you beams of light

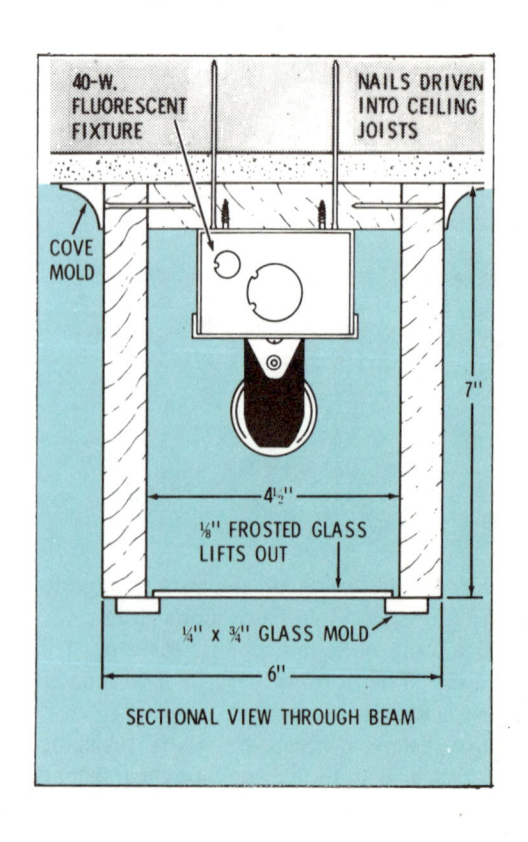

light, night: see night light
light, photo timer: see timer light, photo
light, spot: see spotlight, photo

clever ideas

Barbecue fires will burn more efficiently if you place a piece of hardware cloth over the bottom of the grill to provide a constant draft.

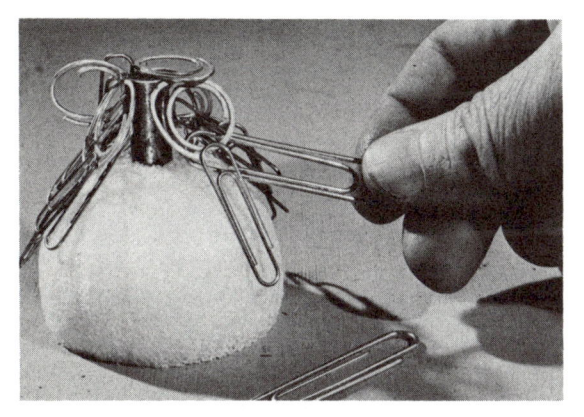

A paper-clip tree for your desk can be made by mounting a small permanent magnet in any suitable base. Just toss the clips on the tree.

This removable guard rail to prevent potted plants from falling from a window ledge is made from a flat curtain rod mounted on the window frame.

To spray wasps' nests under eaves, tape an insect bomb to a pole and mount an L-shaped metal strip over the cap so that you can trigger it with a string.

1641

light stand

A stand for your photo spot

BY J. RAMSEY

■ ADDING THAT PROFESSIONAL highlight to family portraits usually requires a studio-type spot high overhead. But the common frail light stand suitable for holding a photoflood is far from sturdy enough to support such heavy photo lamps.

But this pole-type light stand will serve your purpose. Pipe fittings are used so it can be taken apart for storing and also so it can be jacked against the ceiling for extra rigidity.

The pipe and fittings used are listed below. Assemble them as shown in the photographs. Cut the handle at least 18 in. long from ½-in. plywood, the platform from ¾-in. plywood. Then cut a hex-shaped hole in the handle to fit over the union nut and cement the handle to the nut with epoxy.

The pipe extension is capped with a rubber crutch tip. The ¼-20 bolt that locks it in place is 3 in. long and is bent 90 deg. to form a handle.

See also: darkroom light control; photography; portrait photography; spotlight, photo; timer, photo; timer light, photo.

MATERIALS LIST
For Adjustable Arm

1 pc.—1" x 6" nipple	1 pc.—1" union
1 pc.—1" x 1½" nipple	1 pc.—1" street elbow
1 pc.—1" tee	1 pc.—1" floor flange

For Legs and Center Post
4 pcs.—¾" elbows
4 pcs.—¾" x 1⅜" nipples
1 pc.—¾" 5-way fence fitting
4 pcs.—1" plastic chair tips
12'—¾" pipe (4-18" legs plus 6' center post)

For Adjustable Ceiling Anchor
3'—⅜" pipe
1 pc.—rubber crutch tip

---

lights, yard: see yard lights
linen closet: see remodeling
linoleum: see tile, floor

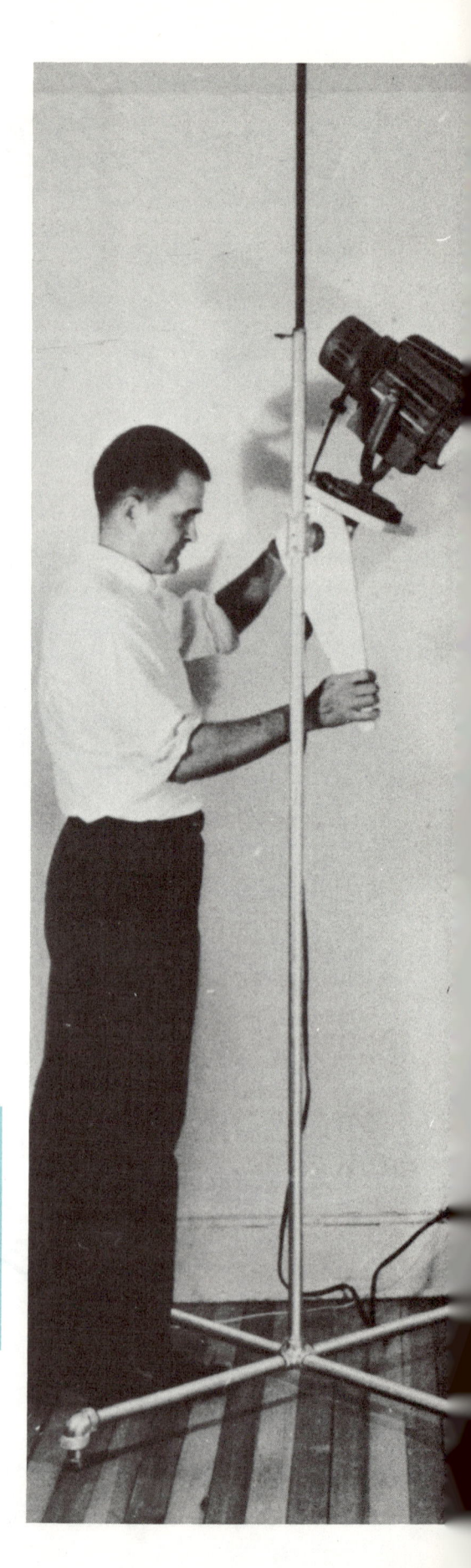

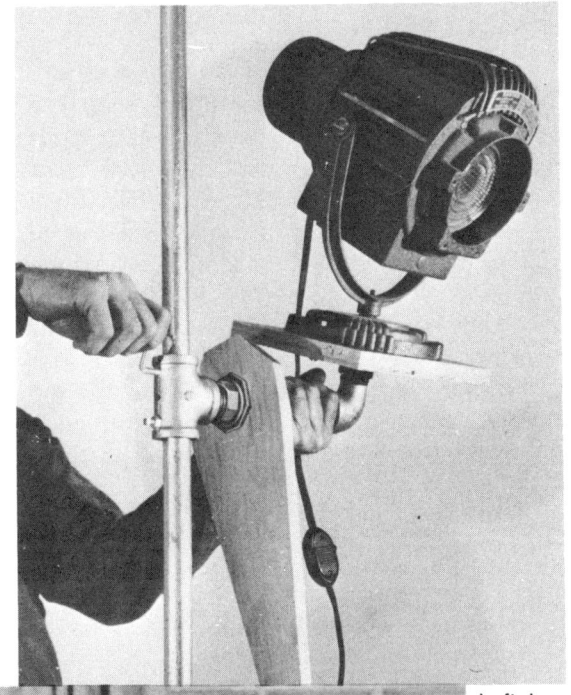

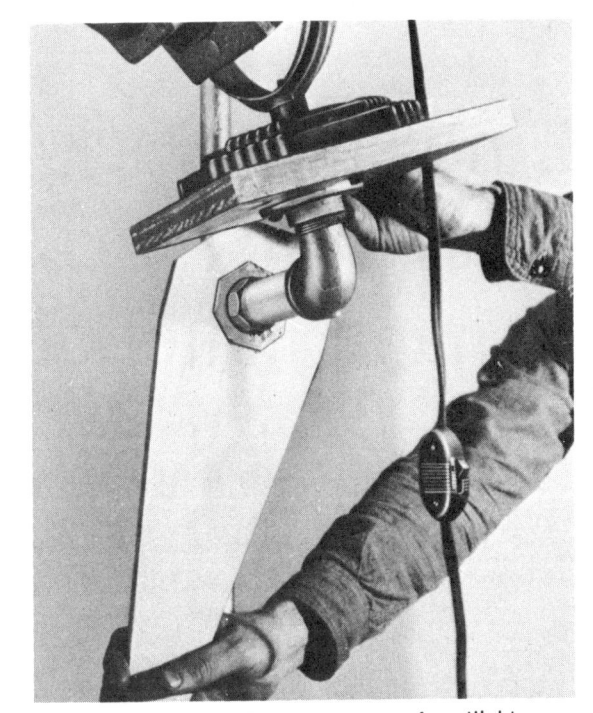

Left, loosening the bolt permits up or down movement of spotlight. Right, a plywood handle provides leverage for turning union nut

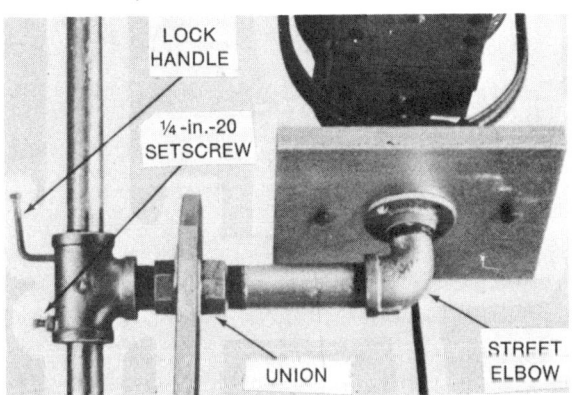

A 1-in. unreamed tee on the movable arm slides on a ¾-in. center post. Setscrew is fitted with a locknut

A 5-way fence fitting joins legs to the center post

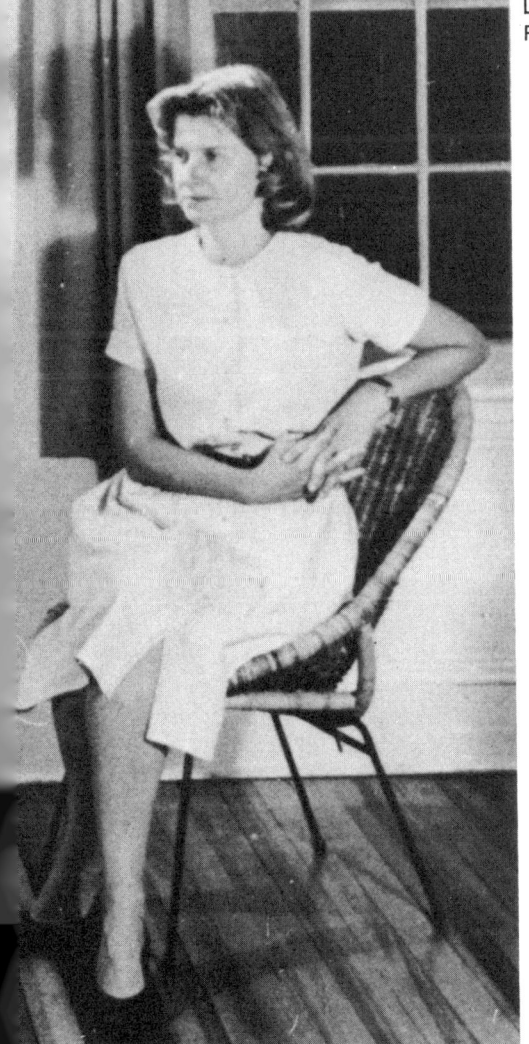

linoleum-block press

Linoleum-block press from at-hand materials

BY MANLY BANISTER

▇ WITH THIS PRESS in your hobby shop you can design and print personalized greeting cards from linoleum blocks, make multiblock color prints, illustrations and bookplates. While you're having fun doing this you can look ahead to printing from wood blocks and zinc engravings. Or, provide yourself with a 5 x 8 chase for the lockup and you can print from any type of your choosing.

The press is fairly simple to build and the important thing to strive for in its construction is a rigid, close-fitting assembly in which there is no rack or end-play. To accomplish this, the side frames, bed and platen carrier are built from

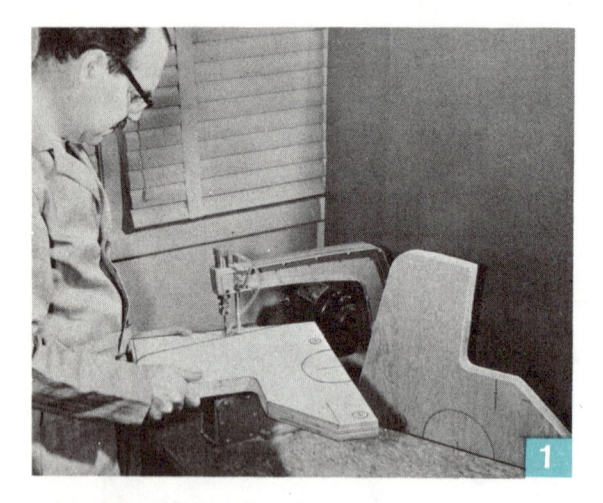

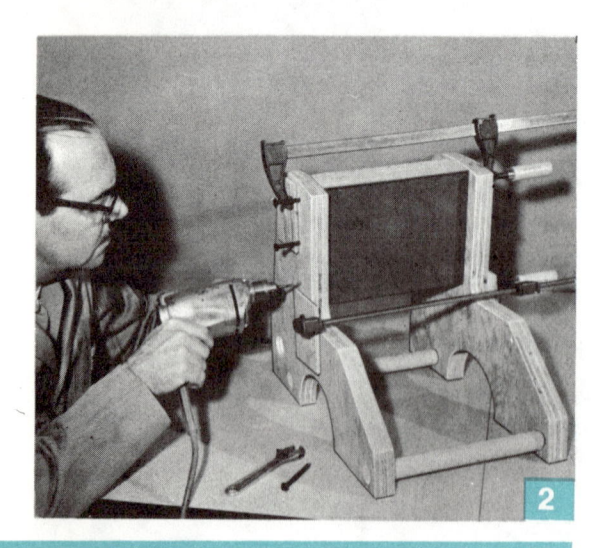

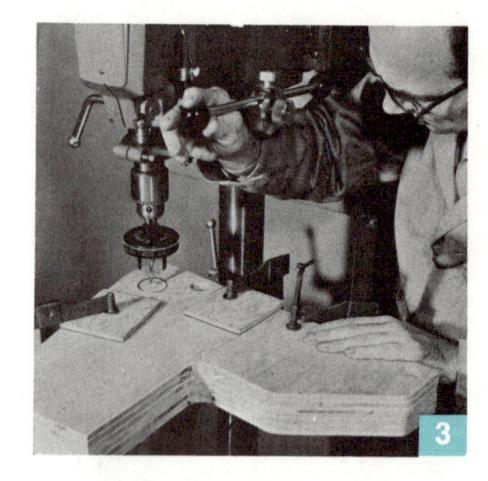

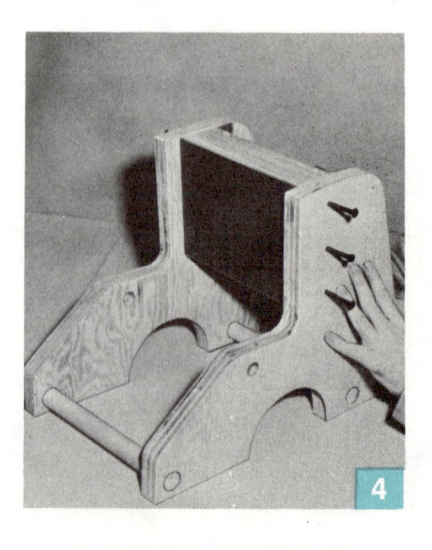

lithographs: see printing press
living room furniture: see step table; tables; weekend projects
locker, storage: see children's furniture

linoleum-block press

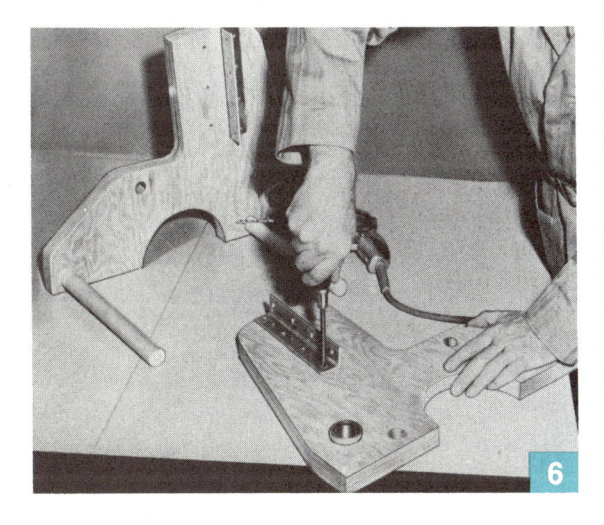

plywood and solid oak and the operating crank and side lever are assembled from standard pipe fittings. Figs. 1 through 8 give you a good idea of the assembly of the side frames and bed. The side frames are detailed in Fig. 16 and are cut from 1⅛-in. plywood. If this thickness in plywood is not readily available, then build up to the required thickness by sandwiching ¾ and ⅜-in. plywood and gluing under pressure.

You can use hardwood-faced plywood or ordinary fir plywood, but if you use the latter be sure to purchase the grade known as "good two sides" and try to pick pieces with the smallest openings, or voids, in the cores.

When laying out the pattern from Fig. 16, note that the inclination of the forward edge of the side frame is not given. Lay this off approximately 7 deg. from the vertical and keep outside the pattern line when sawing to contour. It may be necessary to make some adjustment here later. After sawing to contour as in Fig. 1, fill any voids in the plywood edges with wood putty and then smooth the edges and round the corners slightly using medium-grade sandpaper.

The next step is to drill the hole for the crankshaft bushing in each side frame, using a circle cutter as in Fig. 3. Center the hole 2½

1645

linoleum-block press

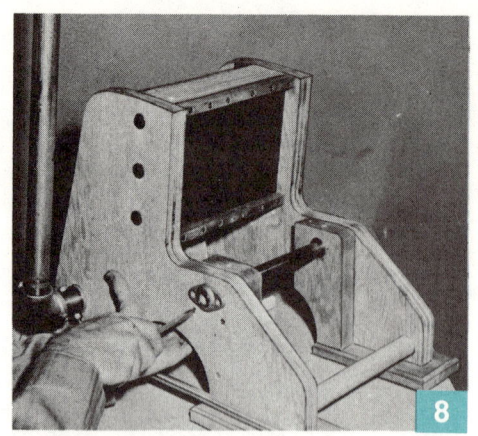

8 This shows the assembly of frames, bed, crank and platen-rocker pivot

9 Waste nuts are tapped to take threaded ends of rocket pivot, which is machined from a nipple

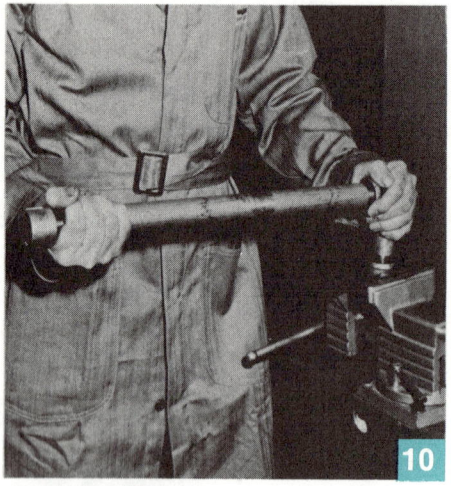

10 When assembling the operating handle, the parts should be drawn up tightly

11 Machine nipple with this setup, chucking it and using coupling and pipe plug as a carrier

linoleum-block press, continued

in. up from the bottom edge and 2 in. in from the back edge. The bushing is shown in place in Fig. 16. It is cut from a 1-in. pipe coupling so be sure to bore the hole to a diameter just under that of the rough coupling (it is machined later) so that the hole will take the bushing in a tight, drive fit. Check the setting of the circle cutter on a piece of waste.

Use much the same procedure in boring the holes for the 1-in. dowels which serve as cross frames in the assembly, Figs. 3 and 4. Do not insert the dowels at this stage as other parts must be completed and in place before this is done.

Next, note the details of the crank, Figs. 13, 15 and 18. This is built up as in Fig. 13, using five 1 x 3-in. nipples, five 90-deg. elbows and two pipe couplings which supply the bushings and collars, Fig. 13. Three of the nipples are machined, Fig. 11, to provide bearing surfaces, one serving as the pin for the connecting link, Fig. 12, and the other two as extensions of the crankshaft. The two collars are cut from the couplings, which then are machined to a drive

1646

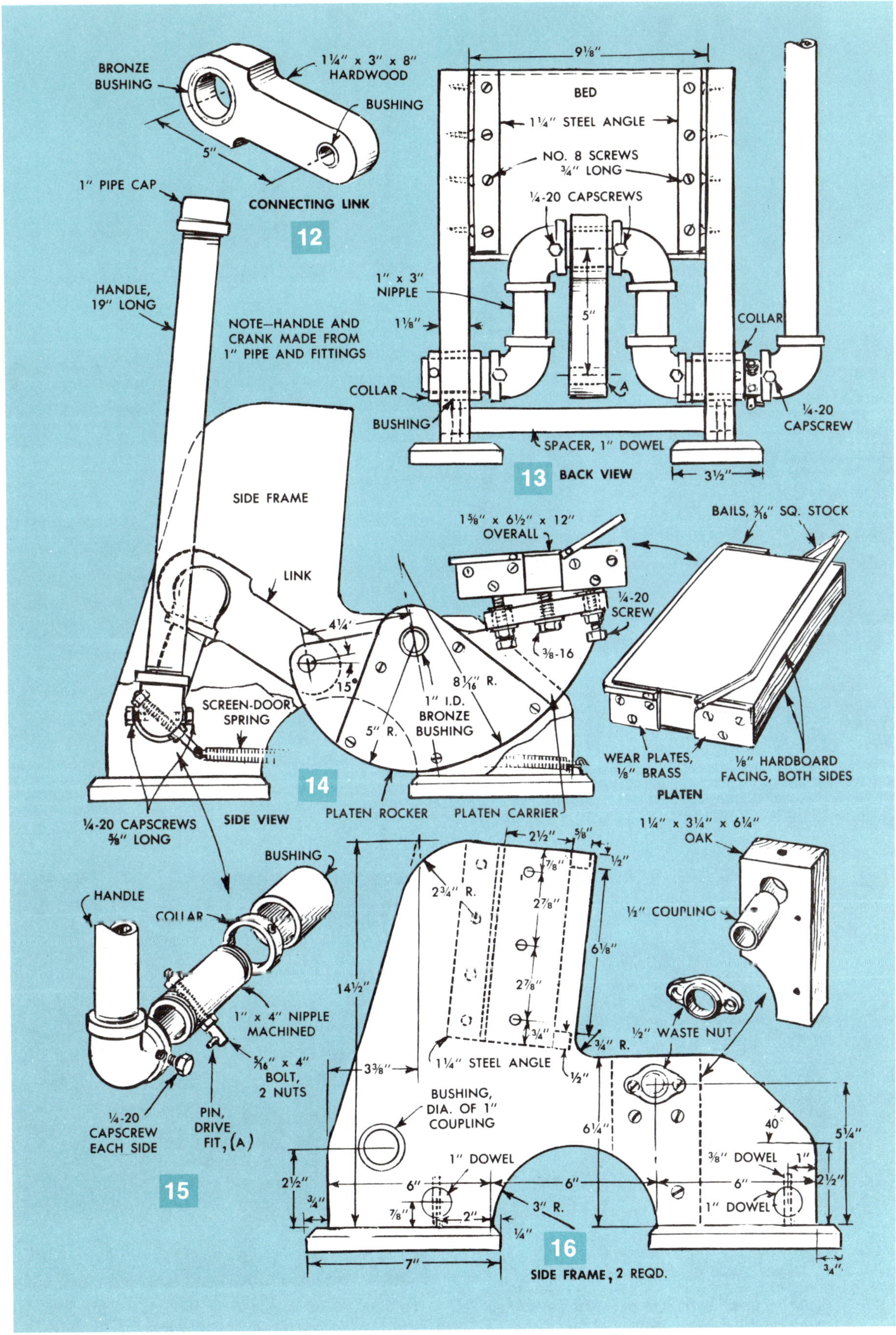
BRONZE BUSHING
1¼" x 3" x 8" HARDWOOD
BUSHING
5"
CONNECTING LINK
12
9⅛"
BED
1¼" STEEL ANGLE
NO. 8 SCREWS ¾" LONG
¼-20 CAPSCREWS
1" x 3" NIPPLE
1⅛"
5"
COLLAR
BUSHING
A
SPACER, 1" DOWEL
¼-20 CAPSCREW
3½"
13
BACK VIEW
1" PIPE CAP
HANDLE, 19" LONG
NOTE—HANDLE AND CRANK MADE FROM 1" PIPE AND FITTINGS
SIDE FRAME
LINK
4¼"
15°
SCREEN-DOOR SPRING
8 1/16" R.
1" I.D. BRONZE BUSHING
5" R.
14
SIDE VIEW
¼-20 CAPSCREWS ⅝" LONG
PLATEN ROCKER
PLATEN CARRIER
1⅝" x 6½" x 12" OVERALL
¼-20 SCREW
⅜-16
BAILS, 3/16" SQ. STOCK
WEAR PLATES, ⅛" BRASS
⅛" HARDBOARD FACING, BOTH SIDES
PLATEN
BUSHING
HANDLE
COLLAR
1" x 4" NIPPLE MACHINED
5/16" x 4" BOLT, 2 NUTS
¼-20 CAPSCREW EACH SIDE
PIN, DRIVE FIT, (A)
15
2½"
⅝"
½"
2¾" R.
7/8"
2⅞"
2⅞"
6⅛"
¾"
¾" R.
14½"
1¼" STEEL ANGLE
½"
3⅜"
BUSHING, DIA. OF 1" COUPLING
6¼"
1" DOWEL
2½"
¾"
6"
7/8"
2"
3" R.
¼"
6"
6"
⅜" DOWEL
1"
1" DOWEL
40°
5¼"
2½"
7"
¾"
1¼" x 3¼" x 6¼" OAK
½" COUPLING
½" WASTE NUT
16
SIDE FRAME, 2 REQD.

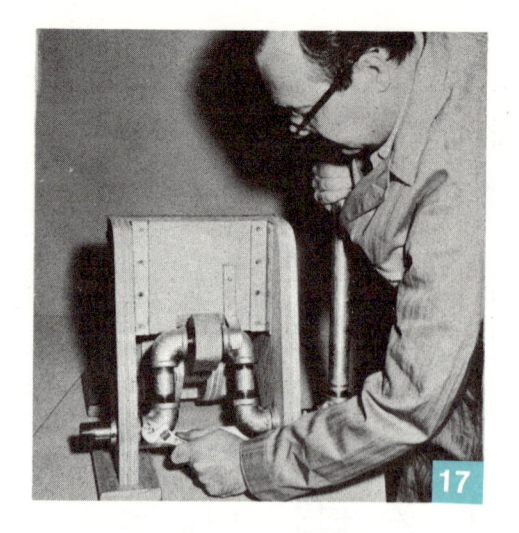

linoleum-block press

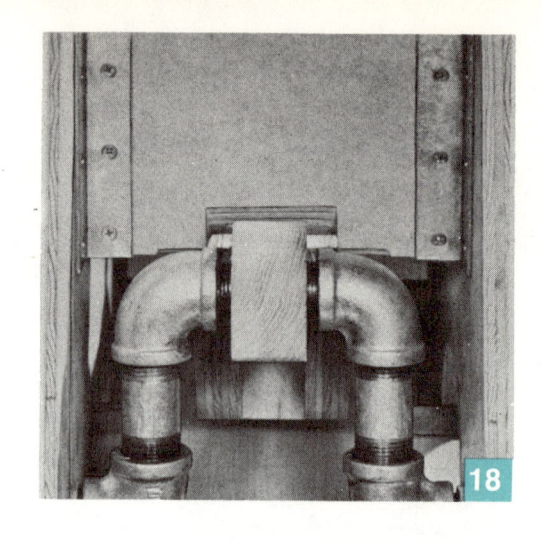

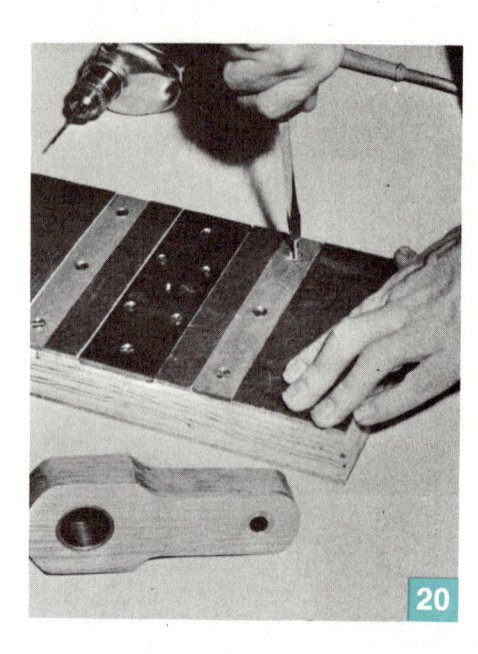

linoleum-block press, continued

21 Finishing touches on lino cut must be worked carefully. It's easy to damage at this stage

22 The finished cut is locked in the bed with printer's furniture and two key-operated quoins

1648

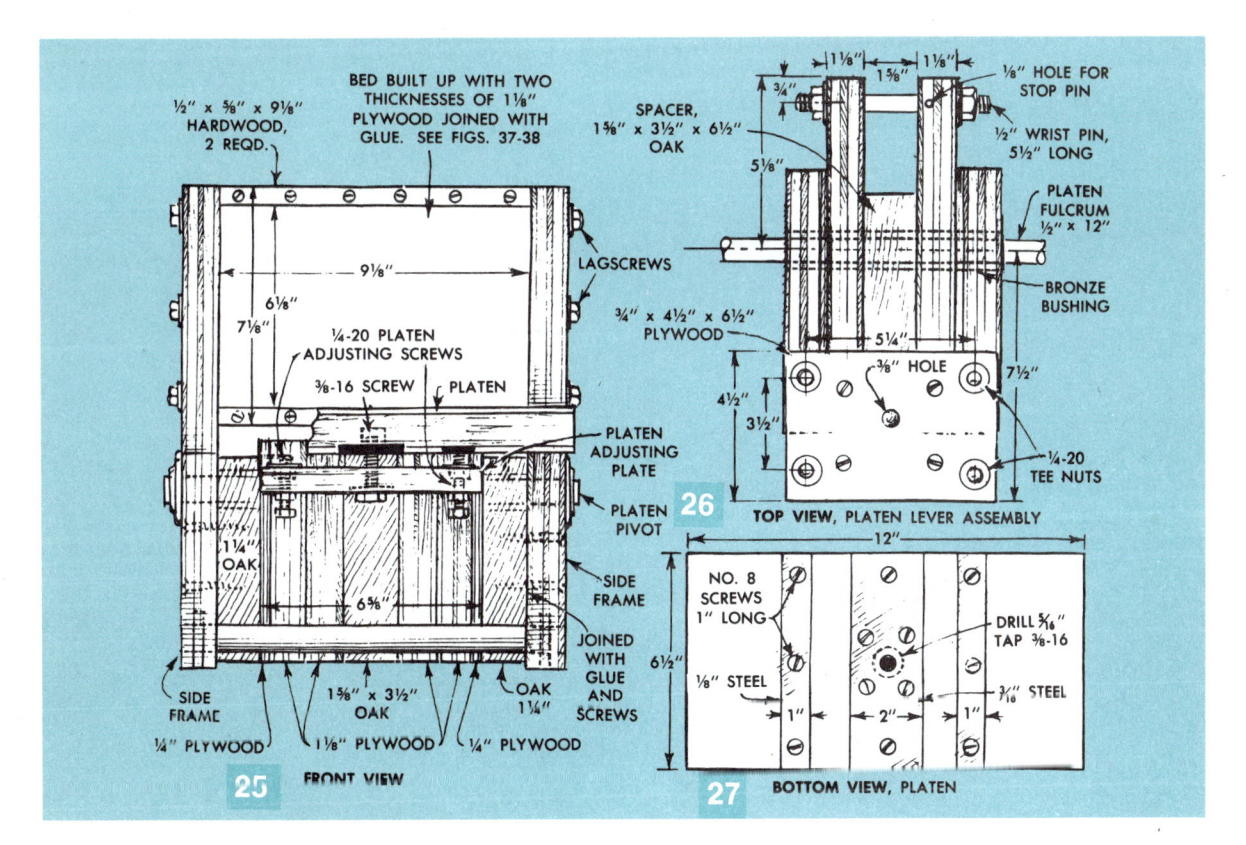

fit in the holes in the side frames. Before insertion, they are bored out to take the machined nipples which are a part of the crankshaft. Both collars are drilled and tapped for setscrews.

Also note that all five elbows, Figs. 13 and 17, are drilled and tapped on one flange for setscrews.

Make a trial assembly of the crank, without the handle, drawing all joints equally tight. Check for squareness and center-to-center distances. These should be reasonably close with all parts tight but due to the allowable variations in the manufacture of pipe fittings it may be necessary to back off one or two of the parts to attain close alignment of the bearing extensions and the crank pin. But if the parts align reasonably close when tight, you will be able to make a permanent assembly.

Figs. 14 and 15, also Fig. 10, show the assembly of the handle. Note that the elbow

linoleum-block press

28 An impression is made when the press is closed as in the photo above

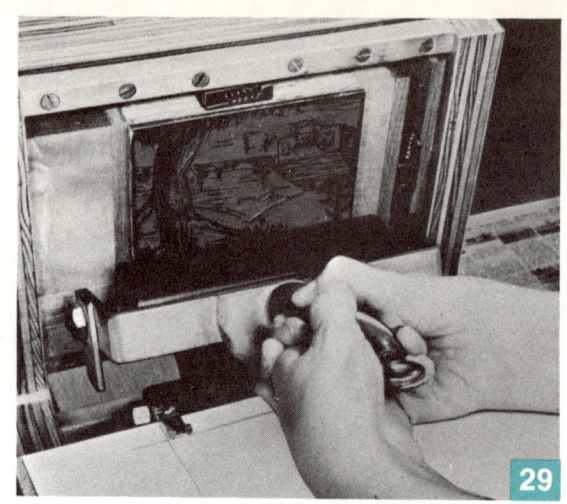

29 Inking the cut with the brayer (above) must be done each time an impression is made as at the left

linoleum-block press, continued

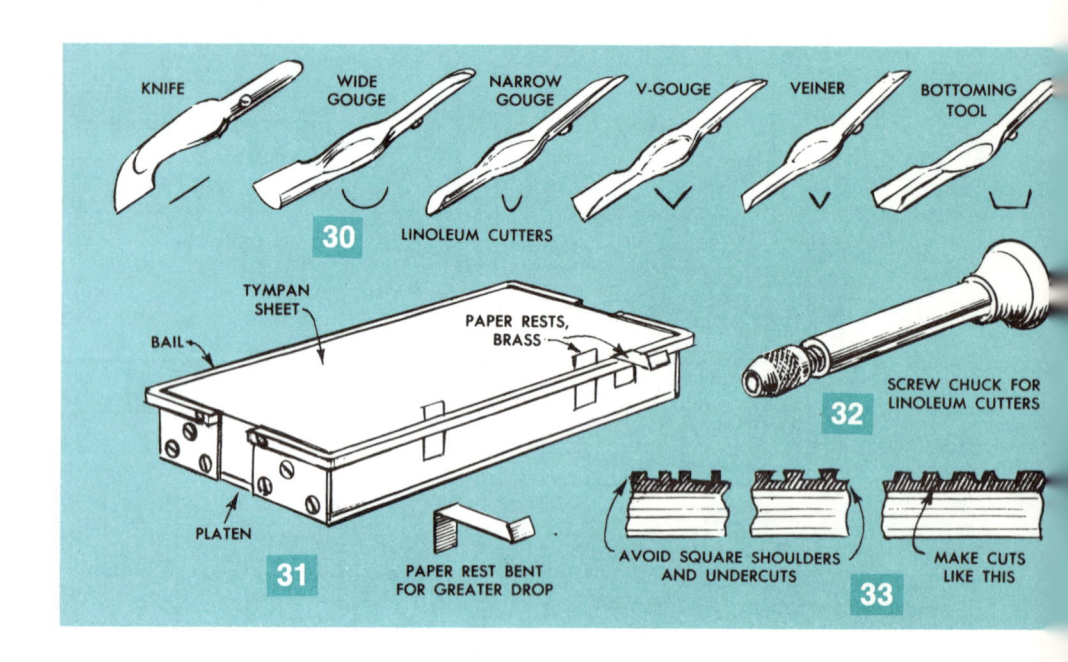

30 LINOLEUM CUTTERS: KNIFE, WIDE GOUGE, NARROW GOUGE, V-GOUGE, VEINER, BOTTOMING TOOL

31 TYMPAN SHEET, PAPER RESTS, BRASS, BAIL, PLATEN, PAPER REST BENT FOR GREATER DROP

32 SCREW CHUCK FOR LINOLEUM CUTTERS

33 AVOID SQUARE SHOULDERS AND UNDERCUTS — MAKE CUTS LIKE THIS

carrying the handle is double-set-screwed to the crankshaft extension and that the extension carries a transverse pin, or stud, which anchors one end of the return spring, Fig. 14.

The bed, Figs. 13 and 16, consists of two thicknesses of 1⅛-in. plywood cut to 7¼ x 9⅛ in. and two pieces of ⅛-in. hardboard of the same size. Sandwich the two pieces of plywood with the hardboard facing pieces, one on each side, and glue together under pressure. Plane the width to about 7⅛ in. and locate between the side members as indicated by the dotted lines in Fig. 16. Locate so that the front face is about ⅞ in. from the inclined front edges of the side frames. The bed is screwed to steel angles attached to the side frames, Figs. 6 and 13, and is also lagscrewed to the side frames as in Figs. 3 and 4. Do not glue in place after fitting.

Next to be made and attached to the sideframes are the waste nuts, the ½-in. couplings

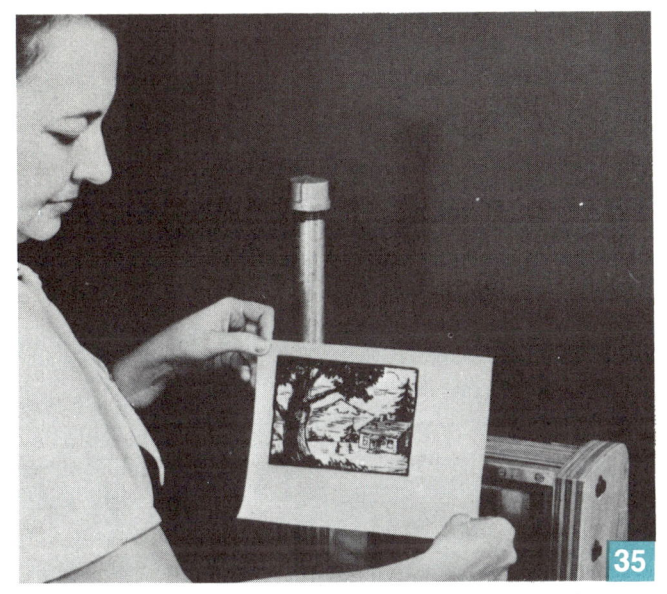

Lifting the print must be done carefully to avoid smearing. Hold one corner and "peel" the print from an opposite corner (left). Note sharpness of a print made from good lino cut

and the supporting blocks, Fig. 16. The pivot, or fulcrum shaft, carrying the platen rocker is a ½ x 12-in. nipple. These parts are shown in position in Fig. 8 and the completed rocker with platen adjusting plate is pictured in Fig. 19. The waste nuts are tapped, Fig. 9, to take the threaded ends of the fulcrum shaft which is machined smooth. The couplings are bored out to a slip fit over the shaft and are machined to

a drive fit in holes in the support blocks, Figs. 8 and 16.

The platen rocker is carried on two bronze bushings of 1 in. outside diameter, Fig. 14. The bushings are bored out to a close fit over the ½-in. fulcrum shaft.

With the side frames, bed, and crank made and trial-assembled refer to Figs. 14 and 19 for the hole locations and how the sandwich type

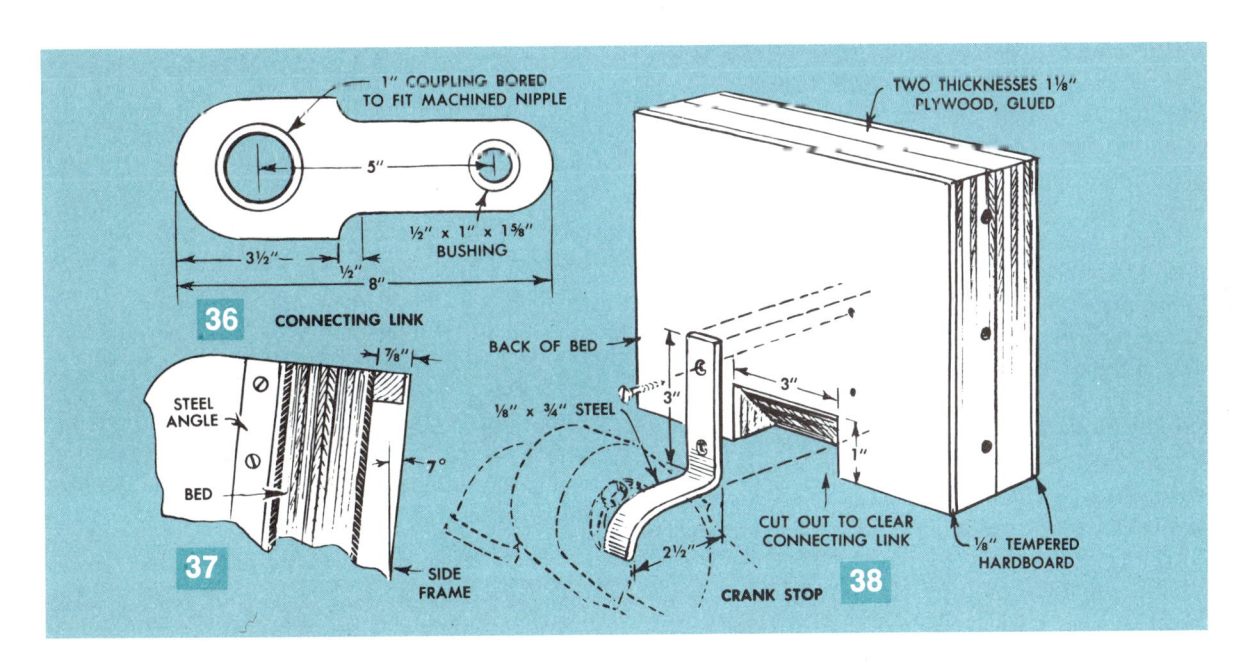

1651

linoleum-block press

linoleum-block press, continued

assembly of the platen rocker and carrier is made. These parts assemble into one piece as you will see from Figs. 25 and 26. Remember when checking the thicknesses of plywood to be used in sandwiching the platen carrier that the 1¼-in. oak members shown in section in Fig. 25 are not a part of the assembly, but are carriers, or supports, for the rocker bushings, Fig. 16. In this connection, note the top view, Fig. 26, and the identification and relationship of these parts will be clear.

must fit properly

When assembled the carrier must fit as indicated in Fig. 25 without any end play and without binding. This may mean that some sanding will have to be done in order to assure a perfect fit. If 1⅛-in. plywood is not readily available, the carrier can be built up from lesser thicknesses of plywood. Cut the two rocker members and finish the edges before gluing the whole together sandwich-fashion. Use a moisture-resistant glue, spread it uniformly and when clamping be sure that the pressure of the clamps is uniformly distributed so that you get sound joints throughout. When the assembly is drilled for the wrist pin taking the forward end of the connecting link, Fig. 36, and the bushings for the fulcrum, or pivot shaft, it is necessary to drill a clearance hole all the way through for the pivot as indicated by the dotted lines in Fig. 26. The size of the hole must be such as to admit the bushings in a drive fit.

The platen-adjusting plate, Figs. 14, 25 and 26, carries five cap-screws, four provided for leveling the platen and the fifth screw at the center serving to hold the assembly rigidly in place. Note in Fig. 27, which shows a bottom view of the platen, that this capscrew turns into a hole tapped in the center of a steel plate inset flush across the bottom of the platen at its center. Wear plates against which the ends of the adjusting screws bear also are inset, one on each side of the center plate, Fig. 27.

faced with hardboard

The platen is faced on both sides with ⅛-in. hardboard, is fitted with metal wear plates at the ends and carries bails of 3/16-in. square steel pivoting on small screws as in Fig. 14.

When made ready, the platen is faced with a sheet of ⅛-in. cork and covered with a sheet of manila paper, the whole being held in place by the tympan bails, Fig. 31. The latter detail also shows the sheet-brass paper rests which hold the paper in place as the impression is made, Fig. 22.

Next step is to attach the lower end of the connecting link to the carrier. The wrist pin, threaded at both ends, must be inserted while the carrier is tilted. It will be necessary to remove the bed, notch it as in Fig. 38 and then make a trial assembly with the bed in position to determine if the notch as dimensioned allows sufficient clearance for the link. If everything checks out, then reassemble with parts in position and you're ready to level the platen.

This is done by bringing it up to the bed and then adjusting the leveling screws until it makes uniform contact. When full contact has been assured, remove the short setscrews from the threaded pipe joints in the crankarm and tap the holes all the way through. Insert longer setscrews to make sure the threaded joints will hold when you exert pressure on the crank handle.

Now note the position of the bed in Fig. 37. The front face of the bed should incline 7 deg. from the vertical and should be about ⅞ in. from the edge of the side frame. If necessary, sand the edges of the side frames to obtain this dimension.

use square members

The square member shown in section in Fig. 37 is a part of the "furniture" of the bed. One piece is screwed to the top of the bed and a duplicate piece at the bottom as in Fig. 25. These pieces permit you to assemble the linoleum cut with blocking and quoins as in Fig. 22 ready for taking the impressions.

Making the linoleum cuts as in Fig. 21 requires the tools detailed in Figs. 30 and 32 and the simple processes of inking and printing are pictured in Figs. 23 and 24, also Figs. 28, 29, 34 and 35. When making cuts in linoleum with the tools avoid making undercuts and leaving any square shoulders at the edges of recesses, Fig. 33. Shoulders should always be sloping 3 to 5 deg. as in the right-hand detail, Fig. 33. Keep tools sharp. Grind out any nicks, however small, as a nick will tend to tear the material when cutting and may cause irreparable damage to an otherwise perfect lino cut.

See also: copy machine; duplicator; printing press; rubber stamps; tracing projector.

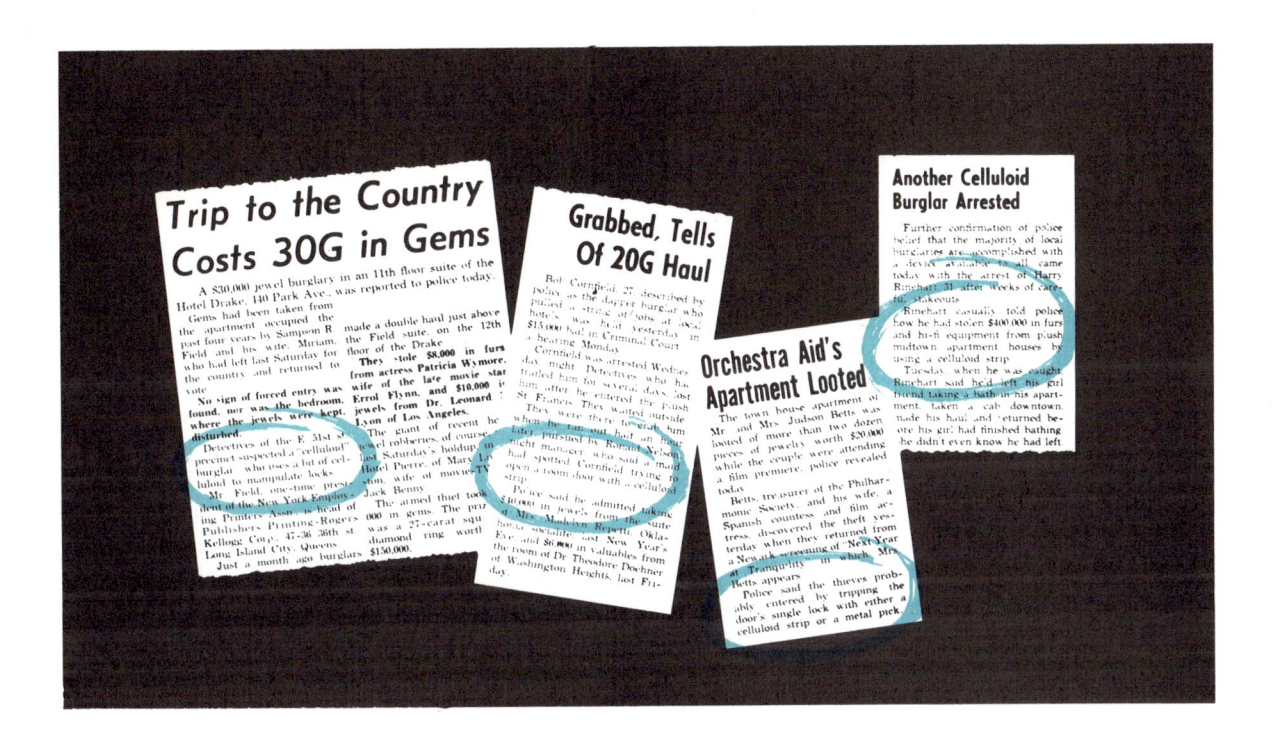

Tricks that foil lock pickers

■ You step out and pull the door shut behind you, testing the knob with a brief twist. Satisfied that the automatic latch set, you turn away with a confident stride. But it may well be a *false confidence*—perhaps you'll return to find unexpected visitors have stripped your home or hotel room of your most valued possessions.

If the current rash of forced entries into luxury hotels, apartment houses and homes teaches us anything, it's that we've put far too much trust in the common door lock. Look at the newspaper clippings, above: in every case, the burglar walked through the front door. And chances are, he wasn't even a skilled lock picker!

A little knowledge of how these through-the-door crooks operate can make you a whole lot less vulnerable to theft—both in your own home, and whenever you must stay in a hotel or motel.

Burglars fall into three categories: the plastic strippers (featured in our four news clips), the lock pickers, and the key forgers—in that order

If the burglar who calls
at your house while you're away
is a "plastic stripper,"
his night will be ruined
if you've pried up the
strike plates on your door jambs

---

locomotive: see train, children's
log furniture: see rustic furniture
lounge, sun: see sun lounge
louvered fences: see fences
low-temperature alarms: see alarm, temperature; heating systems, home
lower units, outboard: see outboard motors, repair

locks

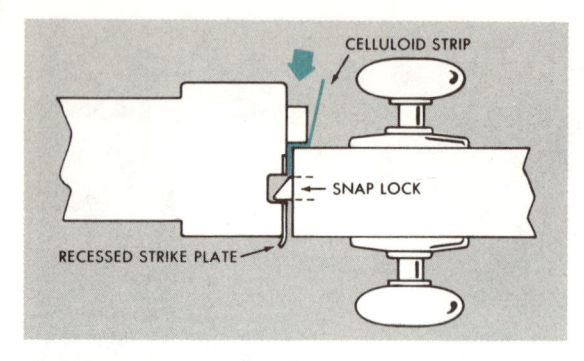

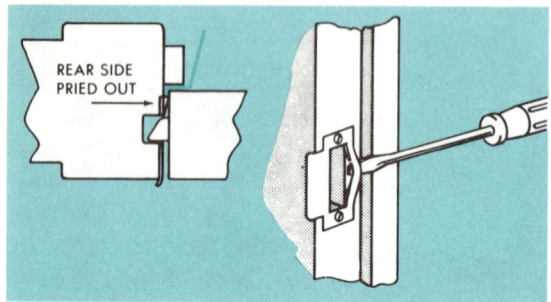

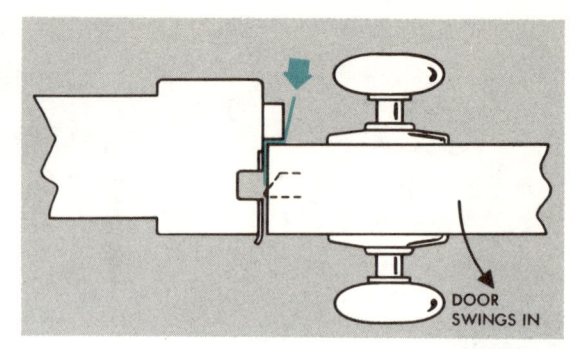

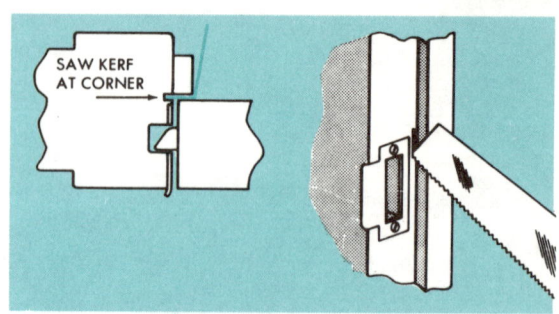

of predominance. In city robberies, the strip boys are the major menace, since any punk can learn the trick. Where only a snap latch prevents a door from being opened, it's not difficult to slide a piece of celluloid between the panel face and the stop strip, urging it around the corner until it bears against the bevel of the latch, as shown in the first sketch, above. Then, as the celluloid continues across the strike plate, it pushes the spring-loaded tongue back. Who needs experience?

Skilled pick men are so much rarer that merely double-locking all doors would prevent over *half* of our burglaries. There's no bevel on the dead bolt. That's why you must turn it into the strike plate by hand, either with a key (from the outside) or with the night-latch knob (from within). A surprising number of people merely slam the

Do the twist—double-lock your door by key. The snap latch sets automatically, but you're not secure until you manually shoot that dead bolt. And check to see that the pushbuttons are set

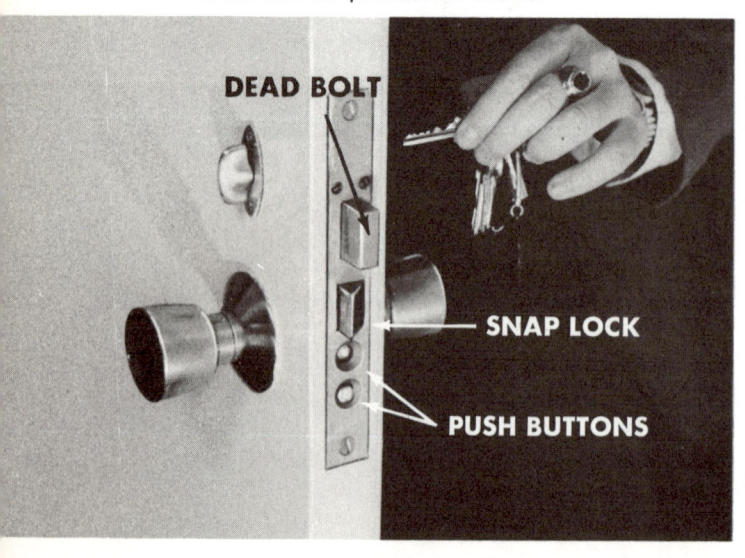

Safest lock? The seven tumblers, spaced around the circular key slot, must be depressed by notches of varying depths in the tubular key. They're not all lined up, waiting to be manipulated by a pick

1654

door behind them as they leave—even though they've just pocketed the key they'll need to get back *in,* and could insure themselves against theft in their absence by simply twisting that key in the lock.

Of course, you don't always have the chance. Some contractors cut costs by installing *only* snap locks—and these economizers include the builders of many respectable hotels and motels.

In such a case, there's a simple precaution you can take to safeguard your valuables while you're out—so simple, in fact, that you can use it on a hotel lock, if you find yourself assigned to a room without a dead bolt. It involves a slight modification of the strike plate so that a plastic strip (or any other flexible insert) will be stopped before it reaches the tongue's bevel. Where the plate is simply recessed into a wood jamb, as in the lower-left sketch, opposite page, you need only dig the blade of a screwdriver under the inner edge of the plate and pry against the stop strip to bow that edge out of the recess. Few doors fit snugly enough to cause any binding on the bent plate.

But where you can't get a pry under the plate, it's equally effective to make a saw kerf beside the stop so that the entering strip seats in it and won't turn the corner. If there's room, you might, instead, drive flathead screws or tacks in front of the plate, letting them protrude enough to halt a strip. Whichever technique you choose, it will give you a sense not only of security, but of smug satisfaction that you're frustrating someone who's out to get you.

Neither double-locking nor strip-stopping will, of course, foil lock pickers or key forgers. And though these are far fewer in number they constitute a threat because we make things too easy for them. There are all kinds of devices on the market for picking locks, and some of them require as little skill to use as the plastic strip. One wicked little gadget looks like a soldering gun. You insert its needle nose in any conventional pin-tumbler lock, pull the trigger and —you're in, without a telltale trace on the lock. To a thief, this item would be cheap at twice its $20 price tag.

sale limited

Manufacturers of such equipment, recognizing its potential danger in the wrong hands, establish conditions of sale to protect the public. This pistol tool, for example, must be ordered on a letterhead from a store or shop owner—or a recognized locksmith (there are about 4000 in the U.S.) Each tool is a registered responsibility.

But such precautions aren't likely to apply to items that cost only a few cents. You can buy a snap pick, for example (sort of a palm-sized safety pin of spring wire), for 65¢—or an elaborate set of flat picks or tension wrenches for under $10. Not all communities have (or enforce) regulations concerning such sales, and even the best-intentioned restrictions can be circumvented —especially via mail order. A professional lock picker would certainly find it worth his while to have a few phony letterheads printed up.

What makes things easy for the key forger, on the other hand, is our obsession with master-key systems. A burglar will often case the building site while a new apartment is under construction. If he can swipe a couple of cylinders before they're installed, he can study the similarity of their tumbler patterns and fashion a key that'll open any door in the place, later.

maximum security

Protecting yourself against the sharpies involves a more drastic measure: changing your lock to one designed for maximum security. One of the best is shown in the photo on page 1654. The circular key slot requires a tubular key that is next-to-impossible to forge, though the lock design is ideally suited to master-keying. The seven pin tumblers, set around the circle—run parallel to the key's shank—not vertical to it, as in standard tumbler locks. Since the pins are actuated by direct pressure from the key, not by a camming action, standard picks are useless.

This type of lock is not new. It's been made by Chicago Lock Co. (under the name "Ace") for nearly 30 years. Cabinet and padlock versions have long been adopted for the confidential files of the U.S. Secret Service and many telephone companies. Perhaps because of such major markets, the manufacturer makes little attempt to introduce the lock to the general public. Yet the "Ace" is offered in a cylinder version with a standard-diameter threaded body so that it can easily be substituted for most existing door locks. Any locksmith can order and install it.

Failing that, your locksmith can put pick-resistant pins in a standard tumbler lock. A skilled —or at least persistent—pick man might still be able to open it, but it will take him much longer, and often that's enough to discourage him. No crook likes to expose himself in the act, and it's hard not to look guilty when you're caught kneeling in front of a stranger's door.

See also: alarms, burglar; door closers.

lumber

Lumber basics for the craftsman

BY W. CLYDE LAMMEY

■ IF YOU LIVE in an average home of wood construction it contains from 1000 to 3000 pieces of lumber in many of the common classified forms. If it's an older structure the chances are it was built of both hard and softwood lumber, the former cut from broad-leaved (deciduous) trees and the latter from the conifers (evergreens).

Hardwood lumber in the structure will likely be in the form of interior trim, floors, doors, stairways, built-in cabinets and moldings in various forms and applications. Softwoods, from the

This man is tallying, or taking inventory of a stack of tongue-and-grooved boards. Such lumber is usually referred to as "manufactured" stock, or lumber

conifers, will be in the framing, sheathing, roof deck, siding, sash frames, exterior trim and also the shingles if the roof is of wood.

The terms board and lumber are often used loosely. Say "board" and you think right away of lumber; or the other way around, "lumber" and one thinks of a board, or perhaps the source of supply, the local lumberyard.

But both terms are a little more specific in the grading and classification of both the hard and softwoods. In general, the term lumber, or yard lumber, refers to individual pieces as cut from the log and dressed (planed, or surfaced) to a given width and thickness and cut to lengths of 8, 10, 12 ft. and so on up to the maximum length available. If the pieces are less than 2 in. thick and less than 8 in. wide they usually are classified as strips. If less than 2 in. thick and 8 in. or more in width they are classed as boards.

Pieces larger in sectional size than strips or boards are usually classified as *dimension* and *timbers*. Dimension lumber is 2 in. and less than 5 in. thick and any width normally supplied. Dimension lumber is commonly supplied as 2 x 4s, 2 x 6s, 2 x 8s, 2 x 10s and 2 x 12s. In sectional size timbers are 4 in. or more on the smaller dimension, as 4 x 6, 4 x 8 and so on.

All these classifications are commonly available in lengths from 6 or 8 up to 20 ft. or more in multiples of 2 ft. Thus to save stock the experienced purchaser of lumber who needs two 7-ft. lengths of 2 x 4, for example, buys one 14-ft. length rather than two 8 ft. lengths. All length dimensions are commonly cut slightly over to allow for trimming to the exact length required.

Lumber is sized as it comes from the saw and is commonly referred to as rough or rough-sawed. As it comes from the saw a 2 x 4 measures a full 2 x 4 in.; a 1 x 8 measures a full 1 in. thick and 8 in. wide. After surfacing (being run through a planer) the 1 x 8 is reduced to a thickness of ¾ in. and a width of 7⅝ in. The board is then referred to as being surfaced on all four sides, that is, on both faces and two edges (S4S). Likewise a rough-sawed 2 x 4 will measure 1⅝ x 3⅝ in. after surfacing. Of course, there may be slight variations in the sectional dimensions due either to swelling or shrinkage.

Common lumber in both the hard and softwoods is priced and sold by the board foot. To visualize the meaning of the term "board foot" think of a piece (cut from a board) which measures 1 in. thick, 12 in. wide and 12 in. long in the rough. A strip 1 in. thick, 6 in. wide and

TABLE 1. Nominal and Minimum Dressed Dry Sizes of Finish, Flooring, Ceiling and Partition, at 19 Percent Maximum Moisture Content.

ITEM	THICKNESSES NOMINAL[1]	THICKNESSES MINIMUM DRESSED	FACE WIDTHS NOMINAL	FACE WIDTHS MINIMUM DRESSED
	Inches	Inches	Inches	Inches
Finish	3/8	5/16	2	1½
	½	7/16	3	2 9/16
	5/8	9/16	4	3 9/16
	¾	5/8	5	4½
	1	¾	6	5½
	1¼	1	7	6½
	1½	1¼	8	7¼
	1¾	1 3/8	9	8¼
	2	1½	10	9¼
	2½	2	11	10¼
	3	2 9/16	12	11¼
	3½	3 1/16	14	13¼
	4	3 9/16	16	15¼
Flooring	3/8	5/16	2	1 3/16
	½	7/16	3	2¼
	5/8	9/16	4	3¼
	1	¾	5	4 3/16
	1¼	1	6	5 3/16
	1½	1¼		
Ceiling	3/8	5/16	3	2¼
	½	7/16	4	3¼
	5/8	9/16	5	4 3/16
	¾	11/16	6	5 3/16
Partition	1	23/32	3	2¼
			4	3¼
			5	4 3/16
			6	5 3/16

TABLE 2. Nominal and Minimum Dressed Dry Sizes of Siding at 19 Percent Maximum Moisture Content.

ITEM	THICKNESSES NOMINAL	THICKNESSES MINIMUM DRESSED	FACE WIDTHS NOMINAL	FACE WIDTHS MINIMUM DRESSED
	Inches	Inches	Inches	Inches
Bevel Siding	½	7/16 butt, 3/16 tip	4	3 9/16
	9/16	15/32 butt, 3/16 tip	5	4½
	5/8	9/16 butt, 3/16 tip	6	5½
	¾	11/16 butt, 3/16 tip	8	7¼
	1	¾ butt, 3/16 tip	10	9¼
			12	11¼
Bungalow Siding	¾	11/16 butt, 3/16 tip	8	7¼
			10	9¼
			12	11¼
Rustic and Drop Siding (shiplapped, 3/8-in. lap)	5/8	9/16	4	3 1/8
	1	23/32	5	4 1/16
			6	5 1/16
Rustic and Drop Siding (shiplapped, ½-in. lap)	5/8	9/16	4	3
	1	23/32	5	3 15/16
			6	4 15/16
			8	6 5/8
			10	8 5/8
			12	10 5/8
Rustic and Drop Siding (dressed and matched)	5/8	9/16	4	3¼
	1	23/32	5	4 3/16
			6	5 3/16
			8	6 7/8
			10	8 7/8

lumber

TABLE 3. Nominal and Minimum Dressed Sizes of Boards, Dimension, and Timbers.

ITEM	THICKNESSES			FACE WIDTHS		
	NOMINAL	MINIMUM DRESSED		NOMINAL	MINIMUM DRESSED	
		DRY	GREEN		DRY	GREEN
Boards	1 1¼ 1½	¾ 1 1¼	25/32 1 1/32 1 9/32	2 3 4 5 6 7 8 9 10 11 12 14 16	1½ 2 9/16 3 9/16 4½ 5½ 6½ 7½ 8½ 9½ 10½ 11½ 13½ 15½	1 9/16 2⅝ 3⅝ 4⅝ 5⅝ 6⅝ 7⅝ 8¾ 9¾ 10¾ 11¾ 13¾ 15¾
2 in. Dimension	2	1½	1 9/16	2 3 4 6 8 10 12 14 16	1½ 2 9/16 3 9/16 5½ 7½ 9½ 11½ 13½ 15½	1 9/16 2⅝ 3⅝ 5⅝ 7⅝ 9¾ 11¾ 13¾ 15¾
Dimension over 2 in. thick DRY OR GREEN	2½ 3 3½ 4		2⅛ 2⅝ 3⅛ 3⅝	3 4 6 8 10 12 14 16		2⅝ 3⅝ 5½ 7½ 9½ 11½ 13½ 15½
Timbers DRY OR GREEN	5 and thicker	½ off		5 and thicker	½ off	

lumber basics, continued

This man is grading lumber as it comes from the surfacing (planing) machine. This work calls for a trained eye and a knowledge of gradings

24 in. long also contains an equivalent volume of lumber, or 1 board foot. Likewise, a 2 x 4 12 ft. long contains 8 board feet.

Lumber is ordinarily graded into two main classifications, *select* and *common*. The select grade is sometimes referred to as clear, meaning it has few or no defects such as knots, checks or discolorations on at least one side of the board; any allowable defects on the opposite face can only be minor. None of these defects interfere in any way with use of the whole board in quality work. But the select grades in most of the common woods are also available in an order of decreasing quality and are designated as A, B, C and D. Many lumberyards combine the first two and refer to the grade as B and Better (B&Btr). If you specify this grade by symbol you'll generally get the best grade the dealer supplies. Some dealers in hardwoods supply a grade AA cut to specified lengths and widths and sold by the piece. Such stock is usu-

TABLE 4. Nominal and Minimum Dressed Sizes of (2-inch and under) Shiplap, Centermatch and D & M.

ITEM	THICKNESSES			FACE WIDTHS		
	NOMINAL	MINIMUM DRESSED DRY	MINIMUM DRESSED GREEN	NOMINAL	MINIMUM DRESSED DRY	MINIMUM DRESSED GREEN
	Inches	Inches	Inches	Inches	Inches	Inches
Shiplap 3/8-inch lap	1	3/4	25/32	4 6 8 10 12 14 16	3 1/8 5 1/16 7 9 11 13 15	3 3/16 5 3/16 7 1/8 9 1/4 11 1/4 13 1/4 15 1/4
Shiplap 1/2-inch lap	1	3/4	25/32	4 6 8 10 12 14 16	3 4 15/16 6 7/8 8 7/8 10 7/8 12 7/8 14 7/8	3 1/16 5 1/16 7 9 1/8 11 1/8 13 1/8 15 1/8
Centermatch 1/4-inch tongue	1 1 1/4 1 1/2	3/4 1 1 1/4	25/32 1 1/32 1 9/32	4 5 6 8 10 12	3 1/4 4 3/16 5 3/16 7 1/8 9 1/8 11 1/8	3 5/16 4 5/16 5 5/16 7 1/4 9 3/8 11 3/8
2" D & M 3/8-inch tongue	2	1 1/2	1 9/16	4 6 8 10 12	3 1/8 5 7 9 11	3 3/16 5 1/8 7 1/8 9 1/4 11 1/4

ally surfaced two sides (S2S) and comes clear with only very minor blemishes permissible on one side.

Common lumber has defects or blemishes that make it unsuited to any job where the project requires a high-grade finish on the exposed parts. However, allowable defects are such that they do not make the materials unsuitable for use as secondary (hidden) parts or as construction parts.

Common lumber is usually graded by number, 1, 2, and 3 being the standard gradings. Some species take gradings of 4 and 5, but are less commonly available. Of the first three No. 1 is, of course, the highest. Numbers 1 and 2 can be used in all suitable applications with no waste. But grade 3, also 4 and 5, usually must be cut to eliminate flaws such as loose knots and checks that would greatly weaken the piece for any use where appreciable stress is present.

Otherwise you should order the select grade for any inside work that requires staining and finishing or finishing in the natural color. The lower grades of select stock will usually be suitable for a paint or enamel finish after assembling and sanding the parts smooth. An opaque finish can usually be depended on to conceal minor surface defects (after filling) and any discolorations that turn up on exposed parts. Quite naturally these rules do not apply when you select woods with normal surface defects, such as knotty pine or wormy cypress, where what are commonly regarded as blemishes in standard gradings are to be exposed and even emphasized with a clear finish, or a stain finish in a light color.

Dimension lumber usually comes in only three grades, 1, 2 and 3. If for example you need a 2 x 4 to use in an exposed location where appearance is of first importance you should ask your dealer for No. 1. This piece will come to you clear and reasonably straight throughout its length.

A point to be kept in mind by the do-it-yourself lumber buyer is that some "softwoods" are actually classed as hardwoods. These are cut from broad-leaved (deciduous) trees and for this reason are classified as hard rather than

lumber

Lumber in a yard neatly stacked for air drying. Notice how each board is stacked with spaced separators to allow free circulation of air

TABLE 5. Worked Lumber, Such as Factory Flooring, Heavy Roofing Decking, and Sheet Piling.
(The thicknesses apply to all widths and all widths to all thicknesses.)
SEE "Note"

THICKNESSES[1]		FACE WIDTHS	
NOMINAL	MINIMUM DRESSED (DRY OR GREEN)	NOMINAL	MINIMUM DRESSED (DRY OR GREEN)
Inches	Inches	Inches	Inches
TONGUE AND GROOVED			
2½	2⅛	4	3⅛
3	2⅝	6	5⅛
3½	3⅛	8	7
4	3⅝	10	9
5	4⅝	12	11
SHIPLAP			
2½	2⅛	4	3
3	2⅝	6	5
3½	3⅛	8	7
4	3⅝	10	9
5	4⅝	12	11
GROOVED-FOR-SPLINES			
2½	2⅛	4	3½
3	2⅝	6	5½
3½	3⅛	8	7½
4	3⅝	10	9½
5	4⅝	12	11½

NOTE: In worked lumber of nominal thicknesses of 2 inch and over, the tongue shall be ⅜ inch wide in tongued-and-grooved lumber and the lap ½ inch wide in shiplapped lumber, with the overall widths ⅜ inch and ½ inch wider, respectively, than the face widths shown in the above table. Double tongued-and-grooved decking may be manufactured with a 5⁄16 inch tongue and double T & G nominal 4 inch thick may be surfaced 3½ inches thick.

[1] See Table 3 for information on 2 inch dimension.

softwoods. A good example is basswood, a fairly common wood of very close grain and fine texture especially suited to paint and enamel finishes. It has many of the characteristics of clear white pine and is just as easily worked with hand or power tools.

Still another point for do-it-yourselfers to remember: don't look for two or more boards of any common lumber exactly alike, or even nearly alike in texture or grain. You'll never find 'em. No two boards cut from the same tree or from any number of trees of the same species are ever precisely alike in surface detail, graining or color.

So when your project calls for parts of similar color and grain pattern, knot pattern, or whatever, that's what you specify or look for when your lumber dealer permits you to select from his stock—boards of *similar* color and grain pattern. These you can usually find just by looking over a relatively few pieces in the lumber rack.

Most lumber dealers will make up a special selection for you at a nominal extra charge. Just be sure to make it clear what you want.

See also: building; framing; home additions; measurements; nails; plywood; sheathing; siding.

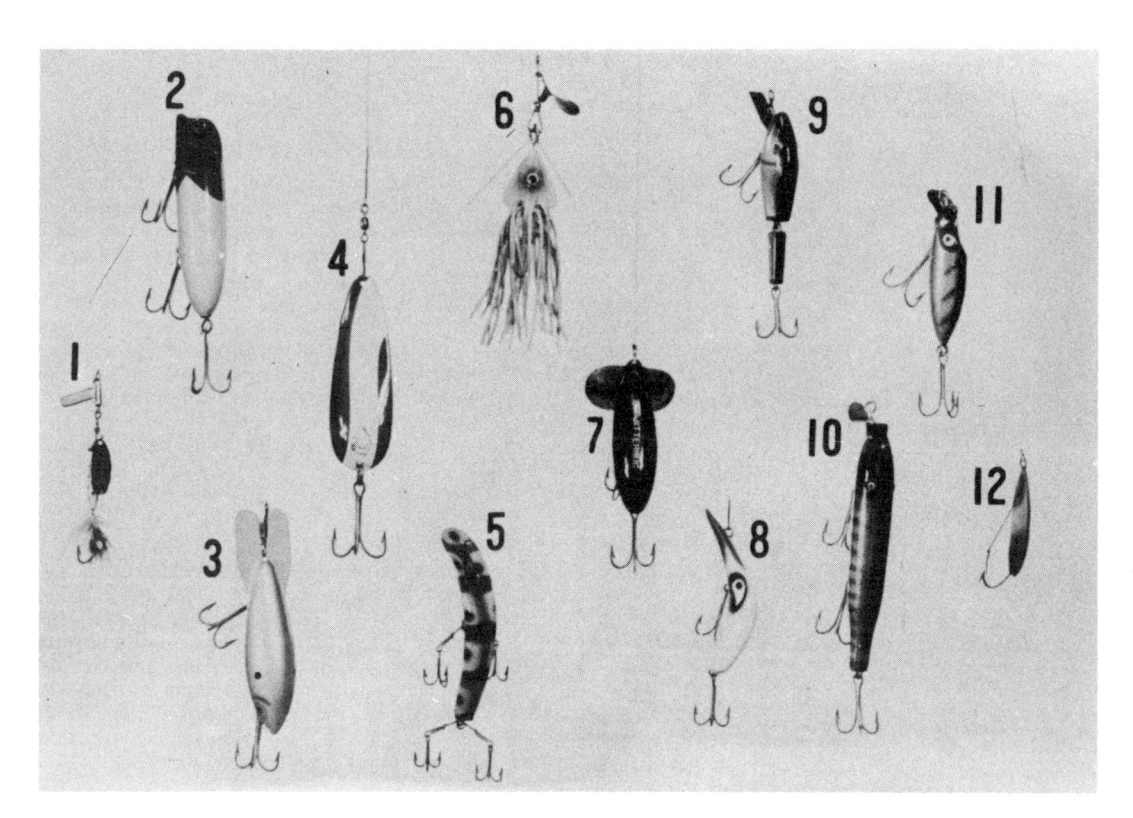

Experts pick fishing's deadly dozen lures

BY DICK KIRKPATRICK

Fishing lures come and go but a few—the great ones—go on forever. We polled a panel of experts to assemble our list of all-time greats, and learned at the same time that most fishermen don't fish the lures right—and won't read the instructions on the box

1. THE ABU REFLEX SPINNER is the newest lure on the list at 5 yrs. old, and the only import. It comes from Sweden through the Garcia Corp. of New York City. The ¼-oz. model shown, with a chrome blade and white body with black spots, is the most popular Seven other models in 10 other combinations. The weedless-hook model shown is a good idea, since spinners are notorious snag-finders. The keel ahead of this lure isn't standard equipment, but helps avoid line twist, though later Abus have a new nontwist eye. Best tip: Fish the Abu just fast enough to keep the blade spinning, and use the "slow roll" method illustrated to cover all depths until you find the fish, then control depth with reeling speed.

2. THE BASS-ORENO is the oldest (60 years) and probably best-known of those listed. It is now made by South Bend Tackle Co., of Chicago, in four sizes from ⅝ to ¼ oz. and in seven finishes. But the original size and style shown—a ⅝-oz. bait-casting size with a red head and white body—is still considered best. Designed as a floating-diving wiggler for bass and northern pike, the lure is still at its best for those species, but has spread to all kinds of shallow-feeding game fish; it's even trolled in the Gulf Stream for big pelagic species. Best tip: By using a reel-pause retrieve, you can make the Bass-Oreno dive and bob near the surface to imitate a struggling, injured baitfish.

lures

3. THE BOMBER, made by The Bomber Bait Co. of Gainesville, Texas, was designed for a specific type of fishing—bottom bouncing down the precipitous dropoffs in southern artificial lakes for smallmouth bass and walleyes. But it has become the hottest thing in deep fishing everywhere. The big ¾-oz. silver-white shad model shown has been most popular, but the line offers 5 sizes in 33 finishes. All but the ¼-oz. spinning size are deep-diving floaters; they dive so sharply that you can reel them under your own boat. Best tip: Bounce the Bomber down slopes as illustrated with a reel-pause retrieve. The diving bill protects the hooks from snags.

4. THE DARDEVLE, made by the Lou J. Eppinger Co., Dearborn, Mich., was the first metal spoon to be designed for casting as well as a fish-catching action, and is indisputably the most imitated lure in the business. It has a reputation for outfishing most spoons. Most popular model in its 50-year history is the familiar red-and-white 1-oz. style with nickel plating on the inside, but there are 22 other sizes and styles in 35 finishes. Best trick is built right into the lure—it can be fished in a variety of ways to get different actions. Three are illustrated; a fast skittering retrieve on the surface, a reel-and-pause retrieve, and a jigging action near the bottom.

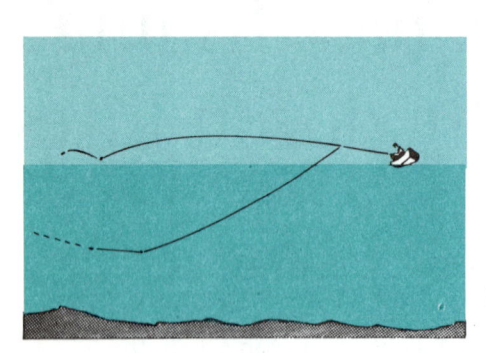

5. THE FLATFISH, developed in 1933 by the Helin Tackle Company of Detroit, is perhaps the most unlikely looking of lures—but probably the biggest seller. Its wild wobbling action is unmatched anywhere; its tiny hooks on spreader bars make it a fine hooker. And almost everyone fishes it wrong. The Flatfish should *never* be fished with a snap between lure and line, and should *always* be fished with a weight about a foot ahead of the lure. It makes casting tricky—unless you learn to stop the cast and let the line straighten out as illustrated. We show the "U-20" model in a green-frog finish; it's probably the most popular, but there are 21 models in all.

6. THE HAWAIIAN WIGGLER, made by the Fred Arbogast Co., of Akron, Ohio, was one of the first really weedless lures made to be fished right in the weeds for shallow-feeding bass and pike. The combination of spinner, wobbling body, and wiggling skirt has kept it popular—and effective—for around 30 years. The Number Two Wiggler, shown, isn't the oldest, but is the most popular in this ⅝ oz. size with a red and green body and black and white "hula skirt." There are 10 other models in six finishes. Best trick: A second hook, trailing behind the main hook, for short-striking fish; the manufacturer supplies a special add-on hook with each lure.

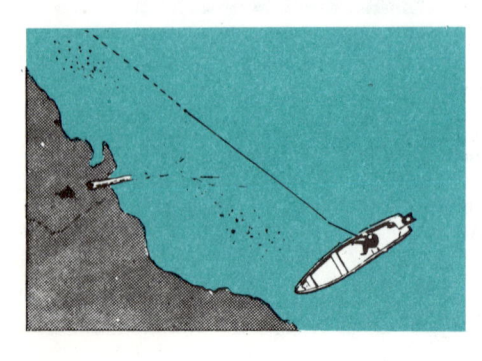

7. THE JITTERBUG, also made by the Arbogast Company, is a double-purpose surface lure. The Jitterbug is intended for a slow, steady, crawling retrieve, but also works well as a surface popper. Most popular model with our experts is the ⅝-oz. black model shown; it's also available in 4 other sizes in 9 finishes. It's been a top-selling surface lure for over 15 years; our experts agree it's because it doesn't require the poppers' maddening wait after the cast, before the retrieve. Best trick: Fish it along weeds *parallel* to shore to keep it in productive water through the entire retrieve. Reel about 3 ft., pause for a few seconds, then reel again.

8. THE LAZY IKE, made by Lazy Ike Corp., of Fort Dodge, Iowa, was developed by the Kautzky Sporting Goods Co. in the early 40's. It's a "sharp" wiggler with an unusual capacity for working at any speed, which became quickly popular with Minnesota trollers, especially for walleye, and spread from there. Most popular size and finish has been the ⅜-oz. red and white model shown, but similar models come in 7 sizes and 12 finishes, plus a good-looking new line of 9 metallic finishes. Two good tips: *Always* fish the Lazy Ikes with a metal snap between the line and lure, and try a worm or a plastic imitation on the rear hook to encourage slow strikers.

9. THE L & S MIRROLURES, made by the L & S Bait Co., of Bradley, Ill., were the first to use the reflective qualities of metallic materials inside clear plastic, and have been very popular, especially in their jointed-minnow models like the ½-oz., black-white-and-silver scale model shown. Their excellent built-in action imitates a live minnow with surprising realism; the slow-sinking plug can be adapted to many retrieving speeds simply by bending the diving lip—forward for a shallow, fast wiggle; back for a slower, deeper action. With the bottom barb taken off both hooks, the lure can be made to crawl along the bottom like a feeding minnow.

10. THE PIKIE MINNOW, made by The Creek Chub Bait Co., of Garrett, Indiana, is another old-timer; it was developed from a customer's suggestion 50 yrs. ago. Its slow, wobbling action was designed for the big northern species—bass, pike, muskies and lake trout, and it holds the world record for largemouth bass and muskies. The ¾-oz. straight-body floater, in the familiar "pike" scale finish, leads the line, but the lure is also made in a dozen other sizes from ⅛ oz. to 4 oz. and 17 finishes. Best tip: One nationally-famous muskie fisherman gets his big ones by trolling a jointed Pikie Minnow as fast and deep as possible—at night!

11. THE RIVER RUNT, made by James Heddon's Sons, Dowagiac, Michigan, was developed from the Heddon Vamp Spook, the first plastic lure. Basically a sinking fast wobbler, it also comes in 9 other styles, including floating and deep-diving models, from ¼ to ⅝ oz., in 8 finishes. The ⅜-oz. Midget River Runt is the most popular size; red and white, yellow, and the perch scale (shown) the most popular finishes. Best tip: Mass-produced lures (of any brand) vary a bit from lure to lure in effective retrieving speed. Since the most violent wobble is most effective, Heddon recommends testing each lure's action to make sure you're retrieving at that speed.

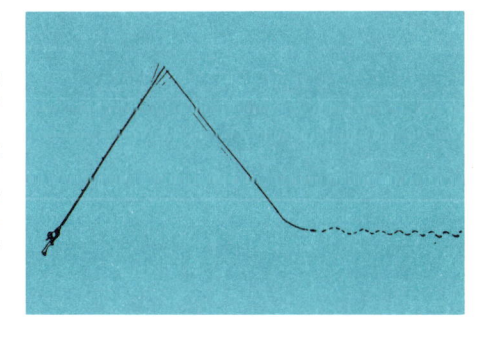

12. THE SILVER MINNOW, made by Lions Johnson Company of Highland Park, Ill., was the source of the old story of the fisherman who made lures from his wife's teaspoons until she caught him at it and forced him to forge his own. The little spoon is probably the most weedless lure on the market, and the best hooker among guarded-hook models. The lure is made in six sizes, from 1/24 oz. to 1⅛ oz., and in 9 finishes. By far the most popular is the ½ and ¼-oz. silver-plated model. Best fished with a bass-sized pork rind strip, the Silver Minnow is becoming popular in the South with a 4 or 6-in. plastic worm trailer, fished slow and deep.

See also: bait, fishing; bass fishing; fishing; fly-casting; ice fishing; trolling motor.

1663

clever ideas

If you have to replace your garden hose this year, don't throw it away—it may still be good enough to make this spray hoop for the kids. Select a length of hose with a female coupling on one end and drill 1/8-in. holes at 3 or 4-in. intervals along one side of this hose. Plug the cut end with a cork and coil the hose on the ground to form one large circle with the holes on the inside surface. Drive two stakes into the ground, the distance apart depending on the size of your hoop, and mount the hoop on these stakes using twine or tape. Then connect the hoop to your garden hose, turn on the water and stand clear!

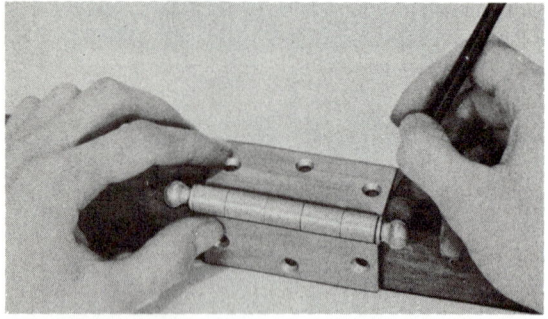

What can you use in a pinch for a try square? Probably a number of things, but one man found that a butt hinge works perfectly for marking small stock. Folded as shown, one leaf of the hinge serves to hold the other leaf square with the edge of the work as it is moved along like a regular square.

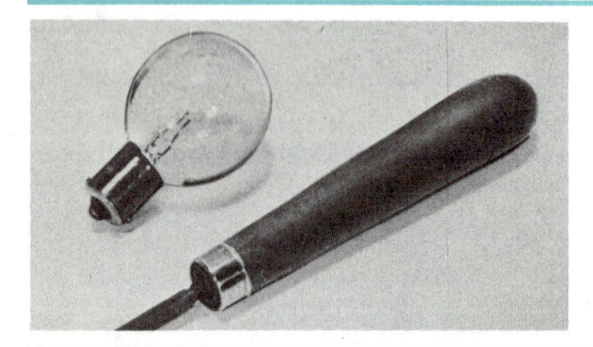

Don't toss away all your used flash bulbs. Save a few. The bases make neat ready-made ferrules for file and other tool handles. Simply file off the two socket pins after removing the glass and drill a hole in the end to suit the tool. Press the base over the end of the handle and polish with fine steel wool. Dimpling the ferrule will hold it secure.

When it comes to ruling equally spaced lines, both horizontally and vertically, cloth-tape measures glued to one side and across the top of a drawing board will make the work go twice as fast. The T-square is merely aligned with the tape calibrations to make it far more convenient than first marking off the lines with dividers or a regular ruler.

1664

machine gun, toy

Machine gun "fires" water bursts

BY THOMAS SIKES

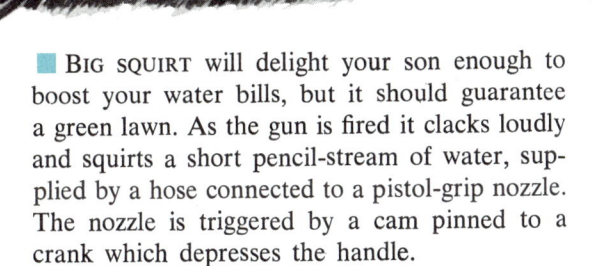

■ BIG SQUIRT will delight your son enough to boost your water bills, but it should guarantee a green lawn. As the gun is fired it clacks loudly and squirts a short pencil-stream of water, supplied by a hose connected to a pistol-grip nozzle. The nozzle is triggered by a cam pinned to a crank which depresses the handle.

The hole locations and the dimensions of the housing may have to be varied slightly to suit the nozzle. The end of the nozzle requires a bit of modification; the flared portion must be cut off and the end of the nozzle tapered with a file so the conduit barrel can be forced over it. The same cut will also remove the valve's cone shaped tip.

A key part of the gun is the 3/32-in. tubing, the end of which is tapered and forced into the nozzle. The tubing's small inside diameter narrows the wide spray into forceful bursts of "fire" that travel a surprisingly long distance.

See also: cannons, toy; children's furniture; duplicator; games, children's; magic shovel, power, toy; toys.

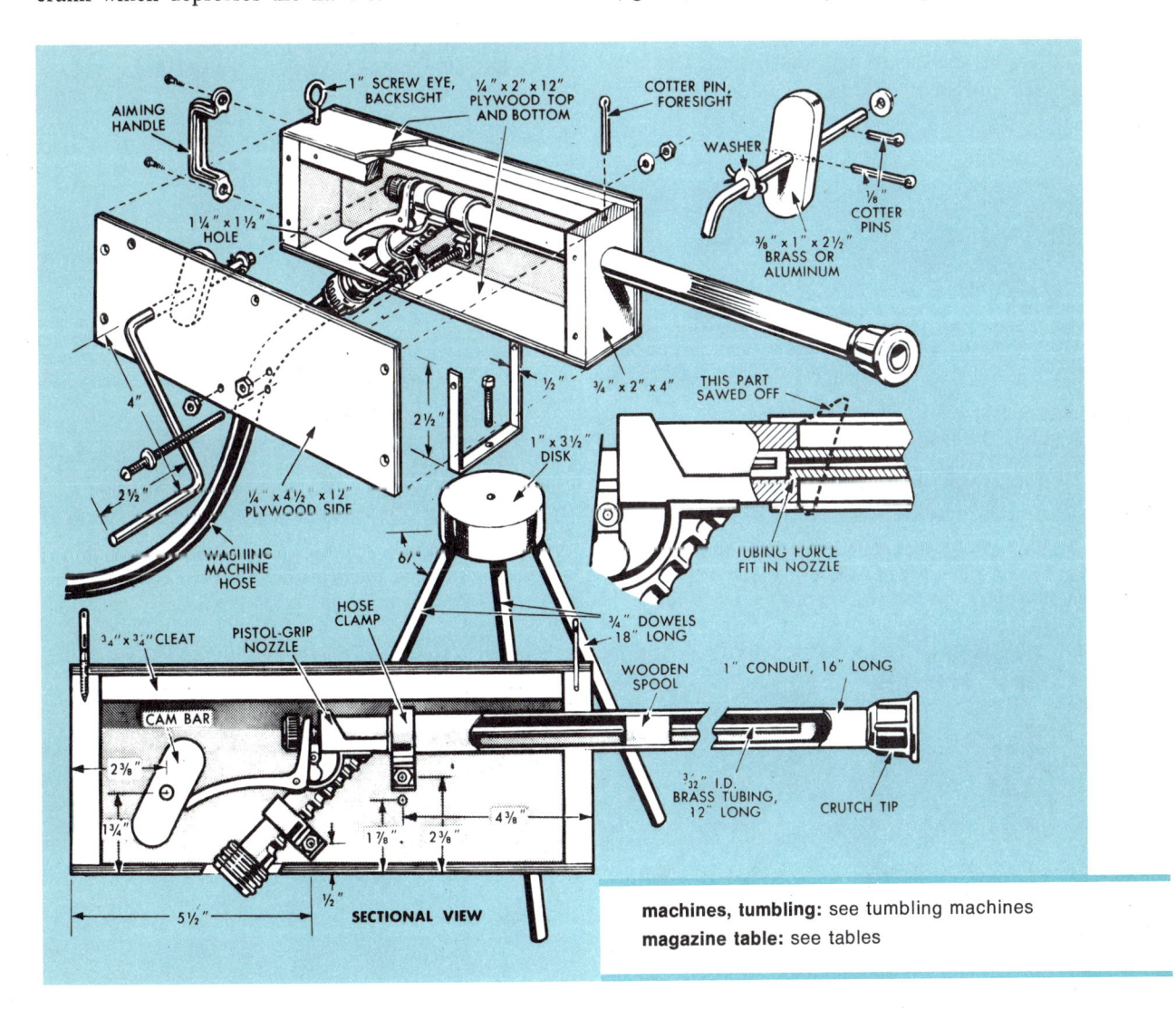

machines, tumbling: see tumbling machines
magazine table: see tables

1665

magic

"Squozen" sponges come to life

BY THOMAS C. THOMAS

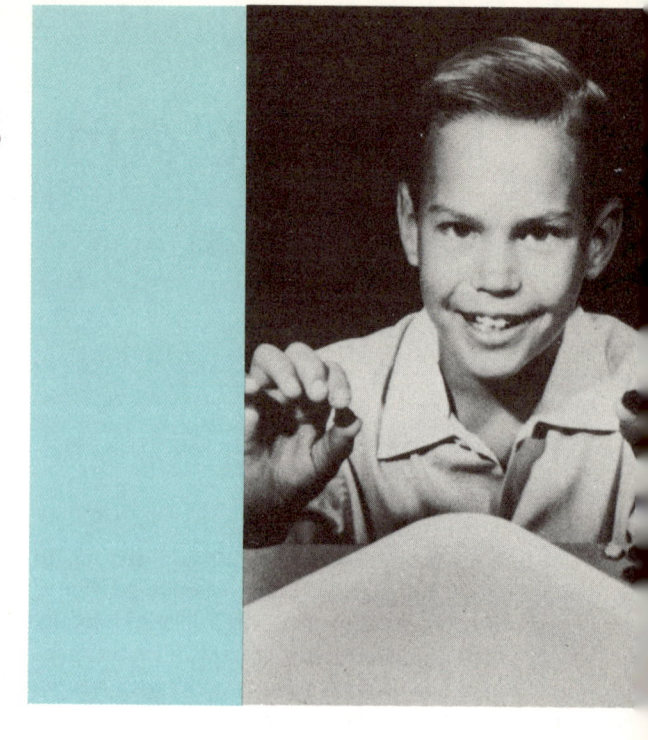

■ WATCHING THESE MAGIC seeds and snake pills come to life holds a curious fascination for both young and old.

What appears to be a tiny inanimate seed wiggling and squirming in water, growing larger and larger by the second and finally stretching out to many times its former size, is simply a highly compressed piece of sponge.

The accompanying picture sequence tells the story. The important thing is that you use only a fine-grain cellulose sponge. Such sponges are readily available at most any local photo shop, and the larger the sponge the better. The compressed pills are "frozen" in compressed form by baking at low heat in the kitchen oven until they are as hard as stones.

See also: games, children's; parade floats; puppet theaters; puzzle; toys.

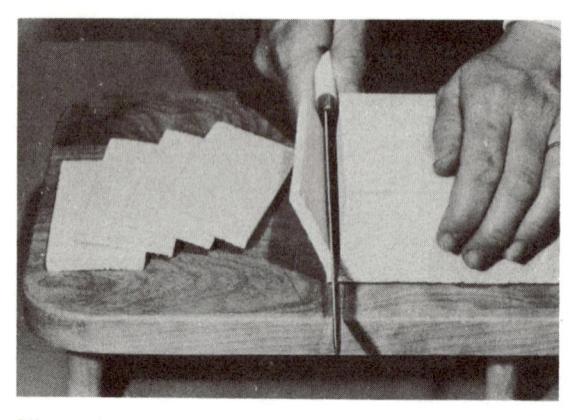

Slices of sponge should be about ¼ in. thick and can be cut with a bread knife or fine-tooth saw. As for the silhouettes (below), shapes are up to you

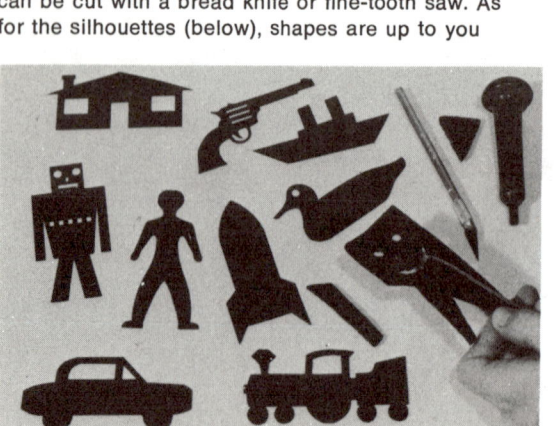

For extra drama, dye the sponge with Rit dye before slicing after the sponge is dry. Bind the compressed sponge with turns of the thread (below)

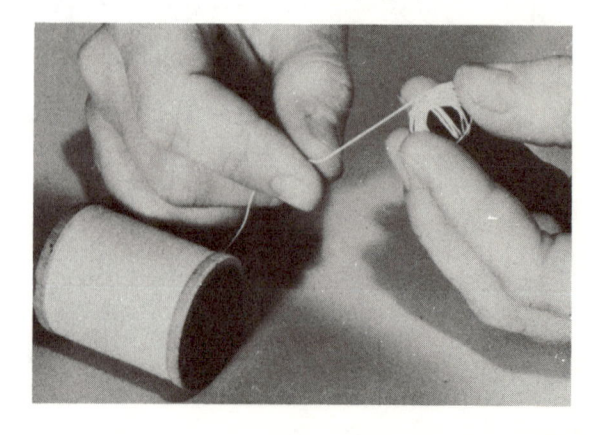

1666

Two little pills dropped in water... HOLY MACKEREL!

Snake pills are easier to make than silhouette ones. After the block of moistened sponge is compressed and dried, punch out pills with paper punch (below)

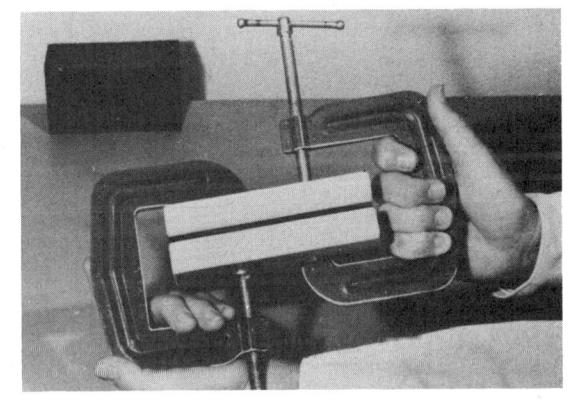

The moistened block of sponge is compressed by clamping between wood blocks until ¼ in. thick. The snakes are resqueezed with a clothespin for reuse

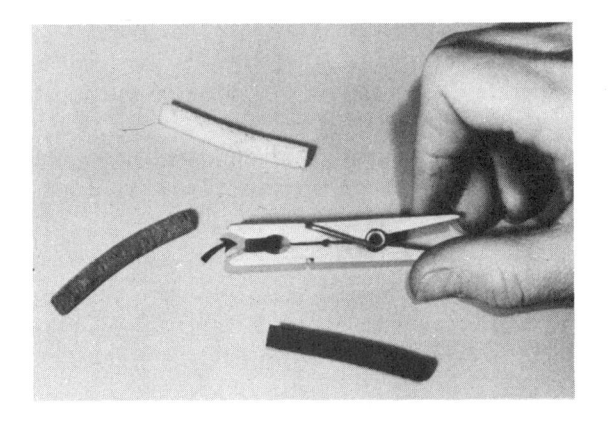

1667

magic

There's magic in these tricks

BY BYRON G. WELS

It's not difficult to master these magic tricks. All you have to do is follow the instructions and keep up a steady "patter" to distract the audience

■ MAGIC! THE WORD has an exciting ring to it, for everybody enjoys the fun of fooling, being fooled and trying to outguess the magician. It's easy to master the mechanics of these tricks, the difficult part is convincing people that you really *are* a magician. Obviously, the boy wearing everyday clothes is an everyday boy, not a magician. But put him in a turban or a top hat and ... well, *there's* a magician.

Remember that an important ingredient in any magic act is "patter," a steady flow of words

magnetic catches: see hardware
magnetic pickup: see preamplifier, stereo
magnetized toy: see toys

1668

to distract the audience. Misleading actions also play a big part. Wave a handkerchief high in the air while shouting "Look!" and you can slip the (supposedly) disappearing object into your pocket without the audience ever noticing.

MAGIC WINE GLASS For this humorous trick you'll need a straight-sided drinking glass with the bottom removed and a thin-walled clear plastic tumbler large enough to hold the bottomless glass. Borrow a hat from the audience, place it brim-up on the table and put the nested glasses inside. Pretend that you are about to pour wine (colored water) into the glass inside the hat, then hesitate and explain that you can't seem to remember the trick, but you think that the glass belongs outside the hat. Slip the bottomless glass out of the plastic tumbler, place it on the table, and pour the liquid into the supposedly empty hat. Next, glance down into the hat, act embarrassed and mutter something about a "mistake." Then brighten up, put the bottomless glass back in the hat (slipping it inside the full tumbler), make a few passes with the wand and lift the full glass(es) out of the hat. Finally, hold up the hat to show that it's empty.

YOUR MAGIC WAND Here are a couple

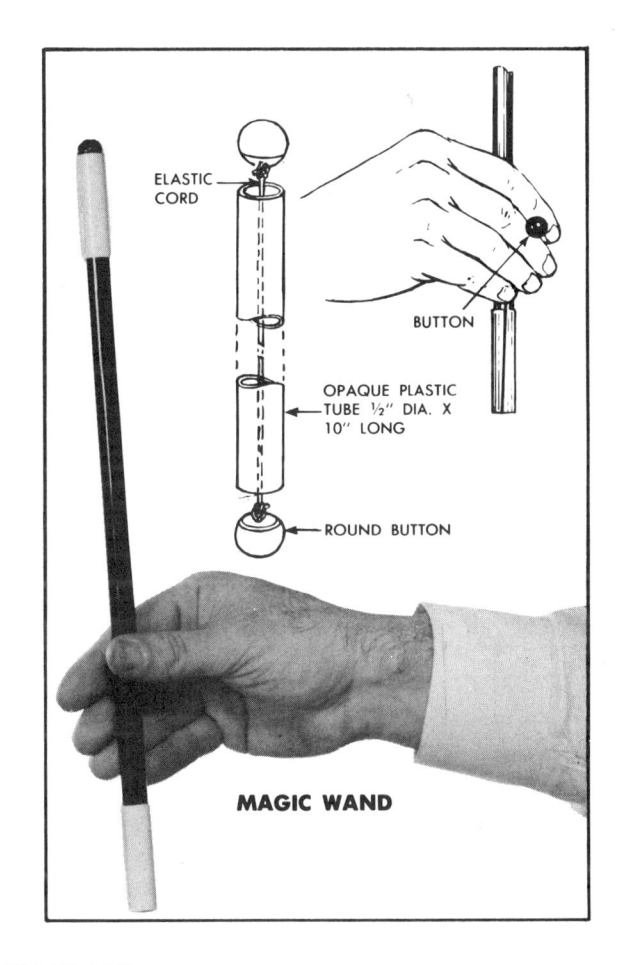

MAGIC WAND

MAGIC WINE GLASS

magic

ELBOW PUMP

magic tricks, continued

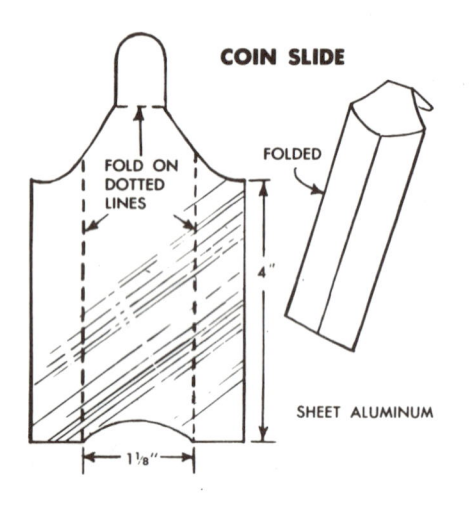

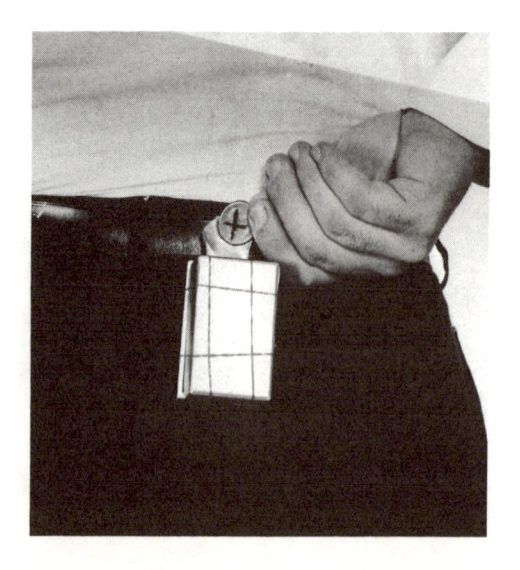

COIN SLIDE

FOLD ON DOTTED LINES
FOLDED
4"
SHEET ALUMINUM
1⅛"

of quick tricks in which the wand itself is the apparatus. Offer to allow a member of the audience to do the next trick, but as you hand him the wand make it jump away from him, toward you. Then explain that you will have to do the trick yourself, as the wand doesn't want to work for him. Or you can roll the wand up in a newspaper, tear the paper to shreds, toss the pieces into the air and the wand will have vanished.

The trick wand is a hollow plastic tube fitted with a button at each end. The two buttons are connected by a rubber band running through the tube. To make the wand jump, hold one of the buttons between your fingers, pull the wand to stretch the rubber and grasp the body of the wand with thumb and forefinger of the same hand. Release the thumb pressure and the wand will move.

For the newspaper trick, pin one button inside the sleeve of your jacket and stretch the rubber band so that you are holding the base of the wand. When you release it the wand will jump back into your sleeve.

ELBOW PUMP People always watch the magician closely, so when you can fool the victim of your trick, you have really accomplished something.

Call for a volunteer and ask him to roll up his sleeve. Examine his arm and exclaim, "Why you poor man! You have water-on-the-elbow." Then grasp his elbow with one hand, hold his wrist with the other and work his forearm like a pump handle. A steady stream of water will spurt from his elbow.

The secret is a small rubber sponge, filled almost to capacity with warm water. Conceal this loaded sponge in your palm and press it against the elbow to make the water flow.

COIN SLIDE The magician borrows a coin from a member of the audience and asks that it be marked in such a way that it can be identified later. A soft lead pencil works well for such marking. Quickly, the magician puts his hand behind his back and brings out a small box bound with rubber bands. The marked coin is no longer in sight.

The magician gives the box to the volunteer and directs him to remove the rubber bands. Inside, he finds a smaller matchbox, also bound with rubber bands. Upon removing these rubber bands and opening the matchbox, he discovers a small cloth pouch securely sealed with another

CAP
KNOT
TASSEL

CHINESE STICKS
(MAKE 2)

PLASTIC TUBE
½" DIA. x 8" LONG

CORD

LEAD WEIGHT

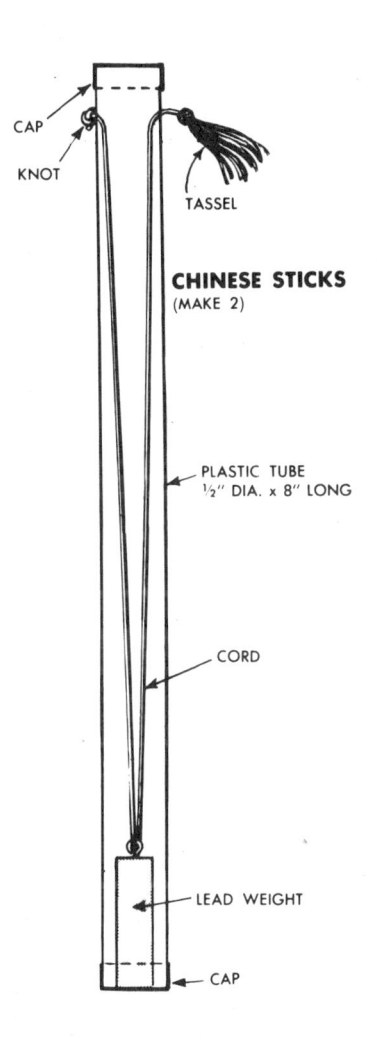

CAP

rubber band. When he opens this pouch, there is the marked coin!

The secret of this trick is a special coin slide made from sheet aluminum. The top of the slide is bent to form a hook. Prepare this trick by placing the straight end of the slide inside the small pouch, and secure the pouch to the slide with a tight rubber band. Next, place the pouch and straight portion of slide in the matchbox and bind with more bands. Don't worry about the box not being fully closed, as the bands will snap it shut when the slide is removed. Place the matchbox inside the last box, and bind it shut. Then suspend the box-slide unit from your belt by the hook. When you receive the marked coin, drop it into the top of the slide and in the same motion pull the box from the slide. The slide will remain suspended from your belt concealed by your coat.

CHINESE STICKS The magician displays a pair of parallel sticks, each with a tassel dangling from one end. As he pulls on one tassel, the other one rises. Then he separates the tasseled

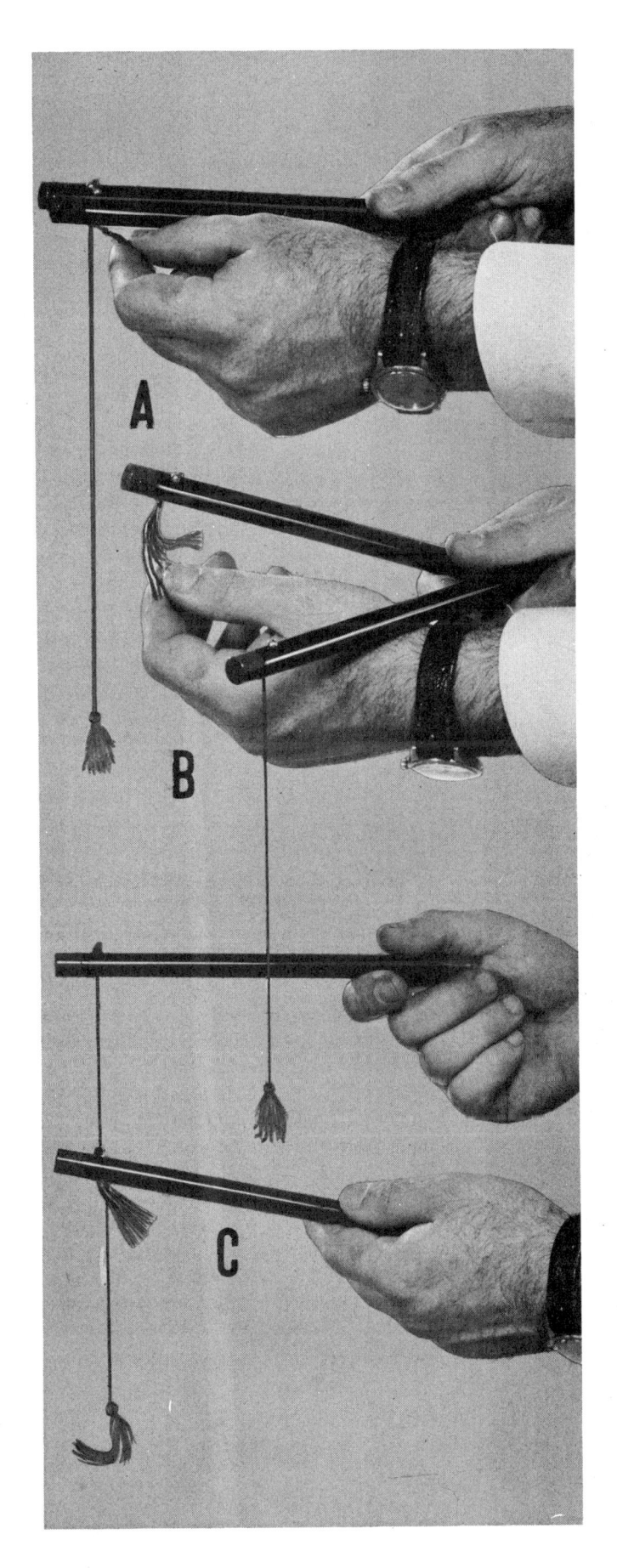

1671

SPIRIT SLATE

ends of the sticks and repeats the tassel-pulling routine. The audience suspects that the string runs through the rear ends of the sticks, and shouts, "Separate the sticks," but the magician pretends to misunderstand and separates the tasseled ends still more. When the audience shouts again, he suddenly appears to understand their meaning and places one stick in his mouth to show that there is no string connecting the two. He pulls the tassel dangling from the stick in his hand, and the other tassel rises!

The sticks are constructed from plastic tubing about ½ in. in diameter, and the movement of the tassels is controlled by small lead weights inside the sticks.

SPIRIT SLATES The magician shows sides of a pair of blank slates, then places them one upon the other and binds them together with a rubber band. After putting the slates on a table and covering them with a handkerchief, he walks out into the audience with a pad and pencil. He then asks a volunteer to write a three-digit number at the top of the pad, moves on to an-

DISAPPEARING QUARTER

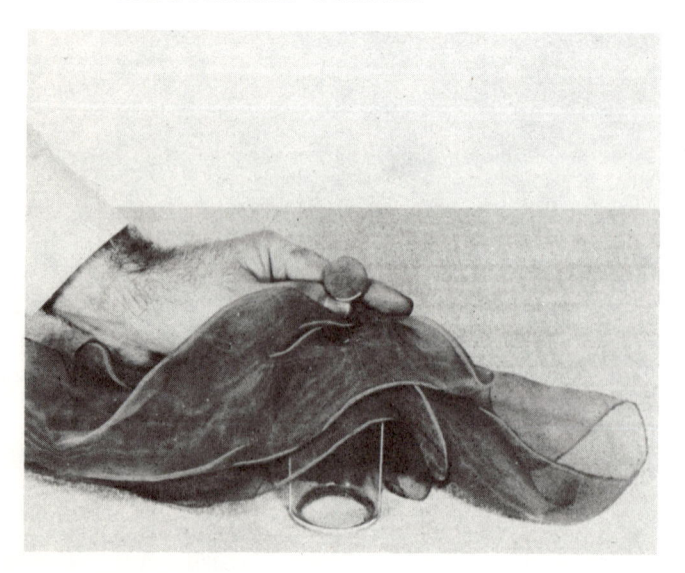

other person who writes a second number under the first and to a third who adds another number. The magician draws a line under the last number and gives the pad to a fourth volunteer who adds up the numbers. When he has arrived at the sum of the three numbers, he calls it out so that the audience can hear it. The magician then returns to the stage, uncovers the slates, removes the rubber band and there, written for all to see, is the total just given.

To prepare the trick, write three three-digit numbers in a column on the pad. Find the total of these numbers and write this number on one of the slates. Now turn over the pad and remove the cardboard backing.

Prepare a piece of black cardboard or poster board to fit inside the frame of the slates. This cardboard covers the number and looks like a part of the slate. Thus, when you show the slates the first time, they appear to be blank. When you unwrap them, tap the back of the numbered slate so the cardboard drops to blank slate.

When you ask volunteers to write numbers on the pad, they will write on the blank side. However, when you recover the pad, draw the line under the numbers *on the other side.*

DISAPPEARING QUARTER Again, the magician borrows a quarter from the audience. He covers the coin with a handkerchief, pulling the kerchief tight so that the audience clearly sees the outline of the coin. Then, holding the handkerchief over the mouth of a glass, he releases the coin and the audience hears a "clink" as it drops into the glass. But when the handkerchief is removed, the coin has vanished!

Actually, the magician substitutes a glass disk the size of a quarter, and slips the quarter into his pocket while the audience is looking at the handkerchief. The disk, which is invisible, drops into the tumbler as the audience is looking for a coin. The flat lens from a small flashlight is an ideal substitute for the quarter in this trick.

magnetos, outboard

Magneto how-to for outboarders

BY HENRY B. NOTROM

To keep your outboard motor running smooth as silk, you should get acquainted with this simple device that puts the spark in sparkplugs

A tester can locate nearly any magneto problem, but lots of jobs are possible without one

■ TELL AN OUTBOARD OWNER that he can do his own ignition trouble-shooting, and he'll look at you as if you'd suggested that he ride shotgun on a space capsule. It's the one part of the engine that causes the staunchest do-it-yourselfer to cringe.

And yet the most common ignition troubles—sparkplug failure and breaker-point breakdown—can usually be handled by the owner himself, if he knows something about the system.

Most small and medium-size outboard engines contain a miniature generating plant called a magneto. Basically, it's nothing more than a magnet that emits a magnetic force, as all magnets do. But this force isn't even strong enough

magnetos, outboard

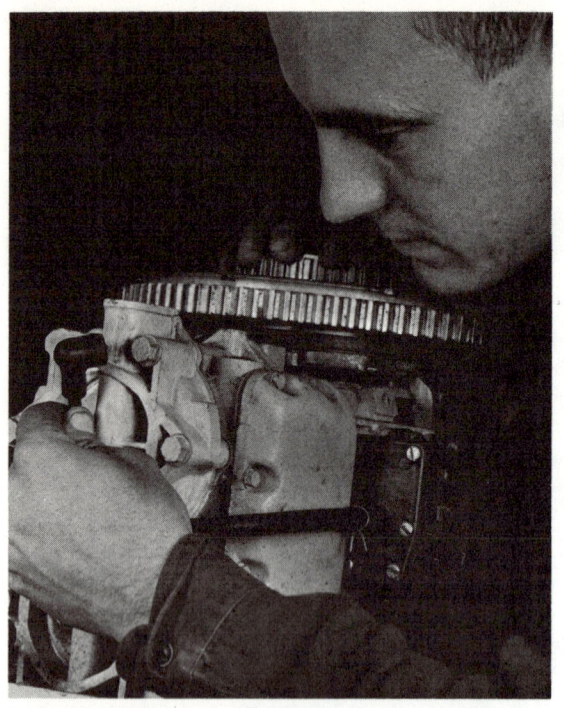

A simple test to verify whether you have magneto trouble involves pulling a plug lead to check spark

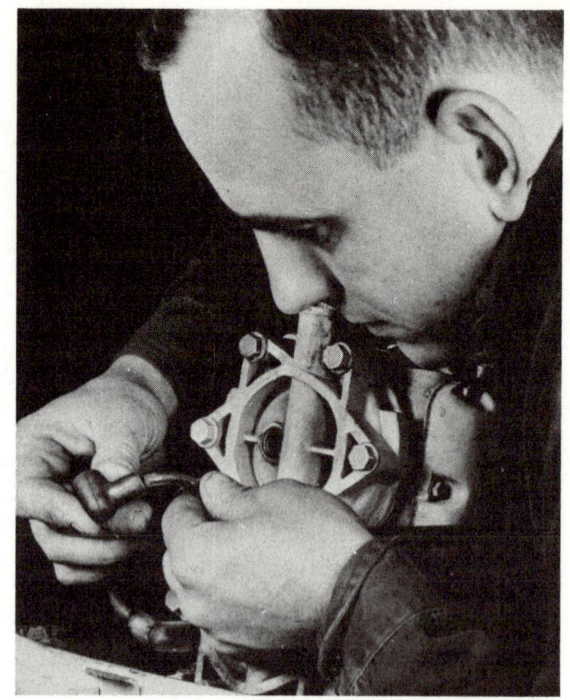

Cracks in the rubber plug boots mean the spark plugs aren't being given the proper protection

magneto how-to, continued

to tickle a baby, let alone ignite fuel. So it's got to be stepped up into something "hot."

This is accomplished by embedding the magnet in the flywheel. As the flywheel rotates on the crankshaft, the magnet passes over a core laminated from sheets of soft metal. Now, instead of traveling through the air from one pole of the magnet to the other, the force passes into the laminations, since they offer less resistance than the air.

The laminations, in turn, are hooked into the coil, which is really two coils, one inside the other. The inner (primary) coil has comparatively few turns of heavy wire. The outer (secondary) coil has a great many more turns of fine wire. As long as the primary circuit is unbroken, the relatively powerless magnetic force flows through and out the circuit. But when this circuit is broken, the force collapses abruptly across the secondary circuit. This induces a current in the secondary coil of a much higher voltage because of the many more turns of finer wire.

Interruption of the magnetic force at the right time is handled by a set of spring loaded breaker points connected into the primary circuit. When the magnetic force in the primary reaches its peak, a cam on the crankshaft forces the points apart, collapsing the magnetic field and producing the current in the secondary—current that's powerful enough to break down the air resistance of the sparkplug and allow a strong spark to jump the gap.

The remaining part in the magneto setup—the condenser—comes into action when the points open to absorb surges of current which otherwise would arc across the open points and ruin them.

Now, suppose the engine's hard to start or doesn't start at all. It could be a fouled-up mag, but it could also be a fuel problem or other internal trouble. To rule out the magneto, remove a sparkplug wire and hold its terminal 3/16 in. away from a ground, such as a bolt on the powerhead. (Be sure to hold the wire by the boot or insulation. The surge can't kill you if you grab it in the wrong spot, but it will be more than a little stimulating.) Crank the engine and look for a spark to jump the gap between terminal and ground. In bright light you may not see a spark, but you should hear a sharp crackle. No spark or crackle? You've got a magneto problem.

Mag troubles can also cause an engine to miss and lose pep at higher speeds. So, with the engine running this time, remove the lead wire,

1674

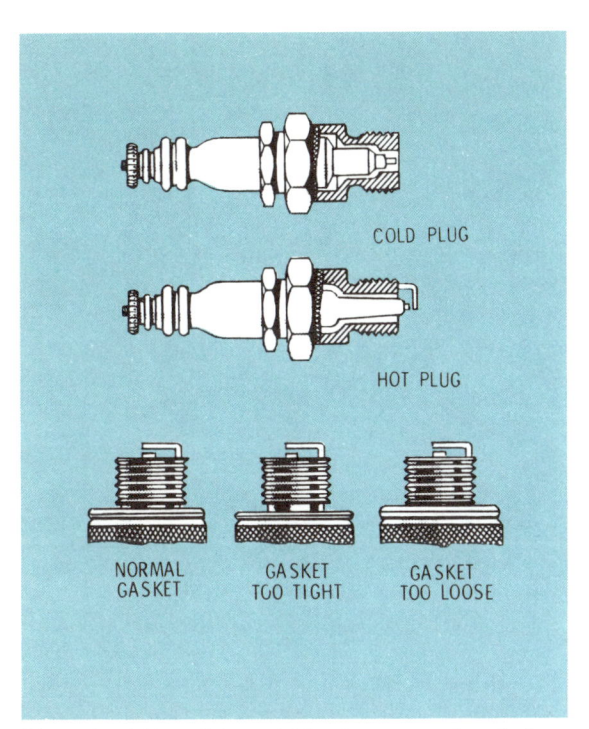

Plugs should be of the right heat range and gaskets should be compressed only enough for a good seal

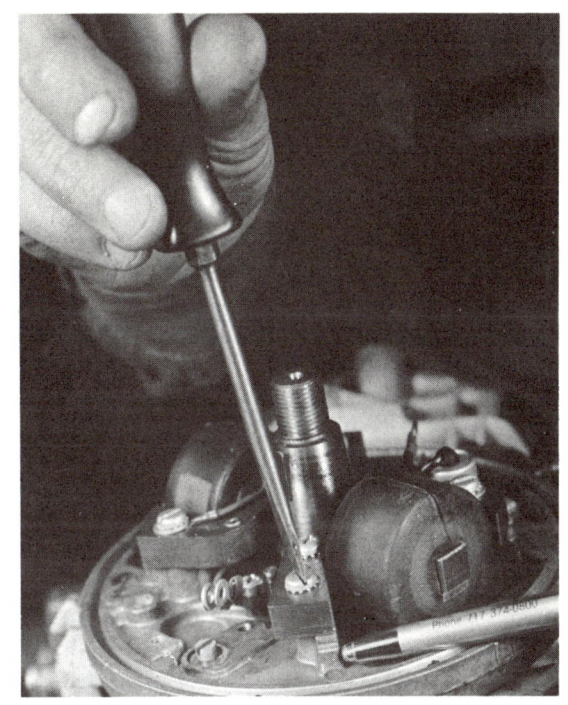

Check the magnet for streaks that warn the core laminations are probably out of line and scraping

hold its terminal 3/16 in. away from the plug terminal and rev the engine for an instant. Snap, crackle or spark? You're okay.

Be careful in doing this test. It puts a terrific strain on the coil and could ruin a perfectly good one if you overdo it. Hold that lead no further away from the plug than 3/16 in. and make the trial only for an instant.

Suppose you get spark or crackle. Does this mean the *entire* ignition system's in good shape? Not by a long shot.

If points aren't to be replaced, clean them well; a little dirt can cause a surprising amount of trouble

It means the mag's okay, but don't overlook that one part of an ignition system which most people take for granted and which, without doubt, causes the most trouble—the sparkplugs.

Every outboard manufacturer stresses that burned, fouled or damaged plugs be replaced with the same type as originally installed in the motor—unless the engine is operated under abnormal conditions.

There's one sure way of telling whether frequent plug troubles are being caused by use of the wrong plugs. Examine the porcelain after the plugs have been in use for some time. Porcelain that's become coffee-colored or dark brown indicates the plug's the right one for operating conditions. If the porcelain retains its natural white color or has formed flakey blisters, it means the plug's too hot. If it's turned black or has an oily coating on the firing end, the plug's too cold for conditions.

To avoid ruining plugs, analyze the conditions under which your engine will be operated. For example, sustained idling periods, much stop and start, and light load operation mean combustion chamber temperatures will be relatively low. To get full combustion, you may need the hotter spark provided by a plug hotter than recommended.

On the other hand, an engine that's going to

1675

magnetos, outboard

After removing the retainers, pull out the movable point and the spring that holds the points closed

The fixed point can be unscrewed if it needs to be replaced. This one still looks all right

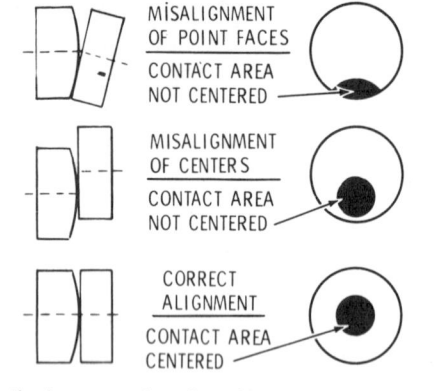

MISALIGNMENT OF POINT FACES — CONTACT AREA NOT CENTERED

MISALIGNMENT OF CENTERS — CONTACT AREA NOT CENTERED

CORRECT ALIGNMENT — CONTACT AREA CENTERED

Be as meticulous as a jeweler when you set the point gap. Adjust it for a slight drag on the feeler gauge

be pushed at high speed for long periods will probably require a colder plug, since chamber temperatures are going to get mighty hot. This type remains cool long enough to avoid engine pre-ignition and plug electrode corrosion. One sure tip-off that a colder plug is called for shows up when you're operating at high speed—the engine suddenly slows down, then picks up speed again, and keeps repeating this erratic operation.

So-called sparkplug problems seldom result from *faulty* plugs. Instead, the trouble usually stems from plugs that aren't installed properly, plugs of the incorrect heat range, or an engine that needs overhaul or adjustment. By the way, outboard plugs should be protected against moisture, and the thing that does this is the rubber sparkplug boot. Once it dries out and begins to crack, get rid of it.

Modern outboard magneto ignitions come in two general types. One, used primarily on small motors, has the magnet embedded in the flywheel. The flywheel sits on top of the stator assembly, which contains the ignition parts. Since this kind is the most common, we'll concentrate on it here. (By the way, it's the only one you should even think of tinkering with unless you have special tools. Even then, you'll need a flywheel puller to get at the stator.)

The other kind, used primarily on bigger engines, is a distributor type in which the flywheel and magneto stator are divorced. The magnet and all other ignition parts are contained in a sealed case. A drive belt connects the flywheel to the shaft. As the flywheel turns, it drives the belt which drives the shaft. The magnet's tied

Two screws hold the condenser—one holding the pigtail and one holding the condenser on its seat

into the shaft, so it turns, too. Everything else operates much the same as discussed earlier.

The one thing that characterizes the distributor-type setup is the need for pinpoint timing. You need a certain amount of dwell, depending on your engine's specifications, which dictates how long the points will remain open. You determine this dwell with a meter.

No matter what type of setup you have, the only way of telling for sure what part of the mag's upsetting the works is with a magneto tester—an all-purpose gadget that tests everything from coil windings to condenser and sells for about $100. Should you get one? That's up to you, but you can have a shop do lots of magneto work for that kind of money.

The magneto tester shown on page 1673 does all of the following jobs:

—tests the general condition of the coils under both high and low speeds.

—tests the coil's secondary for high resistance, open or shorted windings and dampness (continuity).

—tests the coil's primary for open or shorted windings.

—checks out the insulation throughout the whole system.

—tests for high resistance between breaker points, connections in the primary circuit and high-tension leads.

—tests the wiring itself for breaks and current leaks.

—checks the condenser for leakage, shorts and capacity.

—sets engine timing.

But even without this versatile package you can do a major portion of your ignition troubleshooting. Start by removing the flywheel and checking the magnet.

If it's hitting the core laminations, you'll see a telltale black streak.

In many engines, you can set the laminations yourself. Loosen up the screws—there are usually three—and back off the core until its edge is aligned with the edge of the boss on its seat.

Now check the points. Take a piece of clean cardboard and run it lightly between them to remove dirt. If points are pitted or worn, they should be replaced. The moveable point is removed by prying out two spring-type retainers—one on top and one on the side of the point—that keep it from floating. (Don't lose these. You'll want to use them again if your new set doesn't have them in the package.) The fixed point is then removed by unscrewing it.

how to align points

To align points, bend or twist the *fixed point only*. It's best to use a regular point alignment tool—you can buy one for about $1. If you don't have a timing instrument, gapping is the one way of insuring the engine's properly timed. Use a feeler gauge, and consult a mechanic at a local outboard shop for the proper gap.

In the absence of a magneto tester, always replace the condenser when you replace the points. To remove it, simply remove the retaining screw.

In engines equipped with electric starting, the one indication which characterizes a bad starter —no start—can be caused by any of a number of other things. Nine times out of ten you'll find that the first thing to go bad in outboard starters is the armature—it gets burned. However, the brushes, commutator, solenoid or field circuit could also be at fault.

Want to save yourself some money if you suspect a weak starter? Unbolt it and take it to an auto repair shop. The man there will put the starter on a growler, which'll pinpoint the exact trouble area.

You can then buy the one component you need to get cutting across your favorite water—without the delay and expense of leaving your outboard at a shop.

See also: carburetors, outboard; cooling system, outboard; outboard motors, overhauling; outboard motors, repair; outboard motors, storage; outboard motors, used; propellers, boat; remote controls, outboard; sparkplugs, marine; starting system, outboard; trolling motor.

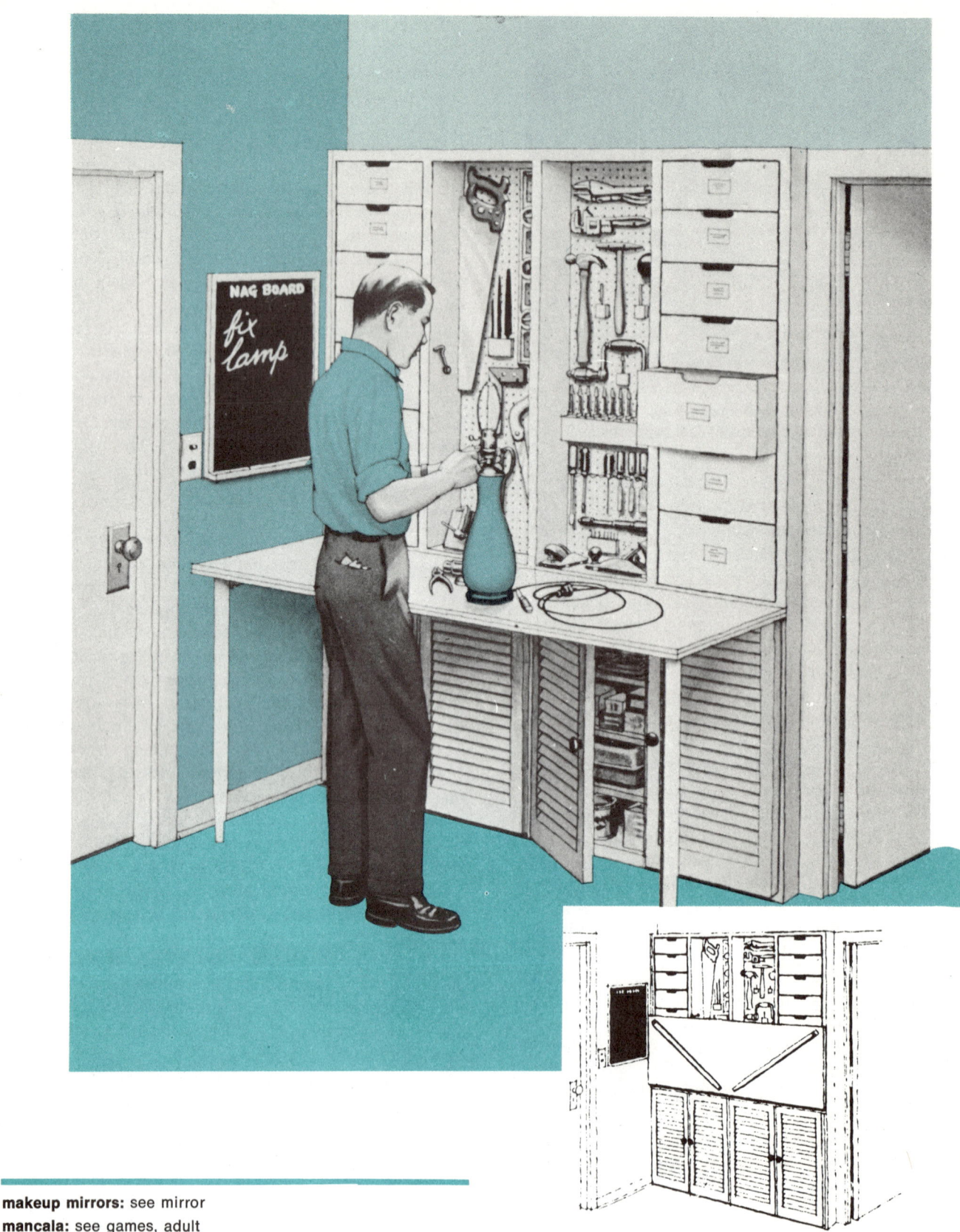

maintenance center

makeup mirrors: see mirror
mancala: see games, adult
manger scene: see Christmas decorations
manifold heat valves: see heat valves, auto

1678

Home maintenance center built into a wall

BY W. CLYDE LAMMEY

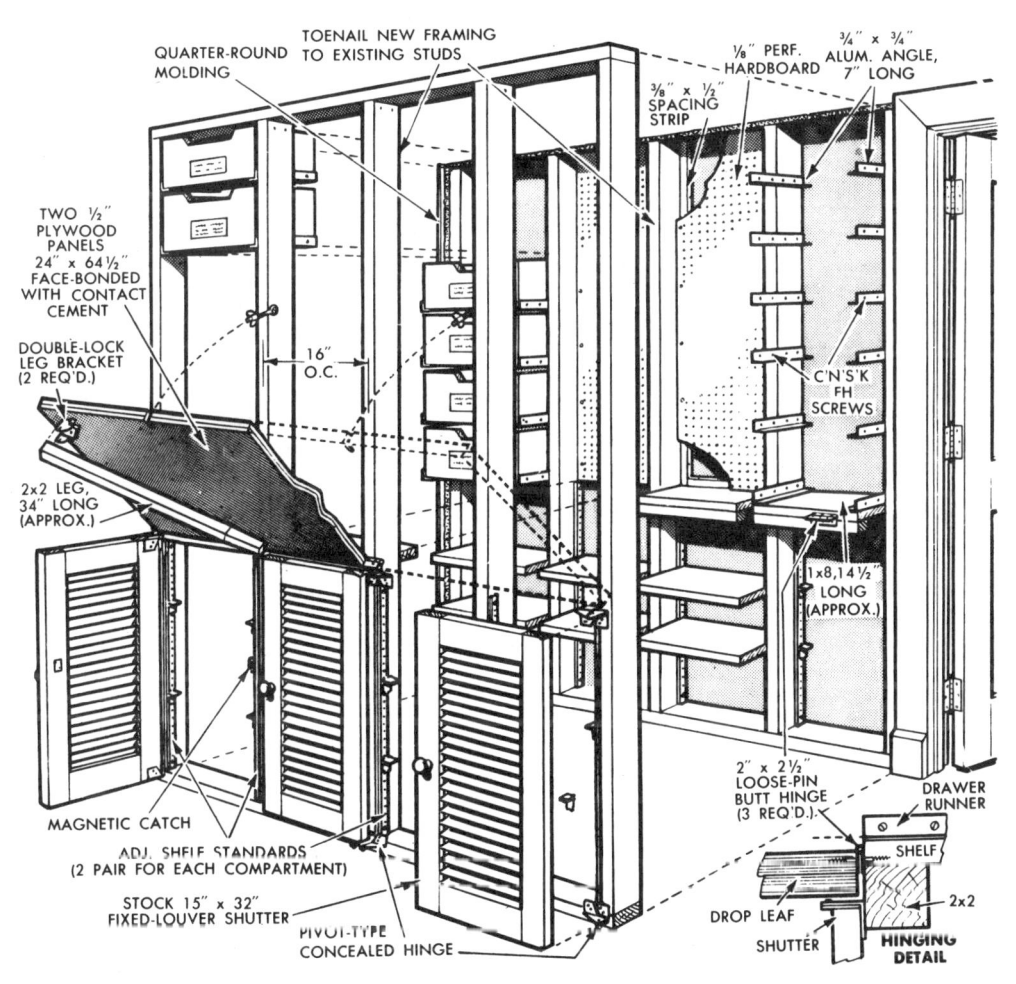

■ EVER STOP to figure out how much time you waste hunting up tools and chasing down supplies you need for maintenance jobs?

A study of this problem produced the built-in shown at the left. Unless you happen to live in a phone booth, you've got space for *this* center. It's tucked right into a partition wall, using the waste space between the studs. All that protrudes into the room is an added frame of 2 x 4s that's glued and toenailed to the wall studs to provide the depth you'll need for storage cabinets and drawers. Every bit of the space gained is put right to work. The drawer fronts and backs are only ⅛ in. thick, and the shutter doors (a stock

This workshop saves space. It's a handy place to store tools and supplies, and simplifies the job of keeping a house shipshape

maintenance center

BASIC HOUSEHOLD TOOLS

- ☐ Claw hammer, 13-oz. head
- ☐ Nail set
- ☐ Hand crosscut saw, 24-in., 12 point*
- ☐ Hand ripping saw, 26-in., 5 point*
- ☐ Jack Plane, 14-in.
- ☐ Block plane, 6-in.
- ☐ Ratchet brace, 8 or 10-in sweep**
- ☐ Auger bit set: ¼ to 1-in. by ⅛ ths**
- ☐ Rosehead countersink***
- ☐ Twist drill set: up to ¼-in.***
- ☐ Hand drill, ¼-in. chuck**
- ☐ Push drill****
- ☐ Screwdriver bit**
- ☐ Screwdrivers, 4-in. and 8-in. blades
- ☐ Screwdrivers, Phillips, medium size
- ☐ Folding rule or metal tape, 6 ft.
- ☐ Combination square, 12-in. blade
- ☐ Wood chisels: ¼, ½, ¾ and 1-in.
- ☐ Adjustable wrenches: 6 and 10-in.
- ☐ Pipe wrenches: 10 and 14-in.
- ☐ Combination pliers, 6"
- ☐ Adjustable locking plier-wrench
- ☐ Long-nose pliers
- ☐ Allen wrench set for socket setscrews
- ☐ Soldering gun, 100-watt minimum, or propane torch
- ☐ Tin snips, plain or duckbill, 10-in.
- ☐ Miter box
- ☐ Keyhole (or compass) saw
- ☐ Hacksaw and blades
- ☐ Carpenter's level, 24-in.
- ☐ Mill file, single cut, 8-in.
- ☐ 3-Corner taper file, 6 or 8-in.
- ☐ Half-round bastard file, medium cut
- ☐ Interchangeable file handle
- ☐ Clamp-on woodworking vise
- ☐ Scratch awl
- ☐ Utility knife with retractable blade
- ☐ Combination oilstone
- ☐ Spout can of light oil
- ☐ Cold chisel
- ☐ Pencil compass
- ☐ Clamps of your choice: C or spring
- ☐ Marking gauge
- ☐ Crowbar
- ☐ Stapling gun

* If you own a portable electric saw, these items may not be essential.

** If you own a portable electric drill, these may not be essential.

*** Can be used with either brace or electric drill.

**** Push drill is good substitute for hand drill and will be useful even if you have an electric drill.

THE IMPORTANT JOB begins after your in-the-wall storage center is built and you start to assemble the tools you'll need. Take a pencil to the basic checklist at left. Once you have this minimum equipment, a few additional items from the specialized lists should complete your shopping. Arrange the tools on the hook board for the best use of space, with most-used tools in easiest reach. If, after several weeks trial, the arrangement seems okay, paint silhouettes on the board to indicate tool positions. This facilitates speedy replacement when you use a variety of tools and shows which tools have strayed and should be tracked down to keep the board complete

HOME PAINTING KIT

- ☐ Brushes: 1, 3 and 4 in. sizes
- ☐ Paint roller and tray
- ☐ Putty knife, scraper—and beer-can opener for cleaning out cracks
- ☐ Spackling compound
- ☐ Sandpaper in fine to coarse grits
- ☐ Steel wool: 2/0 and 4/0
- ☐ Drop cloths
- ☐ Turpentine, denatured alcohol, lacquer thinner or equivalent solvents
- ☐ Paint remover
- ☐ Masking tape

PAPERHANGING KIT

In addition to spackling compound (for plaster patching), sandpaper, paint scraper and putty knife listed elsewhere:

- ☐ Pail for washing walls, mixing paste
- ☐ Wall size
- ☐ Smoothing brush, 12 in.
- ☐ Pastebrush, 6 in.
- ☐ Wheel knife, 1½-in. dia.
- ☐ Oval seam roller, 1½-in.
- ☐ Plumb bob and chalk line
- ☐ Homemade 8-ft. straightedge
- ☐ Large sponge
- ☐ Stepladder, 6 ft.

CONCRETE PATCHING KIT

- ☐ Mason's trowel
- ☐ Tuck-pointing trowel
- ☐ Mason's jointer
- ☐ Groover, edger (for sidewalk patch)
- ☐ Concrete/mortar mixing tray (6" x 24" x 48"—can be homemade)

HOME ELECTRICAL KIT

In addition to the pliers, screwdrivers and soldering gun listed at far left:

- ☐ Pocket knife or wire stripper
- ☐ Lamp cord, 25 ft.
- ☐ Cord plugs
- ☐ Friction tape and rubber tape
- ☐ Solderless connectors (10 or so)
- ☐ Replacement fuses (15-amp for 14-ga. wire, 20-amp for 12-ga. wire)
- ☐ Replacement toggle wall switch
- ☐ Non-acid wire solder (resin core)
- ☐ Neon tester (to check outlets)
- ☐ Spare incandescent and fluorescent bulbs for all household fixtures

HOME PLUMBING KIT

In addition to the 10-in. adjustable wrench, two pipe wrenches and 8-in. screwdriver listed at far left:

- ☐ Plumber's force cup (plunger)
- ☐ 5½-ft. closet-bowl auger
- ☐ Graphited packing
- ☐ Pipe-joint compound
- ☐ Washers, assorted types and sizes
- ☐ Seat reamer

CAULKING AND GLAZING KIT

In addition to the chisels, 1-in. brush and putty knife listed elsewhere:

- ☐ Caulking gun, with spare cartridge
- ☐ Wire brush with attached scraper
- ☐ Glass cutter
- ☐ Glazier's points (box)
- ☐ Linseed oil (pt. can)
- ☐ Glazier's putty (1 to 5 lb. can)
- ☐ Yardstick for measuring, laying out and cutting glass

GENERAL SUPPLIES

- ☐ White polyvinyl glue
- ☐ Epoxy glue
- ☐ Household cement
- ☐ Assorted stove bolts or machine screws
- ☐ Assorted wood screws (½"-#4 through 2"-#10)
- ☐ Mending plates, corner braces
- ☐ Screweyes, screw hooks, picture hooks
- ☐ Tacks, brads; common and finishing nails from 2d to 8d
- ☐ Assorted hollow wall fasteners and fiber, plastic or lead anchors
- ☐ Extra casters, furniture glides
- ☐ Sack of clean rags
- ☐ Pressure-sensitive mending tape
- ☐ Work apron and gloves

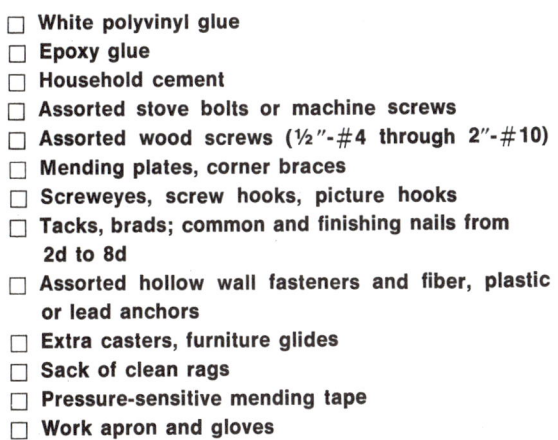

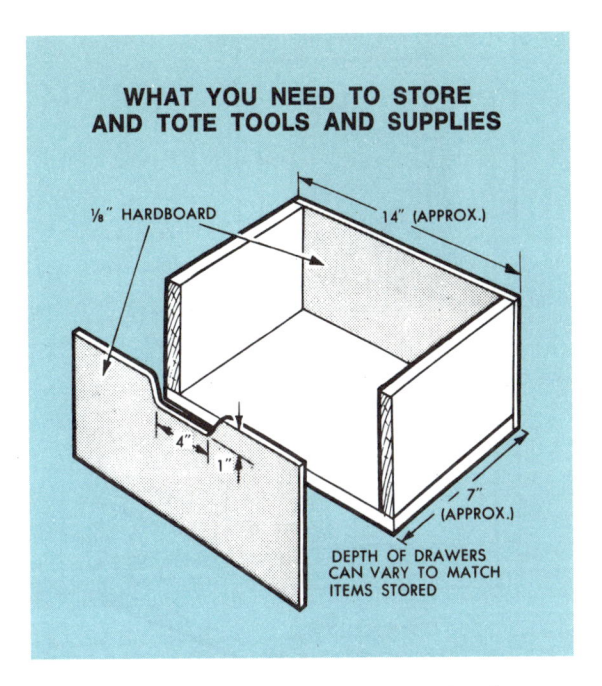

WHAT YOU NEED TO STORE AND TOTE TOOLS AND SUPPLIES

Box construction lets you make drawers of various sizes quickly. When work must be done away from the fix-it center, load up the two-part tool box (below). The tray sections are for a variety of nails, screws

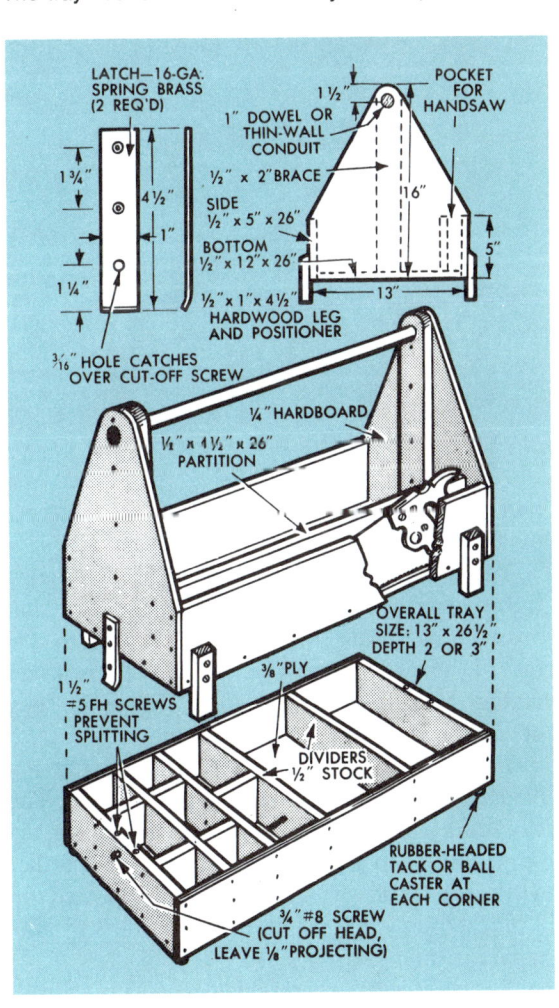

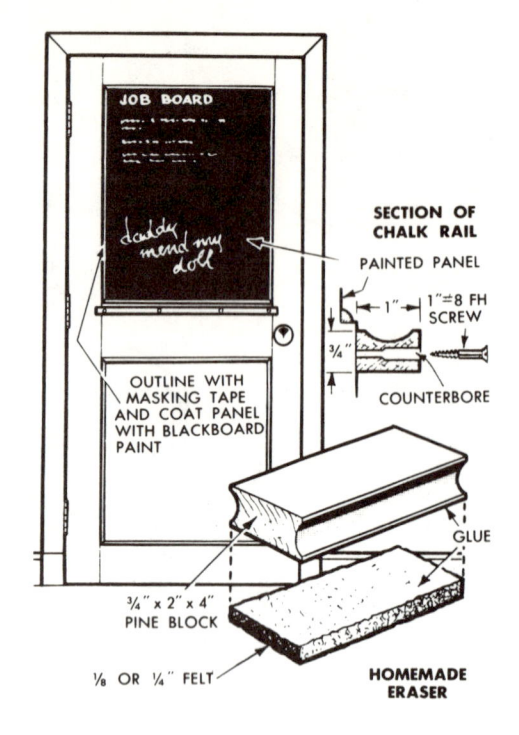

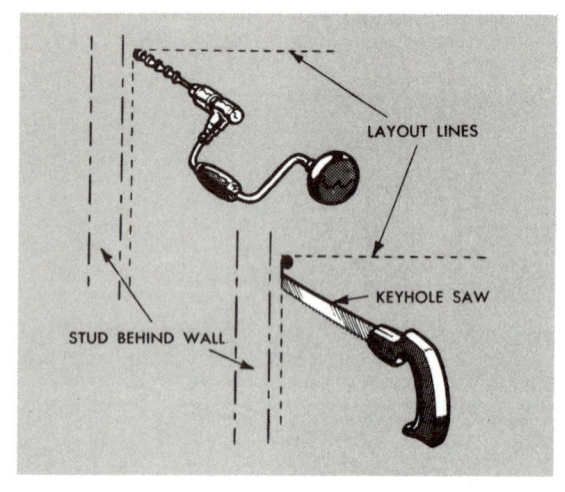

maintenance center

on the space available. About two feet is an ideal width, but it can be as little as a foot wide and still be of practical use. The length can be the full width of the built-in unless you locate your fix-it center in a corner, as shown here. In this case, the table must be shorter, to provide clearance at the corner end.

For rigidity, we bonded two ½-in. plywood panels face-to-face, using contact cement. If you want a more durable work surface, you could face this panel with ⅛-in. tempered hardboard, using the same cement and leaving it unfinished.

Are snoopy small fry a problem in your home? The drawers and toolboard are automatically shielded when the top folds up. Only the upper sections remain exposed, and they're well out of a youngster's reach. The cabinet doors will open whether the worktable is up or down, but two hasps would let you padlock them.

where to place the center

Where you locate your maintenance center depends, of course, on available wall space. In our example, we chose a utility space between two doorways. For appearance and practicality, we let the door frames determine the height of the unit. To run it much higher would only give you inaccessible drawers and out-of-reach space on the perforated-hardboard tool rack.

Note that these perforated panels are spaced ⅜-in. from the rear wall to provide clearance for the many different types of insert hooks and racks available for tool storage. The checklists on the previous pages will help you make a well-rounded selection of tools and supplies. Or simply take a stroll through your home with a memo pad, jotting down the jobs that need doing—and what you'll need to do them.

The method for opening the stud spaces is sketched at left. You need to locate only one stud, either by means of a stud finder, or by drilling test holes through the wall. In normal construction, other studs will be 16 in. on center to either side. Remove the baseboard. Then, with a 1-in. bit in a handbrace, bore a hole along the outside face of one of the border studs. Insert a keyhole saw and carefully cut all the way to the soleplate, with the blade bearing against the face of the stud. (You'll need a guide line for the horizontal top cut only.) In our sketch, we're working on the *inside* face of the left-hand border stud because our corner location made it impractical to cut along the opposite face. After this cut is made, it will be necessary to chop out the wallboard or plaster to expose the full

item with big mail-order houses) are surface-mounted to permit full-depth shelves.

The worktable folds up flat against the facing frame when it's not in use. It's secured in that position by means of eyebolts screwed to the faces of two of the studs so as to pivot down into mating slots in the table edge. Wingnuts snug up against the panel to hold it tight.

The legs are mounted at an angle to avoid any overlap when locked in their folded position. The worktable can be put to extra use by pulling the hinge pins and carrying the panel to another work site. With the hinged edge supported on a blocked-up sawhorse, it makes an ideal pasting table for wallpapering jobs.

The width of the worktable depends, of course,

edge of the stud so the 2 x 4 facing can be toe-nailed to it. The new soleplate should be anchored to the floor, in addition.

After the facing frame is applied, finish the unit to suit your own needs. You might wish to utilize *all* the above-table space for tool panels, or you might prefer open shelves to our angle-runner drawers. The space below the worktable is plenty deep enough to take quart-size cans of paint. Adjustable shelf brackets offer complete flexibility as to the height of items you can store. You might want to leave at least one cabinet free of shelves, for storing tall items.

Another thing you should store in one of the cabinets is an accordion folder with alphabet tabs, for filing all literature that comes with new appliances—installation instructions, warranties or servicing data.

It's a good idea, also, to mount a blackboard near the fix-it center so that you and other members of the family can jot down job reminders. This can be a child's framed slate, or you can simply use a door panel, as shown on the opposite page. For more permanent records—such as when you last cleaned or changed your furnace filters, the number of gallons of paint or paper it takes to decorate certain rooms, etc.—you might also want to hang a roller windowshade above the reminder board, coating the inside surface of the fabric with blackboard paint. You'd then just pull the shade down, scribble your note in chalk and roll it back up. The note will be there, months or years later.

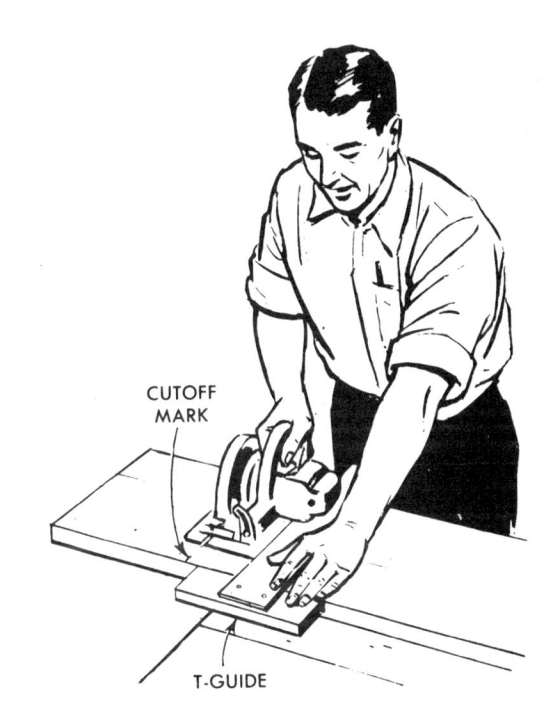

Accurate cut-offs are much easier with a portable electric saw—one of the tool's advantages over hand saws marked (*) in Basic Tool List. Above, two pieces of scrap are lapped at right angles to provide a T-square fence to run saw's base plate along

See also: caulking; concrete; electrical wiring; glazing; painting; plumbing; repairs, home; wallpaper.

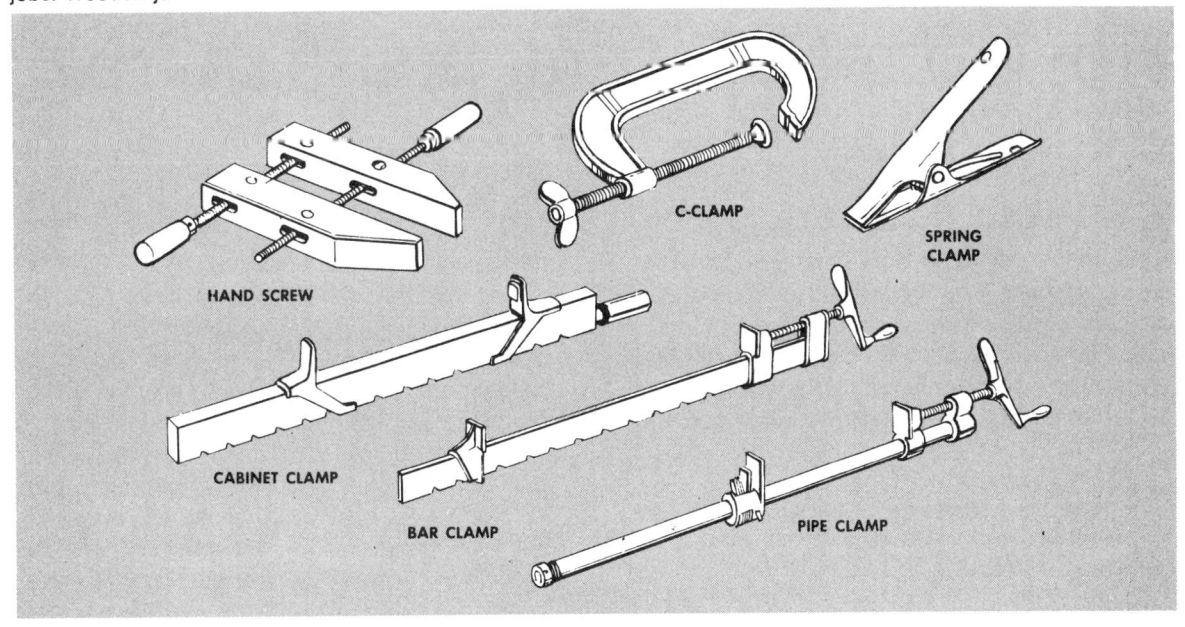

In buying clamps, start with a set of C-clamps, then add several spring clamps for smaller jobs. Wooden-jaw hand screws are for cabinetwork. Three at bottom are for wide, flat work

marble

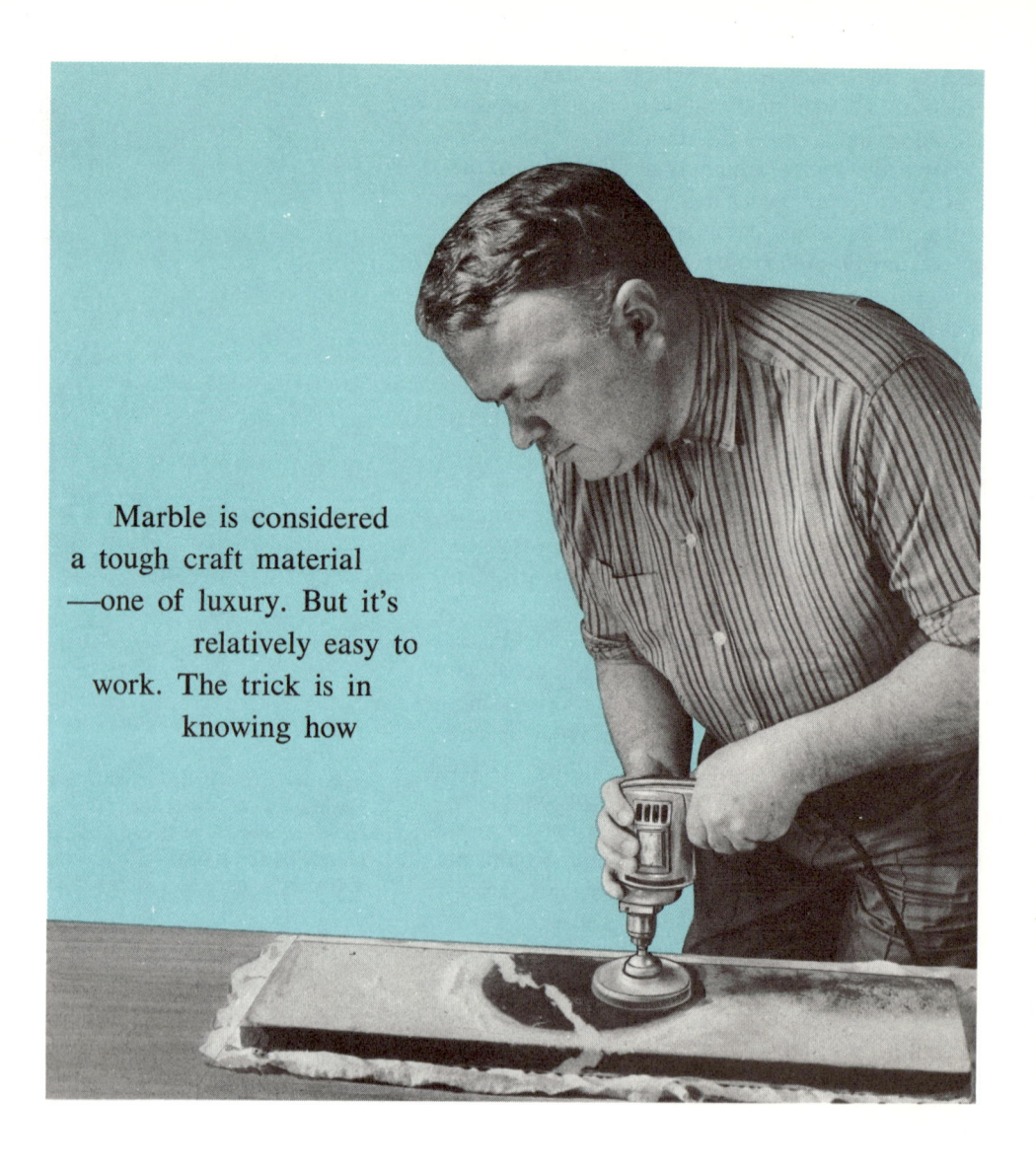

Marble is considered a tough craft material—one of luxury. But it's relatively easy to work. The trick is in knowing how

How to mend, trim, polish marble

BY GEORGE DANIELS

■ WITH A FEW INEXPENSIVE additions to your shop tools, you can work marble almost as easily as wood. A masonry cut-off wheel on your table or portable saw will slice through a 1-ft.-wide slab of 1-in. marble in about 20 seconds. An ordinary carbide-tipped masonry bit in your power drill will penetrate marble almost as fast as concrete block. And standard abrasives on your electric sander disk will polish the scarred surface of a secondhand slab to a mirror finish at about 15 minutes per sq. ft.

You can buy marble new in more than 200 types and color combinations from dealers throughout the country—or used, from any building wrecker's yard. Prices vary, but a typical price per sq. ft. for new ⅞-in. polished marble, cut to size, is $7 or $8. For equivalent used marble, sold "as is," the price ranges from $2 down to as little as 60 cents where the surface may be stained or pitted—conditions you can easily repair. If the marble you buy has to be cut, use a firm guide for the saw. Any veering

marine spark plugs: see spark plugs, marine
marker buoy: see boat repair

POLISHING

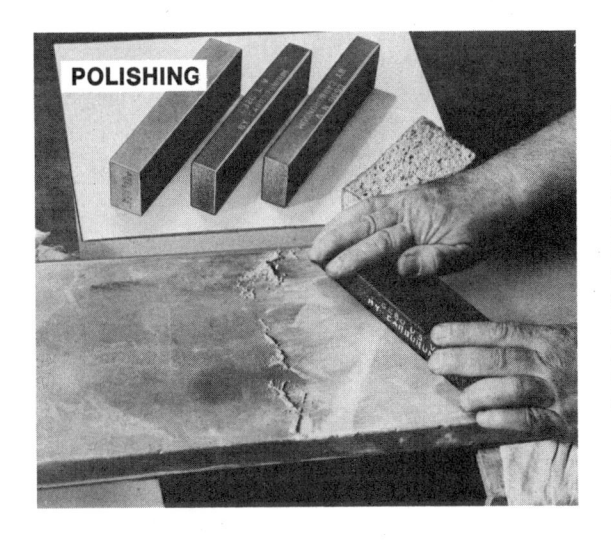

Restoration of a worn slab starts with a block of 80-grit abrasive. This is a back-and-forth hand operation, since power sanding with so coarse an abrasive can cause scooping. Waiting in the background are progressively finer grit sizes: 120, 220, and 320—all available at hardware stores. After the first two stages, you can switch to power sanding. Keep the sander moving uniformly over the surface under moderate pressure

Sponge the surface frequently to avoid clogging and to check progress of abrasive stages. Wetting gives a preview of the final appearance, picking up the pattern and depth of color as much as polishing will do. Change to a finer grit when the abrasive marks are even. Don't skimp on the coarse stages or you'll have to overwork the final ones. If there are any chips or holes to fill, save all the marble dust to mix with the resin

Final abrasive is a thin oxide powder, available from marble dealers and chemical houses. Wet it to form a creamy paste and apply with a saturated cloth. Cover the pad of a power sander with thin felt or flannel. Orbital or reciprocal types are best as they hold the paste under the pad and don't sling it away. Keep the paste moist with a light sprinkling while working; add more as it wears away. Minute scratches will disappear with a final washing

marble

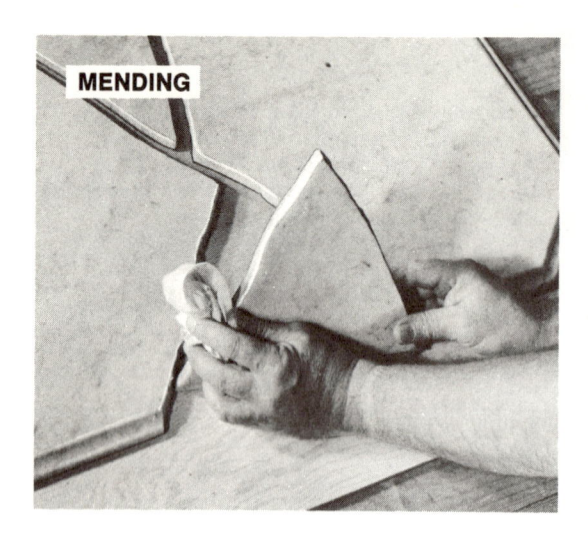

MENDING

Assemble fragments on a flat surface to make sure no large parts are missing. The edges must be wiped thoroughly clean. Use a rag moistened with acetone. Buy a polyester-resin adhesive designed for marble repair, and mix a ¼-oz. test sample to be sure the resin-catalyst proportions recommended on the label allow ample working time. If the sample sets too fast, use less catalyst. The average proportions: 15 drops of catalyst to 2 tablespoons resin

Brush the adhesive on both joining edges of each break and slide the fragments together firmly. Their own weight provides a clamping effect. Scrape off any squeeze-out with a clean putty knife; what remains will fill the small chips along the joint. Other minor chips, gouges and holes should be overfilled so the resin won't "dish" to a hollow as it sets. A half-ounce of the resin did the job here. This catalyst comes in a dropper bottle

Forty minutes later, the adhesive is fully hardened so the excess can be gritted off with a 120-grit abrasive block. Use successively finer grades to polish and blend out the repaired area. The resin is translucent and blends with the marble figuration so repair will be virtually undetectable. Where this is critical, the resin can even be pre-tinted to match the marble. Unmixed leftovers won't go to waste since this adhesive bonds marble to wood

FACTS ABOUT MARBLE

Marble is limestone that's close-textured enough to be polished. It's a unique material, in that impurities increase its value. Pure marble is white; impurities produce the various shades of green, as well as red, black, gray, blue—and attractive mottled effects.

Marble weighs 170 lbs. per cubic foot—about a third as much as cast iron. In average forms, it can withstand up to about 1200 deg. F. without injury, and has a crushing strength of 5 tons per sq. in. Unlike polished metal, marble gets its glasslike luster from the fact that light penetrates the polished surface and is reflected from deeper-lying crystals. Thus wear and time dull the surface, giving marble that lackluster appearance. It's one of the toughest of decorative materials—but keep acids away from it. Remember that acid is poured over marble chips to produce carbon dioxide in laboratories.

---

may shatter the abrasive wheel. Wear goggles, use the saw guard, don't rev the wheel over the peak speed printed on it.

To minimize chipping, don't try to cut the slab in a single pass. Set the blade to bite no deeper than ⅜ in. at a time—and never force the wheel. For curved cuts, make a series of straight cuts tangent to the curve, and grind off the peaks with coarse (No. 3½) floor machine paper on the flexible disk of your ¼ in. drill or a rigid disk in your table saw.

Portable drills with a speed range between 600 and 1250 rpm will bore holes up to ¼ in. diameter in marble. A drill-press stand for the drill assures a perpendicular hole, avoids chipping, and helps get the 25 to 75 lbs. pressure the carbide requires.

If the original surface is only slightly pitted, you can skip the first two abrasive stages described in the polishing captions. If it's merely dull, skip the first three. If it retains considerable polish, with only small areas dulled, you can often restore it with tin oxide alone. Not all marble surfaces require a mirror finish. For hard-use counter tops, stop with the satin polish produced by the 600-grit abrasive.

Marble stains that persist after the first two stages of a polishing job should be removed chemically before further polishing. Organic stains (as from plant leaves or tobacco) can be removed with hydrogen peroxide of hair-bleach strength. To slow evaporation and prolong its effect, mix it to a paste with whiting or talcum and spread it over the stained area. Add a few drops of household ammonia to start the action; wash off the mix when bubbling stops.

Oil and grease stains come off quickly with acetone or mineral spirits. If a color blemish remains, bleach with peroxide, as just described. Iodine stains—likely on bathroom counters—yield to a poultice of denatured alcohol and whiting or talc.

Paint spatters should be removed with a razor blade as soon as discovered.

If you catch rust stains quickly enough, you can usually erase them with energetic hard-cloth rubbing. For deep stains, shake sodium hydrosulfite crystals onto the stained area, moisten with water, and let stand not more than half an hour. Rinse and apply sodium citrate solution. If some stain remains, repeat the process. Slight surface etching may call for repolishing.

For ink stains, rinse with water and follow with alternate wettings of ammonia and alcohol, applied by saturating blotting paper and holding it against the surface for a few minutes. Metallic ink may leave a stain which can be removed by the method described for rust.

The sooner a stain is removed, the easier the job. To keep stain removers from spreading the stain, wet the surrounding area before applying them. If you're timid about mixing chemicals, buy ready-to-use removers from marble dealers.

See also: abrasives; glues.

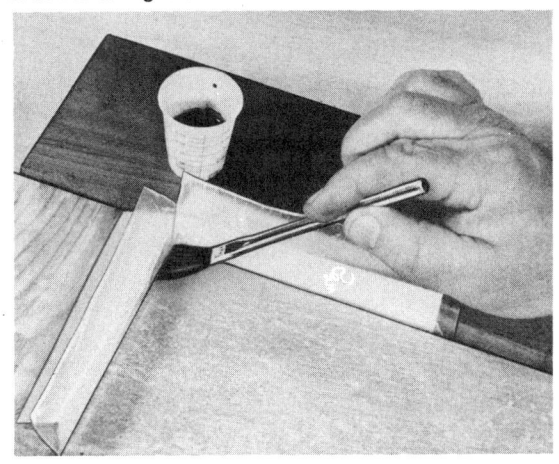

Chipped corners or edges can be patched with a resin mixed with marble dust. Make a dam of scrap-wood blocks, line it with waxed paper. Flow the resin into the depression with a small brush to a slight overfill. Polish flush

marksmanship

Duffer to expert wingshot in minutes

BY GEORGE X. SAND

Whether trapshooter or pheasant hunter,
almost anyone can become expert
using George Carson's surprisingly simple methods

martin birdhouses: see birdhouses
masking screens: see screens, masking
massager, belt: see exercise equipment

With back to target (below), the shooter pivots on his left foot and turns from his hips. Gun stock (right) is held firmly to the chin rather than cheek

■ WITH "SIGHT SHOOTING," a novice can become an excellent wingshooter in just 90 minutes.

Developed by George Carson, a St. Louis, Mo., marksman who has taught more than one thousand people to shoot, sight shooting is based on the principle that aiming a shotgun is the same as pointing your arm at an object.

His method incorporates only two basic rules: (1) The gun is held with the stock touching the chin (rather than in conventional cheek position), and *must* be held in the same position for each shot. It is moved instinctively, in effect, as an extension of the body. (2) In sighting a target *with both eyes open,* the shooter looks slightly above the target. To make it even simpler, the practice weapon is a BB gun.

Using targets such as wafer cookies hanging on thread, ping-pong balls and official 50-ft. paper targets, we asked a 10-year-old who had never fired a gun to try the method. He shot from 10 yards, standing with his back to the targets and turning for each shot. His first shots were wild, but instinctively he began to zero in. We repeatedly reminded him of Carson's two rules. After one hour he used a new target, fired 30 shots and put every one within the scoring rings. He then broke six out of 10 candy wafers, and in another 30 minutes was easily hitting paper plates sailed into the air.

Later on, when we switched to a .410 shotgun and hand-thrown clay targets, the youngster broke 17 out of 25. That would be a respectable performance on any trap range—and it was downright amazing for a beginner.

See also: ammunition; chronograph; deer hunting; pheasant hunting; shotguns; targets.

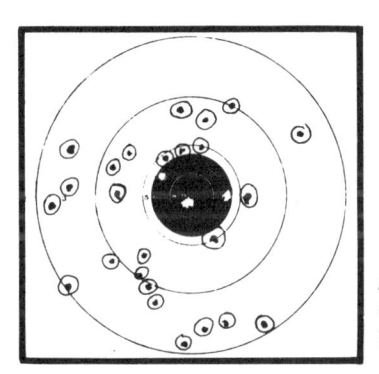

After just one hour of sight-shooting practice, a 10-year-old boy took 30 shots at the paper target (left) from 10 yards, without aiming, and placed every shot within rings

When an older shooter has enough confidence to be able to hit a small wafer thrown into the air, instructor George Carson switches him from BB gun to shotgun for real thing. He throws clay targets into air, and when a student consistently breaks doubles he has graduated

measurements

Guide to the right measurement

WHETHER YOU WANT to remodel your kitchen or add a room to your house, this guide can help you in the planning stage. It provides some basic measurements of common structures, equipment and material and recommended minimum dimensions. Widths are given as the narrower horizontal dimension or as the distance from left to right from the front of an item. Heights are given from the floor or from the bottom of suspended items. Depths are from front to rear. Some measurements are not given since they vary widely.

STAIRS Recommended stairway width 2'10"-3'

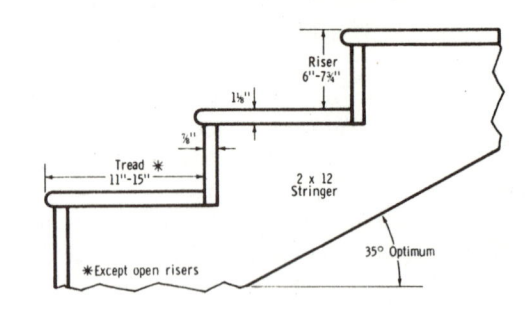

Outside stoop should be 4'6" deep to allow for storm door swing. Minimum step tread is 12" with ¼" pitch. Brick steps should be header fronted

DOORS

FRAMING
Width and height of rough opening are 3½" larger than the door. Head and side casings are ½" x 1¾"; exterior door sill is 1⅝" x 7⅜"; a stock jamb with a ½" rabbet is 1⁵⁄₁₆" or 1⅝" x 5¼".

ENTRANCE DOOR
Standardly 2'6", 2'8", 2'10" and 3' wide, and 6'8" and 7' high; thickness is 1¾"

INTERIOR DOOR
Most commonly 2'4" and 2'6" wide; 6'6", 6'8" and 7' high; thickness is 1⅜" or 1¾"

DOORBELL BUTTON
Commonly 45" above top of doorsill

DOORKNOB
Commonly 36½" from floor

WINDOWS
Placement height is based on aligning with room door top. Measure distance from ceiling to door molding. Window sizes are widely variable. Common wood double-hung sizes: 2', 2'4", 2'8" and 3' wide; 3'2", 3'10" and 4'6" high

RAILINGS
STAIRCASE—Height 2'10"-3'
PORCH AND DECK—Height 3'

HOUSE WIRING
MAJOR EQUIPMENT WATTAGE RATINGS
Air conditioner 850-1200, 3100
Attic fan 500-1500
Clothes dryer .... to 4500
Dishwasher 530-1000
Disposer 380-530
Furnace blower 380-670
Heater 1000-1650
Home freezer 300-670
Motor, ¼ hp. 530
Oil burner 300-550
Range 7000-14,000
Refrigerator 200-670
Television 200-400
Toaster 600-1350
Washer, automatic . . 350-900
Water heater 750-3000

ROOMS—MINIMUM SIZE RECOMMENDATIONS

	WIDTH	LENGTH	HEIGHT THICKNESS	DEPTH
KITCHEN, for 4 persons, depends on layout and equipment	7'	10'		
BATHROOM	5'	7'		
DINING ROOM with 36" chair room	10'	10'		
BEDROOM, including 8' of clothing drawer space per person:				
Single bed	8'	12'	or 10'x10'	
Double bed	12'	13'	or 10'x15'	
Twin beds	12'	15'6"	or 10'x17'6"	
GARAGE without laundry or shop:				
One car with 8' or 9' door	12'	22'		
Two-car with 2-8' or 16' door	19'	22'		
Storage above car hood			4'	5'
Workbench on side, add to width	3'6"		36"	
Floor should pitch toward door ⅛" per foot				

FURNISHINGS & APPLIANCE RECOMMENDATIONS

KITCHEN	WIDTH	LENGTH	HEIGHT THICKNESS	DEPTH	CLEARANCE
Base Cabinet (undersink and corners not included in frontage; height includes counter top)	6'-10'		36"	22"-25"	
Common individual widths: 12", 15", 18", 21", 24", 27", 30", 36", 42", 48"					
Wall cabinet—for 4 persons	6'-10'			12" 13" 14"	
—for service for 12	10'-14'				
Common individual widths: 15", 18", 21", 24", 27" 30", 33", 36", and 44"-60" (triple units)					
Common heights: 15", 18", 21", 24", 27", 30", 31". Top shelf maximum height from floor is 6'					
Cabinet placed above range				30"	
above sink				22"	
above counter				15"-18"	
Counter space needed (not including corners; may be reduced by multiple use)					

	WIDTH	LENGTH	HEIGHT THICKNESS	DEPTH	CLEARANCE
next to: Refrigerator	15″-18″				
Sink, each side	18″				
Food preparation, mixing	36″				
Range	15″				
Oven	15″				
Wall oven—Open door should be 3″-5″ below wife's elbow. Average height from floor to bottom of oven is 27″-32″					
Common kitchen appliance sizes:					
Refrigerator	36″		59″		
1-bowl sink	24″				
2-bowl sink	36″				
Range	30″		36″		
Built-in range	30″				
Built-in oven	24″				
Dishwasher	24″		34½″-36″		
DINING AREA					
Dining table, allow 2′ per person	30″-42″		30″		36″ / 20″ knee
8 persons fit at a 5′ round, a 4′ square or a 3′x8′ rectangle					
Dining counter			36″		
Barstool (footrest 6″-8″ from floor)			24″-25″		12″ knee
Wainscoting			30″		
BATHROOM					
Sinks			31″-36′		
Tubs, square & square corner	3′10″, 4′1½″				
Tubs, rectangular	2′6″-2′9″	4′-5′6″			
Free-standing shower cabinet, square and corner	2′6″-3′6″	6′3″-7′			
Toilets	17¾″-29¼″			26″-31⅜″	18″ front
Shower head			74″		
Curtain rod for tub			78″		
Towel bar			36″-42″		
Medicine cabinet from floor			48″-54″		
Tiling (4¼″x4¼″)—room walls, plus trim			10 tiles		
—tub area from floor, plus trim			16 tiles		
BEDROOM					
Double bed (inside frame measure)	54″	75″, 78″			
Twin bed (inside frame measure)	39″	75″, 78″			
Clothes closet (depth is minimum)			7′-7′6″	22″	
Closet rod			5′3″		
Chest of drawers	36″ up		28″-34″	18″-21″	
WORK AREAS					
Laundry area space in front of washer and dryer	66″			36″	
Space for hand ironing	72″			52″	
Bookshelves and cases (adjustable shelves have pin holes 1″ o.c.)			6′6″ to top shelf	8″-9″	

MATERIALS

BOARD & LUMBER SIZES

Nominal & actual dimensions: 1x2=¾″x1⅝″, 1x3=¾″x2⅝″, 1x4=¾″x3⅝″, 1x5=¾″x4⅝″, 1x6=¾″x5½″, 1x8=¾″x7½″, 1x10=¾″x9½″, 1x12=¾″x11½″; 2x4=1⅝″x3⅝″, 2x6=1⅝″x5⅝″, 2x8=1⅝″x7½″, 2x10=1⅝″x9½″, 2x12=1⅝″x11½″

SHEET MATERIALS

Interior plywood—Most common sizes: 4′x8′, 4′x10′ and 4′x12′; also available, widths 30″-48″, lengths 5′-12′, thicknesses 3⁄16″ and ¼″-¾″ by eighths

Exterior plywood—Same dimensions as interior except in thicknesses: 3⁄16″ and ¼″-1⅛″ by eighths

Gypsum wallboard—Width 4′, lengths 4′ and 8′, thicknesses ¼″-⅝″ by eighths

Asbestos cement wallboard—Width 4′, lengths 4′ and 8′, thicknesses ⅛″ and 3⁄16″

Fiber wallboard—Standard width 4′, lengths 4′-12′, thicknesses ⅜″-¾″ by eighths. Also 4′x14′ & 16′, 8′x14′ & 16′ and 8′x18′

Hardboard, standard & tempered—Widths 2′, 4′ and 5′; lengths 2′-16′; thicknesses ⅛″-5⁄16″ by sixteenths

Plastic laminate—Widths 24″, 30″, 36″, 48″; lengths 60″, 72″, 84″, 96″, 120″, not all combinations; thickness 1⁄16″

MASONRY

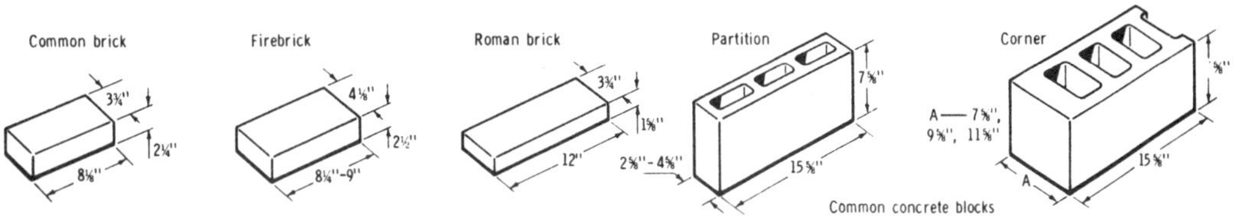

Common brick
3¾″
2¼″
8⅛″
Firebrick
4⅛″
2½″
8¼″-9″
Roman brick
3¾″
1⅝″
12″
2⅝″-4⅝″
Partition
7⅝″
15⅝″
Corner
⅝″
A—7⅝″, 9⅝″, 11⅝″
A
15⅝″
Common concrete blocks

Concrete—General-purpose mix is 1:2¼:3. To make 1 cu. yd., use 6¼ sacks of cement, 14 cu. ft. of sand, 20 cu. ft. of gravel and 6 gal. of water per bag of cement

INSULATION—Commonly available are rolls and loose insulation. Rolls are 16″ o.c. x 36′; loose comes in 4-cu.-ft. bags; also 16″ and 24″ o.c. 4′ batts and 8′ blankets (o.c.=on center)

GUTTERS—4″ and 5″ wide, 10′ long; add connectors, corners and leader adapters to measure length; minimum slope is 1⁄16″ per foot

merry-go-rounds

This go-round puts kids in orbit

BY DAVID A. GATTIS

■ YOU DON'T NEED NASA to put your kids in orbit. They'll really get a blast out of this attachment that adds whiz-around variety to the back-and-forth motion of a set of swings. If your back yard is already graced with a sturdy swingset, you can add the whole pedal-plane unit at a cost of about $14 for materials. The only power tools you'll need: an electric drill and an arc welder. Don't own the latter? Then you can prepare all

metal benders: see benders
metal finishing: see tumbling machines
metal turning: see lathe techniques; tapers, lathe
meter, cam-dwell: see cam-dwell meter
meter, transmitter: see transmitter meter
metronome: see electronics

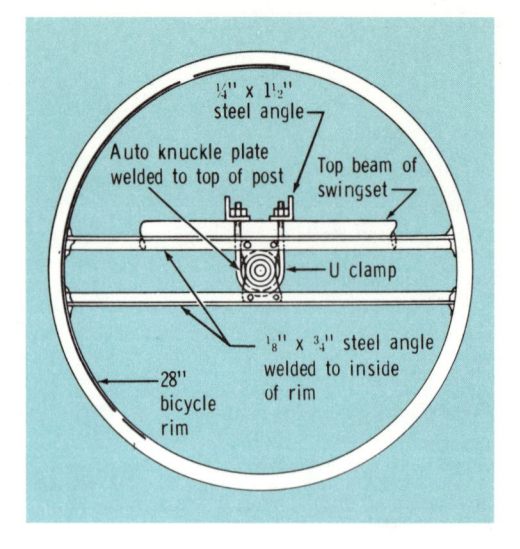

1692

If you have a backyard swing set, you can add this flyer to it and give it all the thrills of a big-time amusement park. No swing set? Then hang it from its own freestanding pole. Either way, you'll be the hero of the local merry-go-round set

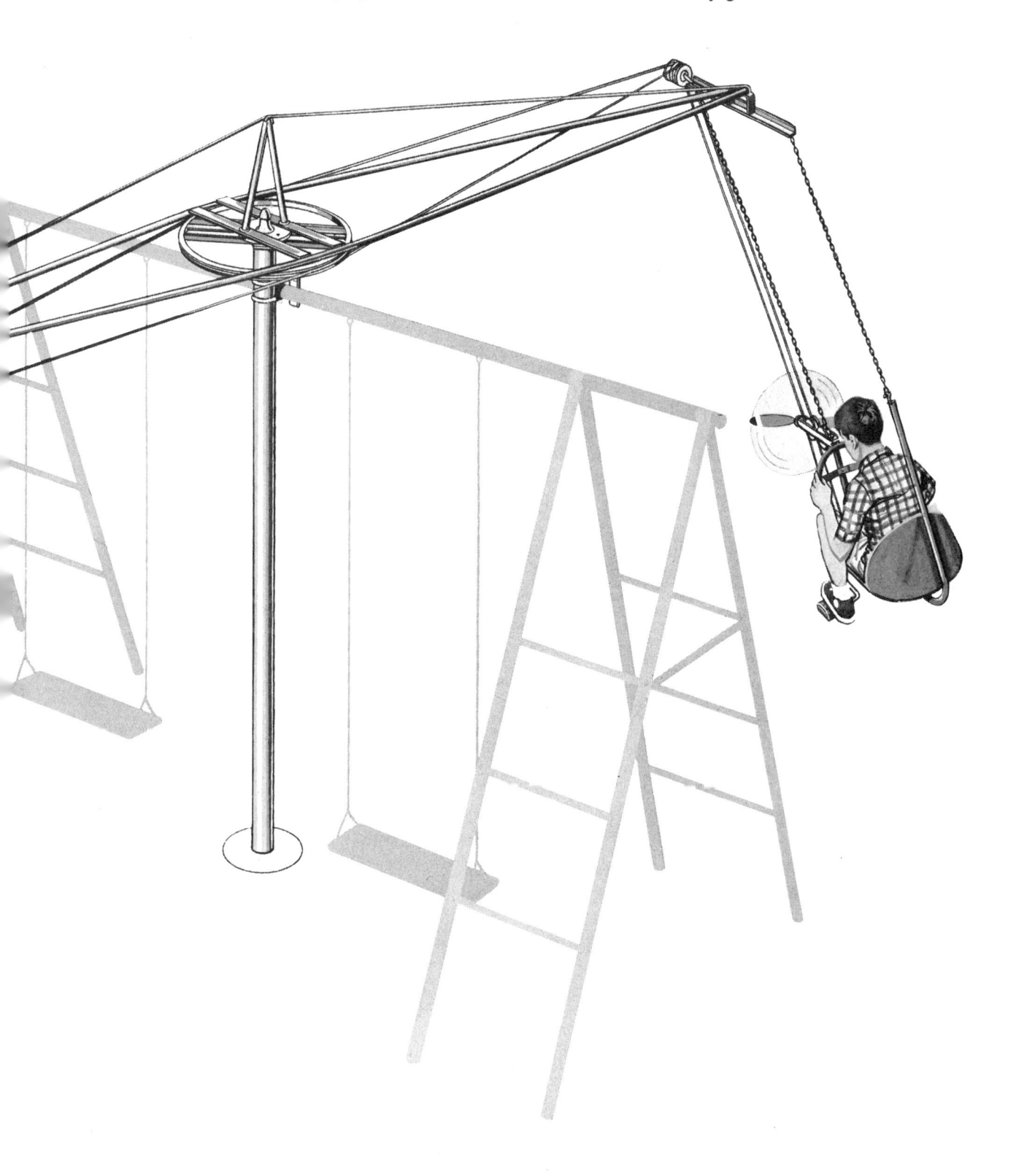

merry-go-rounds

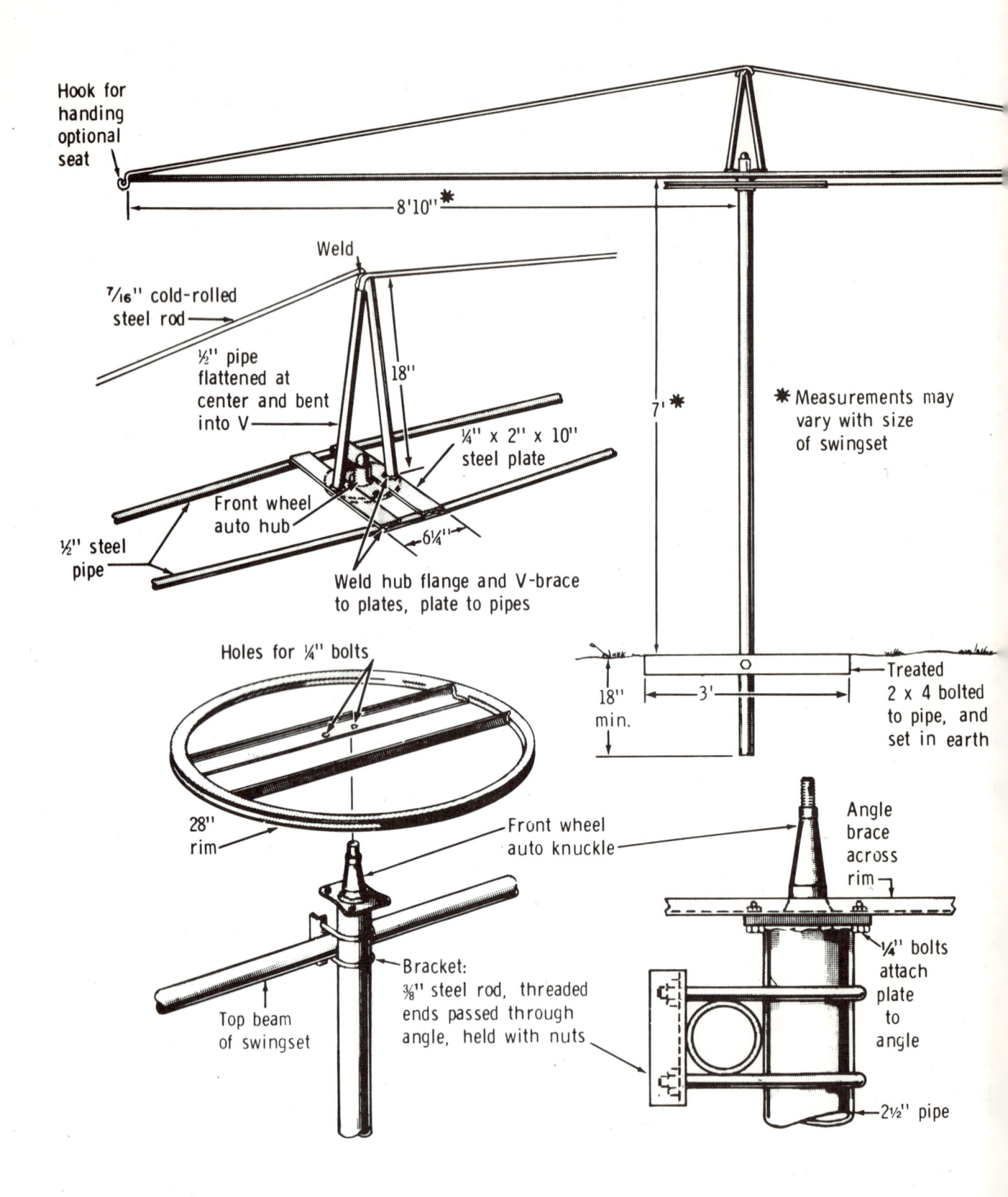

go-round puts kids in orbit, continued

Hook for handing optional seat

8'10"*

Weld

7/16" cold-rolled steel rod

½" pipe flattened at center and bent into V

18"

¼" x 2" x 10" steel plate

Front wheel auto hub

½" steel pipe

6¼"

Weld hub flange and V-brace to plates, plate to pipes

7'*

* Measurements may vary with size of swingset

Holes for ¼" bolts

28" rim

Front wheel auto knuckle

Top beam of swingset

Bracket: 3/8" steel rod, threaded ends passed through angle, held with nuts

18" min.

3'

Treated 2 x 4 bolted to pipe, and set in earth

Angle brace across rim

¼" bolts attach plate to angle

2½" pipe

1694

½"-pipe spacers 4" and 1" long

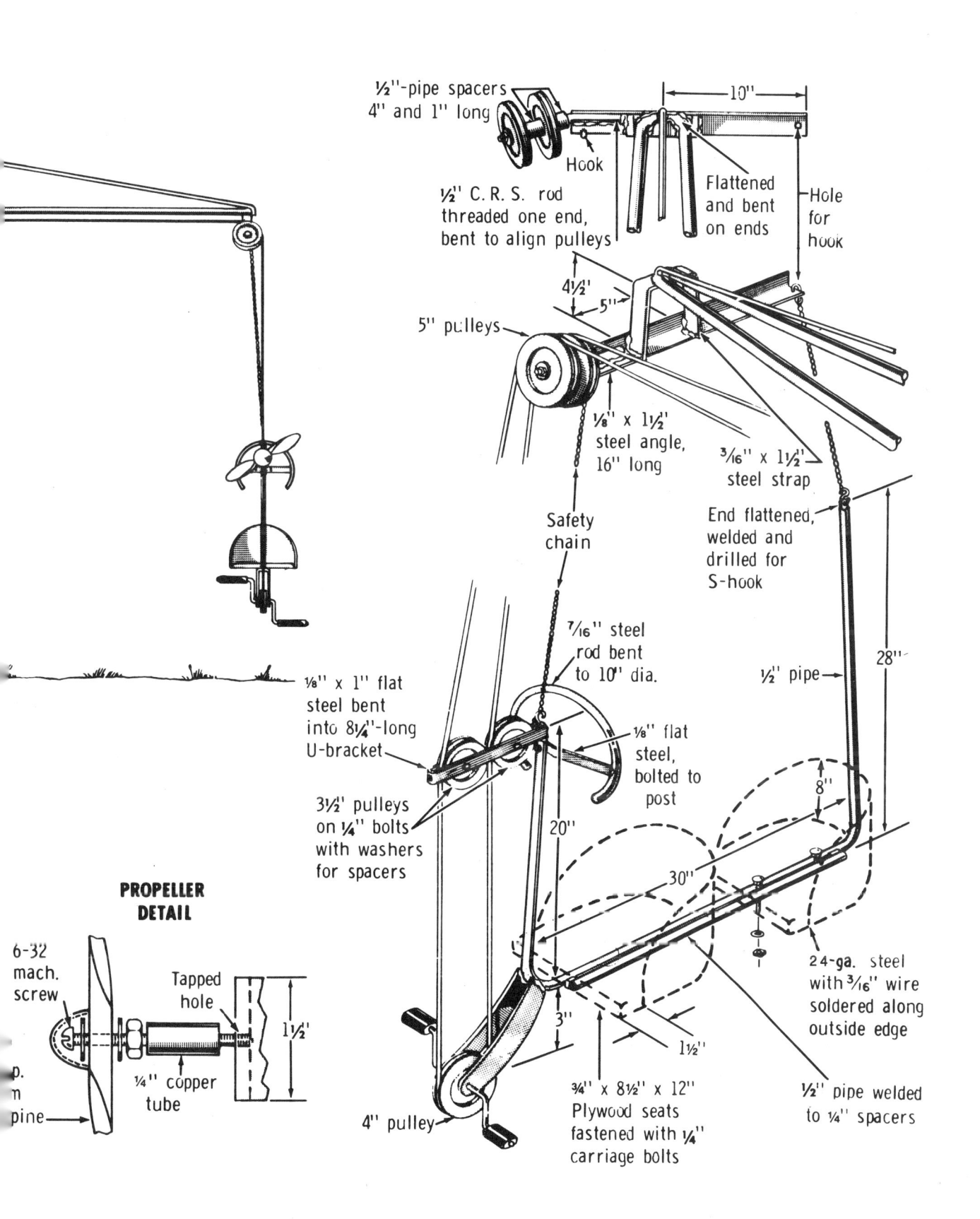

½" C.R.S. rod threaded one end, bent to align pulleys

Hook

Flattened and bent on ends

10"

Hole for hook

5" pulleys

4½"
5"

⅛" x 1½" steel angle, 16" long

³⁄₁₆" x 1½" steel strap

Safety chain

End flattened, welded and drilled for S-hook

⁷⁄₁₆" steel rod bent to 10" dia.

⅛" flat steel, bolted to post

½" pipe

28"

⅛" x 1" flat steel bent into 8¼"-long U-bracket

3½" pulleys on ¼" bolts with washers for spacers

20"

8"

30"

1½"

3"

24-ga. steel with ³⁄₁₆" wire soldered along outside edge

PROPELLER DETAIL

6-32 mach. screw

Tapped hole

1½"

¼" copper tube

p.
m
pine

4" pulley

¾" x 8½" x 12" Plywood seats fastened with ¼" carriage bolts

½" pipe welded to ¼" spacers

merry-go-rounds

go-round puts kids in orbit, continued

pieces for assembly and take them to a welding shop. If you *don't* have a swingset now, you can erect the pedal-plane as a separate unit, taking a bit more care with the "planting" of the pivot pole, and adding prop-type supports.

Roller and ball bearings eliminate virtually all drag, making the rotating mechanism surprisingly easy to operate. A three-year-old can "solo" at speeds up to 15 mph (circular miles) at an altitude of from 1 to 4 ft. The unit is designed for youngsters under 120 lbs., but additional supports could be added to adapt it for larger children. The truss and center post have been tested at over 200 lbs., but with this weight applied, only the most rugged swingset frames will provide necessary bracing.

In the sketch on page 1693, we show a two-seater unit, for small youngsters, balanced by a single-seater for older kids. In this arrangement, you've got a double pedal action, with both drive belts bearing on the same bicycle rim. But as the sketch on page 1694 indicates, a single pedal-plane unit will spin the structure nicely, and you can provide balance by hanging a baby swing, basket, hobby horse or what have you from the other end of the beam. Surprisingly, the extra weight is hardly noticed by the pedaler.

front seat provides tension

The front of the seat unit actually hangs on the endless belt—its weight is what gives this drive loop enough tension against the pivoted bicycle rim to send the whole unit spinning. The belt (¼-in. manila rope for economy) passes around the pedal pulley, up through guide pulleys behind the wind-spun prop, up past pulleys on the end of the support beam and across to the central rim. The front chain is merely a safety factor, since the drive belt is subject to wear and could, in time, break; a small spring between a few top links keeps this chain taut in normal use. The rear chain is, of course, what holds the back of the plane up. It attaches about 2 ft. above the center of gravity, for stabilization.

The belt is made by untwisting 12 in. of rope at one end and weaving the strands back through an untwisted portion of the other end. Trim off the loose ends and you've a splice that can't pull apart. To eliminate belt slippage, rubber electrical tape (or a strip of old inner-tube) is wrapped around the bicycle rim and a vacuum-cleaner belt is snapped over the drive pulley.

The plane unit itself is of the simplest possible construction. The seat frame is a double bend of ½-in. water pipe; the size indicated is adequate for two seats for children 2 to 5 yrs. old, and the seat positions are adjustable.

The fork of an old tricycle provides the drive mechanism. Remove the wheel, but leave the ½-in. shaft at the center. With the crank used, a ⅝-in. hole in the pulley just clears the elbows. After positioning the pulley shim the shaft with sheet-metal strips and, to eliminate slippage, drill the shaft to provide a seat for a setscrew. If no tricycle fork is available, suspend a bicycle crank between two hangers of steel plate, welded to the frame's front bend.

make plywood pulleys

Guide pulleys are made from ¾-in. waterproof plywood, with an old auto generator ball bearing epoxied in the center. Not owning a lathe, you can turn pulleys on a portable drill. Just insert a bolt through the center of each rough disk and chuck it in the drill, which is secured in an upright bracket. Then, with a round file, cut the edge groove about ⅜-in. wide and ½-in. deep. The bearing holes are cut with a circle cutter set for a diameter slightly less than that of the bearing. Degrease the outside of the bearing before applying epoxy and drive it into the hole; before the cement sets, align the bearing so the pulley will spin without wobble.

The support post is 2½-in. steel water pipe—the length determined by the height of your swingset's top beam. Two U-bolts clamp the pipes together, and a length of 2 x 4 is bolted across the post's lower end to keep the pipe from sinking. Or you could provide a concrete footing.

The hub and knuckle (spindle) were from an old Dodge front end; however, almost any type (except a ball joint) could be substituted. All parts attached to the hub and knuckle should be arc-welded to minimize heat distortion. You may have to modify the pipe to insert the knuckle shank. The knuckle-pipe weld should be as strong as possible.

The main beams are two lengths of ½-in. pipe flattened on each end. These ends are bent and welded together after you weld the beams to the hub plates.

If you want to add up-and-down motion, you could tilt the center pole or bolt the bicycle rim off center.

See also: cars, sidewalk; ferris wheel; parade floats; playground equipment; train, children's.

clever ideas

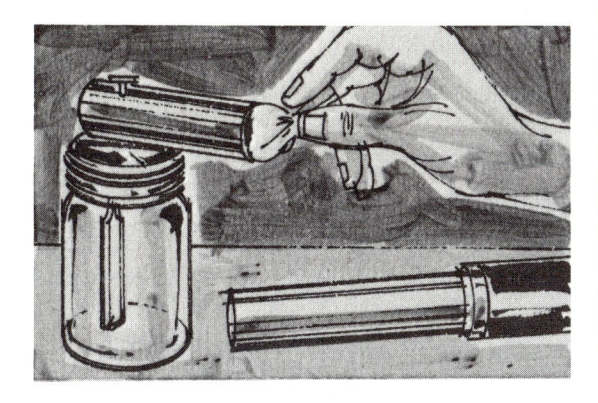

When using a vacuum-cleaner sprayer attachment for painting, dust from the hose sometimes becomes dislodged and gets in the paint, or it may even clog the sprayer nozzle. This can be easily prevented by wrapping a wad of steel wool in a piece of cloth, tying both ends and inserting it in the hose coupling at the top of the sprayer as shown. The tied end of the filter projects slightly for easy removal.

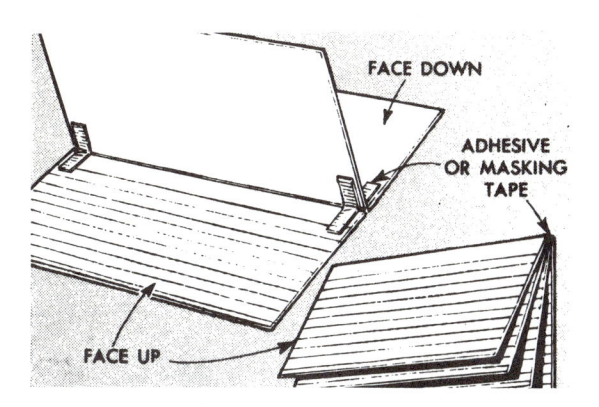

For anyone who keeps an index card file here is a tip on keeping multiple cards in better order. Place the first two cards of a series back-to-back with the upper one facing down, bottom one up. Then, cut a hinge from adhesive or masking tape and apply it across the joint at the outer edges as detailed above. Additional cards are bound into the series in the same manner.

When drafting or drawing paper is fastened to a board and you do not want to pierce the corners with thumbtacks, or risk tearing the paper, simply cut four corners from used stationery envelopes, slip them on the corners of the drafting paper and then tape the corner mounts to the board in the desired position. Since the mounts are easily removed, they can be relocated anywhere on the board to accommodate any size drafting paper.

Small rubber collars cut from a bicycle inner tube and slipped on double-end wrenches as pictured quickly identify the end being used. This saves time and eliminates the annoyance of having frequently to try both ends before finding the right one, especially when a wrench is laid down often while making an adjustment. The collars should be large enough for easy grasping when sliding them to the end of the wrench being used.

microphones

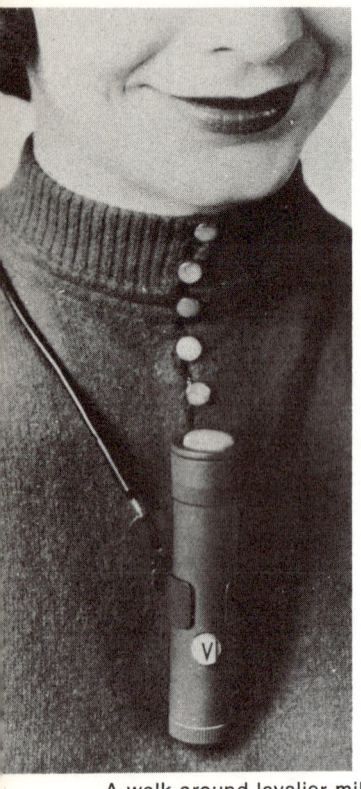

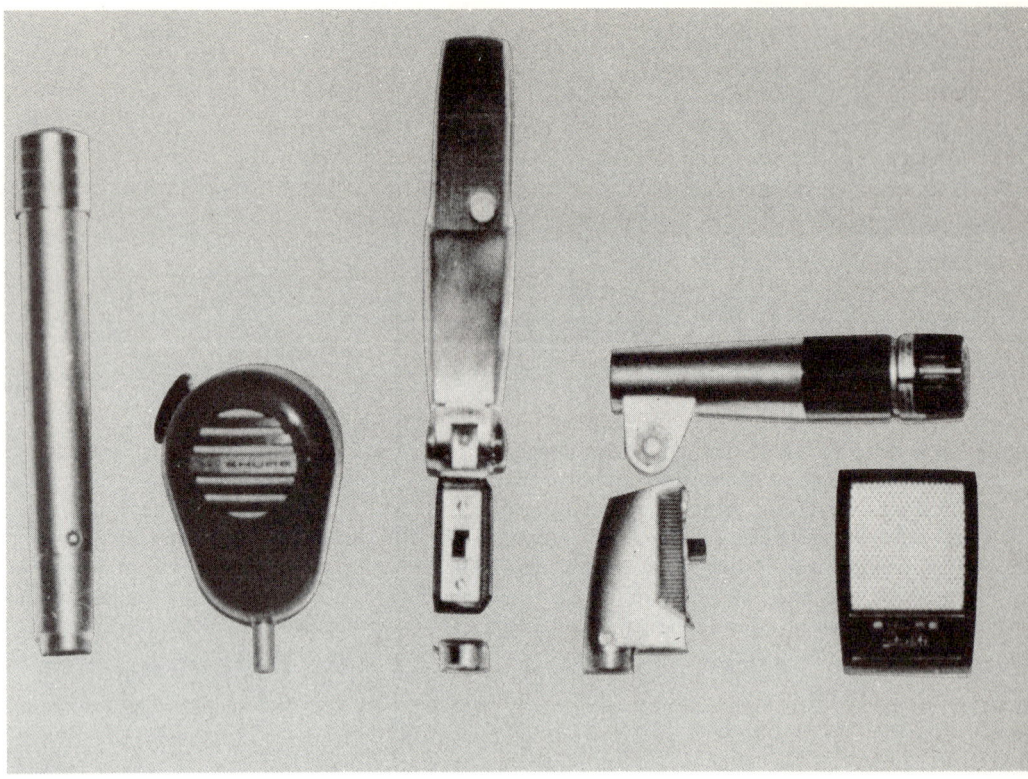

A walk-around lavalier mike hangs on a neck cord. It's convenient when mobile hands-free operation is a must. You talk normally into this mike

Choose your mike for the job

BY ART ZUCKERMAN

The best tape recorder, CB set or PA system is no better than its microphone. Here's how to select the best one for the job

■ A HIGH PRICE TAG is no surefire proof that a particular microphone is just the one you should buy. A super-duper high-fidelity job, perfect for tape recording, would probably be a horrible choice for CB work, for instance. Even a microphone designed specifically for ham use in a home station can come a cropper if you try using it aboard a noisy power boat or on the road. And even in broadcasting and recording, the pickup that does one job best can be all wrong for another.

So check out the various kinds of mikes and how they work before you buy.

The carbon microphone is a sort of living fossil. Still a highly respected workhorse in telephone and other communications jobs, it was the pickup used for the very first wireless voice transmissions, and it was the instrument through which entertainment was funneled into the living rooms of pioneer radio owners.

You might call the carbon mike an electrical valve. A button of carbon granules is attached to its diaphragm, and an electric current is passed through this button. As the diaphragm is pushed in and out by the sound waves hitting it, the granules are alternately squeezed together and released. Since this action changes their electrical resistance, current flow is modified, or modulated, by the movement. The resulting modulated current serves as the audio signal.

Carbon mikes aren't very long on frequency range. Most of them huddle fairly close to a 400 to 4000-cycle spread. This is fine for getting out a clear voice message. Carbon pickups are also pretty efficient, so you don't have to yell to get your point across the airwaves. However, prolonged exposure to vibration can ultimately "age" the pickup and destroy its usefulness.

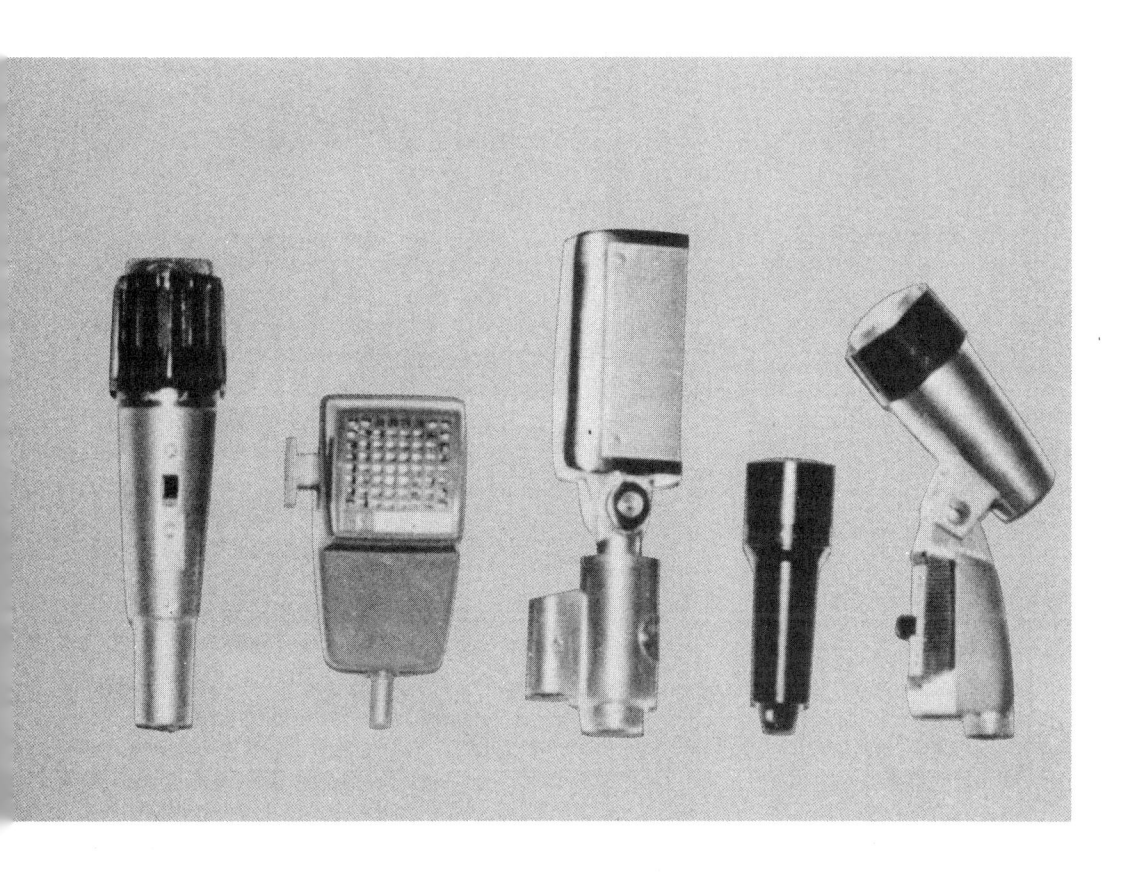

Crystal and ceramic mikes have a lot in common, including a generally low price tag. This explains their popularity as original equipment shipped with lower priced tape recorders.

More important, they are both piezoelectrics. That's the word for a material that, when twisted, compressed or otherwise tortured, generates electricity. The amount generated is in direct proportion to the degree the crystal is stressed. This talent for changing mechanical energy into electrical form gives piezoelectrics the right to membership in the transducer clan.

attached to diaphragm

A slab of piezoelectric material in a microphone is attached directly to the diaphragm, which pushes it around in response to incoming sound vibrations.

Crystal mikes kick out a lusty audio signal in return for the merest whisper of input, so microphone manufacturers can honestly brag about their great sensitivity. When it comes to tonal range, the best of them can reach as high as 10,000 cycles. But most don't get beyond 7000 to 8000 cycles. And it's a rare crystal that doesn't favor certain frequencies over others, a characteristic that creates some degree of tonal coloration. Furthermore, crystal mikes don't take kindly to rough handling, and extreme heat or humidity can ruin them.

Ceramic mikes get around the heat-humidity barrier, and they aren't quite as likely to bruise from physical shock. Some even manage to capture tones well above 10,000 cycles. But they aren't quite as sensitive as crystals.

By far the most popular kind of microphone sold today is the dynamic, also known as the moving-coil microphone. Essentially, it is a permanent-magnet loudspeaker in reverse. A coil of wire is attached to the microphone's diaphragm. As the diaphragm moves, the coil glides back and forth through the field of a permanent magnet. Now any conductor suddenly finds itself carrying an electrical current when it is moved through a magnetic field. The varying current thus produced in a dynamic mike is the audio signal.

Dynamic mikes come in all sizes, shapes and price categories. They can be made to cover the whole range of audible sound, or they can be restricted to a rather limited frequency range. While a shade less sensitive than piezoelectrics,

1699

microphones

moving coil dynamic mike

Most popular mike made is the dynamic, which is extremely rugged and not affected by heat or humidity. It can be tailored to fit any frequency spectrum

crystal mike

Least costly of all is the crystal mike, but severe disadvantages come with it. Heat and moisture can ruin it in short order, and it's easy to damage in use

get the right mike, continued

they are very rugged and completely unaffected by heat or humidity.

Dynamics cost more than piezoelectrics, but this price difference has been trimmed steadily in the past few years and some better home recorders now come with less expensive dynamic models.

For years ribbon microphones were a mainstay of the networks. They are similar in operating principle to dynamics. But instead of a diaphragm and coil combination, they merely have a corrugated ribbon of electrically conductive metal foil suspended in the field of a permanent magnet. When sound waves make it vibrate, the audio signal is generated within the ribbon diaphragm itself.

Because it has little mass, the ribbon mike is exceptionally compliant and responds to each nuance of sound, translating it directly into an audio signal with the greatest fidelity.

Unlike their dynamic cousins, ribbon mikes are usually open on both sides. Performers can be grouped on either side of this instrument, so one mike can do the work of two with ease.

Unfortunately, the ribbon microphone's great delicacy of response is matched by an even greater mechanical delicacy. Many a ribbon element has been ruined because a microphone boom rig was pivoted too rapidly through the air by a studio crew. Ribbon mikes are seldom used outdoors, where they can be undone by a strong wind. And ribbon microphones don't come cheap.

Another expensive pickup is the condenser microphone. Like the quite-different carbon mike, it requires its own power supply. Just as a dynamic mike is the mirror image of a PM speaker, the condenser mike is sort of an electrostatic speaker, backwards.

Its diaphragm is actually one of a condenser's two plates. A change in position of the diaphragm alters the capacitance of the instrument. The constantly changing capacitance creates the audio signal, but this signal is so weak that it needs the help of a preamplifier, which is part of the microphone system.

The condenser mike is possibly the truest

1700

controlled reluctance mike

This type unit is a ribbon mike with an alias. It is excellent where exacting frequency response is a must, but such a unit can be quite expensive

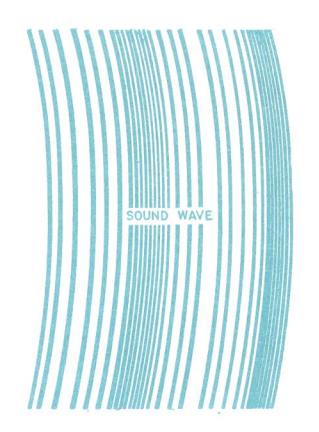

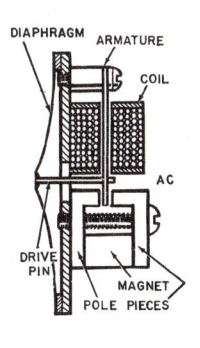

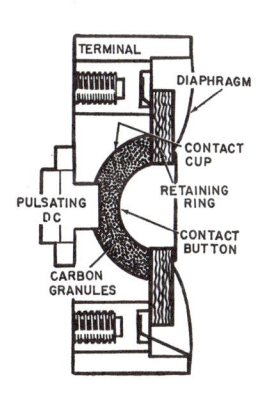

carbon mike

Workhorse of the microphone world, the carbon mike is used in the telephone. For general work, it is rapidly being replaced by the dynamics

of all to original sound. It is the choice of many pros who must have perfection. Some current models are surprisingly compact, but they sport hefty price tags.

When shopping for a mike, make absolutely certain you know what the merchandise you're shown really is. A fancy-looking case may actually conceal a cheap crystal pickup.

Above all, watch out for the salesman who shows you *the perfect microphone* for any job. It doesn't exist. Beware of oversell, too.

If you want a mike for a portable recorder, for example, there's no sense in buying a fancy ribbon mike that can't take a beating and gives you more frequency range than you can use.

Then there's the joker who tells you a microphone is superterrific because it is so fantastically sensitive that it will pick up anything. This is virtually the hallmark of all lower priced mikes, especially when you're working with equipment that has a rather insensitive mike input. But *it is not* a quality hallmark.

As a matter of fact, you may discover that the high-quality mike you want for a modestly priced recorder lacks the necessary output. So always check input sensitivity of your unit and output voltage of the microphone you choose. Sometimes it may pay you to invest in a microphone preamplifier. In that event, you will at least get the benefit of a superior pickup.

Now for the $64 question. How do you know the microphone you select will really be the right one for you?

In this day of the tape recorder, the answer is in-store testing. If the shop is fairly substantial, chances are it has at least one recorder on display with a mike input that suits the instrument you're ogling.

You can also be reasonably sure that a high-fidelity system is available to help in the testing process. Here are some things you should do:

If you're trying a noise-canceling mike, point it toward a hi-fi speaker working full blast. Then talk into the mike, using correct close-talking procedure. On playback, the music should be next to inaudible, while you come through loud and clear.

Where you want to be sure a communications

microphones

mike will overcome severe radio or electronics noise, use the lowest tape speed available on the recorder—ideally 15/16 i.p.s.—and record your voice with the level set too low. This should create lots of background noise to compete with the pickup. If your voice knifes through it all, you have reason to assume it will do a fair job under rotten transmission conditions.

Checking out a cardioid mike requires the services of the store's demonstration hi-fi system. Start with the mike facing dead away from the speaker. Holding it a normal distance from your mouth and at a normal angle, talk into it. Retaining this same mike-to-mouth relationship, turn about 45 deg., calling off your position into the microphone. Then turn another 45 deg. and repeat until you've boxed the compass.

The playback should give a quick clue to the relative sensitivity of the microphone to background noise emanating from different positions.

Do you need a pickup that will render faithful, wide-range reproduction? The obvious test is to lug your instrument down to the store and try it. If this is not practical, the hi-fi system in the store can again be pressed into service.

Use the best speaker in the store and ask the salesman to play a colorful symphonic record through it. Assuming you are choosing between two mikes or more, record this performance with each, then compare the playback results.

A record-and-listen test will also check features such as long-range pickup, wind effect filtration, pop removal and compensatory frequency peaking.

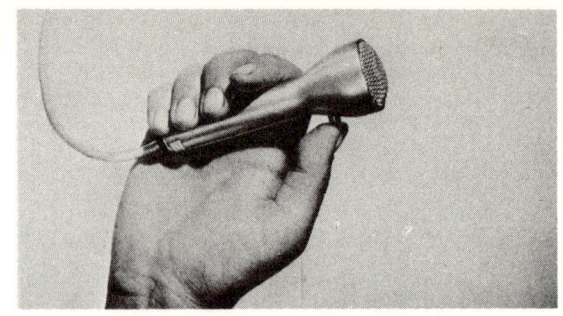

Pushbutton on hand mike is a help when using tape recorder and a must with radio transmitter. It means instant cutoffs without reaching for switches

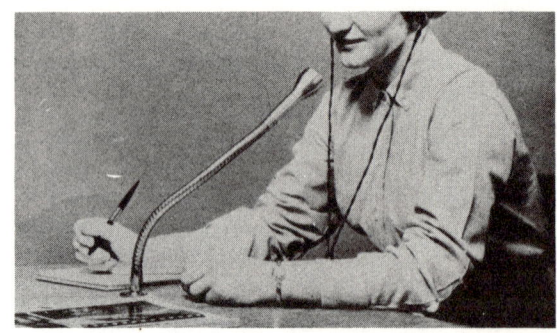

Goosenecks fit almost any mike, are ideal at fixed locations used by different persons, and can be easily adjusted to almost any level or position

MATCHING THE MICROPHONE TO THE JOB

Microphone Type	Job	Advantage
Carbon	Communications (especially mobile)	Good voice clarity, low cost, good output
Crystal	Communications, recording, limited frequency broadcasting, PA	Inexpensive, high output, possible fair quality in non-shock situations
Ceramic	Communications, recording, limited-frequency broadcasting, PA	Inexpensive, high output, less susceptible to shock, climate problems than crystal
Dynamic	Communications, recording, broadcasting, PA	Wide price range, capable of high-fidelity performance, extremely rugged
Ribbon	High-quality recording and broadcasting (studio only)	Superb frequency response, inherent directional control, ability to group performer on both sides
Condenser	High-quality recording and broadcasting	Top frequency response, fairly rugged
Omni-directional	General applications	Broad-area pickup
Cardioid	Public address, broadcasting and recording	Highly directional, providing feedback control, pronounced stereo effects, noise and reverberation control
Noise-canceling	Communications (especially mobile)	Maximum speech clarity under adverse conditions

In all these tests the tape must be played back through the hi-fi music system you've been using, with its tone controls set in the "flat" position.

It is always wise to ask for return privileges when you buy anything as individualistic as a microphone. A reputable store will be willing. Especially if the mike is expensive.

Lastly, you should seek a guarantee—and be sure you know precisely what's guaranteed, and for how long.

See also: electronics; guitar amplifier; high fidelity; tape recorders; transmitter, FM.

microphotography

ADAPTER RING
CARDBOARD DISK
RETAINING RING
POCKET MICROSCOPE

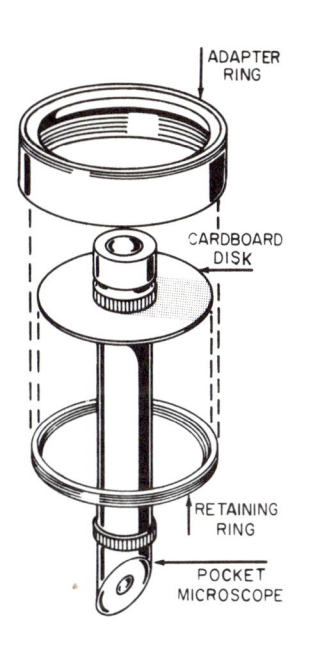

Nearsighted camera shoots fine detail

BY RENE ZENTNER

■ THERE COMES a frustrating time in the life of nearly every photographer when he feels that there just aren't any new subjects for his camera. I know—it happened to me not long ago. But then I decided to try my hand at microphotography, and now I'm convinced that I'll never run out of things to photograph. Even such humdrum items as salt and laundry detergent become exciting subjects when you move in for a close-up with camera and microscope.

A laboratory setup for taking microphotographs can run into thousands of dollars. But that's for the pro. You can outfit yourself for only a few dollars by buying a 50x microscope called the Micro-Pen. It can be ordered from the Edmund Scientific Co., Barrington, N.J. (Catalog no. 30,013). No need to buy a special camera—a 35-mm single-lens reflex is perfect.

The drawing shows how I connected the microscope to the camera. A hole cut in a cardboard disk provided a snug fit for the barrel of the microscope. An adapter ring and retaining ring are used to hold the disk in front of the camera lens. The rings are standard items in any photo shop.

Through trial and error I've found that a 7-watt frosted night-light bulb positioned an inch or so below the microscope objective supplies sufficient illumination for focusing and photographing at reasonable speeds. It's not possible to give any definite recommendations about exposure time; that is something you'll have to determine by experimentation. But as a starting point you may want to consider shooting between 1/25 and 1/100 sec. at f/3.5 on 400 ASA film.

If no microscope slides are available, slide cover glasses of the type used for mounting color transparencies may be used. Your kitchen cabinets and medicine chest should yield a supply of photographic subjects.

Before making the photograph, be sure to place the camera on a sturdy tripod. If you don't, magnification of camera movement may ruin the picture. If your camera has a built-in self timer, use it to trip the shutter. Otherwise, a cable release will do the job.

See also: cameras, used; photography; tripods.

midget autos: see car, midget; cars, sidewalk
midget circular saws: see slitting saws
mildew: see house paints
milling: see keyways; lathe techniques

mirrors

Makeup mirror for powder rooms

Show people know the importance of controlled light in applying makeup, and your wife will feel like a star herself in front of this lamp-studded, back-stage dressing mirror. Controlled from full bright to warm glow by a dimmer switch, the mirror will let her apply her makeup to suit the particular lighting mood. All you need is a fancy picture frame, a dozen or more pin-type plastic sockets with bulbs and a dimmer switch known as Luxtrol.

Replace the picture in the frame with a mirror, then on center line penciled on the back of the frame lay off equal spacings of the sockets. About 4 in. is a good average spacing. Drill holes through the frame on these centers, the holes slightly undersize so that each socket is a press fit. For neatness and ease of wiring take pains to press each socket in to the same level so that all will project the same distance at the back of the frame and present a pleasing symmetry on the front face when the bulbs are in place. When placing the wires be sure that the socket caps are turned to a uniform tension with the wrench supplied so that the points will penetrate the insulation and make contact with the wires.

The control switch is designed to be installed in a two or four-wire outlet as in details A and B below. Switch capacities start at 200 watts so use this as a value when calculating the total wattage.

See also: bathrooms; bedroom furniture; vacation homes.

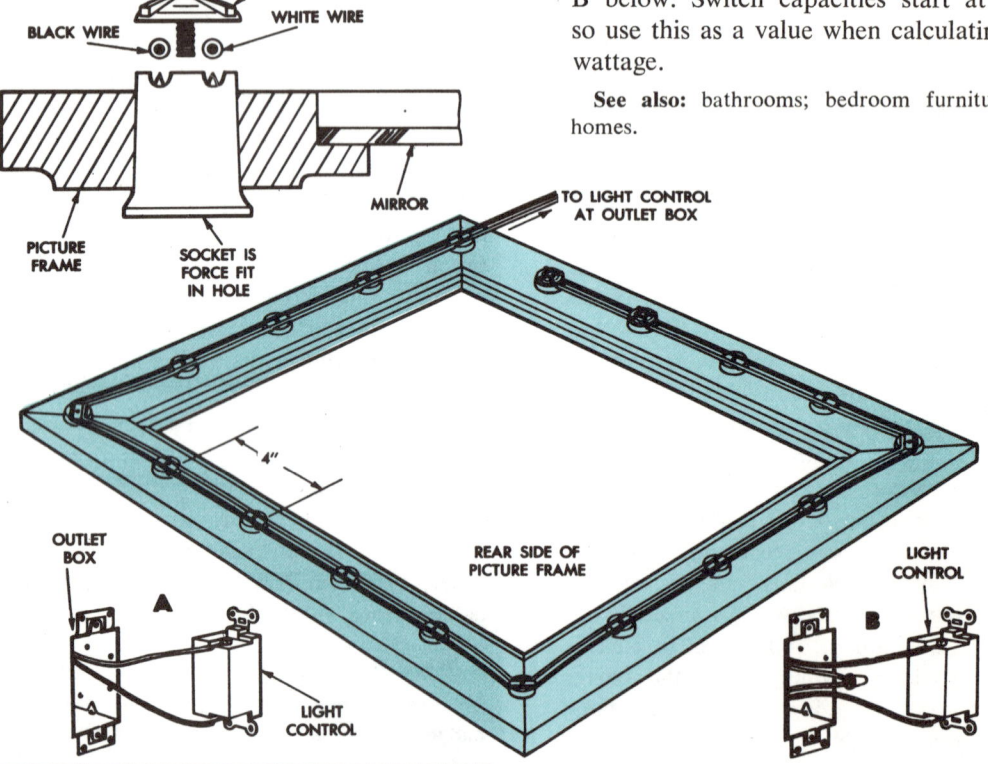

mitering: see picture frames; radial-arm saws; woodworking
mixer, concrete: see concrete mixer

clever ideas

When replacing a sash pane, a torch will soften the old putty so it can be cleaned out with a putty knife. Protect the sash with a metal shield.

Frozen foods will thaw quicker if all surfaces are exposed to free circulation of air at room temperature. A rack used for cooling cakes is ideal for this.

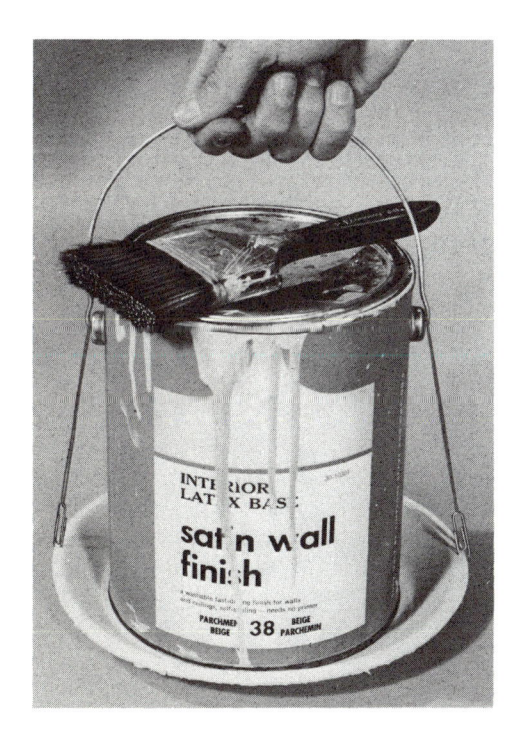

This snap-on drip tray is just a paper plate attached to the paint can with paper clips and rubber bands. Bend the clips so they can be pushed through the rim.

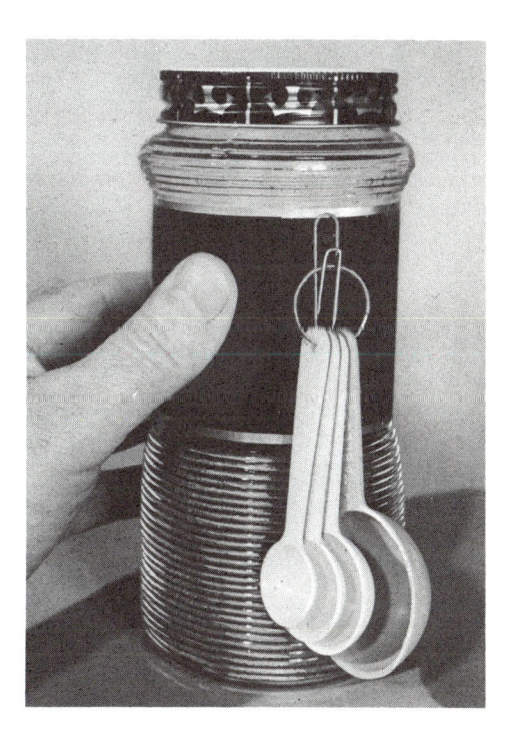

Instant coffee takes time to prepare if you have to hunt for measuring spoons. To save time, tape a paper-clip hanger on the jar to hold them.

1705

mixers, food

How to fix a food mixer

BY JOHN PENNINGTON

That electric mixer
can be kept in good
working condition if
you take the time to
clean it and check
it periodically for worn
or damaged parts

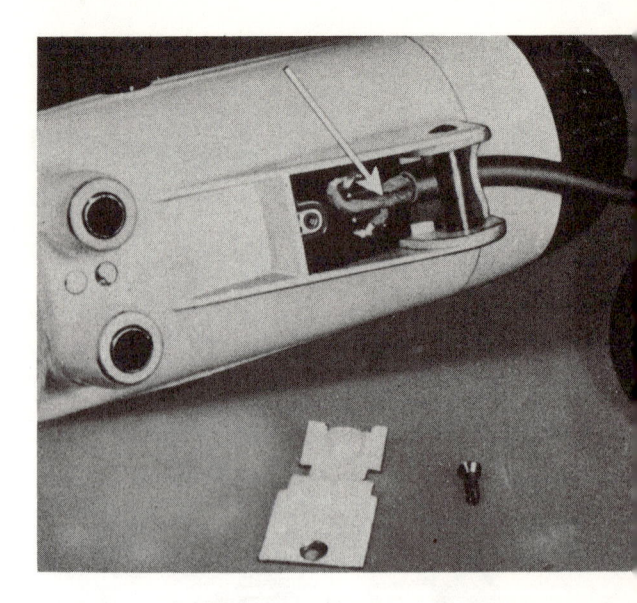

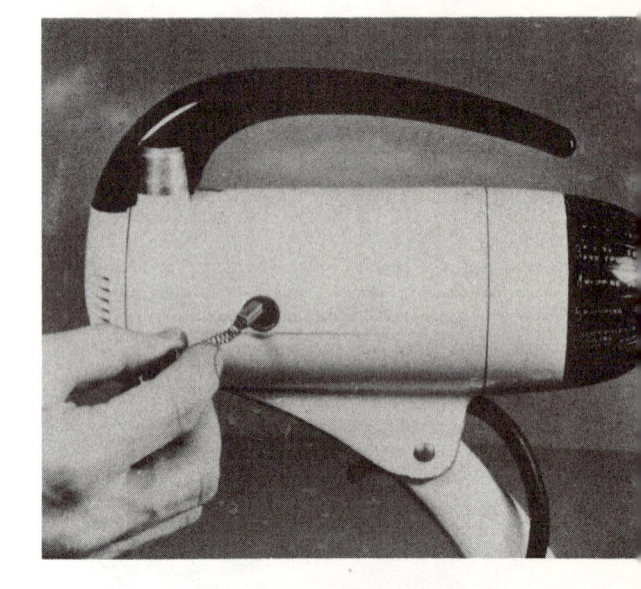

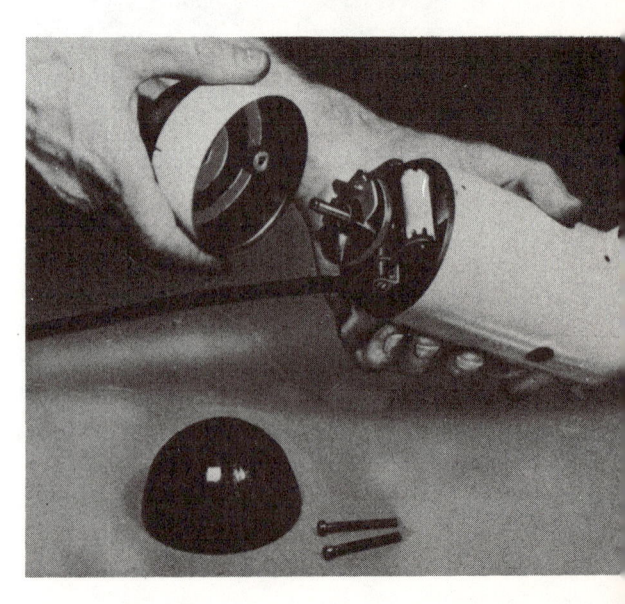

---

mixer, photo chemical: see photography
mobile: see yard decorations
modeling wheel: see potter's wheel
moisture: see basements; condensation; humidifiers; painting

1706

IF YOU EVER drop your electric mixer, one or both the motor brushes may be shattered in the fall. Brushes in a mixer motor will take years of ordinary wear, but the shock of a fall from the table to the floor may break one or both. It's always well to remove both brushes and inspect them before starting the motor.

The center photo at the left shows what the brushes look like. To take them out you unscrew the holder, or retainer, which projects through an opening on each side of the motor housing. There's a screwdriver slot in each holder. Go light on the screwdriver and remember that the brushes are spring-loaded. They'll pop out on the floor unless you grasp the holder as you unscrew it. If the brushes are badly worn, replace them with new ones. If they're okay, be sure they are marked so you can replace them exactly as they were originally.

The cord on a mixer gets rough usage. If the plug end is in good condition, take off the access plate on the underside of the motor (usually it's between the legs of the bracket) and examine the terminals, indicated by the arrow in the upper left photo. Brush away any lint, and if insulation is worn, replace the cord.

clean periodically

Tiny electric motors collect much lint and dust, so take the motor apart periodically for cleaning. Remove the speed-control cone, or wheel, and the access plates as shown in the bottom photo, left. Clear away dust and lint with a soft bristle brush. Inside you'll find a capacitor (arrow, right upper photo). If your mixer causes radio interference, replace this.

Now remove the bearing plate as in the center photo, right. Pull out the armature as in the lower right photo. Brush away all lint and dust from the armature and field coils. You'll see the brush track on the commutator, which is a part of the armature. If the commutator is smooth with no indication of grooving at the edges of the brush track, merely wipe off the loose carbon. Polish the commutator with a very fine sandpaper if you wish. Wipe clean to remove any abrasive. Clean the worm at the end of the armature shaft and relubricate, using a lubricant approved by the manufacturer.

Reassemble all parts in the reverse order. Reoil bearings sparingly, also applying oil at any other point indicated by the word "oil."

See also: appliances; blenders, electric; clothes dryers, electric; coffee-makers; electrical wiring; floor polishers; guarantees; irons; testers, electrical; toasters.

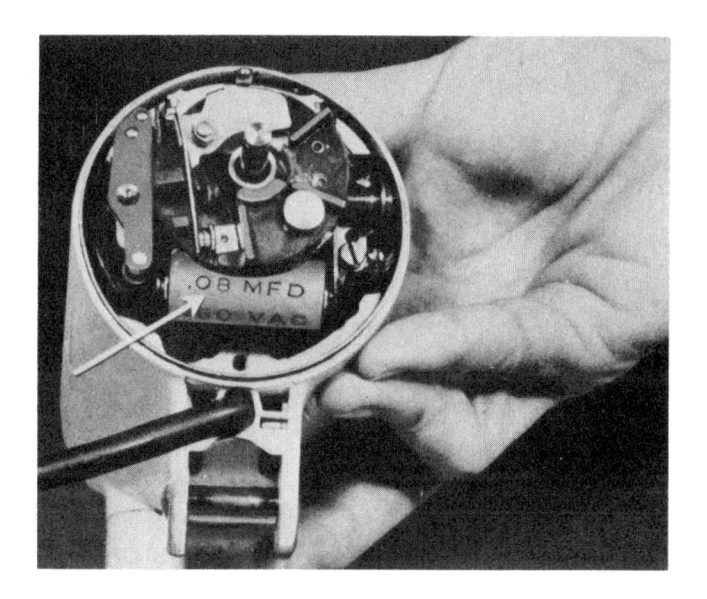

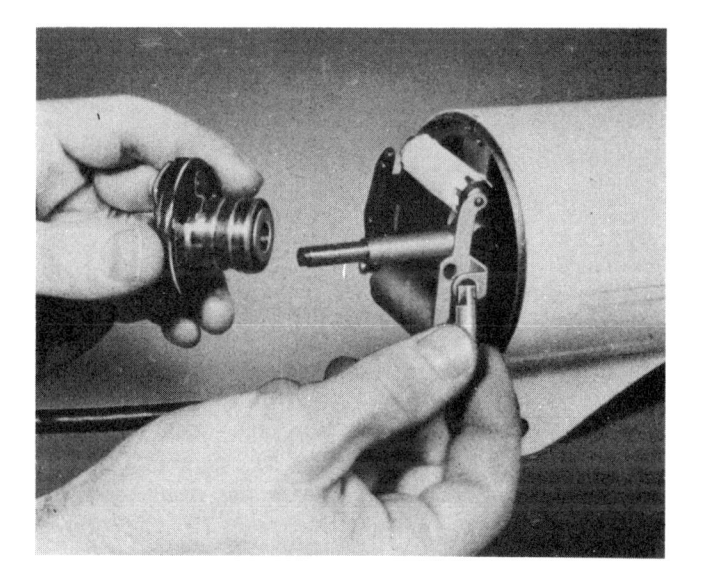

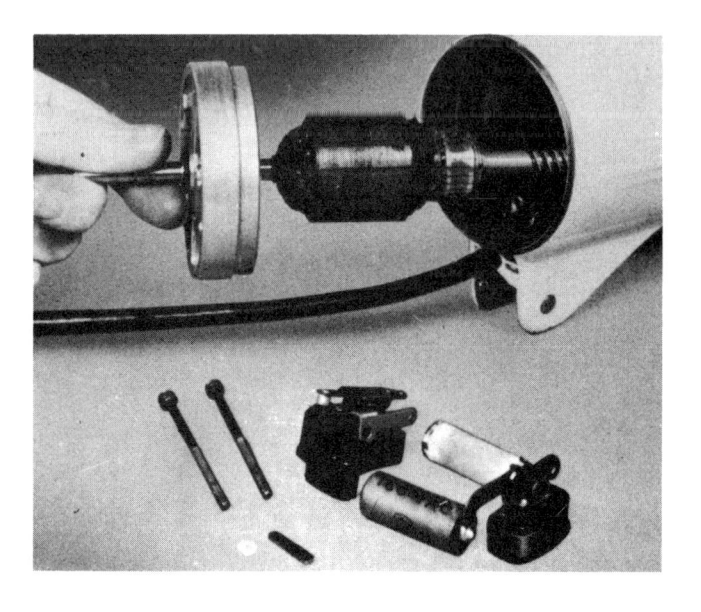

moldings

Moldings—
the finishing touch

BY W. CLYDE LAMMEY

Any woodwork without moldings
has a certain unfinished look,
leaves you with a sense of
incompleteness. Here are the
molding shapes most readily available

■ NO MATTER WHERE located, moldings are a basic of design, an element to be utilized in a wide range of applications. Without moldings almost any structure, anything with dimension, is little more than a box shape with stark overhangs and uninteresting square corners.

But a molding is a shape that catches the eye. It adds something both elemental and decorative, the finishing detail, leaves you with the feeling that the job is complete.

Traditional architecture utilizes a range of applied moldings both inside and outside the structure; inside as a finishing detail in a room, such as picture molding; a coved mold in the corner where wall meets ceiling; as a baseboard with quarter-round and as door and window trim with stops having one molded edge. Outside you see moldings in various forms under cornices, around sash frames and around and over door frames.

Common applied moldings are combinations of curves, reverse curves and plane surfaces generally worked on the face, corners and edges of both hard and softwood lumber. As a rule these shapes come in the form of strips varying in width and thickness and are sold by the lineal foot.

Common among the applied moldings are the simple cove and quarter-round shapes which are cut on small square or rectangular strips. The former shape is ordinarily used as trim under an overhanging member such as a mantel, shelf or similar application. The latter you'll see forming the trim where a baseboard meets flooring. Of course, there are variants in the application and shape of these forms which are commonly known as bed moldings.

Crown and cove moldings are similar in that both shapes are usually cut on one face of stock varying in width from 2 or 3 in. to 5 in. or more in the standard sizes.

As these moldings are usually intended to span a right-angle corner, as in a room where wall meets ceiling, the back corners are cut at a 45-deg. angle and the adjacent corners are trimmed at 90 deg. to the 45-deg. corners, the flats serving as "stops" for the curves cut on the face.

Cove moldings are commonly cut with a single concavity on the face, often the full width of the stock, but these also are cut in combinations of concavity and reverse curve, the former shape usually the wider of the two. A narrow plane surface, or flat, is usually cut between the shapes to serve as a stop at the ends of the curves.

Common crown moldings consist of variations of reverse-curve and cove cuts in combination on the same face of the stock. They come in standard widths from about 1½ in. up. Like the cove moldings, crown moldings in the larger sizes are designed to span a corner.

Half-round moldings, of which there are various sizes, generally are applied as nosings, that is, are nailed or otherwise fastened to square edges to serve either a practical or decorative purpose. On old work you will sometimes see half rounds attached to the outer edges of stair treads. Much the same is true of the combination half-round-and-cove mold which you will often find serving as a nosing on later-type stair treads. These usually have a half-round-and-cove shape cut on the same face of the strip. Such moldings generally come as strips ranging in widths from fractions of an inch to about 2 in. or more.

Stops commonly range in thickness from ⅜ to ½ in. and in widths up to 2 in. or more. These usually come with a reverse-curve molding on one corner but there also are variants of the shapes available. Some are supplied with only one corner slightly rounded to a uniform radius. Stops are used mainly in door and window

CROWNS

WP 49 11/16" x 3-5/8"

WP 52 11/16" x 2-3/4"

WP 60 11/16" x 1-3/4"

WP 74 11/16" x 1-3/4"

COVES

WP 85 11/16" x 1-3/4"

WP 86 11/16" x 1-5/8"

BEDS

WP 90 3/4" x 1-1/8"

WP 93 3/4" x 3/4"

QUARTER ROUNDS

WP 103 1-1/16" x 1-1/16"
WP 105 3/4" x 3/4"
WP 108 1/2" x 1/2"
WP 110 1/4" x 1/4"

HALF ROUNDS

WP 123 5/16" x 5/8"
WP 124 1/4" x 1/2"

BASE SHOE

WP 126 1/2" x 3/4"

shelf edges

WP 142 1/4" x 3/4"

WP 144 1/4" x 3/4"

BRICK MOLDINGS

WP 175 1-1/16" x 2"

WP 180 1-5/16" x 2"

DRIP CAPS

WP 187 1-1/16" x 2"
WP 188 1-1/16" x 1-5/8"

WP 196 11/16" x 1-3/4"
WP 197 11/16" x 1-5/8"

CORNER GUARDS

WP 201 1-3/8" x 1-3/8"

WP 202 1-1/8" x 1-1/8"

WP 203 1-3/8" x 1-3/8"

WP 205 1-1/8" x 1-1/8"

WP 206 3/4" x 3/4"

SHINGLE MOLDINGS

WP 207 11/16" x 2-1/2"
WP 209 11/16" x 2"
WP 210 11/16" x 1-5/8"

WP 212 11/16" x 2-1/2"
WP 213 9/16" x 2"

HAND RAILS

WP 230 1-9/16" x 1-11/16"

WP 231 1-5/8" x 1-3/4"

ROUNDS

WP 232 1-5/8" x 1-5/8"
WP 233 1-5/16" x 1-5/16"
WP 234 1-1/16" x 1-1/16"

S4S STOCK

WP 236 1-5/8" x 1-5/8"
WP 237 1-5/16" x 1-5/16"
WP 238 1-1/16" x 1-1/16"
WP 239 3/4" x 3/4"

WP 246 3/4" x 2-3/4"
WP 248 3/4" x 1-3/4"
WP 249 3/4" x 1-5/8"
WP 251 3/4" x 1-3/8"
WP 254 1/2" x 3/4"

PICTURE MOLDING

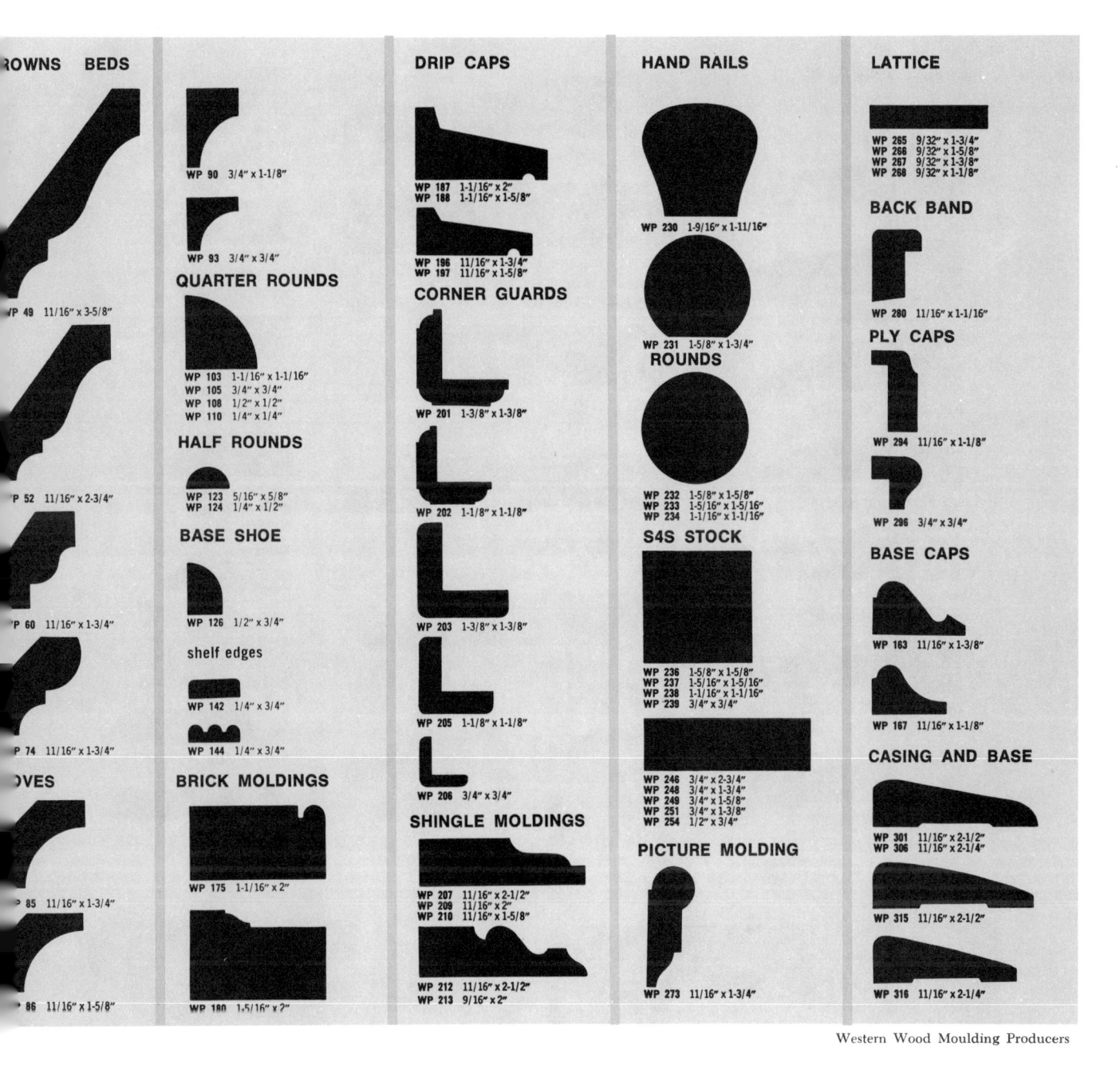

WP 273 11/16" x 1-3/4"

LATTICE

WP 265 9/32" x 1-3/4"
WP 266 9/32" x 1-5/8"
WP 267 9/32" x 1-3/8"
WP 268 9/32" x 1-1/8"

BACK BAND

WP 280 11/16" x 1-1/16"

PLY CAPS

WP 294 11/16" x 1-1/8"

WP 296 3/4" x 3/4"

BASE CAPS

WP 163 11/16" x 1-3/8"

WP 167 11/16" x 1-1/8"

CASING AND BASE

WP 301 11/16" x 2-1/2"
WP 306 11/16" x 2-1/4"

WP 315 11/16" x 2-1/2"

WP 316 11/16" x 2-1/4"

Western Wood Moulding Producers

framing and are ordinarily attached with small finishing nails having the heads set below the surface and the holes puttied flush. On the finest work the stops are attached with ovalhead screws, the heads being countersunk flush or turned down on plated washers.

Other shapes which classify as moldings are full rounds, screen moldings, chair rails, window stools and corner beads to name a few of the many shapes. Some of these are not so commonly used in present-day construction but most are still available as replacements. Full rounds in larger sizes are often utilized as stair rails. A variant (although it does not classify as molding) is the well-known dowel, which is regularly supplied 36 in. long.

If you've ever made screen frames you've used one of the several forms of screen moldings and you'll see many of the other forms illustrated in nearly all old work and occasionally in newer structures.

All the illustrations, which are end views of the shapes, show only one size. But, of course, many of the moldings come in several widths and thicknesses to adapt them to various types of work.

When installing moldings around outside corners the ends are mitered and it's the usual prac-

moldings

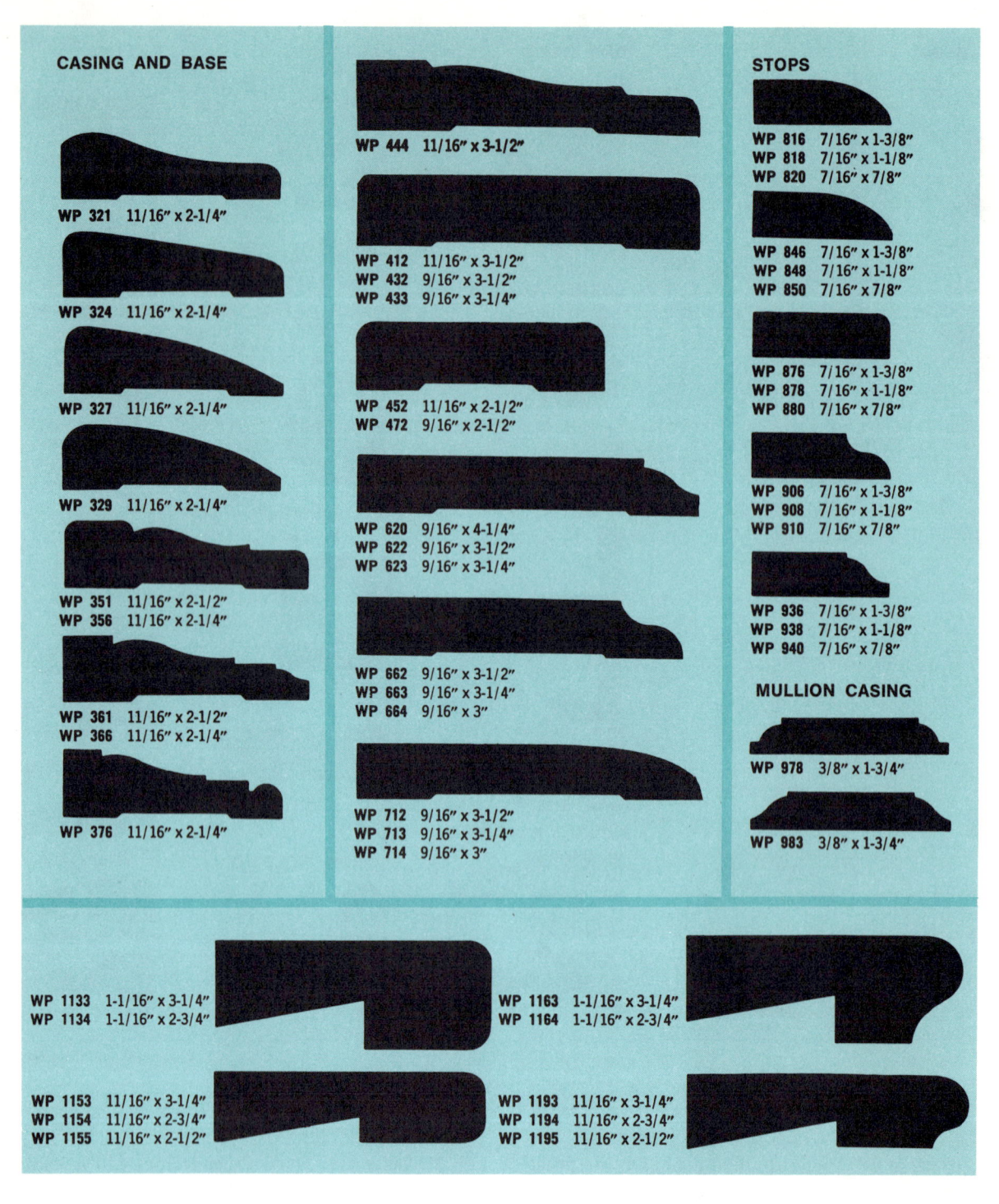

CASING AND BASE

WP 321	11/16" x 2-1/4"
WP 324	11/16" x 2-1/4"
WP 327	11/16" x 2-1/4"
WP 329	11/16" x 2-1/4"
WP 351	11/16" x 2-1/2"
WP 356	11/16" x 2-1/4"
WP 361	11/16" x 2-1/2"
WP 366	11/16" x 2-1/4"
WP 376	11/16" x 2-1/4"
WP 444	11/16" x 3-1/2"
WP 412	11/16" x 3-1/2"
WP 432	9/16" x 3-1/2"
WP 433	9/16" x 3-1/4"
WP 452	11/16" x 2-1/2"
WP 472	9/16" x 2-1/2"
WP 620	9/16" x 4-1/4"
WP 622	9/16" x 3-1/2"
WP 623	9/16" x 3-1/4"
WP 662	9/16" x 3-1/2"
WP 663	9/16" x 3-1/4"
WP 664	9/16" x 3"
WP 712	9/16" x 3-1/2"
WP 713	9/16" x 3-1/4"
WP 714	9/16" x 3"

STOPS

WP 816	7/16" x 1-3/8"
WP 818	7/16" x 1-1/8"
WP 820	7/16" x 7/8"
WP 846	7/16" x 1-3/8"
WP 848	7/16" x 1-1/8"
WP 850	7/16" x 7/8"
WP 876	7/16" x 1-3/8"
WP 878	7/16" x 1-1/8"
WP 880	7/16" x 7/8"
WP 906	7/16" x 1-3/8"
WP 908	7/16" x 1-1/8"
WP 910	7/16" x 7/8"
WP 936	7/16" x 1-3/8"
WP 938	7/16" x 1-1/8"
WP 940	7/16" x 7/8"

MULLION CASING

WP 978	3/8" x 1-3/4"
WP 983	3/8" x 1-3/4"

WP 1133	1-1/16" x 3-1/4"
WP 1134	1-1/16" x 2-3/4"
WP 1153	11/16" x 3-1/4"
WP 1154	11/16" x 2-3/4"
WP 1155	11/16" x 2-1/2"
WP 1163	1-1/16" x 3-1/4"
WP 1164	1-1/16" x 2-3/4"
WP 1193	11/16" x 3-1/4"
WP 1194	11/16" x 2-3/4"
WP 1195	11/16" x 2-1/2"

tice to cut the two members just lightly over at the mitered ends. This assures a tight fit (if the miter is properly cut, of course) and should there be slight shrinkage of the wood, or movement of the framing due to shrinkage, the mitered joint will remain a tight fit.

Moldings that meet in an inside corner should always be coped, that is, one member is cut and nailed in place the full length, the end in the corner being cut square off. Then the end of the meeting mold is cut to a shape that will fit tightly against the first member, using a scroll, or coping saw, and making the cut at a very slight angle. Moldings that fit between walls should not be forced; rather they should be cut slightly under.

See also: dadoes; picture frames; radial-arm saws; walls; woodworking.

moldings

How to cope-cut moldings

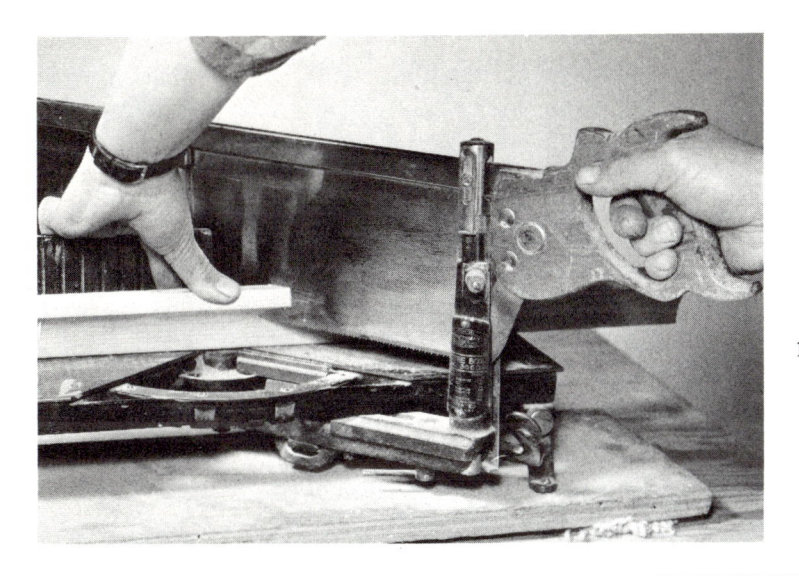

You cope inside moldings and miter the outside ones. Learning this trick can save you countless hours of fitting and make the job perfect

WHEN INSTALLING cove or crown molding around the ceiling of a room, you should remember that while outside corners are generally mitered, inside corners should always be coped —you should never miter both. If you do, the inside ones will later open up when the wood shrinks, making a poor joint.

Coping is the term applied to cutting the reverse shape of one molding to coincide with the profile contour of the adjoining molding when the two are butted together.

Transferring the reverse shape to the molding can pose a perplexing problem. However, there's a simple stunt to follow that will give you a near-perfect fit every time. The line of cut is actually "marked" by placing the molding in a miterbox and sawing the end at a 45-deg. angle. Here you will notice that the molding is set in the miterbox in the same position as it will be installed—the part that fits flat against the wall is placed flat against the back of the box.

The very edge of the 45-deg. cut established the line of cut which is now carefully followed with a coping saw held at right angles to the face of the molding. The waste piece removed will be wedge-shaped. Where all corners of a room are inside corners, only one end of each molding is coped, the other end is simply sawed off square to butt into the corner.

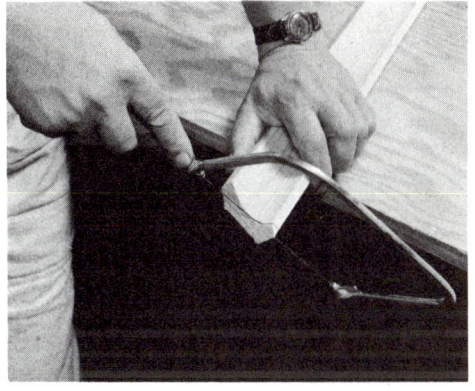

morse code: see electronics; oscillator, audio
mosaic tile: see jewelry case; sewing box
motorbike shelter: see shelters

motorcycles

Winter tuneup for trouble-free cycling

BY MORTON J. SCHULTZ

Winter weather doesn't welcome motorcyclists along the open road—but it does give you an extra opportunity to be certain your machine is in top condition by the time cycle weather returns

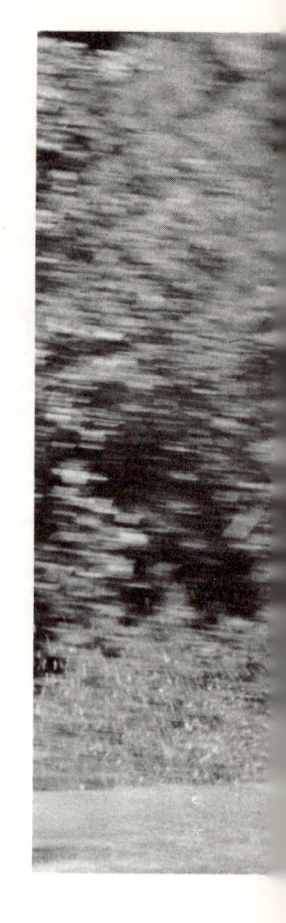

Lightweight and heavyweight motorcycles have more differences than gross weight and engine displacement. Maintenance procedures differ, too. So lightweights will be treated here first. A special section covering tuneup for heavyweights begins on p. 1718.

■ THOSE UNFRIENDLY WEEKENDS of winter offer the ideal opportunity to give your lightweight motorcycle a leisurely, careful, thorough tuneup. And be sure it's careful; while cycle work is less complicated than car servicing, it's more critical.

Before starting to work, break out your owner's manual and study it carefully. This article won't parrot the manual, but will stress especially important services and point out some that the manual may not cover.

Read this article through, as well as the manual. When you're ready to get started, you'll find it's best to attack the various areas in the order in which they're mentioned. And to keep an accurate gauge on your progress, check off each job in the box provided after you complete it.

wheels and tires

☐ Riding a motorcycle with unsafe rubber can be suicide. Give both tires a close inspection. If they are worn or show any breaks, replace them.

Consider switching the tires—putting the back

one on the front wheel and vice versa. A tire kept in continuous service—on the front wheel especially—will begin to wear irregularly and start to peak. This will affect your ability to handle the bike.

☐ Test for loose spokes by striking each spoke individually with a wrench. If they're tight, they'll "ping." A dull response means the spoke is loose. Tighten loose spokes with a spoke nipple torque wrench.

Replace any broken spokes. To do this you must deflate the tire and pull it off the rim in the area of the bad spoke.

☐ Finally, always make sure both tires are inflated to the recommended air pressure.

fuel system

The fuel setup of lightweight motorcycles is quite simple. They have no mass of fuel lines—just a length of hose leading from the gas tank to an uncomplicated carburetor. There's no fuel pump either; gas flows to the carburetor by gravity.

However, a cycle carburetor *is* sensitive and should be checked, cleaned and adjusted at least as often as an auto carb. If one little passage gets plugged, gas stops feeding to the engine cylinder.

Whether you have a four-stroke engine which feeds on raw gas, or a two-stroker which runs on a mixture of gas and oil, servicing is as follows:

☐ Service the air cleaner as outlined in the manual. Many mechanical problems can be traced to a plugged-up cleaner which has thrown the meticulously balanced fuel-air ratio out of whack. The rich fuel mixture that results can lead to loss of power, overheating and high fuel consumption.

☐ Check the fuel strainer. The strainer cleans dirt from the fuel before it enters the carburetor. It's usually located where the fuel line connects into the carburetor bowl. If it gets blocked, fuel is blocked.

To remove the strainer, shut off the fuel supply and unhook the fuel line. Then clean the strainer in gasoline.

☐ Test the functioning of the carburetor idle by letting the engine warm to operating temperature. If the engine races or rough-idles, turn

motorcycles

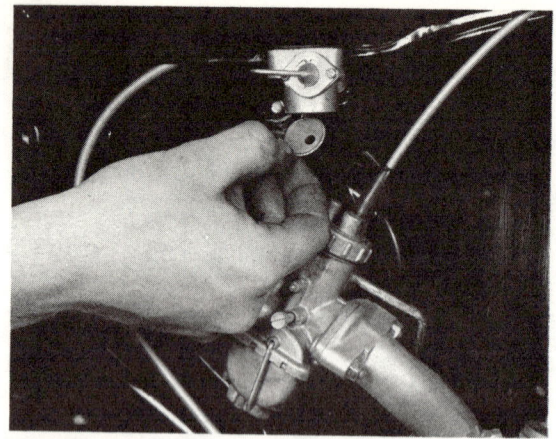

Clean the metal fuel strainer in gasoline. This one is in the gas shutoff on the tank side of the fuel line; some are at the carburetor inlet

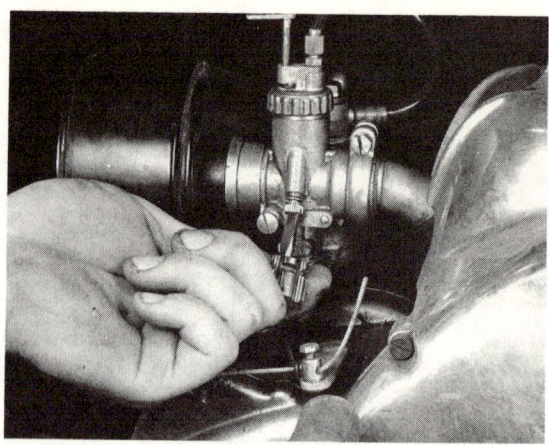

Smooth a rough idle or a racing engine with the idle-speed-stop screw, turning it to the right for a richer mixture and to the left for a leaner mixture

Adjust breaker points (static timing) with a feeler gauge to owner's manual specs. Final adjustment is with a timing light—at a shop if you don't have one

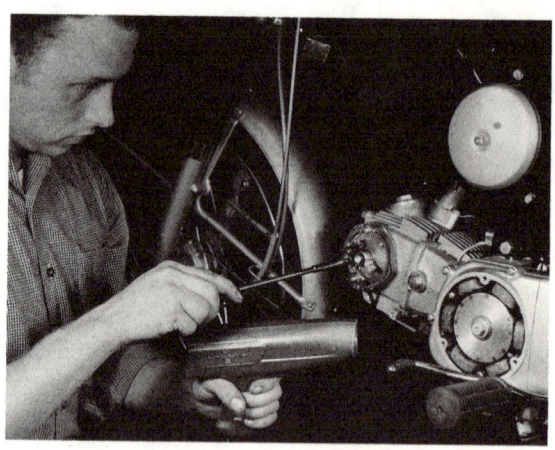

For final fine adjustment of ignition timing, a special timing light is essential. It measures ignition timing and timing at the end of the spark advance

Tighten or loosen the drive chain with the adjusting nut on the rear fork. An over-tight chain hinders power transmission, while a slack chain will slap

To adjust the brakes, operate handlebar lever (front brake) or pedal (rear brake) while taking up on the adjusting nuts at the corresponding bike wheels

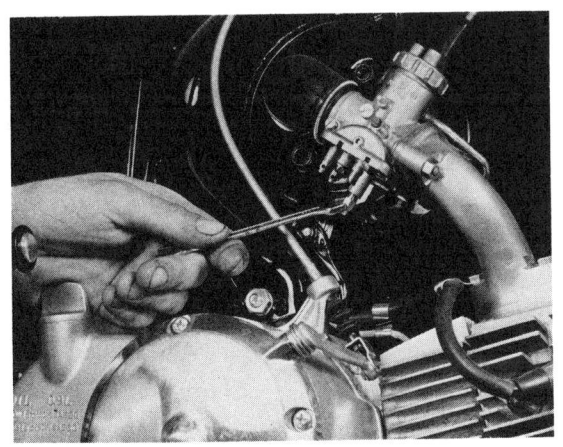

Carburetor dirt can shut off fuel to the engine. Disassemble it by unscrewing the jets as shown, then clean the carb thoroughly in gasoline. But be careful

With the piston (lower right) held at top dead center, a feeler gauge is used to check intake valve adjustment. The exhaust (below the head) is adjusted too

Wheels on a lightweight should be pulled every 5000 to 10,000 miles for brake lining inspection. Any glazed surfaces should be roughened slightly

the idle-speed stop screw in or out. If the carburetor isn't dirt-clogged, the idle will smooth out.

☐ If the carb *is* blocked, disassemble and clean it. This is easily done. In the case of a common four-stroke engine of the type shown in the accompanying photographs, drop the bowl and remove the two jets with a screwdriver. Wash the parts in carburetor cleaner and blow them clean with air pressure. While you're at it, remove the fuel line and clean that too. It might be clogged with residue (varnish).

ignition

Your motorcycle's ignition system has one job: to generate a spark strong enough to jump the plug's electrode gap.

☐ To check whether it's doing its job, remove the plug, reattach the plug wire, ground the plug by holding it to the head, and crank the engine. Unless you see a nice spark, you'll have to search out the trouble.

☐ Even if the ignition circuit seems to check out, look the plug over. If the electrode end is worn or damaged, if the gap is too wide, or if the porcelain is cracked or broken, get a new plug.

☐ Check all the wiring for breaks and fraying and replace any bad leads.

☐ Even if you got a nice spark, time the ignition to the manual specs; a retarded spark costs you power and an advanced spark can damage the engine. If you don't have a timing light, give the job to a cycle shop.

☐ Check the breaker points' condition and gap them to specifications. If they're badly worn or pitted, replace them—and the condenser.

battery

If your bike uses a battery (all four-stroke engines do) check it out like this:

☐ The winter lay-up may have caused the battery to run down. If so, recharge it with a trickle charger. Note: Never use a charger having an ampere-hour rating greater than that of the battery; it *could* cause the battery to explode! Match the rating of the battery (2–15 amp. hrs.; it's on the case) to the rating of the charger.

☐ All cycle batteries are equipped with a vent tube which permits battery gases to escape. This tube must be kept clear. To be sure it is, remove it and blow it out with compressed air.

If the battery has screw-on connectors, remove the terminals from the posts and clean both elements. Apply a thin coat of Vaseline to

1715

motorcycles

the posts and terminals, then reconnect them.

☐ Check the battery electrolyte level. If the battery needs water, use only distilled water.

valves

Adjust the valves at least once every 1,500 miles. The manual will tell you how for your bike. In general, the piston is brought to top dead center, then valve adjustments are made with a feeler gauge to the required specs. This should be done while the engine is cold.

Two-stroke engines have exhaust ports instead of an exhaust valve. Make sure they are clear of carbon. Clean all soot from the muffler too. First remove the exhaust pipe; then move the piston to bottom dead center and scrape carbon from the port.

drive chain

☐ All drive chains lengthen in time. No motorcycle chain should have more than ¾ in. of slack. To tighten it, turn the drive-chain-adjusting nut (on rear fork) to the right. If too little adjustment is available, take off the chain and remove a link, then replace the chain.

brakes

☐ Operate the front brake lever and the rear brake pedal; neither should have more than ½ in. free travel. Turn the appropriate adjusting nut clockwise to reduce lever or pedal travel.

The wheels should be pulled and brakes serviced every 5000 to 10,000 miles, more to recondition glazed linings than to replace worn ones. The glaze cuts down braking power. Remove it with emery cloth or armature paper. At the same time, blow dirt from the drum area and lube wheel bearings.

clutch

☐ The clutch lever should have ¼ to ½ in. of play before the clutch engages. If it doesn't, adjust it at the adjusting nut identified in your manual.

tightening and lubrication

☐ Vibration is the enemy of safe, comfortable cycling, and harmful to the bike as well. With one exception all nuts and bolts on your cycle should be turned down as tight as possible. Head bolts, however, must be torqued to specification (see your manual) with a torque wrench.

☐ Apply grease or oil at every lubrication point. You'll find a lube chart in your manual. But use only a hand grease gun; a high-pressure gun will blow seals.

☐ Carefully examine the rear of the engine for oil leaks. These are extremely dangerous as they can spew oil onto the rear tire and cause the bike to go into a skid. Engine leaks may be caused by a loose bolt or by a ruptured seal in the lower crankcase.

☐ Replace crankcase oil and keep a close check on its level. An undetected loss of a half quart of oil from a motorcycle can spell trouble.

Crusted dirt covering cooling fins will make the engine run hot. Carefully used metal cleaning solvent can loosen the gook so it can be scraped away

Check wheel alignment with straight wood or metal guides parallel to the wheels on each side. The wheel-to-guide distances must equal each other

continued

If measurements show that wheels are out of alignment, turn adjustment nuts on the rear wheel until the front wheel falls squarely between the two guides

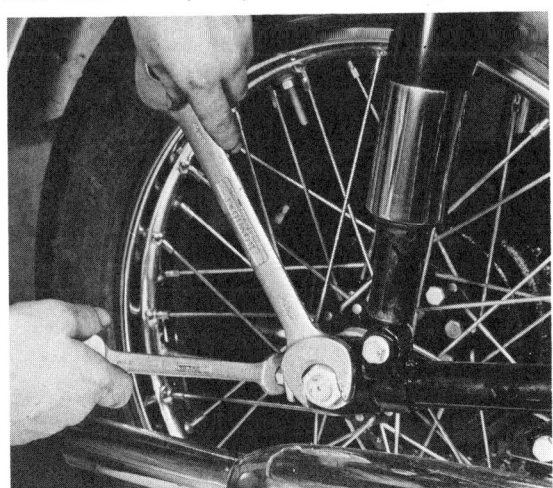

Free play in the rear chain should be exactly ¾ in. Turn the rear chain-adjusting nut until the right amount of slack can be measured at two points

motorcycles

Adjust the rear brake on a heavyweight at the brake-rod adjusting nut while checking pedal play. When the play reaches just 1 in., the brakes are right

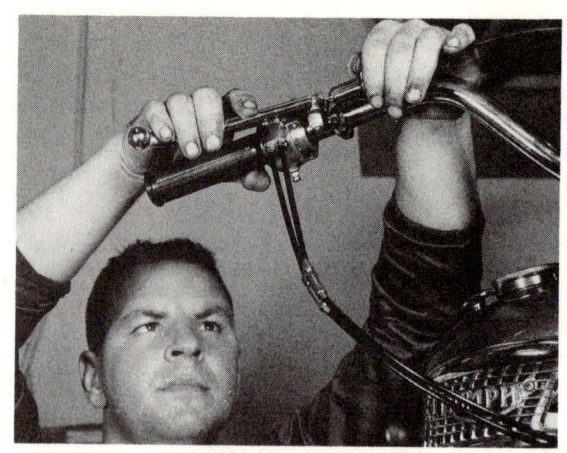

The front brakes are adjusted by taking up on a knurled nut while operating the brake lever. The proper adjustment calls for ½ in. of play

CHECKING OUT THE HEAVYWEIGHTS

Proper maintenance, of course, is at the happy medium—the level that gets the job done. As a rule of thumb with your heavyweight, plan:

—To do everything you can yourself to put your machine in good working order.

—To examine the bike for any major work needed. This should be handled by a competent shop with the special equipment often required.

All set? Let's go. Start to work on the following areas *in the order* in which they're listed, checking off each job as you finish it in the check-off boxes provided.

☐ Give the cycle a thorough washing with hot water and detergent to make it easier to spot the more obvious defects.

Cooling fins filthy? If so, your engine will run hot. Take a putty knife and scrape off the gook.

☐ Starting from the front and working toward the rear, tighten every nut and bolt in sight. Remember, vibration is a bike's worst enemy—and yours too as far as safety and riding comfort are concerned.

At the same time, keep an eye peeled for oil leaks. A little seepage is nothing to worry about, but a largish leak means that a seal has probably failed. If so, hike your bike to the shop.

battery

☐ If the battery's been left in the cycle all winter, remove it now and check the electrolyte level. Scrub the battery clean, then charge it on a trickle charger for seven hours. A gas station can do this job if you lack a charger.

Check battery cables and terminals. Get new cables if the old ones are frayed or worn. File down cable terminals till they're clean and

Periodically remove and clean the main carburetor jets. On some imports, remove the carb top cover to reach and clean the slides as is shown below

Slide adjustments on dual carburetors are made at the slide-control cable. Adjust it until the needle of one slide lines up with its counterpart in the other carb

Check heavyweights' clutch wear by removing the access plate on the primary case, loosening the outer locking nut of the outer plate, and following directions

bright. Trace the battery ground cable back to the frame, disconnect it, file down the terminal and the ground spot on the frame, then hook up the cable, tightly.

grease and oil

☐ Drain old oil from the crankcase and transmission and put in new. Using a hand grease gun and an oilcan—and referring to the lubrication chart you'll find in your owner's manual—use the manufacturer's suggested lubricants.

tires and wheels

☐ Check the tires. They're critical. So don't tolerate worn spots or any cracks in the sidewalls. Replace any tire that shows damage.

If a tire is worn more on one side than on the other, it's a pretty good sign your wheels are out of alignment. This can be corrected with the aid

Timing is easy enough to do yourself with a $3 timing disk that's available from most motorcycle shops. This procedure is a good way to save dollars, safely

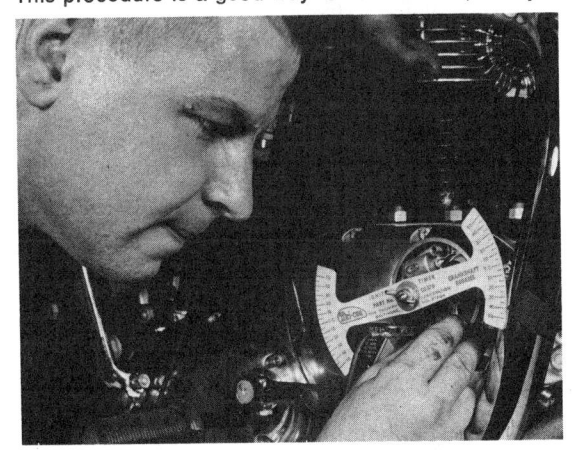

of alignment guides in the form of two straight metal bars or two straight strips of lumber.

☐ Set the bike up straight, then lay an alignment guide on each side of the cycle in a perfectly straight line so both are parallel to and touching the back tire. Using a rule, check the distance between the *front* tire and both alignment devices. The distance between the front tire and each alignment device should be the same. If these distances are not the same, loosen up the *rear* wheel adjusters and adjust the wheel until the front tire is exactly centered between the two alignment guides.

Uneven wear may be corrected also by "flipping" the tires. Flipping a tire means taking the tire off and turning it around. If the worn area, for example, is on the left-hand side of the tire, it will be on the right-hand side after it's turned around. Tire wear is thus equalized.

☐ Check spokes. Replace any that are broken or rusted. Loose spokes can be detected by lightly tapping each in turn with a wrench. A taut spoke will give off a musical "ping." A dull "klunk" indicates a loose spoke that should be tightened with a spoke-nipple wrench.

chains

☐ Check the rear chain for tight spots while someone is sitting on the bike. Adjust the chain until you get ¾ in. free play at *two* points on it.

☐ Inspect the rear sprocket for broken or worn teeth. If it's bad, replace it; bad sprockets chew up rear chains fast. Your manual shows how to replace the sprocket on your model.

☐ Check adjustment of the primary chain which links engine to clutch. Adjustment differs according to the make of motorcycle.

Generally, though, the job is done by first pulling the bottom plug of the primary case and letting the oil run out. This is the access hole to the chain in which the chain adjusting tool is inserted. Using this tool, turn the adjusting nut clockwise while checking the adjustment through the top plug in the case. Loosen or tighten the chain until you get ½ in. of play.

Replace the bottom plug and replenish the oil by unscrewing the check plug and pouring oil in through the fill plug until it runs out the check plug.

brakes

☐ Check the brakes. This is easier to do on a big bike than on a lightweight; on the heavyweights you don't have to pull a wheel unless new brake linings are needed.

1719

motorcycles

winter tuneup, continued

☐ Have someone apply the brake pedal fully while you check the brake arm at the rear wheel. If the arm goes beyond a 90-deg. angle, the linings have worn and require replacing.

Similarly, if there's no more adjustment left in the brake cable of the front brake, you need front brake lining.

☐ To adjust the rear brakes, take up on the nut on the end of the brake rod until you get 1 in. of free pedal.

☐ Adjust the front brakes by taking up on the knurled nut where the brake cable connects to the brake lever. The brake lever should have just ½ in. of free play.

clutch

☐ Check clutch pressure-plate wear. Most cycles have an inspection hole on the primary case. To check clutch pressure plates of most cycles, back off the locking nut of the outer clutch plate, then turn out the screw to release tension on the plate. Now turn the screw back up until you begin to feel tension on the screwdriver. This means the screw is *just touching* the clutch rod (the correct tension).

With the screw in place, tighten up on the locknut. A locknut that doesn't tighten indicates a worn clutch plate. The proper adjustment is reached when the screw has the slightest tension on it and the locknut tightens.

☐ Adjust the clutch lever. This is similar to adjusting the front brake. You'll find the knurled clutch-adjuster nut near the handlebar where the clutch cable connects to the clutch lever. Adjust the nut to ¼-in. play in the lever.

carburetor

☐ Check out the carburetor. Remove the main-jet bottom nut from the carburetor and check for any deposits of dirt. If it's really dirty take the carburetor apart and clean it. If not just remove the main jet and clean that.

(Dual-carburetor models of British and Japanese cycles present a distinct service problem. Make sure that both slides are clean and open easily. If they're dull with carbon deposits remove them and clean them with crocus cloth.)

ignition

☐ To check the points, remove the point cover. If they're not too badly pitted, run a fine point file through them. If they *are* badly pitted, replace them.

A properly timed engine is essential to good performance, yet most cyclists shy away from this job. There's little reason; it's easy with a timing disk, obtainable for about $3 from the shop that sells your model bike. And it pays to do your own timing. Shops charge up to $10.

☐ Check the sparkplugs. In fact, play it safe and replace them with new ones.

☐ Check the coil and secondary wiring. The easy way to do this is to ground a plug and crank the engine. A fat spark should jump the plug gap. If it doesn't, you know you have a bad or loose wire, or a bad coil.

valves and engine

☐ Check valve adjustment—with the plugs out. Shift into top gear, then turn the engine over manually until the valves farthest from you are wide open. Then adjust the valves nearest you with a feeler gauge. Generally this adjustment will be from .002 to .004.

Turn the engine again until the valves nearest you are open all the way, then repeat the adjustment procedure on the remaining valves.

☐ Check engine compression. You can do this yourself if you have a compression tester. Good compression is 160 lbs. in both cylinders. If you don't have your own tester, you can get a pretty good idea of the internal condition of your engine by using your ears:

Start the engine and let it warm up. Get it to a slow, smooth idle, then place a gloved hand lightly over the end of the muffler to drown out exhaust noise. Now listen carefully. A regular tick-tick-tick sound might mean a worn wrist pin—not too serious. It could also be piston slap, a major ailment.

To determine whether it's the piston, advance the ignition—if this is possible on your make cycle—and look at the exhaust; a lot of smoke indicates back pressure past the piston. Also, run your hand beneath the lower part of the engine. Oil there could indicate back pressure.

Retard the ignition. Both wrist-pin noise and piston slap will disappear if either of these is your problem. If ticking persists, suspect the valves. However, a deep booming knock from inside the engine is likely a rod which will *not* disappear by retarding the ignition.

An engine that rumbles and sounds very rough generally means worn main bearings. If you can rule out worn bearings, look for a too-tight primary chain.

See also: bicycles; car; midget; scooter; shelters; unicycle.

mountain climbing

It isn't dangerous and it's not hard. The secret is expert instruction—and once you learn the basics at a good climbing camp, you'll find yourself perched on a pinnacle and rappelling down a sheer wall with the greatest of ease

Up and down of mountain climbing

BY STUART JAMES

■ YOU DON'T HAVE TO BE RUGGED to climb a mountain. I climbed a 13,768-foot peak on the Palisades Glacier, and I'm neither young, strong nor brave. It was my first climb; I did it on my 40th birthday, and I'm the guy who cannot bear to stand near the railing of a high terrace.

Frankly, the hardest thing about climbing a mountain is getting to the mountain. After you have hiked 13 miles—all uphill—with a 50-pound pack to get to the climbing camp, and then trudge another five or six miles—all uphill—to get to the base of the mountain, the actual climbing is just a series of nice long rests.

Like any novice who wants to try his hand at mountaineering, I was concerned about getting expert instruction. There are three excellent climbing schools in the United States. The National Park Service operates schools and camp sessions at Mount Rainier in Washington and Grand Teton National Park in Wyoming. I chose a private camp operated by Larry Williams Mountaineering Guide Service in Big Pine, Calif.

I had my doubts about this venture. By the time I reached the climbing camp at Sam Mack Meadow I was ready to forget the whole thing and go back to a nice, sensible sport like dominoes or basket weaving. I was completely exhausted, I felt at least 70 years old, and I was surrounded by mountain peaks that were very high and straight up and down. The young, muscled college-age boys strutting around the camp did nothing to cheer me up, but when I saw a five-year-old girl who had hiked effortlessly up the same trail with her own little pack, and her 110-pound mother who had done the same thing with a big pack, I was dismayed.

Surrounding Sam Mack Meadow are precipitous rock walls. The college boys kept eyeing

mouth-to-mouth resuscitation: see lifesaving

1721

mountain climbing

them with relish, while I stared at them in disbelief. I felt a moment of panic on the morning of the first session when Larry Williams came forward with great coils of rope over his shoulders, but it passed when I was told that all basic instruction would be held on flat ground.

I was heartened considerably when the entire morning session was devoted to safety.

Bespectacled and soft-spoken, Larry Williams exudes confidence. A high school science teacher during the winter and mountaineering guide in the summer, he teaches with a blending of technique and philosophy. "Climbing a mountain is not a combat," he says, "not man against nature. It is true that the mountain is a challenge, but this is only because it is an obstacle that can be overcome by human technical knowledge. When it is done correctly there is never any danger in mountain climbing."

The first lessons were in handling a rope, tying a few knots such as the half-hitch and figure-eight, and how to belay. Each climber has a 10-foot length of ⅜-inch nylon rope which he ties snugly around his waist. Attached to this is a carabiner, an oval-shaped aluminum ring with a snap link. To tie into a rope, the climber simply makes a loop in the rope with a figure-eight knot and snaps this into the carabiner that is attached to his waist rope.

Learning the belay really takes the terror out of climbing. In a practice session, the belayer sits down with feet solidly braced against a rock.

How to tie knots and handle a rope is the first lesson at climbing camp, where safety is emphasized

Crampons are steel spikes that are strapped to the boots for hiking across slick ice and snow

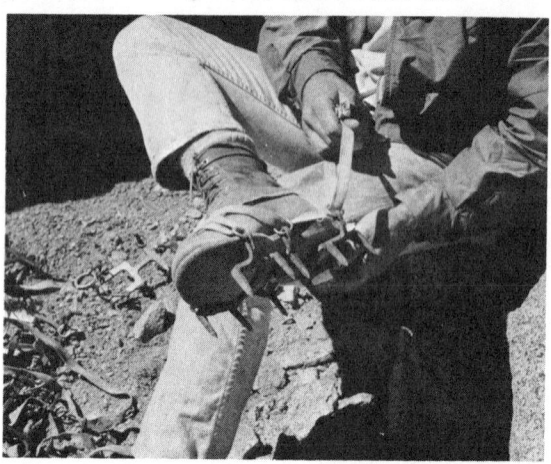

Strength and safety of the friction belay is demonstrated on flat ground by two men using all their power in an attempt to pull the belayer from position. Finally it took the combined strength of five men to dislodge him

He passes the rope behind him, letting it run over his hips and guiding both ends through his hands. As many as three men grip one end of the rope. The man on belay grips this rope firmly in his right hand; the loose end is slack in his left. As one of the young men shouts "Falling!" the belayer crosses his left hand over the right, creating a "friction lock," and the others try to pull him out of his position behind the rock. He cannot be budged.

The next thing to learn is the rappel, a way of lowering yourself down a sheer cliff on a rope looped over a well anchored object on the top. This is practiced on a slight incline. But within an hour of initial introduction, you have to make a rappel off a perilously high rock. Strangely

Young mother put a few of the older men to shame scaling vertical faces, leaping into belays with spilt-second warning to men above her—"Hang on, I'm going to jump!"—and then she would jump

Class in belay technique watches instructor Larry Williams hold a climber who simulated a fall

Ice and snow belays using the ice ax as anchor are practiced on a gentle slope of Palisades Glacier

mountain climbing

Rappel technique of sliding down a stationary rope is first practiced on an easy face

Real thing is accomplished the same day, and after basic training it is a simple maneuver

learning to climb a mountain, continued

enough, the basic instruction is so sound and the method so practical, that you step off into space without a moment of hesitation or a twinge of fear.

The second day, the class takes to the rock walls around the camp, and it is here that theory is taught under actual climbing conditions.

There's the jam hold, for instance. You simply slip your hand into a crack in the rock, flex your fingers and find that you can support your weight with ease. It is also astounding to learn that you can balance yourself quite securely by simply pinching a tiny outcropping of rock between the thumb and index finger.

Like every natural coward, my initial reaction was to press myself as closely as possible to the rock wall and hang on for dear life.

"Lean back," Larry Williams said. He scrambles up and down the rocks like a goat, pausing here and there to give instruction and advice. "Try it. Let your toes take the full weight. You climb with your legs, not your arms."

I leaned out from the wall and, sure enough, it was easier. My feet did the climbing and the hands were used mostly for balance.

After a few days of instruction we were off early in the morning for our first ascent—Mount Winchell. It took us five hours to reach the base of the mountain. All the way there the massive peak towered in the distance, looking like an impossible objective. And if this wasn't discouraging enough, there were the young bucks being helpful with statements like: "Boy, you sure do okay for a man your age."

The actual climb was not difficult. As Larry Williams explained: "You climb a mountain a small piece at a time. It is simply a connected series of small technical problems."

We reached the peak in two hours. The towering mass of rock was no longer so formidable. It had been an experience. I enjoyed the exertion. It was the perfect way to spend a vacation—high in the hills away from campgrounds and crowds. But I had an odd feeling of sadness, there on the peak, and the next time I climb a mountain— and I will—I won't go all the way to the top.

See also: boots; camping; clothing; packs, camping; rope; sleeping bags; tents; wild foods.

clever ideas

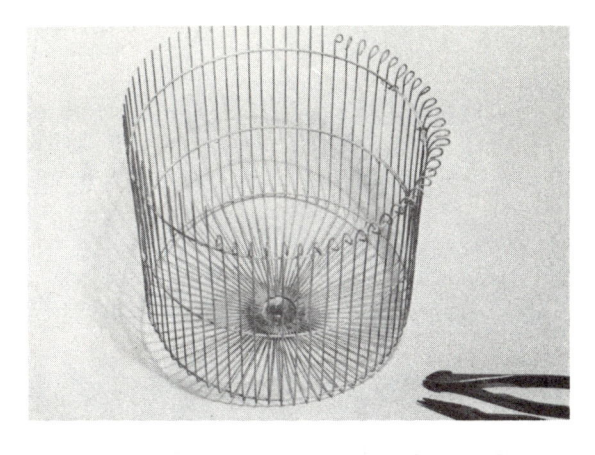

A bird cage can be converted into a hanging basket for plants by removing the bottom, inverting the cage and curling the wire ribs back on themselves with pliers to form ornamental loops.

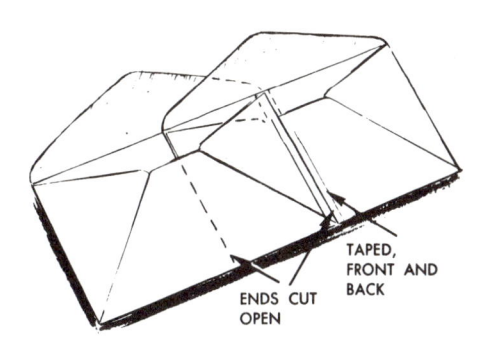

When you need a long envelope and one isn't available, you can make one by slitting the ends of two short envelopes, sliding one into the other and sealing the joint with cellophane tape.

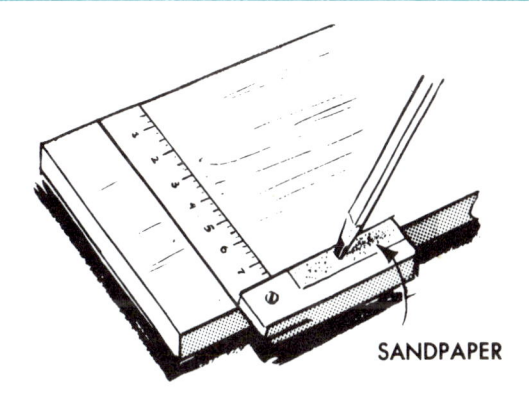

When working to a close dimension you need a fine, flat point on the pencil for accurate scribing. Cement an emery board to the handle of your try square and you'll have a handy means of renewing that worn point quickly.

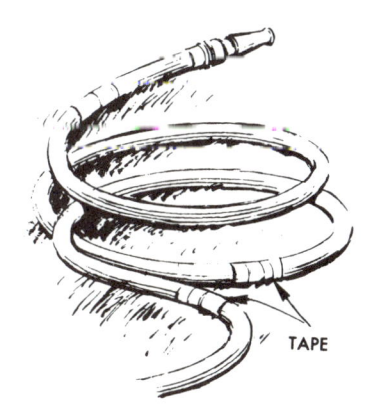

After having two new hoses stolen from his lawn while being used for late-evening sprinkling, a crafty homeowner taped the next hose he purchased with friction tape so that it looked leaky. He hasn't lost one since then.

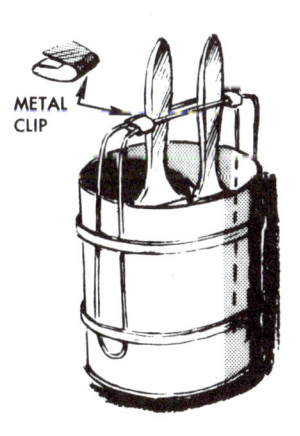

This brush holder is made by folding a length of coathanger wire double and slipping two ¼-in. tubing spacers over it. Flatten the spacers and spread wires between them, then bend the ends and attach them to the can with rubber bands.

movies, sound

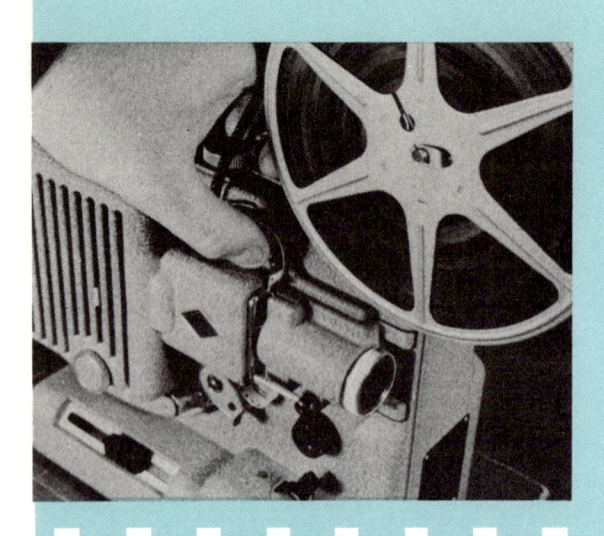

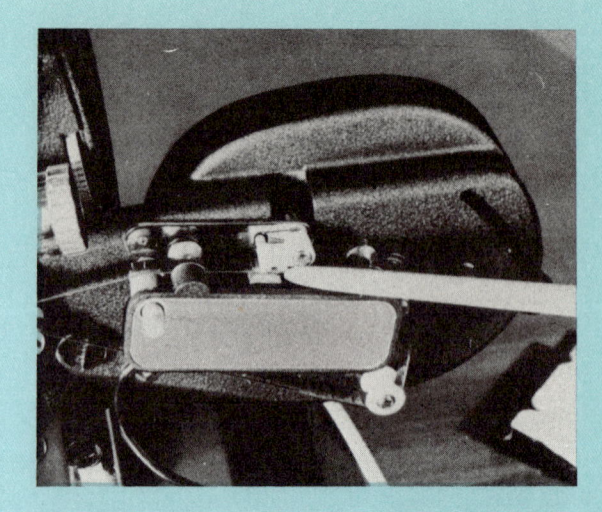

The cue point for film during sound tracking is the joint between the leader and the start of exposed film. Line it up with projector's pressure plate

Sound-on-film recording has the advantage of perfect synchronization without fuss because the sound is wedded to the picture on a magnetic stripe

Soundtrack your home movies

BY ART ZUCKERMAN

You can add a new dimension
to your home movie productions
by introducing sound.
It doesn't cost much today
and it will send your reputation
as a producer right to the top.
Use a tape recorder
or put your sound on the film

---

movies, underwater: see underwater camera cases
movies, zoetrope: see zoetrope
movie titles: see titles, movie
moving targets: see targets

A NEW DIMENSION of interest and fun can be added to your 8-mm home movies with sound. You might have thought of this as an expensive proposition requiring the talents of an advanced amateur, but it just isn't so. A modest outlay for equipment—very modest if you already own a good tape recorder—will put you in business.

If you can do a good film-editing job and have a reasonably good ear for music, you can turn out sound tracks that will make your audiences glow with pleasure.

Truly synchronized sound calls for either a sound-on-film projector or a silent model designed to sync with a tape recorder. (You might do without a projector-recorder link, but only if your projector runs at a flat 16 frames per second without variation.)

Home sound-on-film involves magnetic recording on a thin ribbon of oxide striping that runs along the film just outside the sprocket holes.

The cost of sound-striping the film averages about 6 cents per ft., making the tab for a 400-ft. reel about $24. But there is a do-it-yourself striping device that cuts the cost to about ½ a cent per foot or $2 for a 400-ft. reel.

A sound-striped film has perfect sync, but should be projected at 24 frames per sec. for best audio quality, instead of the standard 16 f.p.s.

1726

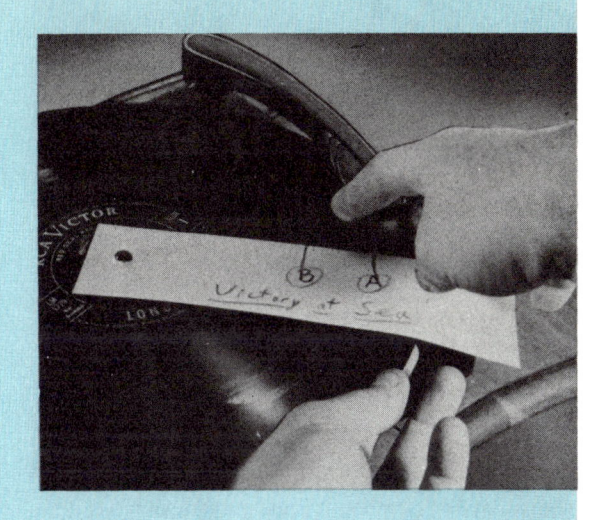

A fragment of splicing tape stuck to the back (shiny side) of magnetic tape is the cue point for sound tracking. Line it up with the recording head

Cue strips locate record grooves on which musical inserts start. For instant cue-ins, hold the record as the turntable spins; let go when recording starts

End result is that a 400-ft. reel runs 20 min. Acceptable reproduction can be produced at 16 f.p.s., however, if you prefer it.

If you already own a good tape recorder you may prefer tape sync. The standard ratio is 16 f.p.s to a 3¾-i.p.s. tape speed.

Whichever way you decide to record, the first caution should be to place your projector far enough from the mike to eliminate projector noise. A directional mike helps; projecting through a glass door from another room is ideal.

There are two approaches to sound tracking: the one-pass system, in which you record all your audio simultaneously; and the sound-on-sound technique, where the first film pass is used to record music and effects, and you add the narrative on a second pass. (During the narration, the volume of the original recording is automatically lowered as you record over it.)

Sound-on-sound takes longer but simplifies the job. It is done by either turning off the erase head or physically isolating it from the tape or film. Most sound-stripe projectors have the sound-on-sound feature built into them as do many tape recorders. But a simple trick will let you do the same thing with a recorder not originally equipped for sound-on-sound.

Cut a 1-in.-wide strip several inches long from an exposed piece of photographic film and double it over to form two layers. Loop the strip around your recorder's erase head and cut off the excess, leaving a bit to spare at the ends. Staple these ends together to form a permanent loop. When making sound-on-sound recordings, slip the loop over the erase head.

The most elementary sound-tracking set-up is a microphone between two self-contained phonographs. To make a musical transition, cut the volume of one phonograph and bring it up on the other. To insert narration, cut back on the phonograph volume and speak into the mike.

For better results use an electronic mixer and two simple turntables or record player attachments. A regular phonograph can be used as a turntable for this system by disconnecting the pickup-arm cable from the set's amplifier and plugging it right into the mixer.

Let's see how to make a sound track, using the all-at-once, electronic-mixer techniques.

First step is to edit your film into a single story-telling reel. Avoid scenic monotony, and be careful not to introduce musical monotony.

Once the film is edited, it must be sound striped if you choose sound-on-film. But footage for tape sync is now ready for the next step.

This consists of screening it, timing each indi-

1727

movies, sound

A mixer makes a smooth blending effect with two record players plus a microphone. Keep the cue sheet near to know what's next and how to set controls

vidual sequence and jotting down notes on subject matter, sequence changes and spots calling for commentary. Next think of the music available in your record collection. Try, mentally, to fit passages to the scenes you've run off and make a tentative list of the records they're on.

Armed with this list, rerun your film, and try each musical selection against its allotted sequence. See how scene and sound play together, and make changes where necessary. Once you've decided on the final layout, make cue strips for each record. These are strips of paper with a spindle hole at one end.

Print the name of the record on the strip, put the disk on the player and place the cue slip over the spindle. Locate the beginning of the chosen passage and stop the turntable. Move the cue strip around until it touches the stylus. Draw a straight line on the strip in front of the point of contact with a crayon pencil. If more than one selection is to be used, print the letter A, circle it, and join it to the lead-off passage's cue mark. Identify the next cue with the letter B and so on.

Prepare a cue sheet next. It labels each sequence, indicates the music selection by record name and identifying letter, if any, and notes the cue-in action to look for while screening. It cues sound effects, too. These can be made live or can be supplied from records or tapes.

The cue sheet also contains your dialogue and indicates where it should be inserted. The fewer and shorter the commentaries the better. Picture, music and sound effects should carry the story burden, leaving narration to establish settings and fill in necessary information.

Now you're ready to record. Stack your records in order of play. First play the musical sections with the loudest passages through the recording system to get proper levels. Once you find the master setting for recorder or projector, all further level juggling should be done at the mixer. Camera or recorder controls should not be varied during the recording session.

Mark the peak setting on the mixer's phono-channel controls. Then do the same thing for the mike channels. Next, using earphones, blend some music with a sample of the narration, gradually cutting back on the music till you get the right background effect. Mark this setting.

start records spinning

Set your first two records on the turntables and start them spinning. Hold the edge of the lead-off record to keep it from turning. Use the cue strip to locate the starting groove and set the needle on it. Then with all other mixer controls at zero, set the turntables' channel level to the play setting. Start the projection-recording system and simultaneously release the disks to get a well-synchronized start.

To insert narrative, drop the music level to the background setting and bring up your mike level. Reverse the process when narration ends. Always keep the mike dead when you're not using it to minimize pickup of spurious noise.

Gradual fades and cross fades make the best normal transitions. But you can sometimes get dramatic effects by bringing up key passages.

In screening your creation for an audience, provide a true theater effect by playing the sound track through an auxiliary speaker placed by or behind the screen.

A stereo recorder used with the tape-sync system offers wonderful opportunities for extra dramatic touches. With two speakers, you can make your music and effects come from the side of the screen where attention should be focused.

One final comment on the cost of sound tracking regular 8-mm film: The home movie industry is developing rapidly, and as a result, new products and new processes are introduced frequently. Therefore, all cost figures quoted here may be made obsolete overnight. Check your photo supply store for the most recent prices on sound tracking—and don't be surprised if they are much lower than we stated.

See also: photography; tape recorders; titles, movie; tripods; underwater camera cases; zoetrope.